Gandhi's Experiments with Truth

STUDIES IN COMPARATIVE PHILOSOPHY AND RELIGION

Series Editor: Douglas Allen, University of Maine

This series is based on the view that significant and creative future studies in philosophy and religious studies will be informed by comparative research. These studies will emphasize aspects of contemporary and classical Asian philosophy and religion, and their relationship to Western thought. This series will feature works of specialized scholarship by new and upcoming scholars in Asia and the West, as well as works by more established scholars and books with a wider readership. The editor welcomes a wide variety of manuscript submissions, especially works exhibiting highly focused research and theoretical innovation.

Varieties of Ethical Reflection: New Directions for Ethics in a Global Context, by Michael Barnhart

Gandhi's Experiments with Truth: Essential Writings by and about Mahatma Gandhi, edited by Richard L. Johnson

Gandhi's Experiments with Truth

Essential Writings by and about Mahatma Gandhi

Edited by
Richard L. Johnson

LEXINGTON BOOKS

A Division of
ROWMAN & LITTLEFIELD PUBLISHERS, INC.
Lanham • *Boulder* • *New York* • *Toronto* • *Oxford*

All images in this volume © Vithalbhai Jhaveri/GandhiServe

LEXINGTON BOOKS

A division of Rowman & Littlefield Publishers, Inc.
A wholly owned subsidary of The Rowman & Littlefield Publishing Group, Inc.
4501 Forbes Boulevard, Suite 200
Lanham, MD 20706

PO Box 317
Oxford
OX2 9RU, UK

British Library Cataloguing in Publication Information Available

Library of Congress Cataloging-in-Publication Data

Gandhi's experiments with truth : essential writings by and about Mahatma Gandhi /
[edited by] Richard L. Johnson.
    p. cm. — (Studies in comparative philosophy and religion)
  Includes bibliographical references and index.
  ISBN 0-7391-1142-6 (hardcover : alk. paper) — ISBN 0-7391-1143-4 (pbk. : alk.
paper)
  1. Gandhi, Mahatma, 1869–1948. I. Johnson, Richard L., 1941– II. Gandhi,
Mahatma, 1869–1948. Selections. 2005. III. Series.
DS481.G3G2774 2005
954.03_5_092—dc22

                                                          2005006420

Printed in the United States of America

⊗™ The paper used in this publication meets the minimum requirements of
American National Standard for Information Sciences—Permanence of Paper
for Printed Library Materials, ANSI/NISO Z39.48-1992.

To Torkom Saraydarian and Jeanne Shoup,
teachers of truth and love,
and to all who experiment with truth.

Contents

Acknowledgments

I wish to acknowledge

- My students in Peace and Conflict Studies at Indiana University-Purdue University Ft. Wayne (IPFW) who have taken courses with me over the past fifteen years, especially the students in my Honors seminars on Gandhi. They know that a writer must be clear about his/her audience. As I worked on this book, I have always had these thoughtful, inquisitive, and creative students in mind as my audience *par excellence*.
- My wife Teresa and our (still at home) children Andrea and Ian, who were patient, gracious, and forgiving during the work on this book for a longer time than any of us had anticipated.
- Douglas Allen, the series editor, who pored over the book and made substantive suggestions for improvements.
- Jason Hallman of Lexington Books, who was quite helpful and thoroughly professional.
- Mahendra Kumar, editor of *Gandhi Marg*, who began coediting this book with me but who, unfortunately, was not able to continue. I am grateful for our discussion of this project in New Delhi in 2000 and for our collaboration in the initial stages of the writing.
- Sue Dirrim, secretary in Modern Foreign Languages at IPFW, who is the best proofreader I have ever met; Fred Jehle, "retired" professor of Spanish and computer wizard, who kept helping me solve computer problems; and Pam Zepp, the Microsoft expert on our campus, who saved me from the morass of headers and footers and even claimed to enjoy it.

Gratefully acknowledged are the following publishers, editors, and authors for their permission to reprint their publications:

Bhikhu Parekh for Bhikhu Parekh, "Ghandhi's Legacy," in *Gandhi: A Very Short Introduction* (New York, Oxford University Press, 2001).

The Center for Global Nonviolence for Glenn D. Paige, "Gandhi's Contribution to Global Nonviolent Awakening," in *To Nonviolent Political Science* (Honolulu: Center for Global Nonviolence Planning Project, Mastunga Institute for Peace, University of Hawaii, 1993).

Kanishka Publishers, Distributors for Douglas Allen, "Ghandhi, Contemporary Political Thinking and Self-Other Relations," in *Contemporary Political Thinking*, ed. B. N. Ray (New Delhi: Kanishka Publishers, Distributors, 2000), 129–70.

Lexington Books for Judith M. Brown, "Gandhi and Human Rights: In Search of True Humanity," in *Gandhi, Freedom, and Self-Rule*, ed. Anthony J. Parel (Lanham, MD: Lexington Books, 2000); and Anthony J. Parel, "Gandhian Freedoms and Self-Rule," in *Gandhi, Freedom, and Self-Rule*, ed. Anthony J. Parel (Lanham, MD: Lexington Books, 2000).

Lloyd I. Rudolph for Lloyd I. Rudolph, "Gandhi in the Mind of America," in *Conflicting Images: India and the United States*, ed. Sulochana Raghaven Glazer and Nathan Glazer (Glenn Dale, MD: Riverdale, 1990).

The Navajivan Trust for excerpts from *An Autobiography, or The Story of My Experiments with the Truth*; *Hind Swaraj*; *Satyagraha in South Africa*; and further spiritual, moral, and political writings by Mahatma Gandhi.

Rowman & Littlefield Publishers, Inc., for Ronald J. Terchek, "Gandhi's Politics," in *Gandhi: Struggling for Autonomy* (Lanham, MD: Rowman & Littlefield, 1998).

Introduction: Gandhi's Experiments with Truth: Private Life, *Satyagraha*, and the Constructive Programme

Richard L. Johnson

Mohandas Karamchand Gandhi (1869–1948), known as the Mahatma (Great Soul), is widely revered for his practice and theory of nonviolence. Most people believe that nonviolence was the primary focus of his life, but it was not. Although nonviolent action was pivotal to Gandhi, he came to it after years of public service and religious striving, and he always believed that the deepest and most abiding meaning of his life was the pursuit of truth. He saw himself as a scientist doing experiential research in a series of "experiments with truth." Nonviolent resistance—*satyagraha* as he called it—was one area of experimentation within a wider spectrum of experiments. He wrote, "Life has . . . become for me a series of experiments with truth. In my pursuit of truth I came across the method of non-violence."[1]

He called his autobiography *The Story of My Experiments with Truth* to suggest how central these experiments were to him. As he explained in the Introduction, "It is not my purpose to attempt a real autobiography. I simply want to tell the story of my numerous experiments with truth, and as my life consists of nothing but these experiments, it is true that the story will take the shape of an autobiography."[2] According to Sissela Bok, Gandhi's experiments

served the purpose of testing his own character and moulding it in directions he saw as desirable. The words "trial" and "test" often enter into his characterization of these experiments. He shows how the most minute, most ordinary, and sometimes most intimate aspects of his own life offer opportunities for testing himself. Nothing, he implies, prevents his readers from viewing their own lives as likewise open to choice and experimentation, making them able to participate in equally astounding personal and social transformation. Some of Gandhi's early experiments involved purely personal change. . . . Gandhi's well-known experiments in the communal [religious], educational, and political realms are closely linked to his efforts at personal change. However different, his experiments in the several realms cannot be pried apart, he claims, since at bottom they are all moral experiments.[3]

Although it is true that his various forms of experimentation "cannot be pried apart," still we can look at them in three closely related realms of his life: his experiments in his private life on the one hand, and on the other his two great experiments in public life, *satyagraha* and the Constructive Programme.

PRIVATE LIFE

Gandhi's first major experiment with truth was undertaken in London where he was studying law. Before leaving for London, he promised his mother that he would not get involved with women, alcohol, or meat eating. As a Hindu, Gandhi had grown up as a vegetarian, but in his youth he had secretly eaten meat several times and was not really committed to vegetarianism. In London he remained true to his vow, but he could not find food that satisfied his hunger. One day he happened upon a vegetarian restaurant, saw Henry Salt's *Plea for Vegetarianism*, and immediately read it. He then read a number of books on diet: "The result of reading all this literature was that dietetic experiments came to take an important place in my life. Health was the principal consideration of these experiments to begin with. But later on religion became the supreme motive."[4]

As he continued his experiments with diet, he began to examine his whole life, making both "internal and external" changes. He "saw that the writers on vegetarianism had examined the question very minutely, attacking it in its religious, scientific, practical and medical aspects. Ethically they had arrived at the conclusion that man's supremacy over the lower animals meant not that the former should prey upon the latter, but that the higher should protect the lower, and that there should be mutual aid between the two as between man and man."[5] The pattern of his experiments is emerging here: careful examination of an issue utilizing several sources, a focus on moral considerations, and then, if warranted, a decision to make internal and external changes as a result of the research. Once Gandhi decided his life needed to change, he changed it. His experiments with truth required action. As he wrote, "action is my domain." He was not one to remain in the realm of theory. He called himself a "practical idealist" because he had to practice his ideals to test out their truthfulness in the world around him. For Gandhi, practice often preceded theory.

As he continued his experiments, he came to believe in God as Truth. Although as a youth he inclined "somewhat towards atheism,"[6] in time his experiments were increasingly animated by a desire to come closer to Absolute Truth. However, Gandhi believed that we can only experience our relative truths and hope at times to pierce through the veil of illusion into Absolute Truth. For many, the fact that we have little access to the Truth serves as a deterrent to action, but not for Gandhi. Experiments with truth are necessary because we cannot know how valid these relative truths are unless we test them out in the laboratory of life. It is necessary to hold to the relative truths, to live by them, for the very effort to live according to them forms a path toward the Truth. He stated, "as long as I have not realized Absolute Truth, so long must I hold by the relative truth as I have conceived it. That relative truth must, meanwhile, be my beacon, my shield and buckler. Though this path is strait and narrow and sharp as the razor's edge, for me it has been the quickest and easiest. Even my Himalayan blunders have seemed trifling to me because I have kept strictly to this path. For the path has saved me from coming to grief, and I have gone forward according to my light. Often in my progress I have had faint glimpses of the Absolute Truth, God, and daily the conviction is growing upon me that He alone is real and all else is unreal."[7]

After his return to India from South Africa, he came to believe not only that God is Truth but also that Truth is God. This change involved a movement from a fundamentally religious assertion—God is Truth—to the belief that everyone on some level pursues truth, whether their point of view is religious or secular. He believed atheists could accept the statement that Truth is God as well as theists.

Gandhi's experiment in London with vegetarianism was the first of many experiments in his private life. He experimented with alternative medicine, farming, sanitation, law, celibacy in marriage, writing, and spinning, indeed every facet of life. In South Africa, as he struggled to form a movement which would liberate Indians there from racist laws, he came upon his practice and theory of *satyagraha*, his most celebrated experiment with truth.

SATYAGRAHA

Gandhi believed his public service was a result of his quest to know Absolute Truth. He wrote often that the origin of his political action was religious, spiritual, moral, words he used interchangeably to describe his experiments with truth. He stated in the Introduction to his *Autobiography:* "I should certainly like to narrate my experiments in the spiritual field which are known only to myself, and from which I have derived such power as I possess for working in the political field. . . . The experiments I am about to relate . . . are spiritual, or rather moral; for the essence of religion is morality."[8] His religious/spiritual/moral experiments were the origin of his work in the political field, of his "experimental politics," Ronald Terchek's term for Gandhi's approach to politics.[9]

In the West, political theories are in the main so thoroughly divorced from moral considerations that it can be difficult to fathom Gandhi's practice of subordinating the political to the moral. His experiments with truth—in politics and all fields of human endeavor—were fundamentally moral. As Judith Brown states, "*satyagraha* was a theory and practice of moral growth that enabled Truth-seekers to deal with situations where clearly his ideals for individuals, for society, and for the operation of political power were not being followed."[10]

Gandhi's belief in nonviolence was an integral part of his ideals for moral growth at all levels of individual and social practice. He was well aware that he did not invent nonviolence. *Ahimsa*, non-harming or nonviolence, has been a central tenet of Hinduism for thousands of years. He often said that nonviolence is as "old as the hills." He was, however, unparalleled as an innovator in the development of nonviolent action as a movement for social and political change. After he and other Indians decided to pursue "passive resistance" to the racist laws in South Africa, he realized that the English term did not properly describe their movement. Many passive resisters he had read about used nonviolent techniques but would also resort to violence, if they felt circumstances warranted it. Gandhi believed that nonviolence had to be a practical technique *and* a spiritual principle of their movement. He therefore asked the readers of *Indian Opinion*, his journal in South Africa, to come up with a new term that would demonstrate the spiritual dimension of their actions. He modified a suggestion his cousin Maganlal Gandhi sent in and coined the term *satyagraha*, which means literally "clinging to Truth." Although the end was always Truth for Gandhi, he discovered that the means must be *ahimsa*. He expanded his concept of *ahimsa* with Love. With Truth as the end and Love as the means, the *satyagrahi*, the nonviolent activist, would be able simultaneously to elevate politics and to ground spirituality in practical living.

Gandhi also decided not to use the term "passive resistance" because he recognized how active nonviolence is. He variously translated *satyagraha* as truth force, love force, compassion force, and soul force to emphasize that it was an actual force which rulers would have to reckon with. He believed that we often remain in our animal nature—the origin of brute force—but we can raise ourselves up into our souls and thereby come in contact with a spiritual force infinitely more powerful than brute force.

Each *satyagrahi* was to look within and discover the deepest spiritual truth possible. Gandhi believed a *satyagrahi* was a scientist of the soul who had to first turn his or her "searchlight inward." Once inner purity and clarity was attained, he or she would then seek to realize truth in the world of politics, which for Gandhi embraced all social and political processes. *Ahimsa* or love was central to this attempt because, given the fact that our truths are relative, we cannot be sure that someone else's truths are necessarily any less valid than ours. We cannot harm them for pursuing their truths just as we do not wish them to harm us for pursuing ours. Even if we differ in our perceptions of truth, we can love others, even our so-called enemies; and instead of making them suffer because of a conflict with us, we are enjoined to suffer in attempt to touch their hearts with our truths. *Satyagraha* was sacrificial suffering in the pursuit of Truth and Love, a way to bring moral living into the political sphere.

THE CONSTRUCTIVE PROGRAMME

The Constructive Programme, an experiment with truth and one of Gandhi's most abiding contributions to humanity, is not as widely known as *satyagraha*. And yet he came to believe that it was even more important. As Michael Nagler argues, Gandhi's nonviolent resistance was non-cooperation with evil, a strong No to laws and practices that deprived Indians of their basic human rights.[11] Saying No to evil was implicitly an affirmation of good, but it did not build up the whole Indian community. He advocated Indian self-help programs in South Africa, but his primary focus there and in the first *satyagraha* campaigns in India was resisting government domination. After he suspended the Non-Cooperation S*atyagraha* against the British in 1922, he thought more deeply about initiating a wide range of programs to uplift the oppressed and to create social harmony: the Constructive Programme. This was saying Yes to India as a community whether or not the British were still present. By the time he wrote *Constructive Programme: Its Meaning and Place* in 1941, Gandhi believed that civil disobedience—or any primarily political action—was less significant in gaining independence than the Constructive Programme.

He wanted the privileged to work on the village level side by side with the underprivileged, forging a union that would ultimately be more powerful than the government. It was Gandhi's conviction that the many initiatives of the Constructive Programme would transform Indian society: Hindu-Muslim unity; fostering the use of Indian languages, not primarily English; spinning *khadi*, homespun cloth; *swadeshi*, supporting local industries; and the uplift of the poor, women, and untouchables. The process of the richer and the poorer working together would itself contribute to overcoming pernicious social divisions, and the productive powers of a united people would be greater than the dominance of oppressive leaders. The day before he was killed, Gandhi called on the members of the Indian National Congress to withdraw from political power and dedicate themselves to the Constructive Programme, a call that very few were inclined to follow.

Gandhi's experiments with truth were designed to bring about *swaraj*, personal self-rule and home rule, which meant not only liberation from foreign rule but also universal social welfare, *sarvodaya*. Gandhi and other *satyagrahis* experimented with truth in their private lives; for without truthful living how could they find their own spiritual essence, and how could they become models of truthful living for others? Gandhi's life-long striving to apply his experiments to his daily life and to practice *satyagraha* and the Constructive Programme in the broader socio-political realm has taken root in the hearts and minds of more and more people. For Gandhi, the personal was the political.

ABOUT *GANDHI'S EXPERIMENTS WITH TRUTH*

Gandhi's Experiments with Truth is the only book containing a biographical introduction to Gandhi, a selection of his essential writings, and recent essays by many highly regarded researchers on Gandhi.

The book consists of three major sections: I. Gandhi's Life and Thought, II. Selections from Writings by Gandhi, and III. Writings about Gandhi. In Section I., a biographical sketch of Gandhi is given in historical context. It is important to understand Gandhi's life. As he wrote, "my life is my message." This first section consists of two chapters, Chapter 1, From Childhood to *Satyagrahi*, and Chapter 2, Return to India.

Section II. Selections from Writings by Gandhi contains excerpts from his books, a major pamphlet, and many short writings. The first four chapters are excerpted from three books, *An Autobiography: The Story of My Experiments with Truth*, *Satyagraha in South Africa*, *Hind Swaraj* (*Indian Home Rule*), and one pamphlet, *Constructive Programme: Its Meaning and Place*. Although his autobiography and *Satyagraha in South Africa* were written after he wrote *Hind Swaraj*, they are included as the first two chapters here because they describe the years before he wrote *Hind Swaraj* in 1909, as well as several years after that time. His autobiography has chapters about his parents, childhood and adolescence, his years in London, his return to India, his coming of age in South Africa, and his first years back in India. As the title suggests, *Satyagraha in South Africa* focuses on the campaigns he led in South Africa. In *Hind Swaraj* Gandhi develops his critique of modern civilization and suggests how Indian home rule can be attained by *satyagraha*. Gandhi's pamphlet *Constructive Programme*, written in 1941 when he was 71, is his definitive statement on the interlocking projects he and his co-workers introduced to reform India from the bottom up. Chapter 5 *Hind Swaraj* and Chapter 6 *Constructive Programme* include additional writings related to central themes in these two works.

Chapter 7, the longest chapter in the book, contains selections from Gandhi's short writings on moral and political topics. The vast majority of Gandhi's extensive writings were short journal articles, letters, and interviews. He was often at his best responding to events and issues in the moment. He did not see himself as a systematic thinker and chose not to describe in depth his whole theory and practice, with the exception of *Satyagraha in South Africa*, *Hind Swaraj* and *Constructive Programme*.

Most of the 100 volumes of his complete works are short pieces on a wide variety of topics. The selections in Chapter 7 are arranged alphabetically by topic and chronologically within each topic. To maintain the continuity of text in all the selections by Gandhi, words or sentences omitted are not indicated by ellipses. However, the selections are as Gandhi wrote them, or had them translated into English, except for an occasional short editorial addition, indicated in square brackets.

Section III. Writings about Gandhi is in two parts: III. A. Gandhi's Practice and Theory of *Satyagraha,* Chapters 8-13, and III. B. Gandhi's Impact on the World, Chapters 14-19. An enormous body of research has been written about Gandhi, possibly more than about any other figure of the twentieth century. Bhikhu Parekh writes in Chapter 17, "opinions about his achievements remain deeply divided." His critics believe, for example, that Gandhi "hampered the emergence of a strong and powerful state" in India, whereas his admirers believe that "he led the greatest anti-colonial struggle in history."[12] In researching Gandhi, many seek to develop the final, ultimate "truth" about his life and work. But Douglas Allen cautions us in Chapter 16 to consider that "there is no exclusive, nondialectical, absolute, static, eternal, true Gandhi or Gandhian political perspective. Therefore, what follows should be seen as several of many possible ways to reinterpret and reconstruct a Gandhian approach to the nature of truth, nonviolence, self, and self-other relations as essential to political reality. Such an approach is consistent with Gandhi's own dynamic, open-ended, relative, experiments with truth."[13] Allen goes on to assert that, although there is no one eternally valid Gandhian perspective, he is *not* saying "anything goes." Rather, the point of view of the researcher, or for that matter of the reader, is an important variable in an interpretation of Gandhi. Gandhi himself wrote that there are "as many religions as minds."[14] If that is true, it would follow that there are as many points of view on Gandhi as there are minds thinking about him.

The writers of the twelve essays in Section III. provide readers with balanced and informative perspectives on Gandhi. These researchers—including several who are nonviolent activists—come from the United States, Canada, Great Britain and India, with academic credentials in several different disciplines— political science, history, literature, philosophy, religious studies, and peace studies. Most of the articles were published in the Eighties and Nineties, and some were written for this book.

There are discussion topics and questions as well as links to other websites on Gandhi and nonviolence at gandhisexperimentswithtruth.com

NOTES

1. Speech at Gandhi Seva Sangh Meeting—III, *Gandhi Seva Sanghke Divitiya Adhiveshan,* 50, 3-3-36.

2. *An Autobiography: The Story of My Experiments with Truth* (Boston: Beacon Press, 1957), xii.

3. In Mohandas K. Gandhi, *An Autobiography: The Story of My Experiments with Truth* (Boston: Beacon Press, 1993), xv-xvi.

4. *Autobiography* (1957), 48-49.

5. *Autobiography*, 55.

6. *Autobiography*, 34.

7. *Autobiography*, xiv.

8. *Autobiography*, xii-xiii.

9. Ch. 10, 219.

10. Ch. 12, 244.

11. Ch. 13, 254.

12. 334.

13. Ch. 18, 315–16.

14. Cited in Terchek, ch. 10, footnote 81, 224.

I

GANDHI'S LIFE AND THOUGHT

Gandhi on a visit to London, 1906

Gandhi with his wife, Kasturbhai, 1913

1

From Childhood to *Satyagrahi*

Richard L. Johnson

THE EARLY YEARS: INDIA, LONDON, AND BACK TO INDIA

Gandhi was born in 1869 in Porbandar, a coastal town in the region of Gujarat in Western India. The family was of the Bania or merchant caste, at a time when the network of caste, subcaste, and clan was the primary factor determining one's place in Indian society. The name Gandhi means grocer, but his grandfather and father were able to become prime ministers of small princely states in Gujarat where the young Gandhi spent the first twenty years of his life. In his *Autobiography* he describes his father, Karamchand (Kaba), as "a lover of his clan, truthful, brave and generous, but short-tempered."[1] Kaba married four times, having lost his first three wives in succession through death. He and his fourth wife, Putlibai, had a daughter and three sons, the last of which was Mohandas. Gandhi wrote, "the outstanding impression my mother has left on my memory is that of saintliness. She was deeply religious."[2]

His parents were Vaishnavites, devotees of the Hindu God Vishnu. His mother belonged to the Pranami sect, which read from Hindu scriptures and the Koran. The family welcomed Muslims, Parsis, and Jains into their home where the young Mohandas heard his father and their guests engage in extended conversations on religious topics. In his adult years, Gandhi carried on the political acumen, strong religious faith, and respect for different religious traditions that were present in his mother and father as he grew up.

He was married at the age of thirteen to Kasturbhai, also thirteen. Gandhi admitted to being "a passionate, jealous, and exacting husband" at an early age, seeking to dominate his wife, who went back at times to her parents' home for respite from him.[3] At sixteen, filled with "carnal lust," he left his father, who was gravely ill, to be with his wife.[4] His father died shortly after his departure, much to Gandhi's shame.

The young Gandhi was "mediocre" in elementary school and painfully shy.[5] He improved academically in high school but found college too difficult and returned home in his first year. His older brother and his mother agreed to send him to London to study law, which at the time did not require an undergraduate degree. Law was a practical course of study for a young man who might follow in his father's footsteps. However, the elders of his caste ordered him to stay in India, believing that an extended stay in London could lead the young Gandhi away from Hindu tradition. They declared him an outcast when he decided to go in spite of their order. He set sail for England without Kasturbhai, the norm for Indian men studying abroad at that time.

In London he aspired at first to be a proper British gentleman but soon realized there was more serious work to be done. He committed himself early on to two experiments with truth: vegetarianism and religion. He had become a vegetarian by choice in his first major experiment in his private life. Now he began to see vegetarianism as a "mission," an experiment in public life. "Full of the neophyte's zeal," he founded a vegetarian club and acquired "some little training in organizing and conducting institutions."[6] The club came to an end when he moved to a different area of London, but he had begun the process of taking his personal convictions out into the wider world.

Religion became his second great experiment with truth, but initially he gave his own faith little thought. In London Gandhi was in many ways more interested in modern British society than in Hinduism. London was the center of the "civilized world," and he believed that the British Empire was in the main a force for good. It is not surprising, then, that it was two British brothers, Theosophists, who stimulated his interest in his own religion. They asked him to help them read the *Bhagavad Gita* in the original Sanskrit along with Edwin Arnold's English translation, *The Song Celestial*. This reading and his subsequent study of theosophical texts, of Arnold's *The Light of Asia*—a celebration of Buddha's life—and of the Bible were the beginning for him of a lifelong fascination with religions, both East and West. Although the Old Testament was boring to him, "the New Testament produced a different impression, especially the Sermon on the Mount which went straight to my heart."[7] Characteristically, he sought to find a common thread among the religious traditions he encountered: "My young mind tried to unify the teaching of the Gita, *The Light of Asia* and the Sermon on the Mount. That renunciation was the highest form of religion appealed to me greatly."[8]

Although his religious studies held greater interest for Gandhi than the study of law, he was able to pass the bar in 1891. He immediately set sail for India. Upon his arrival he learned that his mother had died while he was away. He had not been informed because his brother did not want him to suffer in a foreign land. Her death was "a severe shock" to him, more painful even than the loss of his father.

Gandhi soon suffered a second shock: he was a complete failure as a lawyer. His study of law in England had not prepared him for Indian law, and he had never shed the shyness he felt as a child. He wrote of his first case in a small claims court: "I appeared for the defendant and had thus to cross-examine the plaintiff's witnesses. I stood up, but my heart sank into my boots. My head was reeling and I felt as though the whole court was doing likewise. The judge must have laughed, and the vakils [lawyers] no doubt enjoyed the spectacle. But I was past seeing anything. I sat down and told the agent I could not conduct the case."[9] He tried his hand at drafting legal documents but could not earn a living at it. He applied for a teaching position but was rejected because he had dropped out of college before studying law.

At the tender age of twenty-three, Gandhi's professional life was at a dead end. To be sure, he had a law degree from London but neither the training nor the personality needed to pursue a legal career in India. His family had paid to send him to England, but all he did in his first six months of legal practice was to incur more debt. He had a wife, an infant son, but no money and no clear idea what direction his life should take. According to Judith Brown, Gandhi was, at this juncture of his life, "an Indian nonentity."[10]

Within a short time, however, he received the offer of a job in South Africa from a Muslim firm based in Porbandar. A protracted legal case involving that firm and another Indian firm would require Gandhi's attention, probably more as a legal clerk than as a lawyer. But he leaped at the opportunity to leave India and to try his luck elsewhere. Since he believed he would not remain in South Africa more than a year, he set sail without Kasturbhai and their young son Harilal.

SOUTH AFRICA

When he arrived in South Africa, Gandhi had no idea he would wind up staying there for twenty-one years. In these years he was able to transform himself from "an Indian nonentity" to one of the most respected Indian leaders of the time. How could he have made such extraordinary changes during his South African years? In his *Autobiography*, Gandhi reports the pivotal event that began the process of change barely a week after his arrival in South Africa, a journey by train from Durban to Pretoria:

> A first class seat was booked for me. A passenger came and looked me up and down. He saw that I was a "coloured" man. This disturbed him. Out he went and came in again with one or two officials. They all kept quiet, when another official came to me and said, "Come along, you must go to the van compartment."

"But I have a first class ticket," said I.

"That doesn't matter," rejoined the other. "I tell you, you must go to the van compartment."

"I tell you, I was permitted to travel in this compartment at Durban, and I insist on going on in it."

"No, you won't," said the official. "You must leave this compartment, or else I shall have to call a police constable to push you out."

"Yes, you may. I refuse to get out voluntarily."

The constable came. He took me by the hand and pushed me out. My luggage was also taken out. I refused to go to the other compartment and the train steamed away. I went and sat in the waiting room, keeping my hand-bag with me, and leaving the other luggage where it was. The railway authorities had taken charge of it. . . .

It was winter, and winter in the higher regions of South Africa is severely cold. Maritzburg being at a high altitude, the cold was extremely bitter. My over-coat was in my luggage, but I did not dare to ask for it lest I should be insulted again, so I sat and shivered.

I began to think of my duty. Should I fight for my rights or go back to India, or should I go on to Pretoria without minding the insults, and return to India after finishing the case? It would be cowardice to run back to India without fulfilling my obligation. The hardship to which I was subjected was superficial—only a symptom of the deep disease of colour prejudice. I should try, if possible, to root out the disease and suffer hardships in the process. Redress for wrongs I should seek only to the extent that would be necessary for the removal of the colour prejudice.

So I decided to take the next available train to Pretoria.[11]

Why would the dark-skinned Gandhi refuse to cooperate with the whites when he was told he would be ejected? Most blacks and Indians in South Africa knew their place and would not dare openly oppose white authority. Almost all suffered the humiliation in silence. A "nonentity" would not have defied a deeply entrenched system of racial injustice.

There was clearly a steely resolve in the twenty-three-year-old Gandhi that had not shown itself when he appeared in court in India. It was his devotion to truth, the beginning of a new experiment, which led him to believe he could do something to "root out the disease of colour prejudice." For him to believe that he was experiencing no more than a "superficial . . . symptom" means he knew a deeper truth: all humans are fundamentally equal. Color, race, and creed are insignificant surface phenomena. His upbringing in India and his study of religion in London taught him that he was a child of God no less than the officials who threw him off the train. At that time he knew nothing of *satyagraha*, but out of his devotion to truth he was compelled to seek redress of the wrongs he and others were experiencing.

Gandhi suffered further hardships. On the same trip, a coachman beat him and tried to throw him off the coach until other passengers intervened. Later on he was kicked into the gutter by a sentry when he dared to walk on the sidewalk in front of the home of the president of South Africa. Upon his return from a trip to India he was attacked by a mob of angry whites. Another Indian nearly killed him when he temporarily called off a campaign against the South African government. Throughout all this and more, Gandhi continued his experiments with truth in the private and public spheres.

During his early years in South Africa, his religious experiments became even more central to his life than they had been in London. He was influenced by two Western authors, Leo Tolstoy and John Ruskin, and by an Indian, Rajchandra Ravjibhai Mehta, whom he called Raychandbhai. Early in his years in South Africa, Tolstoy's *The Kingdom of God Is within You* "overwhelmed" him, leaving "an abiding impression."[12] Tolstoy was the first modern writer Gandhi encountered who wrote that the force of truth and love could completely transform culture and politics. It is hard to imagine Gandhi's subsequent political development without Tolstoy's influence. Gandhi read other works by Tolstoy, and they corresponded shortly before Tolstoy died.

Given Ruskin's *Unto This Last* to read on a long train trip in 1904, Gandhi could not put the book down: "It gripped me. Johannesburg to Durban was a twenty-four hours' journey. The train reached there in the evening. I could not get any sleep that night. I determined to change my life in accordance with the ideals of the book."[13] Ruskin's idea that manual labor was essential to the good life made Gandhi think about founding a community based on a shared commitment to working the land and to handicrafts. He decided to found his first ashram, the Phoenix Settlement, the beginning of a series of experiments in communal living.

Raychandbhai's impact on Gandhi was even greater than Tolstoy's and Ruskin's. Their books were influential, but it was Raychandbhai's "living contact" that changed his life.[14] The young Gandhi responded to Raychandbhai's "wide knowledge of the scriptures, his spotless character, and his burning passion for self-realization."[15] Raychandbhai was particularly helpful to Gandhi in South Africa, where he went through a spiritual crisis. Amidst his growing doubts about Hinduism, Gandhi's Muslim and Christian associates sought to convert him to their religions. Raychandbhai's letters to him and the Hindu readings he suggested gave Gandhi the knowledge and confidence he needed to deepen in his own faith.

Under the influence of Raychandbhai, Tolstoy, and Ruskin—moderns from the East and the West—Gandhi took his experience of religion into the political sphere. He blended the spirituality of the East and the political activism of the West into a practice unusual in the East or the West. Indian religious traditions tended to treat the world as an illusion and therefore not worthy of a spiritual seeker's attention. Self-realization, or *moksha*—liberation from the cycle of birth and death—could best be attained by separating oneself from the illusions of the outer world. The tendency in the West was and is to split religion and morality off from politics, the "real world" of individual achievement and

This is incredibly true and [handwritten margin note]

soc..l concern. Gandhi's belief in serving others in the Indian community pro-vided the bridge between religion and politics: "If I found myself entirely ab-sorbed in the service of the community, the reason behind it was my desire for self-realization. I had made the religion of service my own, and I felt that God could be realized only through service."[16] This was the beginning of Gandhi's "Religion of Service" that would become an integral part of *satyagraha.*

It was in South Africa that Gandhi experienced law as an experiment with truth for the first time. Then as now, most lawyers treated law as the clash of interests between two parties in which one would win and the other lose the case. In the case Gandhi worked on, his employer Dada Abdulla "won" af-ter both sides agreed to arbitration. But if Abdulla had insisted on obtaining the financial settlement immediately, Tyeb Sheth, the "loser," would have been ruined. Gandhi got Abdulla to grant

Mediation [handwritten margin note]

> Sheth installments spread over a very long period. . . . Both were happy over the result, and both rose in the public estimation. My joy was boundless. I had learnt the true practice of law. I had learnt to find out the better side of human nature and to enter men's hearts. I realized the true function of a lawyer was to unite parties riven asunder. The lesson was indelibly burnt into me that a large part of my time during the next twenty years of my practice as a lawyer was oc-cupied in bringing about private compromises of hundreds of cases. I lost noth-ing thereby—not even money, certainly not my soul.[17]

Gandhi had moved away from the adversarial model of the law toward a model based on the highest good of both parties. For Gandhi, the true prac-tice of law was to create, in modern terms, a win/win situation where both sides could accept the results. Moreover, "to unite parties riven asunder" was a service to the community, a part of Gandhi's Religion of Service.

wrote for truth [handwritten margin note]

Editing and writing columns for *Indian Opinion*, his journal in South Africa, as well as carrying on correspondence with readers were further experiments for Gandhi. He learned the "real conditions of Indians in South Africa" and studied "human nature in all its casts and shades . . ., es-tablishing an intimate and clean bond between the editor and the readers. . . . I realized that the sole aim of journalism should be service."[18] *Indian Opinion,* important in his public service before *satyagraha,* became es-sential after it had been launched: "Week after week I poured out my soul in its columns, and expounded the principles of Satyagraha as I under-stood it. . . . Satyagraha would probably have been impossible without *In-dian Opinion.*"[19]

After he returned to India, he edited three more journals: *Young India, Navajivan,* and *Harijan.* Gandhi was an extraordinarily prolific journalist who needed the "clean bond between the editor and the readers." His works include a few books, interviews, and correspondence with cowork-ers, the general public in India, opponents, and interested parties from all over the world; but most of his writings—one hundred volumes in *The Col-*

lected Works of Mahatma Gandhi—are articles he published in his journals. He was not concerned with consistency in his ideas but rather with moving from "truth to truth" in the moment. As he wrote in his *Autobiography*, "I am not writing to please critics. Writing is itself one of the experiments with truth."[20]

One of Gandhi's major experiments with truth was the practice of *brahmacharya*, generally translated as celibacy but actually "control of the senses in thought, word and deed."[21] His initial motivation to become a *brahmachari*, one who practices *brahmacharya*, had to do with chastity, the narrower meaning of the word. He wished to expand his dedication to the Indian community in South Africa, and he believed that having more children would stand in the way of his public service.

However, even though he often tried to rein in his passions, he failed until he made a vow of *brahmacharya* in 1906. Gandhi believed this vow transformed his marriage with Kasturbhai. He had been the "blind, infatuated husband"; she had been the "object of his lust."[22] Moreover, as the man of the family, he thought he had the right and responsibility to give her orders. She did not always agree. In 1898, they argued over the cleaning of a chamber pot. Gandhi made it a practice to invite law clerks to live in his home. The conflict came when one of the Indian clerks—a convert to Christianity but from an untouchable family—did not clean his chamber pot. As a caste Hindu, Kasturbhai had been taught that contact with the waste of an untouchable would result in her defilement. Gandhi not only expected her to clean the pot but to do it "cheerfully." When she did not, he dragged and shoved her out to the gate where he planned to push her out into the street. He shouted at her, and "she shouted back: 'Have you no sense of shame? Must you so far forget yourself? Where am I to go?'"[23] Her words brought him back to his senses, and they went back inside. This scene was more violent than other conflicts between them, but to Gandhi it was emblematic of his mistreatment of his wife until he chose to be a *brahmachari*: "with the gradual disappearance in me of the carnal appetite, my domestic life became and is becoming more and more peaceful, sweet and happy."[24]

He slowly learned the deeper meaning of *brahmacharya*, the control of his senses as he strove to come closer to Truth. The process for Gandhi was never ending. He believed that one must learn "control of the palate," choosing a diet which is "limited, simple, spiceless, and, if possible, uncooked."[25] He found fasting essential as well. Since *brahmacharya* was not only controlling sexual passion but also all of the senses, fasting and reducing one's focus on food were just as important to Gandhi.

He believed that the "mind is at the root of sensuality"[26] and that the only path to mental control was complete reliance on God as Truth. The lower self—the body, desires, and the mind—had to be replaced by the divine self. Although control of the lower self, especially the mind, is *very* difficult, "nevertheless, the existence of God within makes even control of the mind possible."[27]

Experiments with truth were the process of learning to replace the lower self with the higher self. Experimentation was needed because the higher self had to be experienced moment by moment to become a viable force in one's life.

Gandhi believed that there was a deep connection between *brahmacharya* and *satyagraha.* The vow of *brahmacharya* was taken in 1906 little more than a month before "the foundation of satyagraha was laid. As though unknown to me, the *brahmacharya* vow had been preparing me for it. Satyagraha had not been a preconceived plan. It came on spontaneously, without my having willed it. But I could see that all my previous steps had led up to that goal."[28] He believed that a spiritual force guided his major and even minor steps in life: "on an examination of the greatest steps I have taken in my life, as also of those that may be regarded as the least, I think it will not be improper to say that all of them were directed by Spirit."[29] These steps brought him to *satyagraha,* the experiment with truth for which he is known worldwide.

The earliest form of s*atyagraha*, passive resistance, began on September 11, 1906, at a mass meeting in Johannesburg. Among the resolutions drafted by Gandhi and others to win rights for Indians in South Africa, the most crucial involved the determination not to submit to a new law which would reduce them to even greater servitude than before. The electrifying moment came when one of the Indian leaders, the Muslim Sheth Haji Habib, "declared in the name of God that he would not submit to that law, and advised all present to do likewise."[30] Gandhi was initially taken aback by Habib's declaration, but soon he welcomed it with enthusiasm, realizing that it brought a new level of commitment to the struggle. Making a solemn pledge in the name of God meant to Gandhi that he would move forward with every fiber of his being to overcome the injustice of the law. He would die rather than submit to it.

All present at the meeting made the solemn declaration, but most fell away from it when the white government increased its pressure on the Indian resisters. The support of the Indian community waxed and waned, but Gandhi and his small band of coworkers continued, no matter how the government responded to their campaign. After 1906 Gandhi reflected about the process of passive resistance, the English term used at the time for their nonviolent resistance movement. He realized that a new term was needed. *Satyagraha*—soul or truth force—was the word Gandhi coined to demonstrate that they were seeking to bring a spiritual force to bear on the political process. This was active resistance to the injustices of the government, not passive resistance.

In 1909, as he was returning to South Africa by ship from England, he set down a full statement of this new approach to political change. He wrote out *Hind Swaraj (Indian Home Rule)* so quickly—in just ten days—that he had to switch at times from the right to the left hand. The book is a dialogue between an Editor, Gandhi, and a Reader, an Indian who believed that terrorist attacks against the British were needed to drive them out of India. The Editor—Gandhi's mouthpiece—explained how violence would wind up strengthening the hand of the British, who were after all more adept at brute force than the Indians. Nonviolence would strengthen the Indians because it would create greater unity and make it possible for India and Great Britain to become, in the long run, allies instead of enemies.

In *Hind Swaraj*, Gandhi sought to demonstrate that home rule, outer *swaraj*, was the direct result of inner *swaraj* or self-rule. He believed outer and inner *swaraj* would make India a strong nation, a model of political change for the whole world. He rejected the widely held notion that the individual and the nation were separate from each other. In a letter written a few months after completing *Hind Swaraj*, Gandhi stated: "Emancipate your own self. Even that burden is very great. Apply everything to yourself. Nobility of soul consists in realizing that you are yourself India. In your emancipation is the emancipation of India. All else is makebelieve."[31]

Gandhi argued in *Hind Swaraj* that the cause of Indians' oppression was not primarily the British but rather Modern Civilization. To be sure, the British were representatives of that civilization, but their exploitation of India was rooted in a deeper malady, modernity itself. As Gandhi stated in the preface to *Hind Swaraj*,

> The British Government in India constitutes a struggle between the Modern Civilization, which is the Kingdom of Satan, and the Ancient Civilization, which is the Kingdom of God. The one is the God of War, the other is the God of Love. My countrymen impute the evils of modern civilization to the English people and, therefore, believe that the English people are bad, and not the civilization they represent. My countrymen, therefore, believe that they should adopt modern civilization and modern methods of violence to drive out the English. 'Hind Swaraj' has been written in order to show that they are following a suicidal policy, and that, if they would but revert to their own glorious civilization, either the English would adopt the latter and become Indianised or find their occupation in India gone.[32]

Modern Civilization was irreligious and immoral, based on materialism. Gandhi reminded his reader that the English were "a nation of shop-keepers" and that "money" was their "God." The only reason they continued to rule India was that Indians kept them for their own "base self-interest."[33] He recognized that blaming the British would perpetuate their power because the very act of blaming acknowledged that it was the British who were in control, not the Indians. Once Indians understood that they had chosen the British Raj, they could then choose to end it. It was necessary first to awaken among a small number of Indians, *satyagrahis,* the awareness that Indians, not the British, were responsible for India's plight.

He emphasized that using the violent means of Modern Civilization produced violent ends. Modern Western thought tends to assume that the ends justify the means. It is commonly asserted in politics that moral people can use immoral means to produce moral ends. Gandhi stated in *Hind Swaraj* that "the means may be likened to a seed, the end to a tree; and there is just the same inviolable connection between the means and the end as there is between the seed and the tree."[34] This conviction, that means and ends are connected as naturally as seed and tree, led him to reject the belief that the ends justify the means.

Gandhi devoted several chapters in *Hind Swaraj* to exposing the dangers of the modern machine craze as well as modern law, medicine, and transportation systems. He believed that modern industry, as well as modern professions, concentrated wealth in the hands of the few at the expense of the many, particularly the poor peasants of India. In *Hind Swaraj*, Gandhi overreacted at times to machines, doctors, lawyers, and railroads, but behind the reaction was a critique of the exploitation of the poor under the guise of material progress. He clarified his position in the years after *Hind Swaraj* by asserting that he was opposed to the "mania for the machine," the tendency in Modern Civilization to place higher value on machines than on people. As long as machines served people, particularly the masses, Gandhi believed that machines were useful.

In his zeal to expose the materialism and violence of modernity, Gandhi tended in *Hind Swaraj* and later in his life to equate Modern Civilization with its evils and to posit traditional Indian culture as inherently spiritual and non-violent. In fact, modernity has strengths and weaknesses, as did ancient India. Gandhi himself learned much from modernity—for example the theory and practice of democracy and human rights—as he acknowledged on many occasions.

In 1913, four years after writing *Hind Swaraj*, Gandhi and his tiny band of *satyagrahis* won major concessions for the Indian community from the South African government. One of the reasons they had remained small and isolated from broader levels of support was that they were a movement of middle-class men. Class and gender divisions were as common among Indians as they were among whites in South Africa. But in his devotion to the uplift of the whole Indian community, Gandhi began moving slowly away from the comfort of class and gender privileges. As a lawyer, he worked with many poor Indians, primarily indentured workers. In the two decades he spent in South Africa, he developed a strong commitment to their well-being. In this same period he worked diligently to accept Kasturbhai as an equal, indeed as his teacher in nonviolence. On his initiative, men and women in the ashrams he founded in South Africa and later in India performed the same tasks, a highly unusual practice in the period.

Only men, however, engaged in the *satyagraha* campaigns until 1913. That year a judge of the Cape Supreme Court decided to limit legal marriage to officially registered Christian unions. The Indian community was outraged that their marriages became illegal with the stroke of a pen. Their children were suddenly considered bastards and their wives concubines. It was at this time that Gandhi asked women to join in the nonviolent resistance because he believed they were as directly affected by the court decision as the men. Several women decided to seek arrest by illegally crossing the border between the Transvaal and Natal. Although they were not arrested as they had hoped, they did win over a number of indentured Indian mineworkers to their cause. The white government had not only nullified non-Christian marriages, but also it had levied a £3 tax, which fell heavily on the indentured workers in South Africa. Thousands of mineworkers, and their wives and children, decided to leave the mines and join the effort of the women to court arrest.

For the first time, then, the small band of middle-class men worked with women and a large number of poor mineworkers and their families to become a force too great for the authorities to ignore. Gandhi and over two thousand women and men embarked on the Great March of 1913, a holy pilgrimage for them which led to mass arrests and strikes at other mines. General Jan Smuts, Minister of the Interior of the South Africa government, realized that the cost of maintaining the anti-Indian laws was greater than their intended benefits. He appointed a commission which recommended ending the laws most offensive to the Indians in South Africa. With the success of their final campaign, Gandhi and many of the *satyagrahis* decided to return to India.

NOTES

1. Gandhi, Mohandas K., *An Autobiography: The Story of My Experiments with Truth*. Boston: Beacon Press, 1993, 3.
2. *Autobiography*, 4.
3. Easwaran, Eknath, *Gandhi the Man: The Story of His Transformation*, 3rd ed., (Tomales, CA: Nilgiri Press, 1997), 15.
4. *Autobiography*, 29.
5. *Autobiography*, 6.
6. *Autobiography*, 58.
7. *Autobiography*, 68.
8. *Autobiography*, 69.
9. *Autobiography*, 94.
10. Brown, Judith, *Gandhi: Prisoner of Hope* (New Haven, CT: Yale University Press), 7.
11. *Autobiography*, 111–12.
12. *Autobiography*, 137.
13. *Autobiography*, 298.
14. *Autobiography*, 90.
15. *Autobiography*, 88.
16. *Autobiography*, 158.
17. *Autobiography*, 134.

18. *Autobiography*, 286–87.

19. *Autobiography*, 286.

20. *Autobiography*, 280.

21. *Autobiography*, 210.

22. *Autobiography*, 278.

23. *Autobiography*, 277.

24. *Autobiography*, 278.

25. *Autobiography*, 209.

26. *Autobiography*, 210.

27. *Autobiography*, 211.

28. *Autobiography*, 208.

29. *Autobiography*, 279.

30. *Satyagraha in South Africa, The Collected Works of Mahatma Gandhi* (New Delhi: Publication Division, Ministry of Information and Broadcasting, 1958–1994), 29:88.

31. Iyer, Raghavan, *The Moral and Political Writings of Mahatma Gandhi* (Oxford: Clarendon Press, 1986), vol. I, 340, 4-2-10.

32. Gandhi, Mohandas, *Hind Swaraj and Other Writings*, ed. Anthony Parel (Cambridge: Cambridge University Press, 1997), 7.

33. *Hind Swaraj and Other Writings*, 41.

34. *Hind Swaraj and Other Writings*, 81.

Gandhi and satyagrahis *on Salt March, 1930*

Gandhi with textile workers in England, 1931

Gandhi sharing a joke with Nehru, 1946

2

Return to India

Richard L. Johnson

FROM LOYALTY TO THE EMPIRE
TO NON-COOPERATION: 1915–1922

In many ways South Africa had been an ideal laboratory for Gandhi's experiments with truth. The Indian community was not very large, and it was relatively unified across religious barriers. Many in India celebrated his work for the Indians in South Africa and hoped he would be able to make further contributions upon his return to India. Believing that *satyagraha* was an approach with potentially universal application, Gandhi looked forward to experimenting in a much larger laboratory, the Indian subcontinent.

He knew, however, that he would face a number of challenges in India. Before his return, he asked himself, "What shall I do with myself?"[1] Having been gone for twenty-one years, he had no experience as a leader in India and no power base. It was also difficult for Gandhi to sort out his long-standing loyalty to the British Empire. Although he believed that the Indian people needed and deserved *swaraj*, he still viewed the Empire overall as a greater force for good than for evil. He had formed close friendships with several of the British in South Africa. In London before returning to India, Gandhi organized an ambulance corps to support the British war effort.[2] After his return to India, he was a "recruiting sergeant" for the British Army in the midst of growing opposition to the British Raj. Two Home Rule organizations had been formed, and most Indians working for independence found Gandhi's support of the Empire contradictory, given his stated belief in *swaraj* and *satyagraha*. He wrote then and later that life was too complex to be able to base one's every action on a single principle. As much as he believed in both *swaraj* and *satyagraha,* his role as citizen of the British Empire required that he support it in times of need. Living as he did under the protection of the British, he felt he had to do his best to support them in World War I. He also wrote that Indian service in the war effort could help Indian aspirations for independence after the war.

Gandhi's greatest problem in his early years back in India was that neither he nor his ideas fit into any established religious or political mold. His desire to combine the religious, spiritual, and moral with the social and political was rare in a country where most holy men, *saddhus*, withdrew from the world. Many educated Indians and British politicians did not believe that he could be both religious and political. They thought he was actually a scheming politician hiding behind a façade of holier-than-thou rhetoric.

The Westernized Indians as a whole were in one of two political camps, the moderates or the extremists. The moderates advocated petitioning the British for gradual political change. This was the method Gandhi used for years in South Africa, a method he ultimately rejected because it did not work. Asking those in power to give it up is—as activists said during the American civil rights movement—like expecting a baseball player to strike himself out. Gandhi developed *satyagraha* because he recognized that *force* had to be employed—not brute force but soul force.

The extremist camp opted for terrorist methods. Believing that the approach of the moderates could not be successful, they were drawn to a belief in revolutionary violence. Gandhi found weaknesses in both camps. He believed that *satyagraha* was the only effective response to moderates and extremists: "I think the growing generation will not be satisfied with petitions, etc. We must give them something effective. Satyagraha is the only way, it seems to me, to stop terrorism."[3] He perceived accurately that moderates and extremists, as different as they seemed to be, were fundamentally Western in their orientation. Indian moderates were similar to British moderates, whereas Indians who espoused revolutionary violence were similar to European extremists, particularly communists. However different the two groups were, they did not, in Gandhi's opinion, understand India's essential nature, *ahimsa*. *Satyagraha* would unite all Indians. The common people more fully embodied *ahimsa* than did the educated elites, he believed, but these elites would ultimately be won over as they witnessed the successes of *satyagraha*.

In Gandhi's view, there are four essential elements of political power. First, *power is based on the consent of the people*. No matter how evil a government is, if the people consent to it, out of fear or the belief that those who govern have a right to do so, that government will remain in power. His approach to political education focused on the consent of the people and their right, indeed their duty, to withdraw that consent if they found a government oppressive: "Oppression is sin but submission to oppression is no less sin. History teaches us that neither the power of the oppressor nor the suffering of the oppressed can last for ever. Both must come to an end."[4]

Second, *satyagraha demonstrates that there are effective ways to withdraw consent*. If the people observe one person withdrawing consent successfully, they begin to believe that they too have that power. As more Indians witnessed the success of *satyagraha*, they were able to find the strength within themselves to noncooperate with the British. *Satyagraha* made liberation from oppression *visible*. Gandhi provided an "ocular demonstration" of free people choosing not to cooperate with a government.

Third, closely related to the withdrawal of consent is *the formation of public opinion*. Whether one person noncooperates, a few dozen, or tens of thousands, the long-term goal is transforming public opinion. Meeting the objectives of a particular *satyagraha* campaign is valuable but of secondary importance to changing how people think about themselves and their government. In South Africa, all the campaigns were unsuccessful until the final victory of the Great March in 1913. In India, whereas several local or regional campaigns were successful, none of the Indiawide campaigns brought British rule to an end. However, all the campaigns contributed to a slow but steady change in the way the Indian public viewed itself and the British. As Gandhi wrote, "*Satyagraha* is a process of educating public opinion such that it covers all the elements of society and in the end makes itself irresistible."[5]

In his early work in India, whether he was engaged in social or political work—it was all the same to him—Gandhi was seeking to form among Indians the belief in their independence and to undermine their belief in the British as legitimate rulers. This fourth element of power, *legitimacy*, is actually the linchpin of a government's hold on the people. The moderates failed to undermine the legitimacy of the British because, in the very act of petitioning the British to change, they continued to place the power to change in the hands of the British. The extremists failed in their terrorist attacks—brute force—because they unwittingly reinforced the legitimacy of the British whose responsibility it was to maintain law and order. As long as the British were recognized as playing a legitimate role in preventing the spread of violence, they could retain political power.

Satyagraha was forceful and active in ways that petitioning could not be; and simultaneously it undermined the legitimacy of the British because it forced *the British* to use brute force to maintain their power. *Satyagrahis* captured the moral high ground, exposing the lie that British rule was motivated by the desire to provide the necessary political leadership in India until Indians themselves could take over the reins of power. How moral is a government which attacks and jails *satyagrahis* for demanding, in a peaceful manner, the political power the British have stated they should have, sooner or later? Although few recognized what was going on in the early stages of *satyagraha* in India, Gandhi was involved in a long-term strategy to legitimize free India and delegitimize the Raj. He engaged the British in a struggle which struck at the roots of their legitimacy, whether they acted with force or allowed the *satyagrahis* to noncooperate. If they acted with force, they exposed the military basis of their power. If they failed to act, they seemed powerless to quell Indians' legitimate desire for freedom. Gandhi was playing a serious game of "heads-we-win, tails-you-lose." The true battle was for the hearts and minds of the Indian people. Increasingly they sided with Gandhi even when the British "won" an individual battle with him.

"The process of educating public opinion" became "irresistible" because the belief grew during the *satyagraha* campaigns that the time had come to replace foreign rule with Indian self-rule. *Satyagraha* dramatized a fundamental contradiction in the British Raj. At home, the British people enjoyed a robust and long-standing tradition of democracy, a democracy which they touted in their colonies as a model form of governance. But the colonials were denied democracy by the presence of British imperial power. As Jonathan Shell asserts, "empire is incompatible with democracy, whether at home or abroad. Democracy is founded on the rule of law, empire on the rule of force. Democracy is a system of self-determination, empire a system of military conquest."[6] The British maintained their legitimacy in India by asserting how benevolently they exercised their imperial power. However, the iron fist in the velvet glove was exposed to ever-wider circles of Indians when the British resorted to military force to stop *satyagraha*.

To prepare himself and other *satyagrahis* for the campaigns to come, Gandhi needed a base of operation in India. Therefore, in 1915 he founded his first ashram in India, the *Satyagraha* Ashram on the Sabarmati River near Ahmedabad, the major industrial center of Gujarat. This new community has generally been called the Sabarmati Ashram. *Satyagrahis* from the Phoenix Settlement and the Tolstoy Farm, his ashrams in South Africa, needed a place to congregate in India, and Gandhi chose a site in Gujarat in part because he and other *satyagrahis* from the region spoke Gujarati. He also discovered a number of industrialists in Ahmedabad who would make major financial contributions to his work. Gandhi's success in receiving financial backing in South Africa was developed even more fully in India.

The need for financial assistance came to the fore early in the formation of the Sabarmati Ashram. Gandhi was asked to accept "a humble and honest untouchable family" in the ashram. He agreed, but two problems came up. First, "all monetary help . . . stopped," until a rich donor drove up to the ashram and made a donation large enough to tide them over for a year.[7] This person was Ambalal Sarabhai, a young mill owner whose family would play a major role in Gandhi's life a few years later. Second, in the ashram there was strong opposition to untouchables, including Kasturbhai and others close to him. He found their opposition particularly painful, but in time all learned to accept this family and other untouchables who later joined the ashram.

Untouchability was a major problem in India, an "excrescence" in Gandhi's term, an unhealthy growth in the body of Hinduism. He wrote in 1920, "It has been argued that the practice of untouchability implies no contempt; the British put forward a similar argument in regard to their attitude toward us. If they force us to occupy separate compartments in trains, it is entirely for 'convenience of hygiene' and there is no ill will in the procedure—such is their claim. I have seen *Vaishnavas* [caste Hindus who worship Vishnu] abusing and beating up *Antyajas* [untouchables] who happened to touch them unintentionally. . . . The practice of untouchability is a blot on Hinduism."[8] Gandhi did not oppose the caste system in its entirety at this time, but he did oppose most vigorously the oppression of untouchables by caste Hindus. He made the removal of untouchability a vow of the Sabarmati Ashram and realized that if it could not be stamped out there, he could hold no hope for progress in India as a whole.

He was equally concerned by the treatment of poor peasants in India. By 1917 Gandhi felt he was ready for his first *satyagraha* campaign in India, a campaign which would become "an ocular demonstration" of the plight of poor peasants in Champaran, a district of Bihar. As always in these early years in India, since he had no political power base, his campaigns depended on local conditions and local leaders. A farmer of some means, Rajkumar Shukla, asked Gandhi to intervene in Champaran because the peasants were suffering from injustice at the hands of the British planters. The peasants had been required to grow indigo; however, after the development of synthetic dyes in Germany, demand for naturally grown indigo declined. The British planters required cash payments or increased rents to recoup their losses from the peasants. Given the steep rise in prices in India during World War I, the suffering of the peasants in Champaran was enormous. When Gandhi came to investigate the problem, the district magistrate ordered him to leave, fearing that he would cause a disturbance to the fragile peace in Champaran. He refused.

The provincial government in Bihar overruled the district magistrate, allowed Gandhi to remain in Champaran, and even authorized his investigation of the conditions there. Using his training as a lawyer, Gandhi assembled a team to carry out a thorough investigation, conducting inquiries not only of the peasants but also of the planters. The peasants were delighted that someone actually listened to them for the first time; the planters were angry at Gandhi for meddling in their affairs.

This careful analysis of the truth in a given situation became a hallmark of Gandhi's *satyagrahas* in India, a new series of experiments with truth. The British central government in Delhi ultimately sided with Gandhi in Champaran and ordered an end to requiring the peasants to grow indigo or to make cash payments. Gandhi learned a great deal about peasants there and deepened his identification with them. He began setting up elementary schools which would become centers of community uplift—an early form of the Constructive Programme—but there were not enough volunteers to continue his plan. The reverence for Gandhi grew among peasants in the area and in all of India.

In its initial stage, the work in Champaran was a *satyagraha* campaign of one person, Gandhi himself. Although others joined him in the investigation later on, he alone refused to comply with the initial order of the district mag-istrate. Asked over the years about a campaign of one *satyagrahi*, he always argued that it could have an enormous impact in the long run: "If one wish-ing to end the empire of evil customs offers non-co-operation that empire will certainly crack up. The question naturally arises as to what purpose will be served if only one person non-co-operates thus. One answer to this is that he who launches non-co-operation wins and becomes free from faults, and the empire is weakened to the extent of the loss of his co-operation. A house does not collapse if a single brick is removed, but everyone realizes that from the day the brick came off, the house has certainly begun to get weakened. While it is difficult for the first brick to get loose, it is not so for the second brick to fall away or get removed."[9] For Gandhi, Champaran was the single brick that would lead ultimately to the cracking up of the Raj.

The next brick was a campaign which took place in 1918 back in Gujarat, but this time among mill workers in Ahmedabad. Anasuya Sarabhai, Am-balal's sister, asked Gandhi to intervene in the conflict between the workers and the mill owners. He sided with the workers in their demand for higher pay, but he also cared about many of the owners, including Ambalal. His vi-sion was of a harmonious relationship between capital and labor, a unity based on the awareness that owners and workers needed each other for their industry to prosper. Gandhi asked the workers to make a solemn vow not to return to work unless their minimum demands were met, but many wavered as their strike continued. He decided to fast for the first time in a *satyagraha* campaign. Within a short time owners and workers agreed to ar-bitration, which led to the increase in wages demanded by the workers. Al-though there were complaints that his fast coerced the owners into an agree-ment, Gandhi felt that it was an act of self-purification and penance, not a form of coercion.

As a result of the Champaran, Ahmedabad, and other small-scale cam-paigns, Gandhi felt ready to take on his first Indiawide campaign in 1919, the Rowlatt *Satyagraha*. After World War I, the British government decided that it needed stronger measures to deal with Indian terrorists. The Rowlatt bills, named after the chair of the government committee which recommended their adoption, seemed reasonable to many as a response to the growing threat of terrorism. However, the British had promised during the war more self-rule in India, and now their first major legislation would involve greater powers for the British government, without including Indians in the decision-making process. Gandhi believed that the Rowlatt bills were immoral and that Indians must resist them with a nationwide *satyagraha*.

The task that lay before him and his coworkers was daunting. There was no effective nationwide organization. To be sure, two Home Rule move-ments had been launched, and the Indian National Congress was seeking wider influence. But the population in India was over three hundred million, mostly poor peasants in villages with no experience in national politics. The

Congress, established in 1885 by British and Indians who favored more rights for educated Indians, was little more than a club of lawyers with no real plan for the achievement of independence. Gandhi had extensive organizational experience in South Africa and the beginning of a following in India, but he was still an unknown quantity in national politics. There was no evidence that *satyagraha* would work with such a large and diverse population, "a multiethnic, multicaste, multireligious, multilinguistic country."[10]

It is a testimony to Gandhi's self-confidence and belief in nonviolence that he chose to initiate the first Indiawide *satyagraha* barely four years after his return to India. He framed the pledge to oppose the Rowlatt bills in characteristically lofty terms: "We solemnly affirm that, in the event of these Bills becoming law . . . we shall refuse civilly to obey these laws . . . and we further affirm that in this struggle we will faithfully follow truth and refrain from violence to life, person and property."[11]

Although the campaign had some success in Gujarat and Bombay, few thought it would spread to other areas in India. However, when Gandhi announced a *hartal*, a traditional Indian form of mourning and work stoppage, for April 6, 1919, a surprising number of people in major cities throughout India chose to observe it. In Bombay, 80 percent of the workers joined the *hartal*. As the *satyagraha* grew, government and Indian violence broke out. Gandhi observed that the government was acting "in the spirit of terrorism,"[12] although ostensibly the Rowlatt bills were to counter terrorism.

As painful as the government's violence was to Gandhi, the violence on the part of Indians was much more disturbing to him. In Amritsar four Europeans were killed and mobs actually took control of the city from the British. After Gandhi learned of the violence in Ahmedabad, he wrote the government, "I see that I overcalculated the measure of the permeation of *satyagraha* among the people."[13] He admitted that he had made a "Himalayan miscalculation" and called off civil disobedience.[14] → b/c of violence

Gandhi assumed that the Rowlatt *Satyagraha* would succeed because *satyagraha* had worked in South Africa and in local campaigns in India. He believed fervently in nonviolent noncooperation with evil, but he did not properly gauge the enormity of the task before him in India. Opposing anti-Indian laws in South Africa or local injustices in India was not the same as a direct challenge to British authority in India, the most prized colony of the most powerful empire in the world.

The Rowlatt campaign of 1919 can be seen as a dress rehearsal for, and a cause of, the Non-Cooperation Campaign of 1920 to 1922. Gandhi learned valuable lessons in 1919, particularly the need for more effective organization and publicity. To a degree surprising to nearly all observers at the time—Indians and British—Gandhi won wide levels of support within the Indian National Congress and initiated major reforms in its operations. Membership was extended beyond educated Indians. After the failure of the Rowlatt *Satyagraha*, Gandhi acquired two weekly papers, *Young India* and *Navajivan*, soon to be his primary means of communication with his followers for the upcoming Non-Cooperation Campaign.

British violence during the Rowlatt campaign led Gandhi to break with the British Empire. The terrorism of the British was the most extreme in Amritsar. General Reginald Dyer ordered his troops to fire on a large crowd of unarmed civilians in Jallianwalla Bagh, an enclosed space from which escape was almost impossible. Nearly four hundred were killed there and more than fifteen hundred were wounded. General Dyer was severely criticized by a commission which investigated the incident. However, Indians played a minor role in the investigation, and widespread racist support of Dyer in England disturbed a number of Indians, including Gandhi.

Another cause of nationwide noncooperation was a Muslim conflict with the British related to the outcome of World War I. Gandhi believed that working to resolve this conflict would contribute to Hindu-Muslim unity. The Sultan of Turkey, the Khalifah or spiritual leader, had been defeated by the Allies in the war, but his central role in Islam led to a pan-Islamic movement to help him retain a degree of temporal and spiritual leadership. Gandhi joined this Khalifat movement, led in India by two brothers, Mohamed and Shaukat Ali. However, there was no lasting increase in Hindu-Muslim unity. Relatively few Indian Muslims were involved in the Khalifat movement, and the Ali brothers turned out to be more violent in their rhetoric than Gandhi had thought they would be.

After the British violence during the Rowlatt *Satyagraha* and British opposition to the Khalifat movement, Gandhi decided that he could no longer trust the British claims that they were working toward Indian Home Rule. From his student days in London, he had learned to appreciate many kindred spirits among the British. The liberal rhetoric of the British government seemed consonant with the men and women he spent time with in London and South Africa. From 1919 through 1921, Gandhi found repeatedly that the authorities said one thing and did another. B. R. Nanda explains,

> Trusting by nature, he could make allowances for the Government as long as his faith in its sincerity remained. But when that faith was shaken, he saw the British rule in an entirely new light. He had once attributed the faults of this rule to aberrations of individuals; now its virtues appeared to him accidental or incidental. 'I said to myself,' he wrote in *Young India* (December 31, 1921) 'there is no state run by Nero or Mussolini which has not good points about it, but we have to reject the whole once we decide to non-co-operate with the system. . . . The beneficent institutions of the British government are like the fabled snake with a brilliant jewel on its head, but which has fangs full of poison."[15]

In September 1920, Gandhi announced a plan to Congress for *swaraj* within one year. The plan was greeted at first with incredulity, but the majority of the newly reorganized Congress adopted his Non-Cooperation Campaign as their official policy. A majority of Congress members chose nonviolence as a tactic, but few took on nonviolence as a way of life. They were decidedly *not satyagrahis,* bur rather politicians who found *satyagraha* a more plausible strategy than the moderates' petitioning or the extremists' terrorism. However, if the campaign did not succeed, most Congress members would abandon Gandhi and *satyagraha* with little or no hesitation.

In the midst of the Non-Cooperation Campaign, as the Congress began to represent a wider spectrum of the Indian population, he chose to wear only the traditional Indian loincloth and, in cold weather, a homespun shawl. He was working consciously to identify himself—spiritually and physically—with the "poorest of the poor" in India. Always acutely aware of the impact of clothing as a political symbol, Gandhi distanced himself even more from Western dress and thinking. He continued his friendship with British men and women and in fact widened his association with those in the West interested in nonviolence, but he chose at this critical juncture in his life and in India's struggle to strike his roots deeper in Indian traditional culture.

The Non-Cooperation Campaign achieved wider success than the Rowlatt *Satyagraha.* A greater number of Indians noncooperated with the British, and for the first time the Indian National Congress became a truly national organization. However, British legitimacy remained strong among moderates, and rural areas were for the most part not yet integrated into the nationalist movement. *Swaraj* was not won in a year. And especially painful for Gandhi, Indian violence broke out as it had at the end of the Rowlatt *Satyagraha,* but with even greater ferocity. Indians killed Europeans in Bombay, and in the most gruesome instance, twenty-two policemen were burned to death in Chauri Chaura. Gandhi called off the campaign in February 1922, much to the dismay of many Congress members, including the young Jawaharlal Nehru.

In March Gandhi was arrested. At his trial he defended himself and admitted he was guilty of sedition. However, he also presented a strong indictment against the Raj: "I came reluctantly to the conclusion that the British connection had made India more helpless than she ever was before, politically and economically. . . . She has become so poor that she has little power of resisting famines. . . . Little do they [Indians] realize that the Government . . . in British India is carried on for this exploitation of the masses. No sophistry, no jugglery in figures can explain away the evidence the skeletons in many villages present to the naked eyes."[16] He was sentenced to six years in prison, for Gandhi a necessary and honorable part of *satyagraha:* "Freedom is to be wooed only inside prison walls and sometimes on gallows."[17]

It appeared to many, British and Indians alike, that Gandhi was a spent political force after the Non-Cooperation Campaign. Lord Birkenhead, Secretary of State for India, stated in 1925, "Poor Gandhi has indeed perished!"[18] However, they underestimated Gandhi and *satyagraha.* While he lived, nothing would stop his experiments with truth. Although Non-Cooperation had been defeated by the superior strength and organization of the British government, Gandhi had become known throughout India as a fearless champion of Indian independence. In prison and apparently defeated, he maintained a nobility of spirit and hope for the future which many Indians recognized and admired.

TURNING INWARD, TRANSFORMING RELATIONSHIPS: 1922–1928

Gandhi's *Autobiography* ended with his description of the Non-Cooperation Campaign. He wrote in its final chapter, "My life from this point onward has been so public that there is hardly anything about it that people do not know."[19] After that campaign, his public life became so all-consuming that he had little time for a private life. Except for his times in jail, his sole focus was *satyagraha* and the Constructive Programme, his public experiments in truth.

The two years he served in prison, from 1922 to 1924, gave him an opportunity to rest and reflect after the heavy strain of the Non-Cooperation Campaign. As the most revered political figure in India, Gandhi was given a cleaner and more spacious prison cell than any he experienced in South Africa. His food was good, and he had the opportunity to read widely. He spent six hours a day reading, completing over one hundred books on a variety of topics, particularly Hindu scriptures and writings on other religions.

In January 1924 he underwent an emergency appendectomy and was released unconditionally from prison. He spoke with allies in the Congress to see if the work for *swaraj* could be revitalized, but the party was in disarray. Factions were fighting each other over the issue of participation in legislative bodies set up by the British to provide Indians a limited degree of self-rule. After several months of effort, he realized that it was not the time for direct political involvement. He decided to focus his attention on the spiritual base of *satyagraha* and on the Constructive Programme. He felt "defeated and humbled" that he could not forge unity in Congress and make collective progress toward *swaraj.* In the years from 1924 to 1928, he suffered bouts of depression, even despair. However, Gandhi was fundamentally an optimist who had spent twenty years working for the Indian community in South Africa before any success was achieved. Believing that "self rule is home rule" and that the social transformation of India was even more significant than Indian independence, he strove for spiritual and moral strength as well as social uplift.

In prison he read Hindu texts, including the massive *Mahabharata*—over six thousand pages long—the *Ramayana,* and the *Upanishads,* and he read and re-read the *Bhagavad Gita,* the wellspring of his faith. He believed he was an orthodox Hindu, but many found him more reformist than orthodox. He subjected all Hindu texts and practices to the light of reason and conscience and believed only what his head and heart told him was true. His experimental approach to Hinduism—testing his faith out in the real world—seemed decidedly unorthodox to many caste Hindus.

He was, however, orthodox in his belief in the unity of all that is, a foundation of Hinduism. As Douglas Allen states, "Gandhi often uses the terms Truth, God and Self interchangeably. Gandhi's political life and political thought are profoundly influenced by the presuppositions of the indivisibility of Truth, the identification of Self with Truth or God, and the essential unity of all existence."[20]

Given his belief in this fundamental unity, particularly in Hindu-Muslim unity, it was a tragedy to Gandhi that Hindu and Muslim fundamentalism was driving the two communities farther apart in the midtwenties. The more literally fundamentalist Hindus and Muslims interpreted their faiths, and the more fanatical their observation of dogmas and rituals, the greater the chasm between them. For Gandhi, who taught and lived the principle of equal regard for all religions, the awareness that he could do nothing to bridge this growing chasm was a source of deep sorrow.

From his years in South Africa and increasingly in India, Gandhi's political and social action revolved around a belief in the transformation of relationships. When he was asked toward the end of his life whether the nonviolent rebellion he advocated was not a program for the seizure of power, he replied: "No. A non-violent rebellion is not a programme of seizure of power. It is a programme of transformation of relationship ending in a peaceful transfer of power. It will never use coercion. Even those who hold contrary views will receive full protection under it."[21] *Satyagraha* was intended to transform the relationship among Indians and between Indians and the British by establishing Indians' capacity for self-rule.

He came to believe that the best way to transform relationships among Indians was the Constructive Programme. If Indians could find unity among themselves through interfaith cooperation, spinning, sharing wealth, removing untouchability, and the uplift of women, true *swaraj* would take place naturally, like a ripe fruit falling from a tree. Relationships would be transformed by overcoming artificial separations of clothing, religion, caste, class, and gender. Gandhi believed that all humans are, as souls, one. If India was not ready in the midtwenties for political unity, then let Indians transform their fractured relationships, and political unity would come in due time. All the many initiatives of the Constructive Programme were experiments with truth that did not depend on cooperation or noncooperation with the British.

Gandhi believed spinning would transform relationships in India. Rich and poor alike could spin. If India would rely primarily on homespun, extreme poverty would be overcome, the reliance on foreign cloth would be broken, and a united India would be forged. In prison he spent four hours a day spinning and carding homespun cloth, or *khadi*. When it became clear that the Congress did not genuinely support a nationwide program promoting *khadi*, he formed a new organization in 1925, the All-India Spinners' Association.

Khadi was a major foundation in Gandhi's work toward moral economics, a decentralized, bottom-up plan to overcome the materialism of Modern Civilization in India. He believed that morality and economics would be brought together as the rich chose not only to spin *khadi* but also to share their wealth with the poor. If wealthy people reduced their wants to the bare minimum and shared their financial resources with the poor, class would no longer be a barrier to unity among Indians. If the rich chose morality over materialism—if they became trustees of their wealth for the Common Good—India's soul force could lead the world into a better future. He envisioned a society dedicated to the well-being of all, *sarvodaya*.

Khadi and trusteeship were fundamental to Gandhi in part because he experienced a deep connection with his compatriots in the act of spinning and because many wealthy Indians supported the Sabarmati Ashram and his various campaigns for national independence. However, neither *khadi* nor trusteeship became the basis of the transformation of relationships in India. Gandhi's idea of moral economics was never adopted by a critical mass of Indians.

In the twenties, after throwing himself into campaigns and organizing for *khadi*, he turned his attention to the removal of untouchability. Although he initially accepted the idea of castes, he grew to believe that caste itself, at least in its modern form, was wrong. The complex and pervasive separations in Hindu society that resulted from caste, particularly the treatment of untouchables as outcastes, went completely against Gandhi's belief in spiritual unity. His beloved Hinduism would destroy itself unless caste Hindus rejected untouchability, heart and soul.

In addition to *khadi* and the removal of untouchability, Gandhi devoted himself in the twenties to one of the major initiatives of the Constructive Programme, the uplift of women. His relationship with women is a contentious area in the research about him. He has been considered an opponent to women's rights and a feminist, a traditional patriarch and an innovator in gender relations. Researchers' assessments of Gandhi can be based more on their philosophical framework than on his actual perspective on women. Moreover, his attitudes shifted over time. His statements to traditional women were generally more conservative than those he shared with women in his ashrams, where women and men performed the same tasks.

Whatever researchers think today, Indian women during his lifetime were in the main moved and sustained by his strong advocacy of their expanded role in public life. He believed that women had a right and a duty to participate in every aspect of the transformation of Indian society. Although most women chose to center their activity in the home, he did not believe in restricting them to the roles of wife and mother if they wished to focus their attention elsewhere. His understanding of women's sexuality was limited, but he did work actively for decades to free women from the sexual bondage imposed by men. Many women, who faced violence from men in their daily lives, found Gandhi's nonviolence comforting. Believing as he did that women and men were absolutely equal as souls, he fostered women's growth in ways few Indian men chose to do in the years leading up to independence.

Gandhi was generally more persuasive with women than with men. Focusing on nonviolence, love, and nurturance was as natural to him as it was to many women. Moreover, given women's central role in sustaining relationships, Gandhi's efforts to transform Indian society by transforming relationships struck a familiar chord in them. Although he may have been wrong that women are inherently more nonviolent and loving than men, it is true that most women supported nonviolence and loving relationships more than most men. From the twenties until his death, Indian women saw in Gandhi a kindred spirit. More than any other man in public life, he accepted and furthered their development as individuals and as coworkers of the independence movement.

Gandhi's constructive work in the midtwenties was more successful than the Rowlatt *Satyagraha* and the Non-Cooperation Campaign. He was actively engaged in the transformation of Indian society. Although he never attained as much change as he hoped for, neither the British nor Congress members stood in the way of the constructive work. Moreover, he felt at home working on the uplift of women, the poor, and untouchables as he rarely felt in politics.

Gandhi's greatest problem in the midtwenties was that he often worked himself to the point of exhaustion. The stress and strain of his many activities could be overwhelming, and careful management of his inner resources did not come easily to Gandhi. Given the enormity of his vision—to transform relationships in a nation of three hundred million people—it is not surprising that he suffered periodic depressions and exhaustion. Fortunately, in the twenties more coworkers joined him in this vast enterprise. There were more than two hundred *satyagrahis* in his ashram, and others all over India were gathering strength for the next campaign. However much help Gandhi had in his social and political work, it is true that increasingly his coworkers and the masses of India looked to the Mahatma to lead them to independence. In the next phase of his life, he would take them far beyond the Non-Cooperation Campaign of 1920–1922.

SALT, "A WORD OF POWER": 1928–1934

It did not appear in 1927 that Gandhi would soon be called to action by the Congress. He wrote that year, "Really the clock has struck for me."[22] However, by 1928 changes in the relationship between the Congress and the Raj led to Gandhi's first "national call" since the beginning of the decade. The period from 1928 to 1934 was in many ways the high-water mark in Gandhi's direct influence on India, Great Britain, and the world. He planned, initiated, and carried out the Salt *Satyagraha* in 1930, the most successful civil disobedience campaign up to that time in history. Although it would be almost two decades before Indian independence was won, after the salt campaign the relationship between India and the British Raj would never be the same.

The end of the twenties and the beginning of the thirties was a time of growing conflict worldwide. The stock market crash in 1928 and other fundamental problems in the advanced economies of the West led to the Great Depression, causing enormous hardship all over the world. Economic decline exacerbated political tensions. A growing number of the British began to question the validity of their imperial power. Was it economically, politically, and morally justifiable, given widespread unemployment, growing conflicts between and within the major political parties, and the discontent among colonial elites over the pace of British reforms? If the citizens of Great Britain could participate in democratic governance, if citizens of predominantly white nations in the British Commonwealth could enjoy democratic rights and prerogatives, why were dark-skinned colonials denied this freedom? Progressives in Great Britain and India increasingly came to the conclusion that British imperialism had more to do with economic exploitation and racism than with the purported moral superiority of their rule.

Gandhi knew the British well, and he knew that they could only maintain political control of India if a majority of the British and Indians believed the Raj to be morally legitimate. He believed that civil disobedience could expose cracks in that legitimacy which would ultimately become too wide to ignore. The British reforms of 1919 had brought a modicum of political power to Indian elites, but by the late twenties few educated Indians found them sufficient. The Simon Commission, set up by the British government in 1927 to explore further reforms, was all white. To many Indians, it was yet another example of British paternalism and racism. Particularly the younger generation of educated Indians found the exclusion of Indians on this commission offensive, given that its members had the power to recommend how much freedom Indians were to have. It was to Gandhi "an organized insult to a whole people."[23]

Motilal Nehru, Jawaharlal's father, and the moderate T. B. Sapru organized a conference of all Indian political parties to come up with an alternative to the Simon Commission. The Nehru Report in 1928 proposed a democratically elected central government with reserved seats for Muslims, although they would lose the separate electorates granted them by the British in the reforms of 1919. The report was widely accepted across major political parties, although there was opposition as well. Many moderates felt it went too far, too fast; young radicals in Congress, including Jawaharlal, felt it did not go far enough toward complete independence.

Gandhi believed that the Nehru Report was a necessary but not sufficient step toward *swaraj*. It was no more than petitioning the British government unless the Congress was willing to initiate an Indiawide noncooperation campaign. He hoped that the British might respond positively to the report; but he knew that if they did not, *satyagraha* would be the only way to bring them around. After the discouraging results of the Non-Cooperation *Satyagraha* in the early twenties, he was finally encouraged that a mass nonviolent campaign might be possible as a result of the Bardoli *Satyagraha* in 1928. Led by Vallabhbhai Patel in a rural district of Gujarat, the Bardoli campaign was able to roll back increased land revenue assessments. Gandhi wrote his friend Charlie Andrews, "Bardoli victory was indeed a victory for Truth and Non-violence. It has almost restored the shattered faith in non-violence on the political field."[24]

The Congress agreed with Gandhi's proposal that if the British did not accept the Nehru Report by the beginning of 1930, a civil disobedience campaign would be implemented. Late in 1929, the viceroy, Lord Irwin, the head of the British government in India, released a major statement promising increased Indian political autonomy. He proposed "Dominion Status," which would involve India remaining within the British Commonwealth but with complete internal and external political power. However, reactions to his proposal were mixed in the British parliament and within the Congress in India.

It was Gandhi's task first to unify Congress around a plan and then to convince moderates that this plan could bring independence. One of his greatest skills was his ability to mediate between opposing camps in Congress and to forge a compromise that most could accept. In January 1930, after it became clear that Lord Irwin's proposal did not have sufficient support in parliament, Gandhi was given the authority in Congress to initiate a civil disobedience campaign. In this his most successful experiment with truth in the political arena, Gandhi was able to find a way to strengthen Indian self-reliance and simultaneously to demonstrate British injustice.

In February 1930 Gandhi decided to offer *satyagraha* against the British tax on salt. Gandhi chose salt as the core issue of the campaign because he realized that salt was a necessity of life for all, especially the poor who suffered most as a result of the salt tax. Many members of Congress were nonplussed by his choice. They did not understand Gandhi's connection with the masses and his ability to "keep himself in tune," as he wrote, "with the voice of his followers."[25] Dennis Dalton lays out the basic facts of the campaign:

> On March 12, 1930, Mohandas Gandhi, age sixty years, left his ashram at Sabarmati with seventy-eight followers, bound for the shores of Dandi, a small village on the coast of Gujarat in western India. Thus began the historic Dandi march and salt satyagraha, one of the most dramatic events of modern Indian history. The march covered over two hundred miles and lasted twenty-four days. Its specific object was to protest against the tax the British Raj had placed on salt. Under the regulations of the India Salt Act 1882, the government enforced a monopoly on the collection of manufacture of salt, restricting its handling to officially controlled salt depots and levying a tax of Rs 1-4-0 (46 cents) on each

maund (82 lbs.). Gandhi defied the monopoly and so broke the law by simply collecting natural salt from the seashore on April 6. The broader object of the march was to spark a campaign of civil disobedience against the Raj in order to attain independence. The salt satyagraha, therefore, begun with Gandhi's act at Dandi, quickly spread throughout India as others followed his example, and intensified with his arrest on May 5. It then continued for almost a year until direct negotiations between Gandhi and Lord Edward Irwin, the Viceroy, ended the campaign."[26]

Years later, as he assessed Gandhi's impact on his own life and on India, Jawaharlal Nehru singled out an image of Gandhi on the Salt March: "the picture that is most dominant and most significant is as I saw him marching, staff in hand, to Dandi . . . in 1930. Here was the pilgrim on his quest of Truth, quiet, peaceful, determined and fearless."[27] Tens of thousands saw Gandhi on this twenty-four-day march, and millions saw him in newsreels throughout India and the world. Nehru, who had been skeptical about salt as the primary focus of the campaign, realized how wrong he was: "Salt suddenly became a mysterious word, a word of power. . . . The abounding enthusiasm of the people . . . spreading like a prairie fire. . . . We marveled at the amazing knack of the man to impress the multitude."[28]

Beyond the expectations of almost all observers, Gandhi succeeded in staging an "ocular demonstration" of the injustice of the salt tax, which he called "inhuman, Satanic."[29] This was high drama, a carefully conceived and brilliantly executed morality play between the British and the *satyagrahis*. The legitimacy of the Raj hung in the balance, with the whole world the audience, not only the Indians and the British. "I want world sympathy," Gandhi stated, "in this battle of Right against Might."[30]

The British understood what was at stake. An officer in the government in Bombay, one of the areas where the civil disobedience campaign was most successful, wrote that growing numbers of Indians joined in "not because they expect any definite results from anti-salt laws campaign but because belief that British connection is morally indefensible and economically intolerable is gaining strength among educated Hindus, Gujaratis mostly but others also." A member of the Delhi government wrote a month after the march, "I confess I have been getting the impression during the last week or two from various parts of India that . . . Government may not be retaining that essential moral superiority, which is perhaps the most important factor in this struggle."[31]

The Raj and Gandhi were vying for the allegiance of the moderates. Most supported the British government before the Salt March, and by the end of the campaign, many had come over to Gandhi's side. A moderate editor of *The Leader*, who had questioned Gandhi's campaign at the outset, came to this conclusion during the campaign: "Mr. Gandhi is in truth a Mahatma by reason of his moral and spiritual greatness, his soul force."[32]

For the first time in India, women played a pivotal role in a political struggle. Lord Irwin saw the growing support among women for independence as a "new and serious feature." A government report indicated that "thousands of them many being of good family and high educational attainments suddenly emerged from the seclusion of their homes and in some instances actually from *purdah*, in order to join Congress demonstrations and assist in picketing; and their presence on these occasions made the work the police was required to perform particularly unpleasant."[33]

Madhu Kishwar states in "Gandhi on Women": "To manufacture salt in defiance of British laws prohibiting such manufacture, became a way of declaring one's independence in one's own daily life and also of revolutionizing one's perception of the kitchen as linked to the nation, the personal as linked to the political. . . . Gandhi's non-violence was a powerful revolutionary weapon because it created a favorable atmosphere for participation of very large numbers of people, especially women, giving them all a meaningful place in the struggle."[34] Kishwar's insight that "the personal" is "linked to the political," a connection that feminists and other activists make,[35] was central to Gandhi: "political life must be an echo of private life and there cannot be any divorce between the two."[36] He had always seen his experiments with truth in private life as inextricably bound to public life. In the Salt *Satyagraha* large segments of the Indian population linked the kitchen and the nation in a campaign which shook, Gandhi believed, "the foundations of the British Empire."[37]

Dalton cites British documents of the period which demonstrate that the British government was shaken. From the viceroy down to police officers, Gandhi's nonviolence created ambivalence in the government about when or whether to jail the Mahatma and about the most effective way to handle nonviolent resistance. The root of the ambivalence was their knowledge that jailing Gandhi might lose moderate support, and not jailing him might lose moderate support; using force against nonviolent resisters might tarnish the legitimacy of the Raj, and not stopping their civil disobedience might tarnish this legitimacy. John Court Curry, a British police officer stationed in India, experienced nausea every time he had to deal with Congress demonstrations in 1930. He stated in his memoirs thirty years later that he resigned from the force because of the ambivalence he had experienced during the salt campaign. He recalled: "I thought then, and I still think, that I was largely influenced by the feeling that whatever we did the result was to the advantage of the Congress policy and that the policy of our Government in dealing with it was wrong."[38]

Curry and British policymakers in London and Delhi realized that terrorism was easier to control than nonviolent resistance. Curry experienced no ambivalence in his work to suppress terrorist organizations in India. It was suppressing nonviolent resistance which made him sick and led to his resignation. Wedgwood Benn, Secretary of State for India, preferred combating violent to nonviolent opponents. He wrote Lord Irwin that if terrorism becomes more prevalent than nonviolence, "it will be a straight fight with the revolver people, which is a much simpler and much more satisfactory job to undertake."[39] The British government knew how to meet violence with violence, but meeting nonviolence with violence threatened their legitimacy.

The salt campaign did not challenge the British monopoly of salt manufacture. However, the concurrent campaign to stop importing foreign cloth did have a major impact on government revenues. Peasants challenged land revenues in a number of areas, and local officials resigned their posts in many villages. Significantly, British control of certain districts was lost, particularly in Gujarat, Bombay, Bengal, and on the Northwest Frontier. In some areas large numbers of peasants refused to pay land revenues, and many village officials resigned their government posts. An unprecedented number of arrests were made, over sixty thousand.

The support of *satyagraha*, strong in the first half of 1930, fell in the second half of the year. By early 1931, the Congress and the British were ready to negotiate. Gandhi met with Lord Irwin in what was the most intimate encounter between the Mahatma and a viceroy. Both were deeply religious men, and both had to contend with divisions within their own camps. Moderates satisfied with limited autonomy were opposed by radical young members of Congress who wanted complete independence. In London, many in the Labor party favored greater self-rule in India, while Conservatives held firm to the belief that the "jewel of the Empire" must not be lost. India was greatly prized as a colony while the Indian people were often held in contempt. It can be difficult for readers now to understand the depth of this contempt among Conservatives in Great Britain and other Western nations at this time. As Lloyd Rudolph states, "Winston Churchill, the empire's great exponent, coined the epithet 'the half-naked fakir,' a phrase that spoke for Americans and Britons who identified Gandhi with India's self-inflicted poverty and with fraudulent spirituality."[40]

In March 1931 Irwin and Gandhi came to an agreement, the Gandhi-Irwin Pact. Neither found it easy to mollify those in their camps most adamantly opposed to the compromise they struck. Civil disobedience was halted. Prisoners were released, and some village officials were reinstated. Peasants who had lost their land due to nonpayment of taxes had their land returned, if it had not already been sold. Congress agreed to participate in a new round of negotiations in London, the second Round Table Conference late in 1931, with Gandhi as their sole representative.

Gandhi had no expectations about the outcome of the conference. He was a consummate negotiator, but as a representative of Congress he would come with a fixed position which allowed him no room for compromise. The Congress required Dominion Status with the right to sever its connection with the British Empire as well as control of defense and finances, a position that the British would not accept, even though Lord Irwin had promised a similar plan in 1929.

At the Round Table discussions in London Gandhi was consistently opposed not only by the British but also by Muslim, untouchable, and princely representatives who vied with each other for power from the British. The Congress, the most powerful organization in India, and Gandhi, the most powerful individual in India, had no real power at the Round Table. Gandhi was deeply troubled that the British were discussing the possibility of granting a separate electorate to untouchables, which in his view would deepen an already major division in Hindu society and religion.

Recognizing that he could accomplish little at the official conference, Gandhi sought to promote the Congress position with a wide range of British people. He spoke with sympathetic Labor members of Parliament, Oxford professors, textile workers in Lancashire, and especially with the poor on London's East End, where he stayed at Muriel Lester's settlement house, Kingsley Hall. On his morning walks, "he made friends with the children. 'Here I am,' he would say, 'doing the real round table work, getting to know the people of England.'"[41] He was considerably more successful in this unofficial role than in the official one. He knew that in the long run, good relations with the British people were of greater significance to the cause of Indian independence than the Round Table discussions.

When the Congress threatened civil disobedience not long after Gandhi's return to India, the new viceroy, Lord Willingdon, had him arrested. Unlike Lord Irwin, Lord Willingdon had no desire to negotiate with Gandhi: "while he may possibly have his saint-like side, on the other he is the most Machiavellian bargaining little political humbug I have ever come across."[42] Clearly the new viceroy believed Gandhi to be more humbug than saint.

Satyagraha sprang up again, with seventy-five thousand Indians convicted of civil disobedience. But now willing to pursue a strong, unambivalent policy of political control, the British were able to crush nonviolent resistance.

While Gandhi and other *satyagrahis* were in prison, the British announced their decision in August 1932 to award separate electorates to untouchables, the issue most disturbing to Gandhi at the Round Table Conference in London. He had opposed separate electorates for Muslims, but he had not been able to stop them. However, separating untouchables and caste Hindus politically was seen by Gandhi as a direct assault on Hindu cultural and religious unity.

The politician most eager for separate electorates was Bhimrao R. Ambedkar, a Western-educated untouchable with a radically different vision from Gandhi's of how untouchables could better their conditions. Ambedkar was an early proponent of identity politics, the belief that oppressed people had to work on their own to overcome oppression. Gandhi, on the other hand, was a proponent of the politics of inclusion, a belief that untouchables would gain most from a broad movement of reconciliation and mutual understanding. If Hindu society were revitalized, returning to its original spiritual roots, then untouchables would no longer be seen as a separate class of people. Ambedkar believed that untouchables had more to gain from separate electorates than from trusting caste Hindus who had been mistreating them for centuries.

Gandhi decided to begin a fast September 20, 1932, unless the British revoked the special award to untouchables. As usual, there was considerable confusion and anger about this fast. Many, even friends within the Congress, were concerned that Gandhi's fast would be perceived as coercing the British and untouchables to accept his position. Gandhi, on the other hand, believed that his fasts were between him and God and that everyone had a right to decide whatever they thought best, even if it led to his death. Ambedkar believed Gandhi was blackmailing others in pursuit of his own political agenda. However, caste Hindus and untouchables, including Ambedkar, agreed on the "Poona Pact," which guaranteed untouchables over twice the seats they would have had under the British plan, but not a separate electorate. Hindu leaders accepted Gandhi's demand that all Hindu institutions be open to untouchables, including temples, wells, and schools. The initial response among caste Hindus across India to the agreement was quite positive, but in time many went back to treating untouchables as impure and unworthy of contact and consideration. After another fast in April 1933, Gandhi was released from prison.

In the aftermath of the Salt *Satyagraha*, Congress became increasingly divided over their relationship with the British. Should they enter the provincial governments and thereby gain needed experience and authority among the people, or should they remain in opposition to an imperial system of control which could co-opt them? The divisions in the Congress were evident in the relationship between Jawaharlal Nehru and Gandhi. Even though they had a deep bond of friendship and love, they also saw politics and religion from different vantage points. After the young Nehru's father Motilal died in 1931, his relationship with Gandhi became even closer, more like father and son. However, in difficult times, their differences could be glaring. Nehru wrote soon after Gandhi survived his last fast in 1933: "As I watched the emotional upheaval during the fast I wondered more and more if this was the right method in politics. It is sheer revivalism and clear thinking has not a ghost of a chance against it. All India, or most of it, stares reverently at the Mahatma and expects him to perform miracle after miracle and put an end to untouchability and get Swaraj and so on—and does nothing itself! And Bapu goes on talking of purity and sacrifice. I am afraid I am drifting further and further away from him mentally, in spite of my strong emotional attachment to him."[43]

Congress as a whole drifted further and further from Gandhi at this time. When Congress leaders decided to end *satyagraha* in 1934, he withdrew from direct involvement with Congress to devote himself to the Constructive Programme, particularly the effort to end untouchability. He began calling untouchables *Harijans*, literally "the children of God," and launched a new journal, *Harijan*.

As difficult as the aftermath of the Salt *Satyagraha* was, there can be no doubt that the Congress had grown into the major political organization in India and that Gandhi had become the pivotal player in the ongoing drama with the Raj. The British, seemingly in control before and after the civil disobedience of the early thirties, were steadily losing legitimacy whether they repressed the Congress or whether they were able to bring it into cooperative governance. The Raj was fighting a rearguard action in India. Indian, British, and world opinion increasingly recognized the legitimate claims of Gandhi and the Congress for Indian independence. Nehru, as he examined the period from Non-Cooperation to the Salt *Satyagraha*, concluded that the greatest impact of these campaigns was on the self-concept of Indians:

> Of course these movements exercised tremendous pressure on the British Government and shook the government machinery. But the real importance, to my mind, lay in the effect they had on our own people, and especially the village masses. . . . Non-co-operation dragged them out of the mire and gave them self-respect and self-reliance . . . . They acted courageously and did not submit so easily to unjust oppression; their outlook widened and they began to think a little in terms of India as a whole. . . . It was a remarkable transformation and the Congress, under Gandhi's leadership, must have the credit for it. It was something far more important than constitutions and the structure of government. It was the foundation on which a stable structure or constitution could be built up.[44]

"WHOLE VILLAGE WORK": 1934–1939

The Government of India Act of 1935 was the last major British reform. Judith Brown calls it "a strategy to salvage and sustain a minimal British raj, but it also gave Indian politicians a whole new range of structures in which to compete for and exercise power."[45] The electorate was greatly expanded, and the provincial governments were relatively free from British control; however, the ability to veto Indian decisions remained in the hand of the British governor of each province, and the British central administration retained important powers. Geoffrey Ashe asserts that even though Gandhi, Nehru, and other Indian leaders criticized the act, "it did in practice concede just enough. The enlarged electorate and the new provincial system gave Congress the leverage it required to heave India over the top. A real transfer of power might be delayed for ten or twenty or thirty years. But it would come. . . . Britain no longer had the will to hold out for ever. To that crucial extent Satyagraha had done what it was meant to do. It had converted the opponent."[46] Congress members participated in this new reform, and they were rewarded with majorities in seven of the eleven provinces.

As the Congress attained political power, Gandhi turned his attention to village work. In the mid- to late thirties he came to believe that if he contributed to the revitalization of one village and developed there a plan of "whole village work," he would offset the exploitation of India's seven hundred thousand villages by the British and educated Indians in the cities. Gandhi chose a small village in central India, Sevagram, as the focus of his Constructive Programme. With time, although he did not plan it, an ashram grew up around him, made up of a diverse group of coworkers and nonworkers who just wanted to be near the Mahatma. He joked that the ashram was really "an asylum for the insane, the infirm, the abnormals and the like."[47] He had disbanded his ashram on the Sabarmati at the beginning of the salt civil disobedience for various reasons, including the fact that many of its inhabitants had not actually chosen to be committed *satyagrahis*. This pattern repeated itself among the "abnormals" at Sevagram.

Gandhi experienced conflict between leading an ashram and leading a national independence movement. On the one hand, he loved forming a community as a model for the new India he envisioned. On the other hand, his work for that new India often took him away from the ashram for long periods of time. When he returned, he was often sick or preoccupied by the crush of all-India work. The traditional Indian ashram required the near-constant presence of a strong leader, a *guru*, and strict discipline among its members. Gandhi was unable to provide that leadership on a regular basis; no matter how hard he tried to enforce the vows he wrote for the ashrams, they were often ignored.

His primary focus at Sevagram was village work: sanitation, health, diet, *Harijan* uplift, economic development, and education. At Wardha, the headquarters of several rural development projects, and at Sevagram, Gandhi and his coworkers were involved in the manufacture of small-scale farm implements for tanning, spinning, weaving, dairy farming, oil-pressing, and rice-husking. Motivated by a belief in fitting machines to human needs, not humans to the "machine craze," Gandhi was a pioneer in a movement which would not become popular until much later, the sustainable technology movement.

One of Gandhi's most innovative ideas was his plan for Basic Education. He proposed a free, compulsory seven-year village educational system based on manual labor. Pupils would learn a trade and produce valuable goods and services which would provide funds needed to maintain their schools. Teachers would be recruited from the educated classes. Gandhi believed that Indians were separated from each other by the education they received. There was the small elite of the Western educated, who focused exclusively on book learning, and the great masses of Indians, who performed manual labor. To bridge the gap, the educated would have to forsake their books, settle in the villages, and devote their lives to the uplift of the poor.

Gandhi's innovations in "whole village work" and educational reform were promising, but to be successful they would require years of work. They would have required a radical departure from traditional rural and modern urban practices. The success of his ideas depended upon the development of thousands of educated volunteers willing to forsake their education, privileges, and way of life in the cities. Even in the ashram at Sevagram, however, relatively few chose to follow Gandhi into the village to work with the poor. Gandhi discovered again in Sevagram that most of his followers were more interested in staring "reverently at the Mahatma" than in doing anything constructive.

In 1939 he was drawn into a conflict in the tiny state of Rajkot in Gujarat, a princely state where his father had been prime minister in his youth. One of the thorniest problems facing India was the relationship between the princely states and the central government. In general the British had used the allegiance of the princes to buttress their rule, but by the mid-thirties they tried unsuccessfully to devise a plan that would integrate these states into a broader Indiawide federation. Although many in Congress sympathized with the desire of Indians in the princely states for liberation from autocratic rule, the Congress Working Committee (CWC) had decided at this time to center their efforts on the provincial governments and postpone work in these states.

Vallabhbhai Patel had reached an agreement for political reform with the ruler in Rajkot. When the ruler then reneged on the agreement, Gandhi went to Rajkot to broker a new agreement between the ruler and Patel. However, after his efforts proved unsuccessful, Gandhi decided to fast until an agreement was made. The new viceroy, Lord Linlithgow, intervened and gave decision-making power to the Chief Justice of India, who chose to support Patel's position. Gandhi broke his fast but ultimately found the whole business exhausting and unproductive. The conflicts between him and many Congress members, who questioned his involvement in a princely state against Congress policy, hurt him and contributed to his alienation from Congress.

In the mid- to late thirties, three conflicts were particularly painful to Gandhi. His conflict with Jawaharlal Nehru became more intense in these years. Nehru was a Cambridge-educated intellectual who believed in socialism and in Modern Civilization, whereas Gandhi had distrusted Western education and modernity for decades. During the times when Nehru tired of communicating with Gandhi, the older man suffered depression and contemplated leaving Congress for good. As in a number of father-son relationships, however, they were able to agree to disagree and to maintain a deep love for each.

Gandhi's second conflict, with his first-born son Harilal, became unbridgeable in these years. Gandhi's three younger sons worked in concert with their father, but not Harilal. In his youth in South Africa, Harilal had wanted a proper Western education similar to the one his father had enjoyed. But by then Gandhi had rejected modern education and refused to provide it to him. As he grew older, Harilal ran up debts, committed sexual indiscretions, drank excessively, converted publicly to Islam and then reconverted to Hinduism. Gandhi decided to end his direct communications with Harilal and blamed himself for his son's dissolute life. His conflict with Harilal was a public embarrassment for Gandhi and a personal tragedy for father and son.

Gandhi's third conflict, with Muslim League leader M. A. Jinnah, was symptomatic of the great political tragedy in India at the time, the widening divide between Muslims and Hindus. Gandhi believed that all religions were fundamentally equal and that the state had to respect the religious choices of every citizen. He shared the belief in Congress that their organization represented all Indians, irrespective of region, ethnic origin, or religion. Although Jinnah had belonged to the Congress in the early twenties and although he was not a religious man, he believed that the Muslim League represented all Muslims in India and that the Congress represented only Hindus. Moreover, he began to advocate the independent Islamic state of Pakistan in the Muslim majority provinces on the Northwest and East of the Indian subcontinent. Gandhi initiated correspondence with Jinnah in 1937, and the two men met in the spring of 1938, but their positions were irreconcilable.

Gandhi's conflicts with Jawaharlal, Harilal, and Jinnah, along with the growing tensions in Congress and the frustrations at Sevagram, weighed heavily on him. Long years of overwork contributed as well to depression and severe self-criticism. His consolation was his faith. He found solace in the first stanza of the *Isha Upanished*, which had become for him the essence of Hinduism:

> At the heart of the phenomenal world,
> within all its changing forms,
> dwells the unchanging Lord.
> So, go beyond the changing,
> and, enjoying the inner,
> cease to take for yourself what to others
> are riches.

In the midst of the gloom that often surrounded him, he relied even more on God. He learned in this stanza and the *Gita* that he could immerse himself in the world and yet simultaneously remain detached from it. By finding the "unchanging Lord" dwelling "at the heart of the phenomenal world," he would be "enjoying the inner" in the act of attending to the outer. As fascism grew in Europe and India drifted away from a nonviolent resolution of its religious, social, and political conflicts, Gandhi continued to believe that God would grant India the honor of teaching the world that nonviolence can prevail even in the seemingly most intractable conflicts.

WORLD WAR II: 1939–1945

The tragedy of World War II was accompanied in India by the dual tragedies of growing Hindu-Muslim hostility and deteriorating relations between the

British and the Congress. The Government of India Act of 1935 had led to a workable cooperative venture between the British and Indian political parties, especially the Congress. Congress members learned to exercise power in several provincial governments, and its major Indian political adversary, the Muslim League, won only five percent of the vote in 1937. Without the extreme threat the war posed to the British, a smooth transition to independence might have taken place in India. It is even possible that a high level of cooperation between the British and the Congress would have engendered more cooperative Muslim leadership.

However, when Lord Linlithgow announced that India was at war in 1939, he failed to involve Indian political leaders in the decision-making process. To many of these leaders, this unilateral decision was yet another instance of imperial domination when a more conciliatory approach might have led to increased British-Indian cooperation. Most Congress members sided with Great Britain in the war, but at the same time they wanted to choose freely India's role in the struggle against fascism. To Indians, British claims to be fighting for freedom, democracy, and justice against the evils of fascist domination and racism seemed hypocritical in the face of ongoing imperial domination and racism in India. As the war progressed, President Franklin Delano Roosevelt and growing numbers of Americans agreed with Congress leaders that the British position in India was incompatible with their stated aims in Europe.

In the summer of 1940 the CWC offered to cooperate with the Raj as long as the British would commit publicly and unequivocally to Indian independence at an unspecified later date. Lord Linlithgow declined the offer and proposed instead that "representative Indians" selected by the British serve on an Executive Council and a War Advisory Council, bodies without any real power.

Gandhi was then asked by the CWC to initiate civil disobedience. He was doubtful that India was ready for a campaign against the British during the war. Rather than challenging the government as a whole, he chose a plan of individual civil disobedience against one element of British rule, the law prohibiting free speech. The campaign would publish a statement: "It is wrong to help the British war effort with men or money. The only worthy effort is to resist all war with non-violent resistance." The British moved swiftly and efficiently to stop the campaign. Gandhi completely controlled the civil disobedience, both what was to be done and who could participate, although he did not participate directly in the campaign because he was needed to direct it. From the fall of 1940 into mid-1941, fewer than thirty thousand were found guilty of opposing the Raj.

Gandhi was generally well satisfied with the campaign, but most in Congress were not. Whereas the Salt *Satyagraha* had galvanized the nation, civil disobedience was not widely supported while the British were struggling against fascism. Congress members agreed overwhelmingly with the British that armed resistance in Europe was necessary. After Japan invaded Burma, a British colony and India's neighbor to the East, most Indians believed that armed defense might be needed in India as well.

In the war years, Gandhi's faith in principled nonviolence was out of step with Indian public opinion, including Congress members. *Satyagraha* seemed weak and ineffectual in the face of Nazi and Japanese terror and Allied carpet bombing. Gandhi had little understanding of international politics in World War II. His faith in nonviolent resistance to the Nazi Final Solution was incomprehensible to all but the most ardent pacifists at the time. As insightful as he generally was in his nonviolent strategies in India, he was unable to comprehend the enormity of the violence of the war or to come up with viable alternatives to it.

By early 1942, it was clear that civil disobedience had not worked, but the Congress could not devise a strategy of cooperation that was acceptable to the British. Nor could they agree on a strategy to demonstrate their disapproval of the way the British excluded them from the decision-making process in India. A decision was made in London to send Sir Stafford Cripps to India in an attempt to achieve wider Indian support in the war effort, but to no avail.

To bring Congress out of their impasse with the British administration, Gandhi developed the idea of a campaign to compel the British to "Quit India" nonviolently. It is difficult to understand what Gandhi believed would come of this campaign. Few thought it would be successful.

The CWC endorsed Gandhi's "Quit India" campaign in August 1942, with his famous call to "do or die." Gandhi and the members of the CWC were arrested, as were other leaders of the Congress. Nonviolent resistance was controlled in short order. However, others outside the Congress and even some within it initiated a wave of violence against the British. Hundreds of government buildings were damaged or destroyed, and communications systems were disrupted. Over 66,000 Indians were detained, and 2,500 were killed or injured.

The government accused Gandhi of planning violent insurrection, a charge which disturbed him deeply. Incarcerated in the Aga Khan's palace near Poona, he decided to fast for three weeks in February and March 1943. The government offered to release him during the fast, fearful that he might die under their jurisdiction; but he refused to leave without unconditional release, and the government would not release him unconditionally. Although many were concerned that he would not survive the fast and he became quite weak, the fast filled him with a profound state of inner peace.

Gandhi experienced two great personal losses during his imprisonment. His secretary, Mahedev Desai, "an associate beyond compare," died while in prison with Gandhi. Even more heart-wrenching to Gandhi was Kasturbhai's death early in 1944. She had joined him voluntarily in prison, and he watched as she grew weaker and weaker in the last weeks of her life. He wrote that this loss affected him more than he had ever expected. Her love and devotion to him seem to have given him a certain balance in life that he found difficult to maintain without her. He was released unconditionally from arrest in May after an attack of malaria. Doctors attending Gandhi believed he was so weak that he would never again participate in politics. He suffered illness and grave doubts about himself for many months after his release.

During the war the Muslim League became a much stronger force in India. Jinnah and Gandhi had extensive discussions in September 1944 to seek some basis for mutual action, but without success. Jinnah believed that Muslims could only be safe from Hindu domination in the independent state of Pakistan. He argued that Pakistan had to be formed *before* the British left India because they were the only power capable of counterbalancing the Congress.

In 1944 the new viceroy, Lord Wavell, tried to come up with a political solution to the conflict between his own government, the Congress, and the League. He recognized that the Raj would end soon after the war and that without proper preparation for that eventuality, the results could be disastrous. He wrote Churchill, "there remains a deep sense of frustration and discontent amongst practically all educated Indians, which renders the present arrangement for government insecure and impermanent."[48] International support for the Raj was waning. It was unlikely that the British people—who had suffered so much loss during the war—would want to continue to shoulder the burden of further occupation of India after the war. However, Churchill remained committed to an imperial India, and Lord Wavell could not break the impasse between the Muslim League and the Congress.

As the war drew to a close, Gandhi became convinced that the British could no longer mediate between the League and the Congress since their positions were mutually exclusive. Either the Congress had to be supported in their concept of a unified India open to all faiths and parties, or the League's desire to split India into two separate states had to be accepted.

Gandhi was turning increasingly from a belief in a political solution in India to a greater reliance on the Constructive Programme. Even civil disobedience without a series of constructive initiatives would not work, as he wrote in 1941 in his pamphlet *Constructive Programme: Its Meaning and Place*. For Gandhi, civil disobedience "without the co-operation of the millions by way of constructive effort is mere bravado and worse than useless."[49] He concluded his pamphlet with the haunting image, "my handling of civil disobedience without the constructive programme will be like a paralysed hand attempting to lift a spoon."[50] Indeed civil disobedience in the war years was in a state of paralysis, with no real impact on either the British or Indians. Gandhi's first item in his *Constructive Programme*, indispensable to true *swaraj*, was "Communal Unity," an "unbreakable heart unity" among all faiths in India. The years immediately following the war would demonstrate how far India was from this heart unity.

GANDHI'S LAST YEARS: 1945-1948

Lord Wavell was even more convinced after the war that British rule in India had run its course: "The administration has declined, and the machine in the Centre is hardly working at all now. . . . While the British are still legally and morally responsible for what happens in India, we have lost nearly all power to control events."[51] Whereas Churchill and other Conservatives still wanted to maintain control of India, the British people as a whole were tired of the economic and military sacrifices needed to remain an imperial power.

Assuming that Indian independence would soon be granted, the Labor Party took over parliament in July 1945. They sent a Cabinet Mission to India in 1946 to develop a plan for an interim representative government which would pave the way for independence. The British, the Congress, and the Muslim League could not agree on an interim plan because the League and the Congress had incompatible visions of India's future. Congress continued to see itself as an all-Indian organization; the Muslim League saw itself as the sole representative of "the Muslim nation," demanding a separate state of Pakistan as a precondition to negotiations with the Congress. The provincial elections of December 1945 confirmed the League's position. Over 90 percent of the Hindu vote went to the Congress, and over 90 percent of the Muslim seats went to the League.

The conflict involving religious identity and political power resulted in an unprecedented bloodbath between Hindus, Muslims, and Sikhs in northern India from 1946 to 1948. At least one million people died in the rioting. Two million fled their homes for relative safety across the Pakistan-Indian border. Hindus streamed out of Pakistan into India, Muslims out of India into Pakistan, leaving communities where their families had lived from time immemorial.

Given that most Indians had lived in relative peace with each other across their religious divides, it is difficult to understand why these massacres occurred. Research indicates that Hindu, Muslim, and Sikh leaders as well as the British administration all share a degree of responsibility for the violence. Hindu leaders could have done much to assuage the fears of Muslims and Sikhs, but many did not. A vocal minority of Hindu leaders spoke for an exclusively Hindu Raj. Some preached and practiced violence against Muslims and Sikhs. If they had agreed with Gandhi that all religions deserve equal respect, this brutal civil war may well have been averted.

Muslim and Sikh leaders also fanned the flames of anger and fear. Throughout their long reign, the British pitted one faith against the other to buttress colonial rule. Toward the end, as the dangers of rioting grew, the British administration sought to find political accommodations among Hindu, Muslim, and Sikh factions; but in Judith Brown's words, by the forties the British "had let loose a tiger they could not control."

It seemed that no one could control the riots. Gandhi was deeply disturbed by the partition of India—he called it India's "vivisection"—and by the riot-

This is an ideal that has yet to become anyone's reality

ing, which was proof to him that his nonviolent efforts had failed. To be sure, India would soon achieve parliamentary *swaraj*, on August 15, 1947. But Gandhi never believed that winning political independence was the sole or even the major aim of *swaraj*. Having worked his entire adult life for "heart unity," the civil war that broke out between Muslims, Sikhs, and Hindus shook him to the core. It did not touch his faith in nonviolence or truth, but it did force him to reevaluate *satyagraha* in India. He wrote in June 1947: "the non-violence that was offered during the past thirty years was that of the weak. India has no experience of the non-violence of the strong."[52] The non-violence of the strong is true *satyagraha* because soul force by its nature is strong, invincible. The "*ahimsa* of the weak" was not really nonviolence at all but rather "passive resistance . . . a preparation for active and armed resistance."[53] The violence engulfing India at that time was the inevitable outcome of passive resistance, he believed, a mere tactic masking the desire to defeat one's enemies and win political power.

By the summer of 1947, the Congress and the British acceded to the League's demand for the separate state of Pakistan. Gandhi fought it to the end but realized he could do nothing to prevent India's partition. He had become irrelevant to the political process. Increasingly isolated, he said at a prayer meeting in the spring of 1947, "Whatever the Congress decides will be done; nothing will be according to what I say. My writ runs no more. . . . No one listens to me any more. . . . I am crying in the wilderness."[54] The new viceroy, the war hero Lord Mountbatten, continued to consult Gandhi, but the decisive negotiations took place between the viceroy and Nehru on the one hand and between the viceroy and Jinnah on the other.

Gandhi left the world of politics in Delhi and his village work in Sevagram to embark on what was surely his greatest experiment with truth, his pilgrimage of nonviolence to riot-torn areas in India. He went to Naokhali in Bengal, to Bihar, to Calcutta, and finally to Delhi. Faced with the failure of nonviolence to unite India as independence drew near, he sought to live so purely and completely as an individual *satyagrahi* that the riots would end. In this effort, he succeeded to a degree that continues to astound those of us who look back at this bloody civil war in India. *He was a light of peace*

In Naokhali he went from village to village seeking to convince Muslims to stay after their villages had been attacked by Hindus. In January 1947 he walked 116 miles, often barefoot, to forty-seven villages in what has been called his "village a day pilgrimage." Eknath Easwaran recounts the story of an encounter in one village with "a notoriously fierce communal agitator [who] came up to Gandhi in front of a crowd of paralyzed onlookers, put his hands around Gandhi's slender throat, and began choking the life out of him. Such is the height to which Gandhi had grown that there was not even a flicker of hostility in his eyes, not a word of protest. He yielded himself completely to the flood of love within him, and the man broke down like a little child and fell sobbing at his feet."[55] *WOW*

[handwritten marginalia at top: "✓. interesting — a way this women in a way objection is an objection to women & a disillusion he has with reality"]

[handwritten marginalia left margin: "at least he was married"]

In Bihar he undertook an experiment that deeply concerned his coworkers throughout India, an experiment that disturbs many today. Given his strong belief in *brahmacharya* as a purifying force not only of an individual but also of a nation, he decided to sleep naked with young women to purify himself and India in his and its darkest hour. This decision was not the exploitation of these women by an older man in the narrow sense of using them for sexual pleasure. But it demonstrates how poorly he understood his enormous power over these young women. He seems not to have reflected about the effects his actions may have had on them. In his constant refusal to regard himself as a Mahatma, Gandhi did not understand that to others he was the most revered person in India, if not the world. These young women simply did not have the social power and sense of self that would have allowed them to say no to Gandhi.

In his last years he had come to think increasingly that he was not really a man but rather more androgynous, even a mother to these women, especially Manu, his grandniece. Lonely and disoriented by the violence surrounding him and by the partition of India, Gandhi lost his balance in this experiment. His weaknesses and strengths came out in high relief toward the end of his life. Sleeping naked with young women was the greatest of his "Himalayan blunders," but one that he never acknowledged as a blunder. And yet, in the same months, he was able to reduce or end the horrendous violence breaking out wherever he went in India.

The riots in Calcutta shocked Gandhi, the nation, and the world. Hindu, Muslim, and Sikh leaders exploited the communal tensions in 1946–1947 for their own political gain. In their fervor for liberation from the Hindu majority, Muslim Leaguers wrote in Calcutta, "Be ready and take your swords. . . . We shall show our glory with swords in hand and will have a special victory." According to Dalton, H. S. Suhrawardy, the chief minister of Bengal and a major Muslim Leaguer in Calcutta, was "appallingly negligent . . . perhaps . . . even deliberately provocative" in the early stages of the killing.[56] The death toll reached four thousand in the four days of the "Great Calcutta Killing" from August 16 to 20, 1946.

Each group blamed the other for the violence. Jinnah blamed "the Viceroy, Mr. Gandhi, and the Congress." Nehru placed the responsibility "for all that has happened" in Calcutta on the Muslim League.[57]

Gandhi, however, believed that blaming others would never resolve the conflict. As a *satyagrahi*, he asserted that separatism and hatred within each person led to violence. He therefore held everyone in Calcutta responsible for the rioting. He admonished all to "turn the searchlights inwards" and to see that the street criminals directly responsible for most of the violence, the *goondas*, were a reflection of the "goondaism" within every Hindu, Muslim, and Sikh.[58]

Gandhi arrived in Calcutta at the end of August 1947. In the face of growing riots that neither the Congress, the League, nor military troops could quell, he proposed to Suhrawardy a joint action, ultimately one of his most daring and successful experiments with truth. The two men would seek to end the killing by becoming a living symbol of Hindu-Muslim unity—setting up a place of reconciliation in an abandoned Muslim mansion and residing there together. Overwhelmed by the sheer magnitude of the rioting, Suhrawardy agreed. On August 31, a crowd of Hindus converged on the mansion and demanded that Gandhi seek retaliation against Muslims for an injury sustained by a Hindu. Dalton reports that Gandhi was unable to quiet the crowd and that he "was almost seriously wounded when the crowd attacked his party" before the police were able to restore order.[59]

On September 1, he decided to fast, "the weapon which has hitherto proved infallible for me." He understood that "an appearance before a yelling crowd does not always work. It certainly did not last night." He chose to "begin fasting from 8:15 tonight to end only if and when sanity returns to Calcutta."[60] That evening, his close friend and Congress leader Rajagopalachari asked, "Can one fast against the *goondas*?" Gandhi replied, "I want to touch the hearts of those who are behind the *goondas*."[61]

Hearts were touched in Calcutta. Amiya Chakravarty, a teacher at the time in Calcutta, described the reaction to Gandhi's fast: "Even while repudiating his method and its efficacy, the one question in people's mind would be, 'How is Gandhiji?' . . . University students . . . would say . . . one thing struck them as curious; after all, if anybody had to suffer for the continued killing and betrayal in the city, it was not Gandhi. He had taken no part in it. So, while others were engaged in crime, it was he who had to suffer like this."[62] Women in Calcutta stopped eating during his fast. Police officers—Hindus, Muslims and Christians, Indians and British—fasted for twenty-four hours in solidarity with Gandhi. By September 3, the rioting had ceased. On September 4, a group of leaders from all faiths came together and promised they would give their lives for continued peace and communal harmony in Calcutta.

Gandhi broke his fast. Rajagopalachari said, "Gandhiji has achieved many things, but in my considered opinion, there has been nothing, not even independence, which is so truly wonderful as his victory over evil in Calcutta." Mountbatten wrote Gandhi, "In the Punjab we have 55 thousand soldiers and large scale rioting on our hands. In Bengal our forces consist of one man, and there is no rioting." According to E. W. R. Lumby, "He had in fact worked a miracle, perhaps the greatest in modern times."[63]

Was this a miracle? Can we explain the phenomenal success of one man fasting for peace in a city of four million? Gandhi wrote: "The conflagration has been caused not by the *goondas* but by those who have *become goondas*. It is we who make *goondas*. . . . The heart of the anti-social elements may or may not be changed; it will be enough if they are made to feel that the better elements of society are asserting themselves in the interest of peace and in the interests of normality."[64] He always believed that humans have a lower and a higher nature. The rioting was an expression of the lower nature found in all people. In Gandhi's view, if "the better elements" could act in concert with their higher nature, they could bring the whole city out of violence and fear.

But why did "the better element of society" respond to Gandhi? Would they have responded to Jinnah, Nehru, or Mountbatten in the same way? Probably not. There was something in Gandhi which spoke to the "heart unity" of all people in Calcutta. It was perhaps his ability to renounce personal gain and to identify himself with the totality of India. He had written in 1910, "Nobility of soul consists in realizing that you are yourself India. In your emancipation is the emancipation of India."[65] To the people of Calcutta and other riot-torn areas, he had become a living symbol of India. As Nehru wrote, Gandhi was the "soul of India"; he could, therefore, touch Indians as no one else could.

Gandhi went to Delhi on his way to quell the riots in the Punjab, but he chose to stay in Delhi because of the widespread violence in the city. If he could end the bloodletting there, India's capitol, he believed the violence all over India could stop. In mid-January 1948, he fasted in Delhi. He called it his "greatest fast." As in Calcutta, the violence abated.

At the same time, fanatical Hindus were plotting to assassinate Gandhi. "These highly-strung young men saw Hinduism menaced by Islam from without and by Gandhi from within."[66] They believed that he stood in the way of a Hindu Raj, a glorious nation that would expel all non-Hindus or convert them to Hinduism. A bomb exploded on January 20 at Gandhi's prayer meeting. Many feared for his life.

Gandhi was well aware that his life was in danger, but he was ambivalent about living on in this time of extreme violence. He had written earlier that he hoped to live to the age of 125; but in the last year of his life, he was overwhelmed at times by the enormity of the violence. It seemed that he would muster all his reserves to put out one fire only to be confronted with another. He said the summer of 1947, "I pray that God may not keep me alive" to witness independence tainted by partition and communal violence.

On January 29, 1948, he called on the Congress to cease being "a propaganda vehicle and parliamentary machine" and to become an organization dedicated completely to the Constructive Programme.[67] Even if he had lived, it is not likely that Congress members as a whole would have chosen to comply. On January 30, Gandhi went to his evening prayer meeting on the grounds of the Birla House where he was staying in Delhi. A young Hindu fanatic forced his way through the crowd and shot the Mahatma three times in the chest at point-blank range.

Gandhi's death sent a shock wave throughout India and the world. Many could hardly comprehend the barbarity of this act of violence against the greatest proponent of nonviolence in history. The historian Suranjan Das called it a "tragic commentary on his cherished principles of non-violence."

However, Dalton states, "Gandhi's assassination, more than any other single event, served to stop the communal violence surrounding partition. . . . Somehow a determination came to stop the killing."[68] It appears that in death, Gandhi caused his compatriots to stop, think, and choose a different course of action. *In death he induced non-violence*

His death can be seen as his final experiment with truth. He had said that he would pass the test he set for himself if he could die with the words "Hé Ram" (Oh God) on his lips. He met the test.

Gandhi's last years show that he was not an ordinary man, as he so often claimed. No ordinary man could quell riots with his fasts or as a result of his death. Nor was he a saint, as many others have claimed.[69] He was an extraordinary man in the depth and breadth of his experiments with truth; however, his "Himalayan miscalculations" are not characteristic of a saint. Rather, he seems to have stood somewhere between ordinary mortals and saints—close enough, perhaps, for us to emulate him but also far enough ahead to spur us on to act for the Common Good.

His ardent faith in soul force inspired millions in his lifetime and tens of millions since then. He spearheaded a movement of *satyagrahis* who carried out a program of national self-determination that has served as a model for nonviolent revolutions all over the world. He was arguably the greatest man of his century and potentially among the most influential in the century to come. Albert Einstein's eloquent statement seems fitting as we look back at Gandhi's life: "Generations to come . . . will scarce believe that such a one as this ever in flesh and blood walked upon this earth."

NOTES

1. Gandhi, Mohandas K., *The Collected Works of Mahatma Gandhi* (CWMG) (New Delhi: Publication Division, Ministry of Information and Broadcasting, 1958–1994) 12:557.

2. Gandhi organized and served in ambulance corps for the British during the Boer War and the Zulu Rebellion in South Africa as well.

3. *CWMG*, 15:107.

4. Iyer, Raghavan, ed., *Moral and Political* Writings, vol. II, 45, 7-28-46. Gandhi's belief that submitting to oppression is sin comes from Tolstoy's *Letter to a Hindoo*, which he read in South Africa. Gandhi translated Tolstoy's *Letter* for *Indian Opinion* and wrote a preface to it. Cf. M. K. Gandhi, *Hind Swaraj and Other Writings*, ed. Anthony J. Parel (Cambridge: Cambridge University Press, 1997), 136–38.

5. "Answers to Questions at Constructive Workers' Conference," Madras, *The Hindu*, 1-26-46.

6. Shell, Jonathan, "Pre-emptive Defeat, or How Not to Fight Proliferation," in *The Iraq War Reader: History, Documents, Opinions*, eds. Micah L. Sifry and Christopher Cerf (New York: Touchstone, 2003), 516.

7. Gandhi, *Autobiography*, 397.

8. Iyer, ed., *Moral and Political Writings*, vol. I, 70–71, 12-12-20.

  9. Iyer, ed., *Moral and Political Writings*, vol. III, 169, 3-14-26.
 10. Parel, ch. 9, 178.
 11. *CWMG*, 15:102, 2-24-19.
 12. *CWMG*, 15:164, 172, 174–75.
 13. Cited in Brown, *Gandhi*, 132.
 14. Gandhi, *Autobiography*, 469.
 15. Nanda, B. R., *Mahatma Gandhi: A Biography* (Boston: Beacon Press, 1958), 199.
 16. Cited in Nanda, *Mahatma Gandhi*, 239.
 17. Cited in Nanda, *Mahatma Gandhi*, 241.
 18. Cited in Brown, *Gandhi*, 176.
 19. *Autobiography,* 503.
 20. Allen, ch. 16, 318.
 21. "Discussion with a Friend," *Harijan*, 2-10-46.
 22. *CWMG*, 33:196.
 23. *CWMG*, 36:67.
 24. *CWMG*, 37:200.
 25. *CWMG*, 42:420.
 26. Dalton, Dennis. *Mahatma Gandhi: Nonviolent Power in Action*. New York: Columbia University Press, 1993, 91–92.
 27. Cited in Brown, *Gandhi*, 237.
 28. Cited in Dalton, *Mahatma Gandhi*, 113.
 29. *CWMG*, 43:162.
 30. *CWMG*, 43:180.
 31. These two quotes cited in Brown, *Gandhi*, 238, 231.
 32. Cited in Dalton, *Mahatma Gandhi*, 127.
 33. Cited in Dalton, *Mahatma Gandhi*, 118 in both quotes.
 34. Kishwar, Madhu, "Gandhi on Women," *Economic and Political Weekly*, 20:40, Oct. 5, and 20:41, Oct. 12, 1985, 1696, 1757–58.
 35. Paranjape writes, "it was only Gandhi who helped me connect the personal with the political," ch. 15, 294.
 36. Cited in Terchek, ch. 10, 214.
 37. Cited in Dalton, *Mahatma Gandhi*, 115.
 38. Cited in Dalton, *Mahatma Gandhi*, 133.
 39. Cited in Dalton, *Mahatma Gandhi*, 132.
 40. Rudolph, ch. 14, 263.
 41. Nanda, *Mahatma Gandhi*, 311–12.
 42. Cited in Brown, *Gandhi*, 262.
 43. Cited in Brown, *Gandhi*, 270.
 44. Cited in Ashe, Geoffrey, *Gandhi* (New York: Stein & Day, 1968), 324–25.
 45. Brown, *Gandhi*, 282.
 46. Ashe, *Gandhi*, 327.
 47. *CWMG*, 70:247.
 48. Cited in Brown, *Gandhi*, 353.
 49. *CWMG*, 75:165.
 50. *CWMG*, 75:166.
 51. Cited in Brown, *Gandhi*, 359–60.
 52. Gandhi, "Non-Violence," *Harijan*, 6-15-47.
 53. Iyer, *Moral and Political Writings*, vol. III, 607, 7-4-47.

54. *CWMG*, 87:187.

55. Easwaran, Eknath, *Gandhi the Man: The Story of His Transformation.* Tomares, CA: Nilgiri Press, 1997, 97.

56. Cited in Dalton, "The Calcutta Fast," *Mahatma Gandhi*, 141.

57. Cited in Dalton, *Mahatma Gandhi*, 147.

58. Cited in Dalton, *Mahatma Gandhi*, 151.

59. Dalton, *Mahatma Gandhi*, 154.

60. *CWMG*, 89:132.

61. Cited in Dalton, *Mahatma Gandhi*, 154.

62. Cited in Dalton, *Mahatma Gandhi*, 156.

63. The quotes in this paragraph are cited in Dalton, *Mahatma Gandhi*, 158–59.

64. *CWMG*, 89:132, 149.

65. Iyer, *Moral and Political Writings*, vol. I, 340, 4-2-10.

66. B. R. Nanda, *Mahatma Gandhi*, 512.

67. "His Last Will and Testament," *Harijan*, 1-29-48.

68. Dalton, *Mahatma Gandhi*, 167.

69. See Rudolph for a discussion of differing views about Gandhi "the saint," ch. 14, 272–82.

II

SELECTIONS FROM WRITINGS
BY GANDHI

3

An Autobiography: The Story of My Experiments with Truth

Mohandas K. Gandhi

> I am not writing the autobiography to please critics. Writing it is itself one of the experiments with truth. (280)

Gandhi's autobiography was written in Gujarati in weekly installments and published in his journal Navajivan *from 1925 to 1929. The English translation appeared, also in installments, in his other journal,* Young India, *in the same years. The autobiography was a Western form of literature, not Indian. Gandhi was intent that his not be self-indulgent, as many other autobiographies were, in his opinion. As the editor states in the introduction to the autobiography in the* Collected Works of Mahatma Gandhi, *the subtitle* The Story of My Experiments with Truth *"makes the moral purpose explicit. The lessons that Gandhiji wished to convey were not only relevant to the India of his time but are of the highest importance to man in his striving towards an integrated way of living."[1] Gandhi wrote in the autobiography: "My purpose is to describe experiments in the science of satyagraha, not to say how good I am. In judging myself I shall try to be as harsh as truth, as I want others also to be."*

References are to An Autobiography: The Story of My Experiments with Truth *(Boston: Beacon Press, 1957).*

PART I

Introduction

It is not my purpose to attempt a real autobiography. I simply want to tell the story of my numerous experiments with truth, and as my life consists of nothing but those experiments, it is true that the story will take the shape of an autobiography. My experiments in the political field are now known, not only to India, but to a certain extent to the "civilized" world. For me, they have not much value. But I should certainly like to narrate my experiments in the spiritual field which are known only to myself, and from which I have derived such power as I possess for working in the political field.

What I want to achieve,—what I have been striving and pining to achieve these thirty years,—is self-realization, to see God face to face, to attain *Moksha*.[2] I live and move and have my being in pursuit of this goal. All that I do by way of speaking and writing, and all my ventures in the political field, are directed to this same end.

The experiments I am about to relate are spiritual, or rather moral; for the essence of religion is morality. If I can narrate them in a dispassionate and humble spirit, many other experimenters will find in them provision for their onward march. Far be it from me to claim any degree of perfection for these experiments. I claim for them nothing more than does a scientist who, though he conducts his experiments with the utmost accuracy, forethought and minuteness, never claims any finality about his conclusions, but keeps an open mind regarding them.

My purpose being to give an account of various practical applications of these principles, I have given the chapters I propose to write the title of *The Story of My Experiments with Truth*. These will of course include experiments with non-violence, celibacy and other principles of conduct believed to be distinct from truth. But for me, truth is the sovereign principle, which includes numerous other principles. This truth is not only truthfulness in word, but truthfulness in thought also, and not only the relative truth of our conception, but the Absolute Truth, the Eternal Principle, that is God. (xii–xiii)

Chapter I: Birth and Parentage

The Gandhis belong to the Bania[3] caste and seem to have been originally grocers. But for three generations, from my grandfather, they have been Prime Ministers in several Kathiawad States.[4]

My father, Kaba Gandhi, married four times in succession, having lost his wife each time by death. He had two daughters by his first and second marriages. His last wife, Putlibai, bore him a daughter and three sons, I being the youngest.

My father was a lover of his clan, truthful, brave and generous, but short-tempered. To a certain extent he might have been given to carnal pleasures. For he married for the fourth time when he was over forty. But he was incorruptible and had earned a name for strict impartiality in his family as well as outside.

The outstanding impression my mother has left on my memory is that of saintliness. She was deeply religious. She would not think of taking her meals without her daily prayers. Going to *Haveli*—the Vaishnava temple[5]—was one of her daily duties. As far as my memory can go back, I do not remember her having ever missed the *Chaturmas*.[6] She would take the hardest vows and keep them without flinching. Illness was no excuse for relaxing them.

Of these parents I was born at Porbandar, otherwise known as Sudama-puri, on the 2nd October, 1869. I passed my childhood in Porbandar. I re-collect having been put to school. It was with some difficulty that I got through the multiplication tables. The fact that I recollect nothing more of those days than having learnt, in company with other boys, to call our teacher all kinds of names, would strongly suggest that my intellect must have been sluggish, and my memory raw. (3–5)

Chapter II: Childhood

I must have been about seven when my father left Porbandar for Rajkot to become a member of the Rajasthanik Court. There I was put into a primary school, and I can well recollect those days, including the names and other particulars of the teachers who taught me. As at Porbandar, so here, there is hardly anything to note about my studies. I could only have been a mediocre student. From this school I went to the suburban school and thence to the high school, having already reached my twelfth year. I do not remember having ever told a lie, during this short period, either to my teachers or to my school-mates, I used to be very shy and avoided all company. My books and my lessons were my sole companions. To be at school at the stroke of the hour and to run back home as soon as the school closed,—that was my daily habit. I literally ran back, because I could not bear to talk to anybody. I was even afraid lest anyone should poke fun at me. (6)

Chapter III: Child Marriage

I know that I shall have to swallow many bitter draughts in the course of this narrative. And I cannot do otherwise, if I claim to be a worshipper of Truth. It is my painful duty to have to record here my marriage at the age of thirteen. As I see the youngsters of the same age about me who are under my care, and think of my own marriage, I am inclined to pity myself and to congratulate them on having escaped my lot. I can see no moral argument in support of such a preposterously early marriage. (8)

Chapter VI: A Tragedy

A wave of 'reform' was sweeping over Rajkot at the time when I first came across this friend. He informed me that many of our teachers were secretly taking meat and wine. He also named many well-known people of Rajkot as belonging to the same company. There were also, I was told, some high-school boys among them.

I was surprised and pained. I asked my friend the reason and he explained it thus: "We are a weak people because we do not eat meat. The English are able to rule over us, because they are meat-eaters. You know how hardy I am, and how great a runner too. It is because I am a meat-eater. Our teach-ers and other distinguished people who eat meat are no fools. They know its virtues. You should do likewise. There is nothing like trying. Try, and see what strength it gives."

All these pleas on behalf of meat-eating were not advanced at a single sitting. They represent the substance of a long and elaborate argument which my friend was trying to impress upon me from time to time. My elder brother had already fallen. He therefore supported my friend's argument. I certainly looked feeble-bodied by the side of my brother and this friend. They were both hardier, physically stronger, and more daring. This friend's exploits cast a spell over me.

All this had its due effect on me. I was beaten. It began to grow on me that meat-eating was good, that it would make me strong and daring, and that, if the whole country took to meat-eating, the English could be overcome.

A day was thereupon fixed for beginning the experiment. It had to be con-ducted in secret. I was extremely devoted to my parents. I knew that the mo-ment they came to know of my having eaten meat, they would be shocked to death. (19–21).

Chapter VII: A Tragedy (Continued)

So the day came. It is difficult fully to describe my condition. There were, on the one hand, the zeal for "reform," and the novelty of making a mo-mentous departure in life. There was, on the other, the shame of hiding like a thief to do this very thing. I cannot say which of the two swayed me more. We went in search of a lonely spot by the river, and there I saw, for the first time in my life—meat. There was baker's bread also. I relished neither. The goat's meat was as tough as leather. I simply could not eat it. I was sick and had to leave off eating.

I had a very bad night afterwards. A horrible nightmare haunted me. Every time I dropped off to sleep it would seem as though a live goat were bleat-ing inside me, and I would jump up full of remorse. But then I would remind myself that meat-eating was a duty and so become more cheerful.

My friend was not a man to give in easily. He now began to cook various delicacies with meat, and dress them neatly.

This bait had its effect. I got over my dislike for bread, forswore my com-passion for the goats, and became a relisher of meat-dishes, if not of meat it-self. This went on for about a year. But not more than half a dozen meat-feasts were enjoyed in all.

Whenever I had occasion to indulge in these surreptitious feasts, dinner at home was out of the question. My mother would naturally ask me to come and take my food and want to know the reason why I did not wish to eat. I would say to her, "I have no appetite today; there is something wrong with my digestion." It was not without compunction that I devised these pretexts. I knew I was lying, and lying to my mother. I also knew that, if my mother and father came to know of my having become a meat-eater, they would be deeply shocked. This knowledge was gnawing at my heart.

Therefore I said to myself: "Though it is essential to eat meat, and also essential to take up food 'reform' in the country, yet deceiving and lying to one's father and mother is worse than not eating meat. In their lifetime, therefore, meat-eating must be out of the question. When they are no more and I have found my freedom, I will eat meat openly, but until that moment arrives I will abstain from it."

This decision I communicated to my friend, and I have never since gone back to meat. My parents never knew that two of their sons had become meat-eaters.

I abjured meat out of the purity of my desire not to lie to my parents, but I did not abjure the company of my friend who almost led me into faithlessness to my wife. I was saved by the skin of my teeth. My friend once took me to a brothel. He sent me in with the necessary instructions. It was all pre-arranged. The bill had already been paid. I went into the jaws of sin, but God in His infinite mercy protected me against myself. I was almost struck blind and dumb in this den of vice. I sat near the woman on her bed, but I was tongue-tied. She naturally lost patience with me, and showed me the door, with abuses and insults. I then felt as though my manhood had been injured, and wished to sink into the ground for shame. But I have ever since given thanks to God for having saved me. I can recall four more similar incidents in my life, and in most of them my good fortune, rather than any effort on my part, saved me. From a strictly ethical point of view, all these occasions must be regarded as moral lapses; for the carnal desire was there, and it was as good as the act. But from the ordinary point of view, a man who is saved from physically committing sin is regarded as saved. And I was saved only in that sense. (22–24)

Chapter IX: My Father's Death and My Double Shame

My father was bed-ridden, suffering from a fistula.[7] My mother, an old servant of the house, and I were his principal attendants. I had the duties of a nurse, which mainly consisted in dressing the wound, giving my father his medicine, and compounding drugs whenever they had to be made up at home. Every night I massaged his legs and retired only when he asked me to do so or after he had fallen asleep. I loved to do this service. I do not remember ever having neglected it.

This was also the time when my wife was expecting a baby,—a circumstance which, as I can see today, meant a double shame for me. For one thing I did not restrain myself, as I should have done, whilst I was yet a student. And secondly, this carnal lust got the better of what I regarded as my duty to study, and of what was even a greater duty, my devotion to my parents. Every night whilst my hands were busy massaging my father's legs, my mind was hovering about the bed-room. I was always glad to be relieved from my duty, and went straight to the bed-room after doing obeisance to my father.

The dreadful night came. My uncle was then in Rajkot. I have a faint recollection that he came to Rajkot having had news that my father was getting worse. No one had dreamt that this was to be the fateful night. The danger of course was there.

It was 10:30 or 11 p.m. I was giving the massage. My uncle offered to relieve me. I was glad and went straight to the bed-room. My wife, poor thing, was fast asleep. But how could she sleep when I was there? I woke her up. In five or six minutes, however, the servant knocked at the door. I started with alarm. "Get up," he said, "Father is very ill." I knew of course that he was very ill, and so I guessed what "very ill" meant at that moment. I sprang out of bed.

"What is the matter? Do tell me!"

"Father is no more." So all was over! I had but to wring my hands. I felt deeply ashamed and miserable. I ran to my father's room. I saw that, if animal passion had not blinded me, I should have been spared the torture of separation from my father during his last moments. I should have been massaging him, and he would have died in my arms.

The shame was the shame of my carnal desire even at the critical hour of my father's death, which demanded wakeful service. It is a blot I have never been able to efface or forget, and I have always thought that, although my devotion to my parents knew no bounds and I would have given up anything for it, yet it was weighed and found unpardonably wanting because my mind was at the same moment in the grip of lust. I have therefore always regarded myself as a lustful, though a faithful, husband. It took me long to get free from the shackles of lust, and I had to pass through many ordeals before I could overcome it.

Before I close this chapter of my double shame, I may mention that the poor mite that was born to my wife scarcely breathed for more than three or four days. Nothing else could be expected. Let all those who are married be warned by my example. (28–31)

Chapter X: Glimpses of Religion

In Rajkot I got an early grounding in toleration for all branches of Hinduism and sister religions. Jain[8] monks also would pay frequent visits to my father, and would even go out of their way to accept food from us—non-Jains. They would have talks with my father on subjects religious and mundane.

He had, besides, Musalman[9] and Parsi[10] friends, who would talk to him about their own faiths, and he would listen to them always with respect, and often with interest. Being his nurse, I often had a chance to be present at these talks. These many things combined to inculcate in me a toleration for all faiths.

Only Christianity was at the time an exception. I developed a sort of dislike for it. And for a reason. In those days Christian missionaries used to stand in a corner near the high school and hold forth, pouring abuse on Hindus and their gods. I could not endure this.

The fact that I had learnt to be tolerant to other religions did not mean that I had any living faith in God. I happened, about this time, to come across *Manusmriti*[11] which was amongst my father's collection. The story of the creation and similar things in it did not impress me very much, but on the contrary made me incline somewhat towards atheism.

But one thing took deep root in me—the conviction that morality is the basis of things, and that truth is the substance of all morality. Truth became my sole objective. It began to grow in magnitude—every day, and my definition of it also has been ever widening. (33–34)

Chapter XIII: In London at Last

I was very uneasy even in the new rooms. I would continually think of my home and country. My mother's love always haunted me. At night the tears would stream down my cheeks, and home memories of all sorts made sleep out of the question. It was impossible to share my misery with anyone. And even if I could have done so, where was the use? I knew of nothing that would soothe me. Everything was strange—the people, their ways, and even their dwellings. I was a complete novice in the matter of English etiquette and continually had to be on my guard. There was the additional inconvenience of the vegetarian vow. Even the dishes that I could eat were tasteless and insipid. I thus found myself between Scylla and Charybdis.[12] England I could not bear, but to return to India was not to be thought of. Now that I had come, I must finish the three years, said the inner voice. (44–45)

PART II

Chapter III

About this time,[13] I took up the case of one Mamibai. This was my *debut* in the Small Causes Court.[14] I appeared for the defendant and had thus to cross-examine the plaintiff's witnesses. I stood up, but my heart sank into my boots. My head was reeling and I felt as though the whole court was doing likewise. I could think of no question to ask. The judge must have laughed, and the vakils[15] no doubt enjoyed the spectacle. But I was past seeing anything. I sat down and told the agent that I could not conduct the case, that he had better engage Patel and have the fee back from me.

I hastened from the Court, not knowing whether my client won or lost her case, but I was ashamed of myself, and decided not to take up any more cases until I had courage enough to conduct them. Indeed I did not go to Court again until I went to South Africa. (94–95)

Chapter XV: Religious Ferment [in South Africa]

Thus if I could not accept Christianity either as a perfect, or the greatest religion, neither was I then convinced of Hinduism being such. Hindu defects were pressingly visible to me. If untouchability could be a part of Hinduism, it could but be a rotten part or an excrescence. I could not understand the *raison d'etre* of a multitude of sects and castes. What was the meaning of saying that the Vedas were the inspired Word of God? If they were inspired, why not also the Bible and the Koran?

As Christian friends were endeavouring to convert me, even so were Musalman friends. Abdulla Sheth had kept on inducing me to study Islam, and of course he had always something to say regarding its beauty.

I expressed my difficulties in a letter to Raychandbhai.[16] I also corresponded with other religious authorities in India and received answers from them. Raychandbhai's letter somewhat pacified me. He asked me to be patient and to study Hinduism more deeply. One of his sentences was to this effect: "On a dispassionate view of the question I am convinced that no other religion has the subtle and profound thought of Hinduism, its vision of the soul, or its charity."

I purchased Sale's translation of the Koran and began reading it. I also obtained other books on Islam. I communicated with Christian friends in England. Tolstoy's *The Kingdom of God is Within You* overwhelmed me. It left an abiding impression on me. Before the independent thinking, profound morality, and the truthfulness of this book, all the books given me by Mr. Coates seemed to pale into insignificance.

Though I took a path my Christian friends had not intended for me, I have remained for ever indebted to them for the religious quest that they awakened in me. I shall always cherish the memory of their contact. The years that followed had more, not less, of such sweet and sacred contacts in store for me. (137–38)

PART III

Chapter VII: Brahmacharya[17] I

What, I asked myself, should be my relation with my wife? Did my faithfulness consist in making my wife the instrument of my lust? So long as I was the slave of lust, my faithfulness was worth nothing. To be fair to my wife, I must say that she was never the temptress. It was therefore the easiest thing for me to take the vow of *brahmacharya*, if only I willed it. It was my weak will or lustful attachment that was the obstacle.

Even after my conscience had been roused in the matter, I failed twice. It became my conviction that procreation and the consequent care of children were inconsistent with public service. The idea flashed upon me that if I wanted to devote myself to the service of the community in this manner, I must relinquish the desire for children and wealth and live the life of a *vanaprastha*—of one retired from household cares. (205–6)

PART IV

Chapter XVIII: The Magic Spell of a Book

Mr. Polak[18] came to see me off at the station, and left with me a book to read during the journey, which he said I was sure to like. It was Ruskin's[19] *Unto This Last*.

The book was impossible to lay aside, once I had begun it. It gripped me. Johannesburg to Durban was a twenty-four hours' journey. The train reached there in the evening. I could not get any sleep that night. I determined to change my life in accordance with the ideals of the book.

I believe that I discovered some of my deepest convictions reflected in this great book of Ruskin, and that is why it so captured me and made me transform my life.

The teachings of *Unto This Last* I understood to be:

1. That the good of the individual is contained in the good of all.
2. That a lawyer's work has the same value as the barber's inasmuch as all have the same right of earning their livelihood from their work.
3. That a life of labour, *i.e.,* the life of the tiller of the soil and the handicraftsman is the life worth living.

The first of these I knew. The second I had dimly realized. The third had never occurred to me. *Unto This Last* made it as clear as daylight for me that the second and the third were contained in the first. I arose with the dawn, ready to reduce these principles to practice. (298–99)

Chapter XIX: The Phoenix Settlement

I talked over the whole thing with Mr. West, described to him the effect *Unto This Last* had produced on my mind, and proposed that *Indian Opinion* should be removed to a farm, on which everyone should labour, drawing the same living wage, and attending to the press work in spare time. Mr. West approved of the proposal, and £3 was laid down as the monthly allowance per head, irrespective of colour or nationality. (300)

PART V

Chapter XII: The Stain of Indigo [after Gandhi's Return to India]

Champaran[20] used to be full of indigo plantations until the year 1917. The Champaran tenant was bound by law to plant three out of every twenty parts of his land with indigo[21] for his landlord. This system was known as the *tin-kathia* system, as three *kathas* out of twenty (which make one acre) had to be planted with indigo.

Early in 1917, we left Calcutta for Champaran. (404–5)

Chapter XIII: The Gentle Bihari

"Having studied these cases," said I, "I have come to the conclusion that we should stop going to law courts. Taking such cases to the courts does little good. Where the ryots[22] are so crushed and fear-stricken, law courts are useless. The real relief for them is to be free from fear. We cannot sit still until we have driven *tinkathia* out of Bihar. I had thought that I should be able to leave here in two days, but I now realize that the work might take even two years." (408)

Chapter XIV: Face to Face With Ahimsa

My object was to inquire into the condition of the Champaran agriculturists and understand their grievances against the indigo planters. For this purpose it was necessary that I should meet thousands of the ryots. But I deemed it essential, before starting on my inquiry, to know the planters' side of the case and see the Commissioner of the Division. I sought and was granted appointments with both.

The very same day we heard that about five miles from Motihari a tenant had been ill-treated. It was decided that, in company with Babu Dharanid-har Prasad, I should go and see him the next morning, and we accordingly set off for the place on elephant's back. We had scarcely gone half way when a messenger from the Police Superintendent overtook us and said that the latter had sent his compliments. I saw what he meant. I got into the hired carriage which the messenger had brought. He then served on me a notice to leave Champaran, and drove me to my place. On his asking me to acknowledge the service of the notice, I wrote to the effect that I did not propose to comply with it and leave Champaran till my inquiry was finished. Thereupon

I received a summons to take my trial the next day for disobeying the order to leave Champaran.

I kept awake that whole night writing letters and giving necessary instructions to Babu Brajkishore Prasad.

The news of the notice and the summons spread like wildfire, and I was told that Motihari that day witnessed unprecedented scenes. My companions proved the greatest help. They occupied themselves with regulating the crowds, for the latter followed me wherever I went.

A sort of friendliness sprang up between the officials—Collector, Magistrate, Police Superintendent—and myself. I might have legally resisted the notices served on me. Instead I accepted them all, and my conduct towards the officials was correct. They thus saw that I did not want to offend them personally, but that I wanted to offer civil resistance to their orders. In this way they were put at ease, and instead of harassing me they gladly availed themselves of my and my co-workers' co-operation in regulating the crowds. But it was an ocular demonstration to them of the fact that their authority was shaken. The people had for the moment lost all fear of punishment and yielded obedience to the power of love which their new friend exercised.

No political work had yet been done amongst the ryots. The world outside Champaran was not known to them. And yet they received me as though we had been age-long friends. It is no exaggeration, but the literal truth, to say that in this meeting with the peasants I was face to face with God, Ahimsa and Truth.

When I come to examine my title to this realization, I find nothing but my love for the people. And this in turn is nothing but an expression of my unshakable faith in Ahimsa. (409–12)

Chapter XV: Case Withdrawn

The trial began. The Government pleader, the Magistrate and other officials were on tenterhooks. They were at a loss to know what to do. The Government pleader was pressing the Magistrate to postpone the case. But I interferred and requested the Magistrate not to postpone the case, as I wanted to plead guilty to having disobeyed the order to leave Champaran and read a brief statement as follows:

"With the permission of the Court I would like to make a brief statement showing why I have taken the very serious step of seemingly disobeying the order passed under Section 144 of Cr. P. C. In my humble opinion it is a question of difference of opinion between the Local Administration and myself. I have entered the country with motives of rendering humanitarian and national service. I have done so in response to a pressing invitation to come and help the ryots, who urge they are not being fairly treated by the indigo planters. I could not render any help without studying the problem. I have, therefore, come to study it with the assistance, if possible, of the Administration and the planters. I have no other motive, and cannot believe that my coming can in any way disturb public peace and cause loss of life. As a law-abiding citizen my first instinct would be, as it was, to obey the order served upon me. But I could not do so without doing violence to my sense of duty to those for whom I have come. I feel that I could just now serve them only by remaining in their midst. I could not, therefore, voluntarily retire. Amid this conflict of duties I could only throw the responsibility of removing me from them on the Administration.

I have disregarded the order served upon me not for want of respect for lawful authority, but in obedience to the higher law of our being, the voice of conscience."

Before I could appear before the Court to receive the sentence, the Magistrate sent a written message that the Lieutenant Governor had ordered the case against me to be withdrawn, and the Collector wrote to me saying that I was at liberty to conduct the proposed inquiry, and that I might count on whatever help I needed from the officials. None of us was prepared for this prompt and happy issue.

The planters engineered against me a poisonous agitation. All sorts of falsehoods appeared in the press about my co-workers and myself. But my extreme cautiousness and my insistence on truth, even to the minutest detail, turned the edge of their sword. (413–15)

Chapter XVI: Methods of Work

The Champaran inquiry was a bold experiment with Truth and Ahimsa. (416)

Chapter XIX: When a Governor Is Good

Sir Edward Gait, the Lieutenant Governor, asked me to see him, expressed his willingness to appoint an inquiry and invited me to be a member of the Committee. I ascertained the names of the other members, and after consultation with my co-workers agreed to serve on the Committee, on condition that I should be free to confer with my co-workers during the progress of the inquiry, that Government should recognize that, by being a member of the Committee, I did not cease to be the ryots' advocate, and that in case the result of the inquiry failed to give me satisfaction, I should be free to guide and advise the ryots as to what line of action they should take.

The Committee found in favour of the ryots, and recommended that the planters should refund a portion of the exactions made by them which the Committee had found to be unlawful, and that the *tinkathia* system should be abolished by law.

Sir Edward Gait had a large share in getting the Committee to make a unanimous report and in getting the agrarian bill passed in accordance with the Committee's recommendations.

The *tinkathia* system which had been in existence for about a century was thus abolished, and with it the planters' *raj*[23] came to an end. The ryots, who had all along remained crushed, now somewhat came to their own, and the superstition that the stain of indigo could never be washed out was exploded. (424–25)

Chapter XXX: That Wonderful Spectacle!

I felt myself at a loss to discover how to offer civil disobedience against the Rowlatt Bill[24] if it was finally passed into law. One could disobey it only if the Government gave one the opportunity for it. Failing that, could we civilly disobey other laws? And if so, where was the line to be drawn?

While these cogitations were still going on, news was received that the Rowlatt Bill had been published as an Act. That night I fell asleep while thinking over the question. Towards the small hours of the morning I woke up somewhat earlier than usual. I was still in that twilight condition between sleep and consciousness when suddenly the idea broke upon me—it was as if in a dream. Early in the morning I related the whole story to Rajagopalachari.[25]

'The idea came to me last night in a dream that we should call upon the country to observe a general *hartal*.[26] Satyagraha is a process of self-purification, and ours is a sacred fight, and it seems to me to be in the fitness of things that it should be commenced with an act of self-purification. Let all the people of India, therefore, suspend their business on that day and observe the day as one of fasting and prayer. The Musalmans may not fast for more than one day; so the duration of the fast should be 24 hours.'

I drafted a brief appeal. The date of the *hartal* was first fixed on the 30th March 1919, but was subsequently changed to 6th April. The people thus had only a short notice of the *hartal*. (459–60)

Chapter XXXI: That Memorable Week! I

But in the meanwhile Delhi had already observed the *hartal* on the 30th March. The wire about the postponement of the *hartal* till the 6th of April had reached there too late. Delhi had never witnessed a *hartal* like that before. Hindus and Musalmans seemed united like one man. Swami Shraddhanandji[27] was invited to deliver a speech in the Jumma Masjid which he did. All this was more than the authorities could bear. The police checked the *hartal* procession as it was proceeding towards the railway station, and opened fire, causing a number of casualties, and the reign of repression commenced in Delhi.

The story of the happenings in Delhi was repeated with variations in Lahore and Amritsar. (460–61)

Chapter XXXII: That Memorable Week! II

I spoke at length on the duty of non-violence and on the limitations of Satyagraha, and said: "Satyagraha is essentially a weapon of the truthful. A Satyagrahi is pledged to non-violence, and, unless people observe it in thought, word and deed, I cannot offer mass Satyagraha."

Anasuyabehn,[28] too, had received news of disturbances in Ahmedabad. Some one had spread a rumour that she also had been arrested. The mill-hands had gone mad over her rumoured arrest, struck work and committed acts of violence, and a sergeant had been done to death.

I proceeded to Ahmedabad. I learnt that an attempt had been made to pull up the rails near the Nadiad railway station, that a Government officer had been murdered in Viramgam, and that Ahmedabad was under martial law. The people were terror-stricken. They had indulged in acts of violence and were being made to pay for them with interest. (467–68)

Chapter XXXIII: 'A Himalayan Miscalculation'

Almost immediately after the Ahmedabad meeting I went to Nadiad. It was here that I first used the expression "Himalayan miscalculation" which obtained such a wide currency afterwards. Even at Ahmedabad I had begun to have a dim perception of my mistake. But when I reached Nadiad and saw the actual state of things there and heard reports about a large number of people from Kheda district[29] having been arrested, it suddenly dawned upon me that I had committed a grave error in calling upon the people in the Kheda district and elsewhere to launch upon civil disobedience prematurely, as it now seemed to me. I was addressing a public meeting. My confession brought down upon me no small amount of ridicule. But I have never regretted having made that confession.

Let us now see what that Himalayan miscalculation was. Before one can be fit for the practice of civil disobedience one must have rendered a willing and respectful obedience to the state laws. A Satyagrahi obeys the laws of society intelligently and of his own free will, because he considers it to be his sacred duty to do so. It is only when a person has thus obeyed the laws of society scrupulously that he is in a position to judge as to which particular rules are good and just and which unjust and iniquitous. Only then does the right accrue to him of the civil disobedience of certain laws in well-defined circumstances. My error lay in my failure to observe this necessary limitation. I had called on the people to launch upon civil disobedience before they had thus qualified themselves for it, and this mistake seemed to me of Himalayan magnitude. (469–70)

Farewell

The time has now come to bring these chapters to a close.

My life from this point onward has been so public that there is hardly anything about it that people do not know.

It is not without a wrench that I have to take leave of the reader. I set a high value on my experiments. I do not know whether I have been able to do justice to them. I can only say that I have spared no pains to give a faithful narrative. To describe truth, as it has appeared to me, and in the exact manner in which I have arrived at it, has been my ceaseless effort. The exercise has given me ineffable mental peace, because, it has been my fond hope that it might bring faith in Truth and Ahimsa to waverers.

This much I can say with assurance, as a result of all my experiments, that a perfect vision of Truth can only follow a complete realization of Ahimsa.

To see the universal and all-pervading Spirit of Truth face to face one must be able to love the meanest of creation as oneself. And a man who aspires after that cannot afford to keep out of any field of life. That is why my devotion to Truth has drawn me into the field of politics; and I can say without the slightest hesitation, and yet in all humility, that those who say that religion has nothing to do with politics do not know what religion means.

Ever since my return to India I have had experiences of the dormant passions lying hidden within me. The knowledge of them has made me feel humiliated though not defeated. The experiences and experiments have sustained me and given me great joy. But I know that I have still before me a difficult path to traverse. I must reduce myself to zero. So long as a man does not of his own free will put himself last among his fellow creatures, there is no salvation for him. Ahimsa is the farthest limit of humility.

In bidding farewell to the reader, for the time being at any rate, I ask him to join with me in prayer to the God of Truth that He may grant me the boon of Ahimsa in mind, word and deed. (503–5)

NOTES

1. 39:vi
2. Liberation from the cycle of birth and death, self-realization
3. Merchant caste
4. Small princely states in Gujarat in western India
5. Temple dedicated to the Hindu God Vishnu
6. A period of four months, a vow of fasting during the four months of the rains
7. An internal abscess
8. A religion closely related to Hinduism, but with a greater emphasis on *ahimsa*
9. An early English word for Muslim
10. The Indian term for a follower of Zoroastrianism
11. The Code of Manu, foundation of Hindu Law
12. A rock and a whirlpool personified in Greek and Roman mythology as female monsters; caught between two hazardous alternatives

13. In 1893, after Gandhi had returned to India from London having earned his law degree

14. Small claims court

15. Lawyers

16. The name Gandhi used for Rajchandra Ravjibhai Mehta, a Jain jeweler

17. Chastity in its narrower meaning, control of all the senses in its wider meaning

18. A journalist and close co-worker with Gandhi in South Africa

19. A widely read British author of the period

20. An area in Bihar and the site of Gandhi's first *satyagraha* campaign in India

21. A plant yielding a deep blue dye; largely obsolete after Germans invented a synthetic dye at this time

22. Peasants

23. Rule; used widely at the time to refer to the British government in India

24. A bill named after the chairman of the committee recommending that strong measures be taken against Indian terrorists

25. C. Rajagopalachariar, also known as Rajaji; one of Gandhi's closest co-workers

26. A temporary work stoppage traditionally associated with Hindu religious purification

27. A Hindu leader. The suffix –ji is used with a name to indicate respect, as in Gandhiji.

28. Anasuya Sarabhai, a social worker who worked with Gandhi

29. A district in Gujarat

4

Satyagraha in South Africa

Mohandas K. Gandhi

Truth (satya) implies love, and firmness (agraha) engenders and therefore serves as a synonym for force. I thus began to call the Indian movement "satyagraha," that is to say, the Force which is born of Truth and Love or non-violence, and gave up the use of the phrase "passive resistance." (92)

Gandhi wrote most of Satyagraha in South Africa *in Yeravda Central Jail in 1923–1924 in India and completed it after his release in 1924. Although he had been involved in public service of the Indian community from the first year he arrived in South Africa in 1893, he and his compatriots did not conceive of* satyagraha *until 1906, and it was not until 1908/1909 that he fully understood the implications of this practice and theory of political change. The ordinance referred to in the first paragraph was the draft of a proposed law requiring that all Indians residing in the Transvaal be fingerprinted and register with the Registrar of Asiatics. They had to carry a certificate of registration with them at all times. Failure to register or to carry the certificate meant they could be deported, involving the loss of property and livelihood. Gandhi believed "it would spell absolute ruin for the Indians in South Africa."*

References are to Satyagraha in South Africa, The Collected Works of Mahatma Gandhi. *39 (New Delhi: Publication Division, Ministry of Information and Broadcasting, 1958–1994).*

CHAPTER XII: THE ADVENT OF SATYAGRAHA

The meeting was duly held on September 11, 1906. It was attended by delegates from various places in the Transvaal. But I must confess that even I myself had not then understood all the implications of the resolutions I had helped to frame; nor had I gauged all the possible conclusions to which they might lead. The old Empire Theatre was packed from floor to ceiling. I could read in every face the expectation of something strange to be done or to happen. The most important among the resolutions passed by the meeting was the famous Fourth Resolution by which the Indians solemnly determined not to submit to the Ordinance in the event of its becoming law in the teeth of their opposition and to suffer all the penalties attaching to such non-submission. The resolution was duly proposed, seconded and supported by several speakers one of whom was Sheth Haji Habib. He was a very old and experienced resident of South Africa and made an impassioned speech. He was deeply moved and went so far as to say that we must pass this resolution with God as witness and must never yield a cowardly submission to such degrading legislation. He then went on solemnly to declare in the name of God that he would never submit to that law, and advised all present to do likewise.

When in the course of his speech Sheth Haji Habib came to the solemn declaration, I was at once startled and put on my guard. I thought out the possible consequences of it in a moment. My perplexity gave place to enthusiasm. And although I had no intention of taking an oath or inviting others to do so, I warmly approved of the Sheth's suggestion. But at the same time it seemed to me that the people should be told of all the consequences and should have explained to them clearly the meaning of a pledge. And if even then they were prepared to pledge themselves, they should be encouraged to do so; otherwise, I must understand that they were not still ready to stand the final test. I therefore asked the President for permission to explain to the meeting the implications of Sheth Haji Habib's suggestion.

"I wish to explain to this meeting that there is a vast difference between this resolution and every other resolution we have passed up to date and that there is a wide divergence also in the manner of making it. It is a very grave resolution we are making, as our existence in South Africa depends upon our fully observing it. We all believe in one and the same God, the differences of nomenclature in Hinduism and Islam notwithstanding. To pledge ourselves or to take an oath in the name of that God or with Him as witness is not something to be trifled with. If having taken such an oath we violate our pledge we are guilty before God and man. Personally I hold that a man who deliberately and intelligently takes a pledge and then breaks it forfeits his manhood."

At last all present, standing with upraised hands, took an oath with God as witness not to submit to the Ordinance if it became law. I can never forget the scene which is present before my mind's eye as I write. The community's enthusiasm knew no bounds.

None of us knew what name to give to our movement. I then used the term "passive resistance" in describing it. I did not then quite understand the implications of "passive resistance" as I called it. I only knew that some new principle had come into being. As the struggle advanced, the phrase "passive resistance" gave rise to confusion and it appeared shameful to permit this great struggle to be known only by an English name. Again, that foreign phrase could hardly pass as current coin among the community. A small prize was therefore announced in *Indian Opinion* to be awarded to the reader who invented the best designation for our struggle. We thus received a number of suggestions. The meaning of the struggle had been then fully discussed in *Indian Opinion* and the competitors for the prize had fairly sufficient material to serve as a basis for their exploration. Shri Maganlal Gandhi was one of the competitors and he suggested the word *sadagraha*, meaning "firmness in a good cause." I liked the word, but it did not fully represent the whole idea I wished it to connote. I therefore corrected it to "satyagraha." Truth *(satya)* implies love, and firmness *(agraha)* engenders and therefore serves as a synonym for force. I thus began to call the Indian movement "satyagraha," that is to say, the Force which is born of Truth and Love or non-violence, and gave up the use of the phrase "passive resistance," in connection with it, so much so that even in English writing we often avoided it and used instead the word "satyagraha" itself or some other equivalent English phrase. (86–88, 91–92)

CHAPTER XXXIII: TOLSTOY FARM I

The satyagrahis now saw that no one could tell how long the struggle would last. On the one hand there were the Boer[1] Generals determined not to yield even an inch of ground and on the other there was a handful of satyagrahis pledged to fight unto death or victory. It was like a war between ants and the elephant who could crush thousands of them under each of his feet. The satyagrahis could not impose a time limit upon their satyagraha.

Whether it lasted one year or many, it was all the same to them. For them the struggle itself was victory. Fighting meant imprisonment or deportation for them. But what about their families in the meanwhile?

There was only one solution for this difficulty, namely, that all the families should be kept at one place and should become members of a sort of co-operative commonwealth. Public funds would be largely saved and the families of satyagrahis would be trained to live a new and simple life in harmony with one another. Indians belonging to various provinces and professing divers faiths would have an opportunity of living together.

But where was the place suitable for a settlement of this nature? The place required must be in the Transvaal and near Johannesburg. Mr. Kallenbach[2] bought a farm of about 1,100 acres and gave the use of it to satyagrahis free of any rent or charge (May 30, 1910). Upon the Farm there were nearly one thousand fruit-bearing trees and a small house at the foot of a hill with accommodation for half-a-dozen persons. Water was supplied from two wells as well as from a spring. The nearest railway station, Lawley, was about a mile from the farm and Johannesburg was twenty-one miles distant. We decided to build houses upon this farm and to invite the families of satyagrahis to settle there. (187–89)

CHAPTER XXXIV: TOLSTOY FARM II

The weak became strong on Tolstoy Farm and labour proved to be a tonic for all.

Everyone had to go to Johannesburg on some errand or other. Children liked to go there just for the fun of it. I also had to go there on business. We therefore made a rule that we could go there by rail only on the public business of our little commonwealth, and then too travel third class. Anyone who wanted to go on a pleasure trip must go on foot, and carry home-made provisions with him. No one might spend anything on his food in the city. Had it not been for these drastic rules, the money saved by living in a rural locality would have been wasted in railway fares and city picnics.

Anyone who wished to go to Johannesburg went there on foot once or twice a week and returned the same day. It was a journey of 21 miles and back. We saved hundreds of rupees by this one rule of going on foot, and those who thus went walking were much benefited. Some newly acquired the habit of walking. The general practice was that the sojourner should rise at two o'clock and start at half past two. He would reach Johannesburg in six to seven hours. The record for the minimum time taken on the journey was 4 hours 18 minutes.

A school was indispensable for the youngsters and the children. This was the most difficult of our tasks and we never achieved complete success in this matter till the very last. The burden of teaching work was largely borne by Mr. Kallenbach and myself. The school could be held only after noon, when both of us were thoroughly exhausted by our morning labour, and so were our pupils.

Religious teaching presented another tough problem. I would like Mussalmans to read the Koran, and Parsis the Avesta. I collected books bearing on Islam and Zoroastrianism. I wrote out the fundamental doctrines of Hinduism according to my light.

This teaching experiment was not fruitless. The children were saved from the infection of intolerance, and learnt to view one another's religions and customs with a large-hearted charity. They learnt how to live together like blood-brothers. They imbibed the lessons of mutual service, courtesy and industry. And from what little I know about the later activities of some of the children on Tolstoy Farm, I am certain that the education which they received there has not been in vain. Even if imperfect, it was a thoughtful and religious experiment, and among the sweetest reminiscences of Tolstoy Farm, the reminiscences of this teaching experiment are no less sweet than the rest. (191–94)

CHAPTER XXXV: TOLSTOY FARM III

Tolstoy Farm proved to be a centre of spiritual purification and penance for the final campaign. I have serious doubts as to whether the struggle could have been prosecuted for eight years, whether we could have secured larger funds, and whether the thousands of men who participated in the last phase of the struggle would have borne their share in it, if there had been no Tolstoy Farm. Tolstoy Farm was never placed in the limelight, yet an institution which deserved it attracted public sympathy to itself. The Indians saw that the Tolstoy Farmers were doing what they themselves were not prepared to do and what they looked upon in the light of hardship. This public confidence was a great asset to the movement when it was organized afresh on a large scale in 1913. (207)

CHAPTER XXXIX: WHEN A MARRIAGE IS NOT A MARRIAGE

As if, unseen by anyone, God was preparing the ingredients for the Indians' victory and demonstrating still more clearly the injustice of the Europeans in South Africa, an event happened which none had expected. Many married men came to South Africa from India, while some Indians contracted marriages in South Africa itself. There is no law for the registration of ordinary marriages in India, and the religious ceremony suffices to confer validity upon them. Although Indians had settled in South Africa for the last forty years, the validity of marriages solemnized according to the rites of the various religions of India had never been called in question. But at this time there was a case in which Mr. Justice Searle of the Cape Supreme Court gave judgment on March 14, 1913, to the effect that all marriages were outside the pale of legal marriages in South Africa with the exception of such as were celebrated according to Christian rites and registered by the Registrar of Marriages. This terrible judgment thus nullified in South Africa at a stroke of the pen all marriages celebrated according to the Hindu, Mussalman and Zoroastrian rites. The many married Indian women in South Africa in terms of this judgment ceased to rank as the wives of their husbands and were degraded to the rank of concubines, while their progeny were deprived of their right to inherit the parents' property. This was an insufferable situation for women no less than men, and the Indians in South Africa were deeply agitated.

According to my usual practice I wrote to the Government, asking them whether they agreed to the Searle judgment and whether, if the judge was right in interpreting it, they would amend the law so as to recognize the validity of Indian marriages consecrated according to the religious customs of the parties and recognized as legal in India. The Government were not then in a mood to listen and could not see their way to complying with my request.

A crisis now arrived, when there could not be any waiting for an auspicious day or hour. Patience was impossible in the face of this insult offered to our womanhood. We decided to offer stubborn satyagraha irrespective of the number of fighters. Not only could the women now be not prevented from joining the struggle, but we decided even to invite them to come into line along with the men. We first invited the sisters who had lived on Tolstoy Farm. I found that they were only too glad to enter the struggle. I gave them an idea of the risks incidental to such participation. I explained to them that they would have to put up with restraints in the matter of food, dress, and personal movements. I warned them that they might be given hard work in jail, made to wash clothes and even subjected to insult by the warders. But these sisters were all brave and feared none of these things. One of them was pregnant while six of them had young babies in arms. But one and all were eager to join and I simply could not come in their way. These sisters were with one exception all Tamilians.[3]

I went to Phoenix,[4] and talked to the settlers about my plans. First of all I held a consultation with the sisters living there. I knew that the step of sending women to jail was fraught with serious risk. (220–23)

CHAPTER XL: WOMEN IN JAIL

The sisters proceeded to Newcastle and set about their work according to the plans previously settled. Their influence spread like wildfire. The pathetic story of the wrongs heaped up by the £3 tax touched the labourers[5] to the quick, and they went on strike. I received the news by wire and was as much perplexed as I was pleased. What was I to do? I was not prepared for this marvellous awakening. I had neither men nor the money which would enable me to cope with the work before me. But I visualized my duty very clearly. I must go to Newcastle and do what I could. I left at once to go there.

Government could not now any longer leave the brave Transvaal sisters free to pursue their activities. They too were sentenced to imprisonment for the same term—three months—and were kept in the same prison as the Phoenix party (October 21, 1913).

The women's bravery was beyond words. They were all kept in Maritzburg jail, where they were considerably harassed.

[One girl] returned from jail with a fatal fever to which she succumbed within a few days of her release (February 22, 1914). How can I forget her? Valliamma R. Munuswami Mudaliar was a young girl of Johannesburg only sixteen years of age. She was confined to bed when I saw her. As she was a tall girl, her emaciated body was a terrible thing to behold.

"Valliamma, you do not repent of your having gone to jail?" I asked.

"Repent? I am even now ready to go to jail again if I am arrested," said Valliamma.

"But what if it results in your death?" I pursued.

"I do not mind it. Who would not love to die for one's motherland?" was the reply.

The imprisonment of many might have been fruitless but the devoted sacrifice of a single pure soul could never go in vain. None can tell whose sacrifice in South Africa was acceptable to God, and hence bore fruit. But we do know that Valliamma's sacrifice bore fruit and so did the sacrifice of the other sisters. (226–28)

CHAPTER XLI: A STREAM OF LABOURERS

I had no means of housing them; the sky was the only roof over their heads. Luckily for us the weather was favourable, there being neither rain nor cold. I was confident that the trader class would not fail to feed us. The traders of Newcastle supplied cooking pots and bags of rice and dal.[6] Other places also showered rice, dal, vegetables, condiments and other things upon us. The contributions exceeded my expectations. Not all were ready to go to jail, but all felt for the cause, and all were willing to bring their quota to the movement to the best of their ability. Those who could not give anything served as volunteer workers. Well known and intelligent volunteers were required to look after these obscure and uneducated men, and they were forthcoming. They rendered priceless help, and many of them were also arrested. Thus everyone did what he could, and smoothed our path.

The strength of the "army" was about five thousand. I had not the money to pay the railway fare for such a large number of persons, and therefore they could not all be taken by rail. And if they were taken by rail, I would be without the means of putting their morale to the test.

The Transvaal border is 36 miles from Newcastle. The border villages of Natal and the Transvaal are Charlestown and Volksrust, respectively. I finally decided to march on foot. I consulted the labourers who had their wives and children with them and some of whom therefore hesitated to agree to my proposal. I had no alternative except to harden my heart, and declared that those who wished were free to return to the mines. But none of them would avail themselves of this liberty. We decided that those who were disabled in their limbs should be sent by rail, and all able-bodied persons announced their readiness to go to Charlestown on foot. The march was to be accomplished in two days. (230–32)

CHAPTER XLIII: CROSSING THE BORDER

The labourers' strike was in full swing at this time. Men as well as women were on the move between the mining district and Charlestown. Of these, there were two women with their little ones one of whom died of exposure on the march. The other fell from the arms of its mother while she was crossing a spruit[7] and was drowned. But the brave mothers refused to be dejected and continued their march. One of them said, "We must not pine for the dead who will not come back to us for all our sorrow. It is the living for whom we must work." I have often come across instances of such quiet heroism, sterling faith and saving knowledge among the poor.

Bread and sugar constituted our sole ration, but how was a supply of bread to be ensured on the eight days' march? The bread must be distributed to the pilgrims every day and we could not hold any of it in stock. The only solution of this problem was that someone should supply us with bread at each stage. But who would be our provider? There were no Indian bakers at all. Again there could not be found a baker in each of the villages, which usually depended upon the cities for their supply of bread. The bread therefore must be supplied by some baker and sent by rail to the appointed station. Volksrust was about double the size of Charlestown, and a large European bakery there willingly contracted to supply bread at each place. The baker did not take advantage of our awkward plight to charge us higher than the market rates and supplied bread made of excellent flour. He sent it in time by rail, and the railway officials, also Europeans, not only honestly delivered it to us, but they took good care of it in transit and gave us some special facilities. They knew that we harboured no enmity in our hearts, intended no harm to any living soul and sought redress only through self-suffering. The atmosphere around us was thus purified and continued to be pure. The feeling of love which is dormant though present in all mankind was roused into activity. Everyone realized that we are all brothers whether we are ourselves Christians, Jews, Hindus, Mussalmans or anything else.

The next day (November 6, 1913) at the appointed stroke of the hour (6:30) we offered prayers and commenced the march in the name of God. The pilgrim band was composed of 2,037 men, 127 women, 57 children. (237, 239–240)

CHAPTER XLIV: THE GREAT MARCH

The caravan of pilgrims thus started punctually at the appointed hour. There is a small spruit one mile from Charlestown, and as soon as one crosses it, one has entered Volksrust or the Transvaal. A small patrol of mounted policemen was on duty at the border gate. I went up to them, leaving instructions with the "army" to cross over when I signalled to them. But while I was still talking with the police, the pilgrims made a sudden rush and crossed the border. The police surrounded them, but the surging multitude was not easy to control. The police had no intention of arresting us. I pacified the pilgrims and got them to arrange themselves in regular rows. Everything was in order in a few minutes and the march into the Transvaal began. (240)

CHAPTER XLV: ALL IN PRISON

A Cape cart came and stopped before us and from it alighted Mr. Chamney, the Principal Immigration Officer of the Transvaal, and a police officer. They took me somewhat aside and one of them said, "I arrest you." I was thus arrested thrice in four days.

"What about the marchers?" I asked.

"We shall see to that," was the answer.

I said nothing further.

The police officer permitted me only to inform the marchers of my arrest. I asked Polak[8] to assume charge of and go with the pilgrims.

At about 9 o'clock in the morning on the 10th the pilgrims reached Balfour where three special trains were drawn up at the station to take them and deport them to Natal. (245–46)

CHAPTER XLVI: THE TEST

The pilgrims were taken on special trains not for a picnic but for baptism through fire. On the way the Government did not care to arrange even to feed them and when they reached Natal, they were prosecuted and sent to jail straightaway. We expected and even desired as much. But the Government would have to incur additional expenditure and would appear to have played into the Indians' hands if they kept thousands of labourers in prison. And the coal mines would close down in the interval. If such a state of things lasted for any length of time, the Government would be compelled to repeal the £3 tax. They therefore struck out a new plan. Surrounding them with wire netting, the Government proclaimed the mine compounds as outstations to the Dundee and Newcastle jails and appointed the mine-owners' European staffs as the warders. In this way they forced the labourers underground against their will and the mines began to work once more. There is this difference between the status of a servant and that of a slave, that if a servant leaves his post, only a civil suit can be filed against him, whereas the slave who leaves his master can be brought back to work by main force. The labourers therefore were now reduced to slavery pure and simple.

But that was not enough. The labourers were brave men, and they flatly declined to work on the mines with the result that they were brutally whipped.

It was then (December 1913)[9] that Lord Hardinge in Madras made his famous speech which created a stir in South Africa as well as in England. The
Viceroy may not publicly criticize other members of the Empire, but Lord
Hardinge not only passed severe criticism upon the Union Government, but
he also wholeheartedly defended the action of the satyagrahis and supported their civil disobedience of unjust and invidious legislation.

The news of the strike and the arrests spread everywhere at lightning
speed, and thousands of labourers unexpectedly and spontaneously came
out on the south as well as on the north coast. When I went to jail, I had
warned my co-workers against allowing any more labourers to go on strike.
I hoped that a victory could be achieved only with the help of the miners. If
all the labourers—there were about sixty thousand of them all told—were
called out it would be difficult to maintain them. We had not the means of
taking so many on the march; we had neither the men to control them nor
the money to feed them. Moreover, with such a large body of men it would
be impossible to prevent a breach of the peace.

But when the floodgates are opened, there is no checking the universal
deluge. The labourers everywhere struck work of their own accord, and volunteers also posted themselves in the various places to look after them.

Government now adopted a policy of blood and iron. They prevented the
labourers from striking by sheer force. (250–52)

CHAPTER XLVII: THE BEGINNING OF THE END

The struggle was now about to close. The Union Government[10] had not the
power to keep thousands of innocent men in jail. The Viceroy would not tolerate it, and all the world was waiting to see what General Smuts[11] would do.
General Smuts saw that there had been injustice which called for remedy, but
he was in the same predicament as a snake which has taken a rat in its mouth
but can neither gulp it down nor cast it out. He must do justice, but he had
lost the power of doing justice, as he had given the Europeans in South Africa
to understand that he would not repeal the £3 tax nor carry out any other reform. And now he felt compelled to abolish the tax as well as to undertake
other remedial legislation. States amenable to public opinion get out of such
awkward positions by appointing a commission which conducts only a nominal inquiry, as its recommendations are a foregone conclusion. It is a general
practice that the recommendations of such a commission should be accepted
by the State, and therefore under the guise of carrying out the recommendations, governments give the justice which they have first refused. General
Smuts appointed a commission of three members, with which the Indians
pledged themselves to have nothing to do so long as certain demands of
theirs in respect of the commission were not granted by the Government.
One of these demands was, that the satyagrahi prisoners should be released,

and another that the Indians should be represented on the commission by at least one member. To a certain extent the first demand was accepted by the commission itself which recommended to the Government "with a view to enabling the enquiry to be made as thorough as possible" that Mr. Kallenbach, Mr. Polak and I should be released unconditionally. The Government accepted this recommendation and released all three of us simultaneously (December 18, 1913) after an imprisonment of hardly six weeks.

I went to Pretoria with Andrews.[12] Just at this time there was a great strike of the European employees of the Union railways, which made the position of the Government extremely delicate. I was called upon to commence the Indian march at such a fortunate juncture. But I declared that the Indians could not thus assist the railway strikers, as they were not out to harass the Government, their struggle being entirely different and differently conceived. Even if we undertook the march, we would begin it at some other time when the railway trouble had ended. This decision of ours created a deep impression, and was cabled to England by Reuter. Lord Ampthill[13] cabled his congratulations from England. English friends in South Africa too appreciated our decision. One of the secretaries of General Smuts jocularly said: "I do not like your people, and do not care to assist them at all. But what am I to do? You help us in our days of need. How can we lay hands upon you? I often wish you took to violence like the English strikers, and then we would know at once how to dispose of you. But you will not injure even the enemy. You desire victory by self-suffering alone and never transgress your self-imposed limits of courtesy and chivalry. And that is what reduces us to sheer helplessness." General Smuts also gave expression to similar sentiments. (255–56, 259)

CHAPTER XLIX: LETTERS EXCHANGED

The commission strongly criticized the Indians for withholding their assistance and dismissed the charges of misbehaviour against the soldiers, but recommended compliance without delay with all the demands of the Indian community, such as for instance the repeal of the £3 tax and the validation of Indian marriages, and the grant of some trifling concessions in addition. Thus the report of the commission was favourable to the Indians as predicted by General Smuts. (265)

CONCLUSION

Thus the great satyagraha struggle closed after eight years, and it appeared that the Indians in South Africa were now at peace. On July 18, 1914, I sailed for England on my way back to India.

NOTES

1. Descendant of Dutch settlers in South Africa
2. A German architect; one of Gandhi's closest friends and co-workers in South Africa
3. From Tamil, an area in southern India
4. Gandhi's first ashram in South Africa
5. Indentured Indians who worked in the mines near Newcastle
6. Lentils
7. A stream
8. A journalist, one of Gandhi's closest associates in South Africa
9. Actually November 24, 1913
10. The central government of South Africa
11. Minister of the Interior in the South African government
12. A minister and a life-long friend of Gandhi
13. A former acting Viceroy of India and a strong supporter of Gandhi

5

Hind Swaraj (Indian Home Rule) and Related Writings

Mohandas K. Gandhi

If we become free, India is free. And in this thought you have a definition of swaraj. (*Hind Swaraj*, 73)

Gandhi wrote Hind Swaraj *in ten days, from November 13 to 22, 1909, on the ship Kildonan Castle on the return voyage from England to South Africa.* Hind Swaraj *was his first book and the only one he translated from the original Gujarati into English. Some critics believe that his indictment of Modern Civilization in* Hind Swaraj *is extreme, but Gandhi held to the views expressed in this book throughout his life.*

In Hind Swaraj *Gandhi achieved for the first time a thoroughgoing understanding of* satyagraha. *He and his coworkers were improvising nonviolent resistance to the laws oppressing Indians in South Africa, and as the practice developed, Gandhi became more aware of its theoretical underpinnings. Although he owed much to contemporary Western and Eastern writers and to the scriptures of major world religions, the application of his readings to the Indian struggle in South Africa was innovative. Gandhi believed that* Hind Swaraj *was "an original work," as he wrote to his friend Hermann Kallenbach in 1909.*

Selections from Gandhi's Hind Swaraj *are followed by passages from other writings relevant to themes introduced in* Hind Swaraj. *References to* Hind Swaraj *are from M. K. Gandhi,* Hind Swaraj and Other Writings, *ed. Anthony J. Parel (Cambridge: Cambridge University Press, 1997).*

Consult chapter 1 in the section on South Africa and chapter 9, Anthony J. Parel's "Gandhian Freedoms and Self-Rule," for further information about Hind Swaraj *and Gandhi's concept of* swaraj.

HIND SWARAJ

Chapter VI: Civilization

EDITOR: This [modern] civilization takes note neither of morality nor of religion. Its votaries calmly state that their business is not to teach religion. Some even consider it to be a superstitious growth. Others put on the cloak of religion, and prate about morality. But, after twenty years' experience, I have come to the conclusion that immorality is often taught in the name of morality.

This civilization is irreligion, and it has taken such a hold on the people in Europe that those who are in it appear to be half mad. They lack real physical strength or courage. (37)

Chapter VII: Why was India Lost?

EDITOR: Some Englishmen state that they took and they hold India by the sword. Both these statements are wrong. The sword is entirely useless for holding India. We alone keep them. Napoleon is said to have described the English as a nation of shop-keepers. It is a fitting description. They hold whatever dominions they have for the sake of their commerce. Many problems can be solved by remembering that money is their God. Then it follows that we keep the English in India for our base self-interest. We like their commerce; they please us by their subtle methods and get what they want from us. To blame them for this is to perpetuate their power. We further strengthen their hold by quarrelling amongst ourselves. (41)

Chapter VIII: The Condition of India

EDITOR: It is my deliberate opinion that India is being ground down, not under the English heel, but under that of modern civilization. It is groaning under the monster's terrible weight. There is yet time to escape it, but every day makes it more and more difficult. Religion is dear to me and my first complaint is that India is becoming irreligious. Here I am not thinking of the Hindu or the Mahomedan[1] or the Zoroastrian[2] religion but of that religion which underlies all religions. We are turning away from God. (42)

Chapter X: The Condition of India (Continued):The Hindus and the Mahomedans

READER: Has the introduction of Mahomedanism[3] not unmade the nation?

EDITOR: India cannot cease to be one nation because people belonging to different religions live in it. The introduction of foreigners does not necessarily destroy the nation; they merge in it. A country is one nation only when such a condition obtains in it. That country must have a faculty for assimilation. India has ever been such a country. In reality, there are as many religions as there are individuals; but those who are conscious of the spirit of nationality do not interfere with one another's religion. If they do, they are not fit to be considered a nation. If the Hindus believe that India should be peopled only by Hindus, they are living in dreamland. The Hindus, the Mahomedans, the Parsis and the Christians who have made India their country are fellow countrymen, and they will have to live in unity, if only for their own interest.

Should we not remember that many Hindus and Mahomedans own the same ancestors and the same blood runs through their veins? Do people become enemies because they change their religion? Is the God of the Mahomedan different from the God of the Hindu? Religions are different roads converging to the same point. (51–53)

Chapter XIII: What Is True Civilization?

READER: What, then, is civilization?

EDITOR: Civilization is that mode of conduct which points out to man the path of duty. Performance of duty and observance of morality are convertible terms. To observe morality is to attain mastery over our mind and our passions. So doing, we know ourselves. The Gujarati equivalent for civilization means "good conduct." (66–67)

Chapter XIV: How Can India Become Free?

EDITOR: If we become free, India is free. And in this thought you have a definition of *swaraj*.

It is *swaraj* when we learn to rule ourselves. It is, therefore, in the palm of our hands. Do not consider this *swaraj* to be like a dream. There is no idea of sitting still. The *swaraj* that I wish to picture is such that, after we have once realized it, we shall endeavour to the end of our life-time to persuade others to do likewise. But such *swaraj* has to be experienced, by each one for himself. (73)

Chapter XV: Italy and India

READER: At first, we shall assassinate a few Englishmen and strike terror; then, a few men who will have been armed will fight openly. We may have to lose a quarter of a million men, more or less, but we shall regain our land. We shall undertake guerilla warfare, and defeat the English.

EDITOR: That is to say, you want to make the holy land of India unholy. Do you not tremble to think of freeing India by assassination? It is a cowardly thought, that of killing others. (77)

Chapter XVII: *Satyagraha*—Soul-Force

EDITOR: The force of love is the same as the force of the soul or truth. We have evidence of its working at every step. The universe would disappear without the existence of that force. But you ask for historical evidence. It is, therefore, necessary to know what history means. The Gujarati equivalent means: "It so happened." If that is the meaning of history, it is possible to give copious evidence. But, if it means the doings of kings and emperors, there can be no evidence of soul-force or passive resistance in such history. You cannot expect silver ore in a tin mine. History, as we know it, is a record of the wars of the world, and so there is a proverb among Englishmen that a nation which has no history, that is, no wars, is a happy nation. How kings played, how they became enemies of one another, how they murdered one another, is found accurately recorded in history, and if this were all that had happened in the world, it would have been ended long ago.

The fact that there are so many men still alive in the world shows that it is based not on the force of arms but on the force of truth or love. Therefore, the greatest and most unimpeachable evidence of the success of this force is to be found in the fact that, in spite of the wars of the world, it still lives on.

Thousands, indeed tens of thousands, depend for their existence on a very active working of this force. Little quarrels of millions of families in their daily lives disappear before the exercise of this force. Hundreds of nations live in peace. History does not and cannot take note of this fact. History, then, is a record of an interruption of the course of nature. Soul-force, being natural, is not noted in history.

If man will only realize that it is unmanly to obey laws that are unjust, no man's tyranny will enslave him. This is the key to self-rule or home rule.

It is a superstition and ungodly thing to believe that an act of a majority binds a minority. Many examples can be given in which acts of majorities will be found to have been wrong and those of minorities to have been right. All reforms owe their origin to the initiation of minorities in opposition to majorities.

Real Home Rule is possible only where passive resistance is the guiding force of the people. Any other rule is foreign rule.

READER: From what you say, then, it would appear that it is not a small thing to become a passive resister, and, if that is so, I should like you to explain how a man may become one.

EDITOR: Chastity is one of the greatest disciplines without which the mind cannot attain requisite firmness. A man who is unchaste loses stamina, becomes emasculated and cowardly. He whose mind is given over to animal passions is not capable of any great effort. This can be proved by innumerable instances. What, then, is a married person to do is the question that arises naturally; and yet it need not. When a husband and wife gratify the passions, it is no less an animal indulgence on that account.

Just as there is necessity for chastity, so is there for poverty. Pecuniary ambition and passive resistance cannot well go together.

Passive resistance has been described in the course of our discussion as truth-force.

Passive resistance cannot proceed a step without fearlessness. Those alone can follow the path of passive resistance who are free from fear, whether as to their possessions, false honour, their relatives, the government, bodily injuries or death. (89–90, 92, 95–98)

Chapter XIX: Machinery

READER: When you speak of driving out Western civilization, I suppose you will also say that we want no machinery.

EDITOR: It is machinery that has impoverished India. It is difficult to measure the harm that Manchester[4] has done to us. It is due to Manchester that Indian handicraft has all but disappeared.

Machinery has begun to desolate Europe. Ruination is now knocking at the English gates. Machinery is the chief symbol of modern civilization; it represents a great sin.

The workers in the mills of Bombay have become slaves. The condition of the women workers in the mills is shocking. When there were no mills, these women were not starving. If the machinery craze grows in our country, it will become an unhappy land. (107–8)

PASSAGES RELATED TO HIND SWARAJ (IN CHRONOLOGICAL ORDER)

There is no impassable barrier between East and West. There is no such thing as Western or European civilization, but there is a modern civilization, which is purely material. The people of Europe, before they were touched by modern civilization, had much in common with the people of the East; anyhow, the people of India and, even today, Europeans who are not touched by modern civilization are far better able to mix with the Indians than the offspring of that civilization. It is not the British people who are ruling India, but it is modern civilization, through its railways, telegraphs, telephones, and almost every invention which has been claimed to be a triumph of civilization. If British rule was replaced tomorrow by Indian rule based on modern methods, India would be no better, except that she would be able then to retain some of the money that is drained away to England; but, then, Indians would only become a second or fifth edition of Europe or America. (Letter to H. S. L. Polak, SN 5127, 10-14-09)

Opposed as I am to violence in any shape or form, I have endeavoured specially to come into contact with the so-called extremists who may be better described as the party of violence. This I have done in order if possible to convince them of the error of their ways. I have noticed that some of the members of this party are earnest spirits, possessing a high degree of morality, great intellectual ability and lofty sacrifice. They wield an undoubted influence on the young Indians here.

Some consider that the time for violence is not yet. I have practically met no one who believes that India can ever become free without resort to violence. (Letter to Lord Ampthill, SN 5152, 10-30-09)

Your argument tends to show that there must be complete divorce between politics and religion or spirituality. That is what we see in everyday life under modern conditions. Passive resistance seeks to rejoin politics and religion and to test every one of our actions in the light of ethical principles. (Letter to W. J. Wybergh, *Indian Opinion*, 5-10-10)

I, for one, bear no ill-will against the British or against any people or individuals. All living creatures are of the same substance as all drops of water in the ocean are the same in substance. I believe that all of us, individual souls, living in this ocean of spirit, are the same with one another with the closest bond among ourselves. A drop that separates soon dries up and any soul that believes itself separate from others is likewise destroyed. For myself, I am an uncompromising enemy of the present-day civilization of Europe. I tried to elaborate my view in *Hind Swaraj* and show that it is not the British that are responsible for the misfortunes of India but we who have succumbed to modern civilization. India can be free this very moment if we turn our back on this modern civilization and go back to our ancient way of life, which embodied the right ethical principles.

The key to an understanding of *Hind Swaraj* lies in the idea that worldly pursuits should give way to ethical living. This way of life has no room for violence in any form against any human being, black or white. (Preface to *Hind Swaraj, Indian Opinion*, 4-29-14)

I would warn the reader against thinking that I am today aiming at the *swaraj* described therein [in *Hind Swaraj*]. I know that India is not ripe for it. It may seem an impertinence to say so. But such is my conviction. I am individually working for the self-rule pictured therein. But today my corporate activity is undoubtedly devoted to the attainment of parliamentary *swaraj* in accordance with the wishes of the people of India.

The only part of the programme which is now being carried out in its entirety is that of non-violence. But I regret to have to confess that even that is not being carried out in the spirit of the book. If it were, India would establish *swaraj* in a day. If India adopted the doctrine of love as an active part of her religion and introduced it in her politics, *swaraj* would descend upon India from heaven. But I am painfully aware that

that event is far off as yet. (*Hind Swaraj* or the "Indian Home Rule," *Young India*, 1-26-21)

I would favour the use of the most elaborate machinery if thereby India's pauperism and resulting idleness be avoided. ("Co-Operation," *Young India*, 11-3-21)

Our non-violence need not be of the strong, but it *has* to be of the truthful. We must not intend harm to the English or to our co-operating countrymen if and whilst we claim to be non-violent. But the majority of us *have* intended harm, and we have refrained from doing it because of our weakness or under the ignorant belief that mere refraining from physical hurt amounted to due fulfilment of our pledge.

Swaraj by non-violence must be a progressively peaceful revolution such that the transference of power from a close corporation to the people's representatives will be as natural as the dropping of a fully ripe fruit from a well-nurtured tree. I say again that such a thing may be quite impossible of attainment. But I know that nothing less is the implication of non-violence. And if the present workers do not believe in the probability of achieving such comparatively non-violent atmosphere, they should drop the non-violent programme and frame another which is wholly different in character. ("Non-Violence," *Young India*, 3-9-22)

Before the [violent] revolutionary, I have urged non-violence not on the highest ground of morality but on the lower ground of expedience. I contend that the revolutionary method cannot succeed in India. If an open warfare were a possibility, I may concede that we may tread the path of violence that the other countries have and at least evolve the qualities that bravery on the battlefield brings forth. But attainment of *swaraj* through warfare I hold to be an impossibility for any time that we can foresee. Warfare may give us another rule for the English rule but not self-rule in terms of the masses. The pilgrimage to *swaraj* is a painful climb. It requires attention to details. It means vast organizing ability, it means penetration into the villages solely for the service of the villagers. In other words it means national education, i.e., education of the masses. It means an awakening of national consciousness among the masses. ("On the Verge of It," *Young India*, 5-21-25)

My freedom from hatred—I would even go so far as to claim for myself individually— my love of those who consider themselves to be my enemies, does not make me blind to their faults. That is no love which is extended simply because of the possession of some virtues fancied or real in the beloved. If I am true to myself, if I am true to mankind, if I am true to humanity, I must understand all the faults that human flesh is heir to. I must understand the weaknesses of my opponents, the vices of my opponents and, yet, in spite of these vices, not hate but even love them. It is by itself a force.

Do not for one moment consider that I condemn all that is Western. For the time being I am dealing with the predominant character of modern civilization, do not call it Western civilization, and the predominant character of modern civilization is the exploitation of the weaker races of the earth. The predominant character of modern civilization is to dethrone God and enthrone Materialism.

Your non-co-operation is intended not to encourage evil. That is the meaning. One of the greatest writers has said that if the world ceases to encourage evil, evil will die of inanition. If we simply find out for ourselves to what extent we are responsible for the evil that exists in society today, we will soon see that evil will soon be gone from society.

The secret is suffering, but not to subject the evil-doers to suffering, but to take the suffering upon our own shoulders.

In my humble opinion hatred is not essential for nationalism. Race hatred will kill the real national spirit.

Let us understand what nationalism is. We want freedom for our country. We do not want sufferings for other countries: we do not want the exploitation of other countries; we do not want the degradation of other countries. For my part I don't want the freedom of India if it means the disappearance of Englishmen, if it means the extinction of Englishmen. I want the freedom of my country so that other countries may learn something from this free country of mine. I want freedom of my country so that the resources of my country might be utilized for the benefit of mankind. (Speech at Meccano Club, Calcutta, *Forward*, 8-29-25)

The peoples of Europe have no doubt political power but no *swaraj*. Asian and African races are exploited for their partial benefit, and they, on their part, are being exploited by the ruling class or caste under the sacred name of democracy. At the root, therefore, the disease appears to be the same as in India. The same remedy is, therefore, likely to be applicable. Shorn of all the camouflage, the exploitation of the masses of Europe is sustained by violence. ("What of the West?," *Young India*, 9-3-25)

Hind Swaraj is not a mere political book. I have used the language of politics, but I have really tried to offer a glimpse of *dharma*. What is the meaning of *"Hind Swaraj"*? It means rule of *dharma* or *Ramarajya*. ("Talks to Ashram Women," *Bapuna Patro—Ashrami Behnone*, 1926)

I hold that the machinery method is harmful when the same thing can be done easily by millions of hands not otherwise occupied. It is any day better and safer for the millions spread in the seven hundred thousand villages of India scattered over an area nineteen hundred miles long and fifteen hundred broad that they manufacture their clothing in their own villages even as they prepare their own food. These villages cannot retain the freedom they have enjoyed from time immemorial, if they do not control the production of prime necessaries of life. ("Superstitions Die Hard," *Young India*, 7-2-31)

Without entering upon an elaborate argument, I would categorically state my conviction that the mania for mass production is responsible for the world crisis. ("Interview with Callendar, An American Correspondent," *Harijan*, 11-2-34)

I would prize every invention of science made for the benefit of all. There is a difference between invention and invention. I should not care for the asphyxiating gases capable of killing masses of men at a time. The heavy machinery for work of public utility which cannot be undertaken by human labour has its inevitable place, but all that would be owned by the State and used entirely for the benefit of the people. I can have no consideration for machinery which is meant either to enrich the few at the expense of the many, or without cause to displace the useful labour of many. ("A Discussion," *Harijan*, 6-22-35)

"What shall it avail a man if he gain the whole world and lose his soul?" In modern terms, it is beneath human dignity to lose one's individuality and become a mere cog in the machine. I want every individual to become a full-blooded, fully developed member of society. The villages must become self-sufficient. ("Discussion with Maurice Frydman," *Harijan*, 1-28-39)

The foreign power will be withdrawn before long, but for me real freedom will come only when we free ourselves of the domination of Western education, Western culture and Western way of living which have been ingrained in us, because this culture has made our living expensive and artificial, both for men and for women. Emancipation from this culture would mean real freedom for us. ("Talk with Englishwomen," *Biharni Komi Agman*, 226–27, 4-19-47)

NOTES

1. Muslim
2. A religion originating in Persia; In India followers of Zoroastrianism are called Parsis.
3. Islam
4. The textile industry of Manchester

6

Constructive Programme: Its Meaning and Place and Related Writings

Mohandas K. Gandhi

I was born for the constructive programme. It is part of my soul. Politics is a kind of botheration for me.

Speech at Gandhi Seva Sangh, 2-21-40

Gandhi wrote the Constructive Programme: Its Meaning and Place *in December 1941 and thoroughly revised it in 1945. Though relatively short—only twenty pages in* The Collected Works of Mahatma Gandhi—*this pamphlet contains one of Gandhi's most important contributions to the theory and practice of nonviolent social change. The pamphlet was the culmination of years of action and thought on the Constructive Programme, which he also called constructive work, constructive effort, and constructive activities. He not only defined the Constructive Programme here, but he also set down its relationship to civil disobedience. He believed that the Constructive Programme was essential to Indian independence and that civil disobedience, though often needed, was not absolutely necessary to win freedom. Civil disobedience had its rightful place, but it was more a handmaiden of the Constructive Programme, not the primary mode of winning independence. Civil disobedience within the context of the Constructive Programme could lead to political revolution, but social revolution—Gandhi's real aim—is only possible through the Constructive Programme. His fundamental concept was that the haves and the have-nots could unite in constructive work, and in that joint effort they would free themselves from social divisions and lead the nation to freedom.*

References are to Constructive Programme: Its Meaning and Place, The Collected Works of Mahatma Gandhi, 75 *(New Delhi: Publication Division, Ministry of Information and Broadcasting), 1958–1994.*

92

Consult chapter 2, 40–43, for more information about the biographi-
cal and historical background of the pamphlet, and chapter 13, "The
Constructive Programme," by Michael Nagler, for an analysis of the
importance of the Constructive Programme in Gandhi's time and in
ours.

CONSTRUCTIVE PROGRAMME: ITS MEANING AND PLACE

Introductory

The constructive programme may otherwise and more fittingly be called construction of *poorna* swaraj or complete independence by truthful and non-violent means.

Effort for construction of independence so called through violent and, therefore, necessarily untruthful means we know only too painfully. Look at the daily destruction of property, life and truth in the present war.

Complete independence through truth and non-violence means the independence of every unit, be it the humblest of the nation, without distinction of race, colour or creed. This independence is never exclusive. It is, therefore, wholly compatible with interdependence within or without. Practice will always fall short of the theory, even as the drawn line falls short of the theoretical line of Euclid. Therefore, complete independence will be complete only to the extent of our approach in practice to truth and non-violence.

Let the reader mentally plan out the whole of the constructive programme, and he will agree with me that, if it could be successfully worked out, the end of it would be the independence we want. (146–47)

1. Communal[1] Unity

Everybody is agreed about the necessity of this unity. But everybody does not know that unity does not mean political unity, which may be imposed. It means an unbreakable heart unity. The first thing essential for achieving such unity is for every Congressman, whatever his religion may be, to represent in his own person Hindu, Muslim, Christian, Zoroastrian, Jew, etc., shortly, every Hindu and non-Hindu. He has to feel his identity with every one of the millions of the inhabitants of Hindustan.[2] In order to realize this, every Congressman will cultivate personal friendship with persons representing faiths other than his own. He should have the same regard for the other faiths as he has for his own.

There would be no separate rooms or pots for Hindus and non-Hindus in schools and colleges, no communal schools, colleges and hospitals. The beginning of such a revolution has to be made by Congressmen without any political motive behind the correct conduct. Political unity will be its natural fruit.

We have long been accustomed to think that power comes only through Legislative Assemblies. I have regarded this belief as a grave error brought about by inertia or hypnotism. A superficial study of British history has made us think that all power percolates to the people from parliaments. The truth is that power resides in the people and it is entrusted for the time being to those whom they may choose as their representatives. Parliaments have no power or even existence independently of the people. It has been my effort for the last twenty-one years to convince the people of this simple truth. Civil disobedience is the storehouse of power. (147–49)

2. Removal of Untouchability

At this time of the day it is unnecessary to dilate upon the necessity of the removal of this blot and curse upon Hinduism. Congressmen have certainly done much in this matter. But I am sorry to have to say that many Congressmen have looked upon this item as a mere political necessity and not something indispensable, so far as Hindus are concerned, for the very existence of Hinduism. (149)

3. Prohibition

Although like communal unity and removal of untouchability prohibition has been on the Congress programme since 1920, Congressmen have not taken the interest they might have taken in this very vital social and moral reform. If we are to reach our goal through non-violent effort, we may not leave to the future government the fate of lakhs[3] of men and women who are labouring under the curse of intoxicants and narcotics. (149)

4. Khadi[4]

Khadi is a controversial subject. Many people think that in advocating khadi I am sailing against a headwind and am sure to sink the ship of swaraj and that I am taking the country to the dark ages. I do not propose to argue the case for khadi in this brief survey. I have argued it sufficiently elsewhere. Here I want to show what every Congressman, and for that matter every Indian, can do to advance the cause of khadi. It connotes the beginning of economic freedom and equality of all in the country. Khadi must be taken with all its implications. It means a wholesale swadeshi[5] mentality, a determination to find all the necessaries of life in India and that too through the labour and intellect of the villagers.

This needs a revolutionary change in the mentality and tastes of many. Easy though the non-violent way is in many respects, it is very difficult in many others. It vitally touches the life of every single Indian, makes him feel aglow with the possession of a power that has lain hidden within himself, and makes him proud of his identity with every drop of the ocean of Indian humanity. This nonviolence is not the inanity for which we have mistaken it through all these long ages; it is the most potent force as yet known to mankind and on which its very existence is dependent.

Moreover, khadi mentality means decentralization of the production and distribution of the necessaries of life. Therefore, the formula so far evolved is, every village to produce all its necessaries and a certain percentage in addition for the requirements of the cities.

Heavy industries will needs be centralized and nationalized. But they will occupy the least part of the vast national activity which will mainly be in the villages. In this scheme of nationwide spinning as a sacrifice, I do not expect the average man or woman to give more than one hour daily to this work. (150–52)

5. Other Village Industries

These stand on a different footing from khadi. There is not much scope for voluntary labour in them. Each industry will take the labour of only a certain number of hands. These industries come in as a handmaid to khadi. They cannot exist without khadi, and khadi will be robbed of its dignity without them. Village economy cannot be complete without the essential village industries such as hand-grinding, hand-pounding, soap-making, paper-making, match-making, tanning, oil-pressing, etc. When we have become village-minded, we will not want imitations of the West or machine-made products, but we will develop a true national taste in keeping with the vision of a new India in which pauperism, starvation and idleness will be unknown. (152–53)

6. Village Sanitation

Divorce between intelligence and labour has resulted in criminal negligence of the villages. And so, instead of having graceful hamlets dotting the land, we have dung-heaps. The approach to many villages is not a refreshing experience. Often one would like to shut one's eyes and stuff one's nose; such is the surrounding dirt and offending smell. If the majority of Congressmen were derived from our villages, as they should be, they should be able to make our villages models of cleanliness in every sense of the word. But they have never considered it their duty to identify themselves with the villagers in their daily lives. A sense of national or social sanitation is not a virtue among us. (153)

7. New or Basic Education

This is a new subject, a big field of work for many Congressmen. This education is meant to transform village children into model villagers. It is principally designed for them. The inspiration for it has come from the villages.

Congressmen who want to build up the structure of swaraj from its very foundation dare not neglect the children. Foreign rule has unconsciously, though none the less surely, begun with the children in the field of education. Primary education is a farce designed without regard to the wants of the India of the villages and for that matter even of the cities. Basic education links the children, whether of the cities or the villages, to all that is best and lasting in India. It develops both the body and the mind, and keeps the child rooted to the soil with a glorious vision of the future, in the realization of which he or she begins to take his or her share from the very commencement of his or her career in school. (153–54)

8. Adult Education

This has been woefully neglected by Congressmen. Where they have not neglected it, they have been satisfied with teaching illiterates to read and write. If I had charge of adult education, I should begin with opening the minds of the adult pupils to the greatness and vastness of their country. My adult education means, therefore, first, true political education of the adult by word of mouth. Side by side with the education by the mouth will be the literary education. (154)

9. Women

I have included service of women in the constructive programme, for though satyagraha has automatically brought India's women out from their darkness as nothing else could have in such an incredibly short space of time, Congressmen have not felt the call to see that women become equal partners in the fight for swaraj. They have not realized that woman must be the true helpmate of man in the mission of service. Woman has been suppressed under custom and law for which man was responsible and in the shaping of which she had no hand. In a plan of life based on non-violence, woman has as much right to shape her own destiny as man has to shape his. But as every right in a non-violent society proceeds from the previous performance of a duty, it follows that rules of social conduct must be framed by mutual co-operation and consultation. They can never be imposed from outside. Men have not realized this truth in its fulness in their behaviour towards women. They have considered themselves to be lords and masters of women instead of considering them as their friends and co-workers. It is the privilege of Congressmen to give the women of India a lifting hand. Women are in the position somewhat of the slave of old who did not know that he could or ever had to be free. And when freedom came, for the moment he felt helpless. Women have been taught to regard themselves as slaves of men. It is up to Congressmen to see that they enable them to realize their full status and play their part as equals of men.

This revolution is easy, if the mind is made up. Let Congressmen begin with their own homes. Wives should not be dolls and objects of indulgence, but should be treated as honoured comrades in common service. To this end those who have not received a liberal education should receive such instruction as is possible from their husbands. The same observation applies, with the necessary changes, to mothers and daughters.

It is hardly necessary to point out that I have given a one-sided picture of the helpless state of India's women. I am quite conscious of the fact that in the villages generally they hold their own with their menfolk and in some respects even rule them. But to the impartial outsider the legal and customary status of woman is bad enough throughout and demands radical alteration. (155)

10. Education in Health and Hygiene

Having given a place to village sanitation, the question may be asked why give a separate place to education in health and hygiene? It might have been bracketed with sanitation, but I did not wish to interfere with the items. Mention of mere sanitation is not enough to include health and hygiene. The art of keeping one's health and the knowledge of hygiene is by itself a separate subject of study and corresponding practice. In a well-ordered society the citizens know and observe the laws of health and hygiene. It is established beyond doubt that ignorance and neglect of the laws of health and hygiene are responsible for the majority of diseases to which mankind is heir. The very high death-rate among us is no doubt due largely to our gnawing poverty, but it could be mitigated if the people were properly educated about health and hygiene.

Mens sana in corpore sano is perhaps the first law for humanity. A healthy mind in a healthy body is a self-evident truth. There is an inevitable connection between mind and body. If we were in possession of healthy minds, we would shed all violence and, naturally obeying the laws of health, we would have healthy bodies without an effort. I hope, therefore, that no Congressman will disregard this item of the constructive programme. The fundamental laws of health and hygiene are simple and easily learnt. The difficulty is about their observance. Here are some:

Think the purest thoughts and banish all idle and impure thoughts.
Breathe the freshest air day and night.
Establish a balance between bodily and mental work.
Stand erect, sit erect, and be neat and clean in every one of your acts, and
let these be an expression of your inner condition.
Eat to live for service of fellow-men. Do not live for indulging yourselves.
Hence your food must be just enough to keep your mind and body in
good order. Man becomes what he eats. (156)

11. Provincial Languages

Our love of the English language in preference to our own mother tongue has caused a deep chasm between the educated and politically-minded classes and the masses. The languages of India have suffered impoverishment. We flounder when we make the vain attempt to express abstruse thought in the mother tongue. There are no equivalents for scientific terms. The result has been disastrous. The masses remain cut off from the modern mind. We are too near our own times correctly to measure the disservice caused to India by this neglect of its great languages. It is easy enough to understand that unless we undo the mischief the mass mind must remain imprisoned. The masses can make no solid contribution to the construction of swaraj. It is inherent in swaraj based on non-violence that every individual makes his own direct contribution to the Independence movement. The masses cannot do this fully unless they understand every step with all its implications. This is impossible unless every step is explained in their own languages. (156–57)

12. National Language

And then for all-India intercourse we need, from among the Indian stock, a language which the largest number of people already know and understand and which the others can easily pick up. This language is indisputably Hindi. It is spoken and understood by both Hindus and Muslims of the North. It is called Urdu when it is written in the Urdu character. (157)

13. Economic Equality

This last is the master-key to non-violent independence. Working for economic equality means abolishing the eternal conflict between capital and labour. It means the levelling down of the few rich in whose hands is concentrated the bulk of the nation's wealth on the one hand, and the levelling up of the semi-starved naked millions on the other. A non-violent system of government is clearly an impossibility so long as the wide gulf between the rich and the hungry millions persists. The contrast between the palaces of New Delhi and the miserable hovels of the poor labouring class nearby cannot last one day in a free India in which the poor will enjoy the same power as the richest in the land. A violent and bloody revolution is a certainty one day unless there is a voluntary abdication of riches and the power that riches give and sharing them for the common good.

I adhere to my doctrine of trusteeship in spite of the ridicule that has been poured upon it. It is true that it is difficult to reach. So is non-violence.

This non-violent experiment is still in the making. We have nothing much yet to show by way of demonstration. It is certain, however, that the method has begun to work though ever so slowly in the direction of equality. And since non-violence is a process of conversion, the conversion, if achieved, must be permanent. Those who think that major reforms will come after the advent of swaraj are deceiving themselves as to the elementary working of non-violent swaraj. It will not drop from heaven all of a sudden one fine morning. But it has to be built up brick by brick by corporate self-effort. We have travelled a fair way in that direction. But a much longer and weary distance has to be covered before we can behold swaraj in its glorious majesty. (158–59)

14. Kisans

The programme is not exhaustive. Swaraj is a mighty structure. Eighty crores[6] of hands have to work at building it. Of these *kisans*, i.e., the peasantry, are the largest part. In fact, being the bulk of them (probably over 80%) the *kisans* should be the Congress. But they are not. When they become conscious of their non-violent strength, no power on earth can resist them.

They must not be used for power politics. I consider it to be contrary to the non-violent method. Those who would know my method of organizing *kisans* may profitably study the movement in Champaran[7] when satyagraha was tried for the first time in India with the result all India knows. It became a mass movement which remained wholly non-violent from start to finish. (159–60)

15. Labour

Ahmedabad Labour Union is a model for all India to copy. Its basis is non-violence, pure and simple. It has never had a set-back in its career. It has gone on from strength to strength without fuss and without show. It has its hospital, its school for the children of the mill-hands, its classes for adults, its own printing press and khadi depot, and its own residential quarters. Almost all the hands are voters and decide the fate of elections. (161)

16. Adivasis (Original Peoples of India)

Service of *adivasis* is also a part of the constructive programme. Though they are the sixteenth number in this programme, they are not the least in point of importance. Our country is so vast and the races so varied that the best of us cannot know all there is to know of men and their condition. As one discovers this for oneself, one realizes how difficult it is to make good our claim to be one nation, unless every unit has a living consciousness of being one with every other. (161–62)

17. Lepers

Leper is a word of bad odour. India is perhaps a home of lepers next only to Central Africa. Yet they are as much a part of society as the tallest among us. But the tall absorb our attention though they are least in need of it. The lot of the lepers who are much in need of attention is studied neglect. I am tempted to call it heartless, which it certainly is in terms of non-violence. If India was pulsating with new life, if we were all in earnest about winning independence in the quickest manner possible by truthful and non-violent means, there would not be a leper or beggar in India uncared for and unaccounted for. (162)

18. Students

I have reserved students to the last. I have always cultivated close contact with them. They know me and I know them. They have given me service. Many ex-collegians are my esteemed co-workers. I know that they are the hope of the future. In the heyday of non-co-operation they were invited to leave their schools and colleges. Some professors and students who responded to the Congress call have remained steadfast and gained much for the country and themselves. The call has not been repeated for there is not the atmosphere for it. But experience has shown that the lure of the current education, though it is false and unnatural, is too much for the youth of the country. College education provides a career. It is a passport for entrance to the charmed circle. Pardonable hunger for knowledge cannot be satisfied otherwise than by going through the usual rut.

But I am myself a fellow-student, using the word in its broader sense. My university is different from theirs. They have a standing invitation from me to come to my university and join me in my search. (162–63)

Place of Civil Disobedience

I have said in these pages that civil disobedience is not absolutely necessary to win freedom through purely non-violent effort, if the co-operation of the whole nation is secured in the constructive programme. But such good luck rarely favours nations or individuals. Therefore, it is necessary to know the place of civil disobedience in a nationwide non-violent effort.

It has three definite functions:

1. It can be effectively offered for the redress of a local wrong.
2. It can be offered without regard to effect, though aimed at a particular wrong or evil, by way of self-immolation in order to rouse local consciousness or conscience.

3. In the place of full response to constructive effort, it can be offered as it was in 1941. Though it was a contribution to and part of the battle for freedom, it was purposely centred round a particular issue, i.e., free speech. Civil disobedience can never be directed for a general cause such as for independence. The issue must be definite and capable of being clearly understood and within the power of the opponent to yield. This method properly applied must lead to the final goal.

I have not examined here the full scope and possibilities of civil disobedience. I have touched enough of it to enable the reader to understand the connection between the constructive programme and civil disobedience. In the first two cases, no elaborate constructive programme was or could be necessary. But when civil disobedience is itself devised for the attainment of independence, previous preparation is necessary, and it has to be backed by the visible and conscious effort of those who are engaged in the battle. Civil disobedience is thus a stimulation for the fighters and a challenge to the opponent. It should be clear to the reader that civil disobedience in terms of independence without the co-operation of the millions by way of constructive effort is mere bravado and worse than useless. (165)

Conclusion

This is not a thesis written on behalf of the Congress or at the instance of the Central Office. It is the outcome of conversations I had with some co-workers in Sevagram. They had felt the want of something from my pen showing the connection between the constructive programme and civil disobedience and how the former might be worked. I have endeavoured to supply the want in this pamphlet. It does not purport to be exhaustive, but it is sufficiently indicative of the way the programme should be worked.

Let not the reader make the mistake of laughing at any of the items as being part of the movement for independence. Many people do many things, big and small, without connecting them with non-violence or independence. They have then their limited value as expected. The same man appearing as a civilian may be of no consequence, but appearing in his capacity as General he is a big personage, holding the lives of millions at his mercy. Similarly, the charkha[8] in the hands of a poor widow brings a paltry pice[9] to her, in the hands of a Jawaharlal it is an instrument of India's freedom. It is the office which gives the charkha its dignity. It is the office assigned to the constructive programme which gives it an irresistible prestige and power.

Such at least is my view. It may be that of a mad man. If it makes no appeal to the Congressman, I must be rejected. For my handling of civil disobedience without the constructive programme will be like a paralysed hand attempting to lift a spoon. (165–66)

Related Writings (in chronological order)

If we were to analyse the activities of the Congress during the past twelve years, we would discover that the capacity of the Congress to take political power has increased in exact proportion to its ability to achieve success in the constructive effort. That is to me the substance of political power. Actual taking over of the Government machinery is but a shadow, an emblem.

We have everywhere emphasized the necessity of carrying on the constructive activities as being the means of attaining *swaraj*. I am convinced that whenever legal prohibition of drinks, drugs and foreign cloth comes, it will come because public opinion had demanded it. It may be said that public opinion demands it today but the foreign Government does not respond. This is only partly right. Public opinion in this country is only now becoming a vital force and developing the real sanction which is *satyagraha*. ("Power not an End," *Young India*, 7-2-31)

I do visualize electricity, shipbuilding, ironworks, machine-making and the like existing side by side with village handicrafts. But the order of dependence will be reversed. Hitherto the industrialization has been so planned as to destroy the villages and village crafts. In the State of the future it will subserve the villages and their crafts.

I hold that the coming into power of the proletariat through violence is bound to fail in the end. What is gained by violence must be lost before superior violence. India is within an ace of achieving the end, if only Congressmen will be true to their creed of non-violence and live up to it. The working of the Constructive Programme is the test.

Thirty-four years of continuous experience and experimenting in truth and non-violence have convinced me that non-violence cannot be sustained unless it is linked to conscious body-labour and finds expression in our daily contact with our neighbours. This is the Constructive Programme. It is not an end, it is an indispensable means and therefore is almost convertible with the end. The power of non-violent resistance can only come from honest working of the Constructive Programme. ("*Ahimsa* in Practice," *Harijan*, 1-27-40)

I know that in this country all constructive activities are part of politics. In my view that is true politics. Non-violence can have nothing to do with the politics of power.

We have adopted a novel policy. We must adopt novel means to follow that policy. I have been trying to find out what these means could be. I am only experimenting. I have to change my methods as situations change. But I have no ready-made formula. Our experiment is absolutely new. The order in which the steps may be taken is not fixed. I am a person with an inquiring mind. With great patience I am discovering and developing the science of *satyagraha*.

I was born for the constructive programme. It is part of my soul. Politics is a kind of botheration for me. (Speech at Gandhi Seva Sangh, *Gandhi Seva Sanghke Chhathe Adhiveshan (Malikanda-Bengal) ka Vivaran*, cited in R. Iyer, *The Moral and Political Writings of Mahatma Gandhi*, I, 416, 419, 2-21-40)

Everyone should do some constructive work over and above parliamentary work. And the aim of parliamentary work should also be to advance constructive work. (Letter to Anasuyabai Kale, in *Pyarelal Papers*, 12-18-45)

Independence is now as good as come. But it is only political independence. Unless poverty and unemployment are wiped out from India, I would not agree that we have attained freedom. Real wealth does not consist in jewellery and money, but in providing for proper food, clothes, education, and creating healthy conditions of living for every one of us. A country can be called prosperous and free only when its citizens can easily earn enough to meet their needs. But today the situation is so tragic that on the one hand there are people who roll in pomp and luxury and on the other there are people who do not have enough clothes to cover their bodies and who live on the brink of starvation. Today men are sitting idle having no work to do. A man should have full opportunity to develop himself. That will happen only when there is an awakening among the constructive workers.
If we do not do our duty, we will be giving a chance for the people to say that slavery was better than this freedom. To the extent the constructive workers are bold and fearless, these qualities would be reflected in their actions and through their work spread in the atmosphere. ("Advice to Constructive Workers," *Biharni Komi Agman*, 346–47, 5-13-47)

NOTES

1. Religious
2. India
3. Hundreds of thousands
4. Handspun cloth
5. Self-sufficiency, self-reliance; relying on local products
6. Tens of millions
7. Cf. ch. 3, 64–67
8. Spinning wheel
9. A penny

7

Short Moral and Political Writings

Mohandas K. Gandhi

"My life is my message."

"Message to Shanti Dal," *The Hindustan Standard*, 9-7-47

"Out of my ashes a thousand Gandhis will arise."

"Message to Students," *Harijan*, 1-16-37

Most of Gandhi's writings were short articles in the journals he edited in South Africa and India, along with letters, interviews, and speeches. Generally he wrote for the moment and made no effort to develop a systematic philosophy. The following selections are arranged alphabetically by topics, and chronologically within each topic.

Abbreviations include

CW	*Archives of the Office of the Collected Works of Mahatma Gandhi, New Delhi*
EWMG	*The Essential Writings of Mahatma Gandhi, Ed. Raghavan Iyer*
GN	*Gandhi Memorial Museum and Library, New Delhi*
MMU	*Mobile Microfilm Unit, Gandhi Smarak Nidhi and Sangrahalaya, New Delhi*
MPW	*The Moral and Political Writings of Mahatma Gandhi, Ed. Raghavan Iyer*
SN	*Sabarmati Sangrahalaya, Ahmedabad*

ASHRAMS

True Education in the Ashrams

True education is that which helps us to know the *atman*, our true self, God and Truth. To acquire this knowledge, some persons may feel the need for a study of literature, some for a study of physical sciences and some others for art. But every branch of knowledge should have as its goal knowledge of the self. That is so in the Ashram. We carry on numerous activities with that aim in view. All of them are, in my sense of the term, true education. In an activity carried on as education, a proper understanding of its meaning, devotion to duty and the spirit of service are necessary. The first necessarily brings about development of the intellect. In doing any piece of work, however small, we should be inspired by a holy aim and, while doing it, we should try to understand the purpose which it will serve and the scientific method of doing it. There is a science of every type of work—whether it be cooking, sanitation, carpentry or spinning. Everybody who does his work with the attitude of a student knows its science or discovers it.

If the inmates of the Ashram understand this, they would see that the Ashram is a great school in which the inmates receive education not for a few hours only but all the time. Every person who lives in the Ashram to attain knowledge of the self—of Truth—is both a teacher and a pupil. He is a teacher in regard to what he knows, and a pupil in regard to anything about which he needs to learn. ("Education," MMU/II, 7-10-32)

BRAVERY

The True Bravery of the Martyr

To fight with the sword does call for bravery of a sort. But to die is braver far than to kill. He alone is truly brave, he alone is martyr in the true sense who dies without fear in his heart and without wishing hurt to his enemy, not the one who kills and dies. If our country, even in its present fallen state, can exhibit this type of bravery, what a beacon light will it be for Europe with all its discipline, science and organization! (Address to the Officers of the Red Shirts, *A Pilgrimage for Peace*, 57, 10-10-38)

BUDDHISM

Buddha Taught Trust in Truth and Love

The only reason for inviting me to preside at this meeting is, I presume, that I am more than most people endeavouring to popularize the truth for which Gautama Buddha lived and died.

For the moment, however, I would like to tell the meeting what I believe about Buddhism. To me it is a part of Hinduism. Buddha did not give the world a new religion; he gave it a new interpretation. He taught Hinduism not to take but to give life.

Religion to me is a living faith in the Supreme Unseen Force. That Force has confounded mankind before, and it is bound to confound us again. Buddha taught us to defy appearances and trust in the final triumph of Truth and Love. This was his matchless gift to Hinduism and to the world.

He taught us also how to do it, because he lived what he taught. The best propaganda is not pamphleteering, but for each one of us to try to live the life we would have the world to live. (Speech at the Buddha Jayanti, CW, 5176, 5-18-24)

CHRISTIANITY

Christianity's Impact on India

In my opinion Christian missionaries have done good to us indirectly. Their direct contribution is probably more harmful than otherwise. I am against the modern method of proselytizing. Years' experience of proselytizing both in South Africa and India has convinced me that it has not raised the general moral tone of the converts who have imbibed the superficialities of European civilization, and have missed the teaching of Jesus. I must be understood to refer to the general tendency and not to brilliant exceptions. The indirect contribution, on the other hand, of Christian missionary effort is great. It has stimulated Hindu and Mussalman religious research. It has forced us to put our own houses in order. The great educational and curative institutions of Christian missions I also count, amongst indirect results, because they have been established, not for their own sakes, but as an aid to proselytizing.

The world, and therefore we, can no more do without the teaching of Jesus than we can without that of Mohamed or the Upanishads. I hold all these to be complementary to one another, in no case exclusive. ("A Student's Questions," *Young India*, 12-17-25)

Jesus, One of the World's Mighty Teachers

I say in one sentence that for many many years I have regarded Jesus of Nazareth as one amongst the mighty teachers that the world has had, and I say this in all humility. (Speech at Central College, Jaffna, *The Hindu*, 12-2-27)

The Sermon on the Mount, Jesus' Message

The message of Jesus, as I understand it, is contained in his Sermon on the Mount unadulterated and taken as a whole. I can tell you that in my humble opinion, much of what passes as Christianity is a negation of the Sermon on the Mount. (Speech at YMCA, Colombo, *Young India*, 12-8-27)

CONSCIENCE/INNER VOICE

Conscience a Result of Discipline

Conscience is the ripe fruit of strictest discipline. Irresponsible youngsters therefore who have never obeyed anything or anybody save their animal instincts have no conscience, nor therefore have all grown-up people. Conscience can reside only in a delicately tuned breast. There is no such thing therefore as mass conscience as distinguished from the consciences of individuals. ("Under Conscience's Cover," *Young India*, 8-21-24)

Conscience Not the Same for All

Stripped of the eloquence, this religion of Truth again resolves itself into its component parts—Hinduism, Islam, Christianity, etc. For Truth will appear to most sincere and conscientious Hindus, Mussalmans and Christians as Hinduism, Islam and Christianity, respectively, *as they believe them.*

The golden rule of conduct, therefore, is mutual toleration, seeing that we will never all think alike and that we shall always see *Truth* in fragment and from different angles of vision. Conscience is not the same thing for all. Whilst, therefore, it is a good guide for individual conduct, imposition of that conduct upon all will be an insufferable interference with everybody else's freedom of conscience. It is a much-abused term. Have all people a conscience? Has a cannibal a conscience? Must he be allowed to act according to the dictates of his conscience which tells him that it is his duty to kill and eat his fellows? Now the etymological meaning of conscience is "true knowledge." The dictionary meaning is "faculty distinguishing between right and wrong and influencing conduct accordingly." Possession of such a faculty is possible only for a trained person, that is, one who has undergone discipline and learnt to listen to the inner voice. But even amongst the most conscientious persons, there will be room enough for honest differences of opinion. ("Religion of Volunteers," *Young India*, 9-23-26)

Unwise to Believe One Is Always Listening to God

The more I listen, the more I discover that I am still far away from God. While I can lay down rules, the observance of which is essential for people listening, the reality still escapes me. When we say we are listening to God and getting answers, though we say it truthfully, there is every possibility there of self-deception. I do not know that I am myself altogether free from self-deception. People sometimes ask me if I may not be mistaken, and I say to them, "Yes, very likely, what I say may be just a picture of my elongated self before you."

I say this in order to warn you how unwise it may be to believe that you are always listening to God. I am not at all against the endeavour, but I warn you against thinking that this is a kind of "open sesame" which has just to be shown to the millions. No one will contradict me when I say I have tried my very best to make India listen to the way of God. I have had some success but I am still far away from the goal. (Discussion with Members of Oxford Group, *Harijan*, 10-7-39)

Conscience Must Be Awakened

Conscience has to be awakened. There are rules and observances for the purpose. Not everyone can be said to have his conscience awakened. (Note to Gope Gurbuxani, GN, 1320)

DUTIES AND RIGHTS

Rights Naturally Follow Duties

Received your cable. I have carefully read your five articles. You will permit me to say you are on the wrong track. I feel sure that I can draw up a better charter of rights than you have drawn up. But of what good will it be? Who will become its guardian? If you mean propaganda or popular education you have begun at the wrong end. I suggest the right way. Begin with a charter of Duties of Man and I promise the rights will follow as spring follows winter. I write from experience. As a young man I began life by seeking to assert my rights and I soon discovered I had none not even over my wife. So I began by discovering and performing my duty by my wife, my children, friends, companions, and society. And I find today that I have greater rights, perhaps than any living man I know. If this is too tall a claim then I say I do not know anyone who possesses greater rights than I. (Cable to H. G. Wells, in response to Wells' "Charter of Right," *The Hindustan Times*, 4-16-40)

ECONOMICS

True Economics Involve Religious and Moral Living

[Gandhi's speech on the topic "Does economic progress clash with real progress?"]

In South Africa, where I had the privilege of associating with thousands of our countrymen on most intimate terms, I observed almost invariably that the greater the possession of riches, the greater was their moral turpitude. Our rich men, to say the least, did not advance the moral struggle of passive resistance as did the poor. The rich men's sense of self-respect was not so much injured as that of the poorest. If I were not afraid of treading on dangerous ground, I would even come nearer home and show you that possession of riches has been a hindrance to real growth. I venture to think that the scriptures of the world are far safer and sounder treatises on laws of economics than many of the modern text-books.

The question we are asking ourselves this evening is not a new one. It was addressed to Jesus two thousand years ago. St. Mark has vividly described the scene. Jesus is in his solemn mood; he is earnest. He talks of eternity. He knows the world about him. He is himself the greatest economist of his time. He succeeded in economising time and space—he transcended them. It is to him at his best that one comes running, kneels down, and asks: "Good Master, what shall I do that I may inherit eternal life?," And Jesus said unto him: "Why callest thou me good? There is none good but one, that is God. Thou knowest the commandments. Do not commit adultery, Do not kill, Do not steal, Do not bear false witness, Defraud not, Honour thy father and mother." And he answered and said unto him: "Master, all these have I observed from my youth." Then Jesus beholding him, loved him and said unto him: "One thing thou lackest. Go thy way, sell whatever thou hast and give to the poor, and thou shalt have treasure in heaven—come take up the cross and follow me." And he was sad at that saying and went away grieved—for he had great possessions. And Jesus looked round about and said unto his disciples: "How hardly shall they that have riches enter into the kingdom of God." And the disciples were astonished at his words. But Jesus answereth again and saith unto them: "Children, how hard it is for them that trust in riches to enter into the kingdom of God. It is easier for a camel to go through the eye of a needle than for a rich man to enter into the kingdom of God!"

Here you have an eternal rule of life stated in the noblest words the English language is capable of producing. "Who then can be saved?" [the disciples asked.] And Jesus looking upon them saith: "With men it is impossible but not with God, for with God all things are possible." Then Peter began to say unto him: "Lo, we have left all, and have followed thee." And Jesus answered and said: "Verily I say unto you there is no man that has left house or brethren or sisters, or father or mother, or wife or children or lands for my sake and the Gospels, but he shall receive one hundred fold."

Perhaps the strongest of all the testimonies in favour of the affirmative answer to the question before us are the lives of the greatest teachers of the world. Jesus, Mahomed, Buddha, Nanak, Kabir, Chaitanya, Shankara, Dayanand, Ramkrishna[1] were men who exercised an immense influence over and moulded the character of thousands of men. The world is the richer for their having lived in it. And they were all men who deliberately embraced poverty as their lot.

I should not have laboured my point as I have done, if I did not believe that, in so far as we have made the modern materialistic craze our goal, in so far are we going downhill in the path of progress. I hold that economic progress in the sense I have put it is antagonistic to real progress.

Under the British aegis, we have learnt much, but it is my firm belief that there is little to gain from Britain in intrinsic morality, that if we are not careful, we shall introduce all the vices that she has been a prey to, owing to the disease of materialism. We can profit by that connection only if we keep our civilization, and our morals, straight, i.e., if instead of boasting of the glorious past, we express the ancient moral glory in our own lives and let our lives bear witness to our past. Then we shall benefit her and ourselves. If we will but clean our houses, our palaces and temples of the attributes of wealth and show in them the attributes of morality, we can offer battle to any combinations of hostile forces without having to carry the burden of a heavy militia. Let us seek first the kingdom of God and His righteousness and the irrevocable promise is that everything will be added with us. These are real economics. May you and I treasure them and enforce them in our daily life. (Speech at Muir College Economic Society, Allahabad, *The Leader,* 12-25-16)

EQUAL DISTRIBUTION

Equal Distribution Based on Trusteeship of Wealthy

At the root of this doctrine of equal distribution must lie that of the trusteeship of the wealthy for the superfluous wealth possessed by them. For according to the doctrine they may not possess a rupee more than their neighbours. How is this to be brought about? Non-violently? Or should the wealthy be dispossessed of their possessions? To do this we naturally have to resort to violence. This violent action cannot benefit society. Society will be the poorer, for it will lose the gifts of a man who knows how to accumulate wealth. Therefore the non-violent way is evidently superior. The rich man will be left in possession of his wealth, of which he will use what he reasonably requires for his personal needs and will act as a trustee for the remainder to be used for the society. In this argument honesty on the part of the trustee is assumed.

As soon as a man looks upon himself as a servant of society, earns for its sake, spends for its benefit, then purity enters into his earnings and there is *ahimsa* in his venture. Moreover, if men's minds turn towards this way of life, there will come about a peaceful revolution in society, and that without any bitterness.

If, however, in spite of the utmost effort, the rich do not become guardians of the poor in the true sense of the term and the latter are more and more crushed and die of hunger, what is to be done? In trying to find the solution to this riddle I have lighted on non-violent non-co-operation and civil disobedience as the right and infallible means. The rich cannot accumulate wealth without the co-operation of the poor in society. Man has been conversant with violence from the beginning, for he has inherited this strength from the animal in his nature. It was only when he rose from the state of a quadruped (animal) to that of a biped (man) that the knowledge of the strength of *ahimsa* entered into his soul. If this knowledge were to penetrate to and spread amongst the poor, they would become strong and would learn how to free themselves by means of non-violence from the crushing inequalities which have brought them to the verge of starvation. ("Equal Distribution," *Harijanbandhu*, 8-24-40)

EDUCATION

Education of Mind, Body, Spirit

Man is made of three constituents, the body, mind and spirit. Of them, spirit is the one permanent element in man. The body and the mind function on account of it. Hence we can call that education which reveals the qualities of spirit. That is why the seal of the Vidyapith[2] carries the dictum "Education is that which leads to *moksha*."

Education can also be understood in another sense; that is, whatever leads to a full or maximum development of all the three, the body, mind and spirit, may also be called education. ("What Is Education?," *Navajivan*, 2-28-26)

Character-Building, the Object of Education

In character-building, which is the object of education, the relationship between the *guru*[3] and his disciples is of utmost importance and where there is no *gurubhakti* [devotion to the teacher] in its pure form, there can be no character-building. ("Question of Education—I," *Navajivan*, 6-3-28)

Manual Labour Central to Balanced Education

One of the complaints that has been made by one of you is that too much emphasis is laid here on manual work. I am a firm believer in the educative value of manual work. Our present educational system is meant for strengthening and perpetuating the imperialist power in India. Those of you who have been brought up under it have naturally developed a taste for it and so find labour irksome. No one in Government schools or colleges bothers to teach the students how to clean the roads or latrines.

Useful manual labour, intelligently performed, is the means *par excellence* for developing the intellect. One may develop a sharp intellect otherwise too. But then it will not be a balanced growth but an unbalanced distorted abortion. It might easily make of one a rogue and a rascal. A balanced intellect presupposes a harmonious growth of body, mind and soul. That is why we give to manual labour the central place in our curriculum of training here. An intellect that is developed through the medium of socially useful labour will be an instrument for service and will not easily be led astray or fall into devious paths. (Address to Trainees of Basic Teachers' Camp, *Harijan*, 9-8-46)

FASTING

Fasting, a Method of Love

Think of last Tuesday, when I began my fast. Why did I take that step? There were three ways open to me:

1. PUNISHMENT: I could have followed the easy road of corporal punishment. Usually a teacher on detecting errors on the part of pupils would flatter himself with having done a good thing if he punished them. I have been a teacher myself, though my preoccupations prevent me from teaching you during these days. As a teacher I had no option but to reject this accepted method for I know by experience it is futile and even harmful.
2. INDIFFERENCE: I could have left you to your fate. Not unoften does a teacher do so. "It is enough," he argues, "that the boys do their lessons tolerably well and reproduce what they are taught. Surely I am not concerned with their private behaviour. And even if I was, how am I to keep watch over them?" This indifference could not appeal to me.
3. The third was the method of LOVE. Your character is to me a sacred trust. I must therefore try to enter into your lives, your innermost thoughts, your desires and your impulses, and help you to detect and eradicate impurities, if any. For inward cleanliness is the first thing that should be taught, other things must follow after the first and most important lesson has gone home. I discovered irregularities amongst you. What was I to do? Punishing you was out of the question. Being the chief among the teachers, I had to take the punishment on myself in the form of the fast which breaks today.

I have learnt a lot during these days of quiet thinking. What have you? Could you assure me that you will never repeat your mistake? You may err again but this fast will be lost on you if you do not realize the way out of it.

Truthfulness is the master-key. Do not lie under any circumstances whatsoever. Keep nothing secret, take your teachers and your elders into your confidence and make a clean breast of everything to them. Bear ill will to none, do not say an evil thing of anyone behind his back, above all "to thine own self be true," so that you are false to no one else. Truthful dealing even in the least little things of life is the only secret of a pure life.

You must have noticed that I receive my inspiration on such occasions from the hymn, *Vaishnava Jana to tene kahiye* (He is the true Vaishnava etc.). That hymn is enough to sustain me, even if I were to forget the *Bhagavad Gita*. To tell you the truth, however, there is one thing which is even simpler, but which may possibly be difficult for you to understand. But that has been my pole star all along during life's journey—the conviction that Truth is God and untruth a denial of Him. (Speech to Students, *Young India*, 12-10-25)

The Permanent Effect of Fasting

Fasting is never intended to affect another's body. It must affect his heart. Hence it is related to the soul. And in this sense the effect, such as it is, cannot be described as temporary. It is of a permanent character. ("Implications of Fasting," *Harijan*, 10-5-47)

FEARLESSNESS

Fearlessness, Freedom from Fears and Attachment

Fearlessness connotes freedom from all external fear, fear of disease, bodily injury and death, of dispossession, of losing one's nearest and dearest, of losing reputation or giving offence, and so on. One who overcomes the fear of death does not surmount all other fears, as is commonly but erroneously supposed. Some of us do not fear death, but flee from the minor ills of life. Some are ready to die themselves, but cannot bear their loved ones being taken away from them.

Perfect fearlessness is almost impossible to cultivate. It can be attained only by him who has realized the Supreme, as it implies freedom from delusion. One can always progress towards this goal by determined and constant endeavour and by cultivating self-confidence. As I have stated at the very outset, we must give up all external fears. But the internal foes we must always fear. We are rightly afraid of animal passion, anger and the like. External fears cease of their own accord when once we have conquered these traitors within the camp. All such fears revolve round the body as the centre, and will therefore disappear as soon as we get rid of attachment for the body. (Letter to Narandas Gandhi, CW, 8123, 9-2-30)

HINDUISM

Dharma, a Quality of the Soul

Dharma does not mean any particular creed or dogma. Nor does it mean reading or learning by rote books known as *shastras* or even believing all that they say.

Dharma is a quality of the soul and is present, visibly or invisibly, in every human being. Through it we know our duty in human life and our true relation with other souls. It is evident that we cannot do so till we have known the Self in us. Hence *dharma* is the means by which we can know ourselves. ("*Dharma*," *Shrimad Rajchandra*, 11-5-26)

Proof of Belief in Reincarnation

Without a belief in reincarnation it would be almost impossible to prove that the world is governed by justice. Moreover, one soul cannot have experience of the world within the span of one life, which is but a moment in a vast cycle of time. I can practically say that I have direct proof every moment of the truth of the belief in reincarnation. (Letter to Santosh Majaraj, SN, 12323, 7-2-27)

The *Gita*, the Gospel of Service

The *Gita* contains the gospel of *karma* or work, the gospel of *bhakti* or devotion and the gospel of *jnana* or knowledge. Life should be a harmonious whole of these three. But the gospel of service is the basis of all. But you must approach it with the five necessary equipments, viz., *ahimsa* (non-violence), *satya* (truth), *brahmacharya* (celibacy), *aparigraha* (non-possession), and *asteya* (non-stealing). (Speech to Students, *The Hindu*, 10-25-27)

Removal of Untouchability a Complete Revolution in Hindu Thought

The work of removal of untouchability is not merely a social or economic reform whose extent can be measured by so much social amenities or economic relief provided in so much time. Its goal is to touch the hearts of the millions of Hindus who honestly believe in the present-day untouchability as a God-made institution, as old as the human race itself. This, it will be admitted, is a task infinitely higher than mere social and economic reform. Its accomplishment undoubtedly includes all these and much more. For it means nothing short of a complete revolution in the Hindu thought and the disappearance of the horrible and terrible doctrine of inborn inequality and high-and-lowness, which has poisoned Hinduism and is slowly undermining its very existence. Such a change can only be brought about by an appeal to the highest in man. And I am more than ever convinced that that appeal can be made effective only by self-purification, i.e., by fasting conceived as the deepest prayer coming from a lacerated heart. ("All About the Fast," *Harijan*, 7-8-33)

Purification of the Heart through Work

Personally I am convinced that man can achieve real and enduring purification of heart only through work. I again feel tempted to quote the *Gita*. Verse 18 of Chapter IV meant that he who sees action in inaction and inaction in action is the wise man, he is the true *yogi* and the true man of *karma*. I have, however, explained here what I have found in my own experience. I have quoted the *Gita* verses because I have found the truth of their teaching in my experience. I never quote anything from the *shastras* which I have not tested in experience. (Letter to Darbari Sadhu, *Mahadevbhaini Diary*, I, 380, 8-23-32)

The Self, Source of the Good

Personality, i.e., the quality of being oneself, can be good or bad. If it is in conformity with the Self it is good and if it disregards the Self it is bad. It becomes good and develops by meditating on the Self and understanding its attributes. (Note to Gope Gurbuxani, GN, 1334, 3-24-45)

Ahimsa, the Chief Glory of Hinduism

When I was in detention in the Aga Khan Palace, I once sat down to write a thesis on India as a protagonist of non-violence. But as I proceeded with my writing, I could not go on. I had to stop. There are two aspects of Hinduism. There is, on the one hand, the historical Hinduism with its untouchability, superstitious worship of stocks and stones, animal sacrifice and so on. On the other, we have the Hinduism of the *Gita*, the Upanishads and Patanjali's[4] *Yoga Sutra* which is the acme of *ahimsa* and oneness of all creation, pure worship of one immanent, formless imperishable God. *Ahimsa* which to me is the chief glory of Hinduism has been sought to be explained away by our people as being meant for *sannyasis*[5] only. I do not share that view. I have held that it is *the* way of life and India has to show it to the world. Where do I stand? Do I represent this *ahimsa* in my person? If I do, then deceit and hatred that poison the atmosphere should dissolve. It is only by going into isolation from my companions, those on whose help I have relied all along, and standing on my own feet that I shall find my bearings and also test my faith in God. ("A Talk," *Harijan*, 12-8-46)

ISLAM

Islam's Place in World Won by Mohamed's Virtues

I became more than ever convinced that it was not the sword that won a place for Islam in those days in the scheme of life. It was the rigid simplicity, the utter self-effacement of the Prophet, the scrupulous regard for pledges, his intense devotion to his friends and followers, his intrepidity, his fearlessness, his absolute trust in God and his own mission. ("My Jail Experiences—XI," *Young India*, 9-11-24)

The Contribution of Islam to India

Islam's distinctive contribution to India's national culture is its unadulterated belief in the oneness of God and a practical application of the truth of the brotherhood of man for those who are nominally within its fold. I call these two distinctive contributions. For in Hinduism the spirit of brotherhood has become too much philosophized. Similarly though philosophical Hinduism has no other god but God, it cannot be denied that practical Hinduism is not so emphatically uncompromising as Islam. (Interview with Dr. John Mott, *Young India*, 3-21-29)

LABOUR AND CAPITAL

Developing the Power of Workers

We know that the employers have crores[6] of rupees and the workers have nothing. If workers have no money however, they have hands and feet with which they can work, and there is no part of the world which can do without workers. Hence, if only he knows it, the worker holds the key to the situation. Wealth is unavailing without him. If he realizes this, he can be sure of success. But the worker who would wield such power must possess certain qualities of character, without which he would be at the mercy of others. Let us see what these qualities are.

1. The worker should be truthful.
2. He should possess courage.
3. He should have a sense of justice.
4. He will not be angry with his employer nor bear him any grudge. After all, when everything is over, the worker is to serve under him. Every human being is liable to err.
5. Every worker should remember that the struggle is bound to involve suffering. But happiness follows suffering voluntarily undertaken.
6. Lastly, the poor have their saviour in God. Our duty is to make the effort and then, fully assured that we are bound to get what He has ordained

for us, remain peaceful while our request is not yet granted. "Ahmed-abad Mill-Hands' Strike," (Leaflet No. 2, *Ek Dharmayuddha*, 2-27-18)

Labour and Capital Should Help Each Other

It is a pleasure to me to identify myself with the labouring classes, because without labour we can do nothing.

My identification with labour does not conflict with my friendship with capital.

At Ahmedabad I have had much to do with the capitalists and workmen, and I have always said that my ideal is that capital and labour should sup-plement and help each other. (Speech at Indian Association, Jamshedpur, *Amrita Bazar Patrika*, 8-14-25)

Capitalists as Trustees of the Masses

God forbid that India should ever take to industrialism after the manner of the West. The economic imperialism of a single tiny island kingdom (En-gland) is today keeping the world in chains. If an entire nation of 300 mil-lions took to similar economic exploitation, it would strip the world bare like locusts. Unless the capitalists of India help to avert that tragedy by becoming trustees of the welfare of the masses and by devoting their talents not to amassing wealth for themselves but to the service of the masses in an altru-istic spirit, they will end either by destroying the masses or being destroyed by them. (Discussion with a Capitalist, *Young India*, 12-20-28)

Seeking to Destroy Capitalism, not the Capitalist

By the non-violent method we seek not to destroy the capitalist, we seek to destroy capitalism. We invite the capitalist to regard himself as a trustee for those on whom he depends for the making, the retention and the increase of his capital. Nor need the worker wait for his conversion. If capital is power, so is work. Either power can be used destructively or creatively. Ei-ther is dependent on the other. Immediately the worker realizes his strength, he is in a position to become a co-sharer with the capitalist instead of re-maining his slave. ("Questions and Answers," *Young India*, 3-26-31)

MEANS AND ENDS

Pure Means Lead to Real Progress

We [in India] cannot rise again till our political condition changes for the better; but it is not true that we shall necessarily progress if our political con-ditions undergo a change, irrespective of the manner in which it is brought about. If the means employed are impure, the change will be not in the direction of progress but very likely in the opposite. Only a change brought about in our political condition by pure means can lead to real progress. (Forward to volume of Gokhale's speeches, *Gopal Krishna Gokhalenan Vyakhyano*, 1, 1916)

Ahimsa the Means, Truth the End

Ahimsa is the means and Truth is the end. Means to be means must always be within reach, and so *ahimsa* becomes our supreme duty and Truth becomes God for us. If we take care of the means, we are bound to reach the end sooner or later. If we have resolved to do this, we shall have won the battle. (Letter to Narandas Gandhi, MMU, I, 7-28/31-30)

Three Brief Statements on Means and Ends

For me it is enough to know the means. Means and end are convertible terms in my philosophy of life. *Young India*, 12-24

We always have control over the means but not over the end. *Young India*, 7-24

They say "means are after all means." I would say "means are after all everything." As the means so the end. *Young India*, 7-24. (MPW, 362)

NON-POSSESSION

Non-Possession, the Ideal of Total Renunciation

Non-possession is allied to non-stealing. A thing not originally stolen must nevertheless be classified as stolen property if we possess it without needing it. Possession implies provision for the future. A seeker after truth, a follower of the law of love, cannot hold anything against tomorrow. God never stores for the morrow; He never creates more than what is strictly needed for the moment. The rich have a superfluous store of things which they do not need, and which are therefore neglected and wasted; while millions starve to death for want of sustenance. If each retained possession only of what he needed, no one would be in want and all would live in contentment. As it is, the rich are discontented no less than the poor. The poor man would fain become a millionaire, and the millionaire a multi-millionaire. The poor are not content if they get their daily needs. They have a right, however, to get enough for their daily needs and it is the duty of society to help them to satisfy them.

Civilization, in the real sense of the term, consists not in the multiplication, but in the deliberate and voluntary reduction of wants. This alone promotes real happiness and contentment, and increases the capacity for service. The soul is omnipresent; why should she care to be confined within the cage-like body, or do evil and even kill for the sake of that cage? We thus arrive at the ideal of total renunciation and learn the use of the body for the purposes of service so long as it exists, so much so that service, and not bread, becomes for us the staff of life.

We should remember that non-possession is a principle applicable to thoughts as well as to things. A man who fills his brain with useless knowledge violates that inestimable principle. Thoughts which turn us away from God or do not turn us towards Him are unnecessary possessions and constitute impediments in our way. Every moment of our life should be filled with mental or physical activity, but that activity should be *sattvik*,[7] tending towards truth. One who has consecrated his life to service cannot be idle for a single moment. But we have to learn to distinguish between good activity and evil activity. This discernment goes naturally with a single-minded devotion to service. (Letter to Narandas Gandhi, MMU/I, 8-26-30)

NON-STEALING

Truth and Love Necessary in Non-Stealing

Asteya means non-stealing. It is impossible that a person should steal and simultaneously claim to know Truth or cherish love. Yet every one of us is consciously or unconsciously, more or less, guilty of theft.

It is theft to take something from another even with his permission if we have no real need of it. We should not receive any single thing that we do not need. Theft of this description generally has food for its object. It is theft for me to take any fruit that I do not need, or to take it in a larger quantity than is necessary. We are not always aware of our real needs, and most of us improperly multiply our wants and thus unconsciously make thieves of ourselves. If we devote some thought to the subject we shall find that we can get rid of quite a number of our wants. One who follows the observance of non-stealing will bring about a progressive reduction of his wants. Much of the distressing poverty in this world has arisen out of breaches of the principle of nonstealing. (Letter to Narandas Gandhi, MMU, I, 8-19-30)

NON-VIOLENCE/LOVE/*AHIMSA*

Buddha, Christ, and Non-violent Resistance

What was the "larger symbiosis" that Buddha and Christ preached? Buddha fearlessly carried the war into the enemy's camp and brought down on its knees an arrogant priesthood. Christ drove out the money-changers from the temple of Jerusalem and drew down curses from Heaven upon the hypocrites and the Pharisees. Both were for intensely direct action. But even as Buddha and Christ chastised they showed unmistakable gentleness and love behind every act of theirs. They would not raise a finger against their enemies, but would gladly surrender themselves rather than the truth for which they lived. Buddha would have died resisting the priesthood, if the majesty of his love had not proved to be equal to the task of bending the priesthood. Christ died on the Cross with a crown of thorns on his head defying the might of a whole Empire. And if I raise resistances of a non-violent character I simply and humbly follow in the footsteps of the great teachers named by my critic. ("Neither a Saint nor a Politician," *Young India*, 5-12-20)

Non-violence, the Law of Humanity

I do believe that where there is only a choice between cowardice and violence I would advise violence. Thus when my eldest son asked me what he should have done, had he been present when I was almost fatally assaulted in 1908, whether he should have run away and seen me killed or whether he should have used his physical force which he could and wanted to use, and defended me, I told him that it was his duty to defend me even by using violence.

But I believe that non-violence is infinitely superior to violence, forgiveness is more manly than punishment. *Kshama virasya bhushanam.* "Forgiveness adorns a soldier." But abstinence is forgiveness only when there is the power to punish; it is meaningless when it pretends to proceed from a helpless creature. A mouse hardly forgives a cat when it allows itself to be torn to pieces by her. I, therefore, appreciate the sentiment of those who cry out for the condign punishment of General Dyer[8] and his ilk. They would tear him to pieces if they could. But I do not believe India to be helpless. I do not believe myself to be a helpless creature. Only I want to use India's and my strength for a better purpose.

Let me not be misunderstood. Strength does not come from physical capacity. It comes from an indomitable will. An average Zulu is any way more than a match for an average Englishman in bodily capacity. But he flees from an English boy, because he fears the boy's revolver or those who will use it for him. He fears death and is nerveless in spite of his burly figure. We in India may in a moment realize that one hundred thousand Englishmen need not frighten three hundred million human beings. A definite forgiveness would therefore mean a definite recognition of our strength.

I am not a visionary. I claim to be a practical idealist. The religion of non-violence is not meant merely for the *rishis* and saints. It is meant for the common people as well. Non-violence is the law of our species as violence is the law of the brute. The spirit lies dormant in the brute and he knows no law but that of physical might. The dignity of man requires obedience to a higher law—to the strength of the spirit.

I have therefore ventured to place before India the ancient law of self-sacrifice. For *satyagraha* and its off-shoots, non-co-operation and civil resistance, are nothing but new names for the law of suffering. The *rishis*, who discovered the law of non-violence in the midst of violence, were greater geniuses than Newton. They were themselves greater warriors than Wellington. Having themselves known the use of arms, they realized their uselessness and taught a weary world that its salvation lay not through violence but through non-violence.

Non-violence in its dynamic condition means conscious suffering. It does not mean meek submission to the will of the evil-doer, but it means the putting of one's whole soul against the will of the tyrant. Working under this law of our being, it is possible for a single individual to defy the whole might of an unjust empire to save his honour, his religion, his soul and lay the foundation for that empire's fall or its regeneration.

And so I am not pleading for India to practise non-violence because it is weak. I want her to practise non-violence being conscious of her strength and power. No training in arms is required for realization of her strength. We seem to need it because we seem to think that we are but a lump of flesh. I want India to recognize that she has a soul that cannot perish and that can rise triumphant above every physical weakness and defy the physical combination of a whole world.

If India takes up the doctrine of the sword, she may gain momentary victory. Then India will cease to be the pride of my heart. I am wedded to India because I owe my all to her. I believe absolutely that she has a mission for the world. She is not to copy Europe blindly. India's acceptance of the doctrine of the sword will be the hour of my trial. I hope I shall not be found wanting. My religion has no geographical limits. If I have a living faith in it, it will transcend my love for India herself. My life is dedicated to service of India through the religion of non-violence which I believe to be the root of Hinduism. ("The Doctrine of the Sword," *Young India* 8-11-20)

Non-Violence, the Greatest Force in the World

My study and experience of non-violence have proved to me that it is the greatest force in the world. It is the surest method of discovering the truth and it is the quickest because there is no other. It works silently, almost imperceptibly, but none the less surely. It is the one constructive process of Nature in the midst of incessant destruction going on about us. I hold it to be a superstition to believe that it can work only in private life. There is no department of life public or private to which that force cannot be applied. But this non-violence is impossible without complete self-effacement. (Message to *World Tomorrow*, Mahadev Desai's Diary, 11-14-24)

Attachment Causes Violence, Detachment Non-Violence

Non-violence is a quality of the heart. Whether there is violence or non-violence in our actions can be judged only by reference to the spirit behind them. There is violence always in the attachment to one's ego. When doing anything, one must ask oneself this question: "Is my action inspired by egoistic attachment?" If there is no such attachment, then there is no violence. ("Problem of Non-Violence," *Navajivan*, 6-6-26)

Renunciation, a Spirit of Detachment in and through Action

I hold that renunciation should be sought for in and through action. That action is the *sine qua non* of life in the body, that the Wheel of Life cannot go on even for a second without involving some sort of action goes without saying. Renunciation can therefore in these circumstances only mean detachment or freedom of the spirit from action, even while the body is engaged in action. A follower of the path of renunciation seeks to attain it not by refraining from all activity but by carrying it on in a perfect spirit of detachment and altruism as a pure trust. Thus a man may engage in farming, spinning, or any other activity without departing from the path of renunciation provided one does so merely for selfless service and remains free from the taint of egoism or attachment.

It remains for those therefore who like myself hold this view of renunciation to discover for themselves how far the principle of *ahimsa* is compatible with life in the body and how it can be applied to acts of everyday life. The very virtue of a *dharma* is that it is universal, that its practice is not the monopoly of the few, but must be the privilege of all. And it is my firm belief that the scope of truth and *ahimsa* is world-wide. That is why I find an ineffable joy in dedicating my life to researches in truth and *ahimsa* and I invite others to share it with me by doing likewise. ("Jain *Ahimsa*," *Navajivan*, 10-21-28)

Non-Violence, a Ceaseless Conscious Struggle

It takes a fairly strenuous course of training to attain to a mental state of non-violence. In daily life it has to be a course of discipline though we may not like it, like for instance the life of a soldier. But I agree that unless there is a hearty cooperation of the mind, the mere outward observance will be simply a mask, harmful both to the man himself and to others. The perfect state is reached only when mind and body and speech are in proper coordination. But it is always a case of intense mental struggle. It is not that I am incapable of anger, for instance, but I succeed on almost all occasions to keep my feelings under control. Whatever may be the result, there is always in me a conscious struggle to follow the law of non-violence deliberately and ceaselessly. Such a struggle leaves one stronger for it. Non-violence is a weapon of the strong.

My daily experience is that every problem would lead itself to solution if we are determined to make the law of truth and non-violence the law of life. For truth and non-violence are, to me, faces of the same coin. ("From S. S. Rajputana—III," *Young India*, 10-1-31)

Brotherhood, Loving All

Brotherhood is just now only a distant aspiration. To me it is a test of true spirituality. All our prayers, fasting and observances are empty nothings so long as we do not feel a live kinship with all life. But we have not even arrived at that intellectual belief, let alone a heart realization. We are still selective. A selective brotherhood is a selfish partnership. Brotherhood requires no consideration or response. If it did, we could not love those whom we consider as vile men and women. In the midst of strife and jealousy, it is a most difficult performance. And yet true religion demands nothing less from us. Therefore each one of us has to endeavour to realize this truth for ourselves irrespective of what others do. (Letter to Esther Menon, *Mahadevbhaini Diary*, I, 345, 8-4-32)

Non-Violence, the Law of Life for Human Beings

Non-violence for me is not a mere experiment. It is part of my life and the whole of the creed of *satyagraha*, non-co-operation, civil disobedience, and the like are necessary deductions from the fundamental proposition that non-violence is the law of life for human beings. For me it is both a means and an end and I am more than ever convinced that in the complex situation that faces India, there is no other way of gaining real freedom. In applying my mind to the present situation I must, therefore, test everything in terms of non-violence. (Letter to M. Asaf Ali, SN 19108, 6-26-33)

Five Axioms of Non-Violence

Let me lay down five simple axioms of non-violence as I know it:

1. Non-violence implies as complete self-purification as is humanly possible.
2. Man for man the strength of non-violence is in exact proportion to the ability, not the will, of the non-violent person to inflict violence.
3. Non-violence is without exception superior to violence, i.e., the power at the disposal of a non-violent person is always greater than he could have if he was violent.
4. There is no such thing as defeat in non-violence. The end of violence is surest defeat.

5. The ultimate end of non-violence is surest victory—if such a term may be used of non-violence. In reality where there is no sense of defeat, there is no sense of victory. ("The Greatest Force," *Harijan*, 10-12-35)

Non-violence, the Greatest and Activist Force in the World

Q. Is non-violence from your point of view a form of direct action?

A. It is not one form, it is the only form. I do not of course confine the words "direct action" to their technical meaning. But without a direct active expression of it, non-violence to my mind is meaningless. It is the greatest and the activest force in the world. One cannot be passively non-violent. In fact "non-violence" is a term I had to coin in order to bring out the root meaning of *ahimsa*. In spite of the negative particle "non," it is no negative force. It is a force which is more positive than electricity and more powerful than even ether. At the centre of non-violence is a force which is self-acting. *Ahimsa* means "love" in the Pauline sense, and yet something more than the "love" defined by St. Paul, although I know St. Paul's beautiful definition is good enough for all practical purposes. *Ahimsa* includes the whole creation, and not only human. Besides, love in the English language has other connotations too, and so I was compelled to use the negative word. Supposing I cannot produce a single instance in life of a man who truly converted his adversary, I would then say that is because no one had yet been found to express *ahimsa* in its fullness.

Q. Then it overrides all other forces?

A. Yes, it is the only true force in life.

Q. Forgive the weakness, but may I ask how are we to train individuals or communities in this difficult art?

A. There is no royal road, except through living the creed in your life which must be a living sermon. Of course the expression in one's own life presupposes great study, tremendous perseverance, and thorough cleansing of one's self of all the impurities. If for mastering of the physical sciences you have to devote a whole lifetime, how many lifetimes may be needed for mastering the greatest spiritual force that mankind has known? But why worry even if it means several lifetimes? Seek ye first the Kingdom of Heaven and everything else shall be added unto you. (The Kingdom of Heaven is *ahimsa*. Interview with American Negro Delegation, *Harijan*, 3-14-36)

Gandhi's Wife, his Teacher in Non-violence

I used to let loose my anger upon her. But she bore it all meekly and uncomplainingly. I had a notion that it was her duty to obey me, her lord and master, in everything. But her unresisting meekness opened my eyes and slowly it began to dawn upon me that I had no such prescriptive right over her. If I wanted her obedience, I had first to persuade her by patient argument. She thus became my teacher in non-violence. And I dare say, I have not had a more loyal and faithful comrade in life. I literally used to make life a hell for her. She had been brought up in an orthodox family where untouchability was observed. Muslims and untouchables used to frequent our house. I made her serve them all regardless of her innate reluctance. But she never said "no." She was not educated in the usual sense of the term and was simple and unsophisticated. Her guileless simplicity conquered me completely.

You have all wives, mothers and sisters at home. You can take the lesson of non-violence from them. (Talk to Khudai Khidmatgars, *A Pilgrimage for Peace*, cited in *MPW*, II, 365, 10-23-38)

Non-Violent Organization

The principles on which a non-violent organization is based are different from and the reverse of what obtains in a violent organization. For instance, in the orthodox army, there is a clear distinction made between an officer and a private. The latter is subordinate and inferior to the former. In a non-violent army the general is just the chief servant—first among equals.

The second difference between a military organization and a peace organization is that in the former the rank and file have no part in the choice of the general and the officers. These are imposed upon them and enjoy unrestricted power over them. In a non-violent army, the general and the officers are elected or are as if elected when their authority is moral and rests solely on the willing obedience of the rank and file.

So much for internal relations between the general of a non-violent army and his soldiers. Coming to their relations with the outside world, the same sort of difference is visible between these two kinds of organizations. Just now we had to deal with an enormous crowd that had gathered outside this room. You tried to disperse it by persuasion and loving argument, not by using force and, when in the end we failed in our attempt, we withdrew and sought relief from it by getting behind closed doors in this room. Military discipline knows nothing of moral pressure.

Here [in a non-violent organization], to consider the opponent, or, for the matter of that, anybody, even in thought, as your enemy would, in the parlance of non-violence or love, be called a sin. Far from seeking revenge, a votary of non-violence would pray to God that He might bring about a change of heart in his opponent, and if that does not happen he would be prepared to bear any injury that his opponent might inflict upon him, not in a spirit of cowardice or helplessness, but bravely with a smile upon his face. I believe implicitly in the ancient saying that "non-violence real and complete will melt the stoniest hearts." ("Talk to Khudai Khidmatgars," *Harijan*, 11-19-38)

Non-violence Possible in Nazi Germany

Herr Hitler is but one man enjoying no more than the average span of life. He would be a spent force if he had not the backing of his people. I do not despair of his responding to human suffering even though caused by him. But I must refuse to believe that the Germans as a nation have no heart or markedly less than the other nations of the earth.

A single Jew bravely standing up and refusing to bow to Hitler's decrees will cover himself with glory and lead the way to the deliverance of the fellow Jews. ("Is Non-Violence Ineffective?" *Harijan*, 1-7-39)

Non-Violence Is the Means, the End Is Complete Independence

All society is held together by non-violence, even as the earth is held in her position by gravitation. But when the law of gravitation was discovered the discovery yielded results of which our ancestors had no knowledge. Even so when society is deliberately constructed in accordance with the law of non-violence, its structure will be different in material particulars from what it is today. But I cannot say in advance what the government based wholly on nonviolence will be like.

What is happening today is disregard of the law of non-violence and enthronement of violence as if it were an eternal law. The democracies, therefore, that we see at work in England, America and France are only so called, because they are no less based on violence than Nazi Germany, Fascist Italy or even Soviet Russia. The only difference is that the violence of the last three is much better organized than that of the three democratic powers. Nevertheless we see today a mad race for outdoing one another in the matter of armaments. And if when the clash comes, as it is bound to come one day, the democracies win, they will do so only because they will have the backing of their peoples who imagine that they have a voice in their own government whereas in the other three cases the peoples might rebel against their own dictatorships.

Holding the view that without the recognition of non-violence on a national scale there is no such thing as a constitutional or democratic government, I devote my energy to the propagation of non-violence as the law, of our life—individual, social, political, national and international. I fancy that I have seen the light, though dimly. I write cautiously, for I do not profess to know the whole of the Law. If I know the successes of my experiments, I know also my failures. But the successes are enough to fill me with undying hope.

I have often said that if one takes care of the means, the end will take care of itself. Non-violence is the means, the end for every nation is complete independence. There will be an international League only when all the nations, big or small, composing it are fully independent. The nature of that independence will correspond to the extent of non-violence assimilated by the nations concerned. One thing is certain. In a society based on non-violence, the smallest nation will feel as tall as the tallest. The idea of superiority and inferiority will be wholly obliterated. ("Working of Non-Violence," 2-11-39)

Jesus' Life Teaches the Law of Love

I am unprepared to find the view expressed by *The Statesman* writer that the example of Christ proved once and for all that in a worldly and temporal sense it [non-violence] can fail hopelessly!! Though I cannot claim to be Christian in the sectarian sense, the example of Jesus' suffering is a factor in the composition of my undying faith in non-violence which rules all my actions, worldly and temporal. And I know that there are hundreds of Christians who believe likewise. Jesus lived and died in vain if he did not teach us to regulate the whole of life by the eternal Law of Love. ("Is Non-violence Ineffective?" *Harijan*, 1-7-39)

Ongoing Research in the Science of Non-violence

You are all my fellow-students and co-workers, fellow-servants and fellow-researchers. Forget the idea of being followers. Nobody is leading and nobody is following. Nobody is a leader and nobody is a follower.

We want to bring about a new social order based on truth and non-violence. We need experts to develop this into a science. The world as it functions today represents a mixture of violence and non-violence. The external surface of the world suggests its internal state. A country like Germany which regards violence as God is engaged only in developing violence and glorifying it. We are watching the efforts that the votaries of violence are making. We must also know that those given to violence are watching our activities. They are observing what we are doing for developing our science. The science of non-violence is yet taking shape. We are still not conversant with all its aspects. There is a wide scope for research and experiment in this field. You can apply all your talents to it.

Every day I have a new vision and I experience a new joy. I am certain that non-violence is meant for all time. It is an attribute of the *atman* and is, therefore, universal since the *atman* belongs to all. Non-violence is meant for everybody and for all time and at all places. (Speech at Gandhi Seva Sangh, *Gandhi Seva Sanghke Chhathe Adhiveshan (Malikanda-Bengal) ka Vivaran*, 2-22-40)

Ahimsa Unifies: No Sects, No Gandhism

I have a horror of "isms," especially when they are attached to proper names. Even if all that you say of me is true, it does not make a new sect. My effort is to avoid not only new sects but even to do away with old and superfluous ones. *Ahimsa* abhors sects. *Ahimsa* is a unifying force. It discovers unity in diversity. All that you say is derivable from *ahimsa*. To bring into being a new cult is repugnant to *ahimsa*, to the very experiment I am making. Thus you will, I hope, see that there is no room for "Gandhism." ("Question Box," *Harijan*, 3-16-40)

Non-violent Education of Haves and Have-Nots

It must be realized that the reform cannot be rushed. If it is to be brought about by non-violent means, it can only be done by education both of the haves and the have-nots. The former should be assured that there never will be force used against them. The have-nots must be educated to know that no one can really compel them to do anything against their will, and that they can secure their freedom by learning the art of non-violence, i.e., self-suffering. ("Jayaprakash's Picture," *Harijan*, 4-20-40)

Mankind Steadily Progressing Towards *Ahimsa*

If we turn our eyes to the time of which history has any record down to our own time, we shall find that man has been steadily progressing towards *ahimsa*. Our remote ancestors were cannibals. Then came a time when they were fed up with cannibalism and they began to live on chase. Next came a stage when man was ashamed of leading the life of a wandering hunter. He therefore took to agriculture and depended principally on mother earth for his food. Thus from being a nomad he settled down to civilized stable life, founded villages and towns, and from member of a family he became member of a community and a nation. All these are signs of progressive *ahimsa* and diminishing *himsa*.

Prophets and *avatars* have also taught the lesson of *ahimsa* more or less. Not one of them has professed to teach *himsa*. And how should it be otherwise? *Himsa* does not need to be taught. Man as animal is violent, but as spirit is non-violent. The moment he awakes to the spirit within he cannot remain violent. Either he progresses towards *ahimsa* or rushes to his doom. That is why the prophets and *avatars* have taught the lessons of truth, harmony, brotherhood, justice, etc.—all attributes of *ahimsa*.

If we believe that mankind has steadily progressed towards *ahimsa*, it follows that it has to progress towards it still further. Nothing in this world is static, everything is kinetic. If there is no progression, then there is inevitable retrogression. ("Is Non-Violence Impossible?" *Harijanbandhu*, 8-10-40)

Non-Violent Police Will Be the Servants of the People

If all Congressmen had been true to their creed, we would not be vacillating between violence and non-violence as we are today. The fruits of *ahimsa* would be in evidence everywhere: There would be communal harmony, the demon of untouchability would have been cast out, and, generally speaking, we should have evolved an ordered society. But the reverse is the case just now. There is even definite hostility to the Congress in certain quarters. The word of Congressmen is not always relied on. The Muslim League and most of the Princes have no faith in the Congress and are in fact inimical to it. If Congressmen had true *ahimsa* in them, there would be none of this distrust. In fact the Congress would be the beloved of all.

Therefore I can only place an imaginary picture before the votaries of *ahimsa.*

So long as we are not saturated with pure *ahimsa* we cannot possibly win *swaraj* through non-violence. We can come into power only when we are in a majority or, in other words, when the large majority of people are willing to abide by the law of *ahimsa.* When this happy state prevails, the spirit of violence will have all but vanished and internal disorder will have come under control.

Nevertheless I have conceded that even in a non-violent State a police force may be necessary. This, I admit, is a sign of my imperfect *ahimsa.* I have not the courage to declare that we can carry on without a police force as I have in respect of an army. Of course I can and do envisage a state where the police will not be necessary; but whether we shall succeed in realizing it, the future alone will show.

The police of my conception will, however, be of a wholly different pattern from the present-day force. Its ranks will be composed of believers in non-violence. They will be servants, not masters, of the people. The people will instinctively render them every help, and through mutual cooperation they will easily deal with the ever-decreasing disturbances. The police force will have some kind of arms, but they will be rarely used, if at all. In fact the policemen will be reformers. Their police work will be confined primarily to robbers and dacoits. Quarrels between labour and capital and strikes will be few and far between in a non-violent state, because the influence of the non-violent majority will be so great as to command the respect of the principal elements in society. Similarly there will be no room for communal disturbances. ("My Idea of a Police Force," *Harijanbandhu*, 8-31-40)

Constructive Work, "Arms" of a Non-Violent Man

A non-violent man has to keep himself engaged usefully during all waking hours and, therefore, *constructive work is for him what arms are for the violent man.* (Fragment of a Letter to Abdul Ghaffar Khan, *Harijan*, 1-18-42)

Action, the Basis of *Ahimsa*

A friend suggests that I should resume writing my autobiography from the point where I left off and, further, that I should write a treatise on the science of *ahimsa.*

How can I find time to bring the remainder of my experiments with truth up to date? But if it is God's will that I should write them, He will surely make my way clear.

To write a treatise on the science of *ahimsa* is beyond my powers. I am not built for academic writings. Action is my domain, and what I understand, according to my lights, to be my duty, and what comes my way, I do. All my action is actuated by the spirit of service. Let anyone who can systematize *ahimsa* into a science do so, if indeed it lends itself to such treatment. The world does not hunger for *shastras*. What it craves, and will always crave, is sincere action. ("Two Requests," *Harijan*, 3-3-46)

India's Experiment in Non-violence Fairly Successful

No man can stop violence, God alone can do so. Men are but instruments in His hands. Here material means cannot stop violence but this does not mean that material means should not be employed for the purpose. The deciding factor is God's grace. He works according to His law and, therefore, violence will also be stopped in accordance with that law. Man does not and can never know God's law fully. Therefore we have to try as far as lies in our power. I hold that our experiment in non-violence has succeeded to a fair extent in India. ("How Can Violence Be Stopped?" *Harijan Sevak*, 5-19-46)

Discriminating between *Ahimsa* and *Himsa*

If I wish to be an agriculturist and stay in the jungle, I will have to use the minimum unavoidable violence in order to protect my fields. I will have to kill monkeys, birds and insects which eat up my crops. If I do not wish to do so myself, I will have to engage someone to do it for me. There is not much difference between the two. To allow crops to be eaten up by animals in the name of *ahimsa* while there is a famine in the land is certainly a sin. Evil and good are relative terms. What is good under certain conditions can become an evil or a sin under a different set of conditions.

Man is not to drown himself in the well of *shastras* but he is to dive into their broad ocean and bring out pearls. At every step he has to use his discrimination as to what is *ahimsa* and what is *himsa*. ("Religion v. no Religion," *Harijanbandhu*, 6-9-46)

PEACE

Qualifications for Membership in Peace Brigade

Some time ago I suggested the formation of a Peace Brigade whose members would risk their lives in dealing with riots, especially communal. The idea was that this Brigade should substitute the police and even the military. This reads ambitious. The achievement may prove impossible. Yet, if the

Congress is to succeed in its non-violent struggle, it must develop the power to deal peacefully with such situations.

Let us therefore see what qualifications a member of the contemplated Peace Brigade should possess.

(1) He or she must have a living faith in non-violence. This is impossible without a living faith in God. A non-violent man can do nothing save by the power and grace of God.

(2) This messenger of peace must have equal regard for all the principal religions of the earth.

(3) Generally speaking this work of peace can only be done by local men in their own localities.

(4) The work can be done singly or in groups. Therefore no one need wait for companions. Nevertheless one would naturally seek companions in one's own locality and form a local brigade.

(5) This messenger of peace will cultivate through personal service contacts with the people in his locality or chosen circle, so that when he appears to deal with ugly situations, he does not descend upon the members of a riotous assembly as an utter stranger liable to be looked upon as a suspect or an unwelcome visitor.

(6) Needless to say, a peace-bringer must have a character beyond reproach and must be known for his strict impartiality.

(7) Generally there are previous warnings of coming storms. If these are known, the Peace Brigade will not wait till the conflagration breaks out but will try to handle the situation in anticipation.

(8) Whilst, if the movement spreads, it might be well if there are some whole-time workers, it is not absolutely necessary that there should be. The idea is to have as many good and true men and women as possible.

(9) There should be a distinctive dress worn by the members of the contemplated Brigade so that in course of time they will be recognized without the slightest difficulty. ("Qualifications of a Peace Brigade," *Harijan*, 6-18-38)

Realizing Peace through Renunciation

Not to believe in the possibility of permanent peace is to disbelieve the godliness of human nature. Methods hitherto adopted have failed because rock-bottom sincerity on the part of those who have striven has been lacking. If the recognized leaders of mankind who have control over engines of destruction were wholly to renounce their use, with full knowledge of its implications, permanent peace can be obtained. This is clearly impossible without the great Powers of the earth renouncing their imperialistic design. This again seems impossible without great nations ceasing to believe in soul-destroying competition and to desire to multiply wants and therefore increase their material possessions. It is my conviction that the root of the evil is want of a living faith in a living God. It is a first-class human tragedy that peoples of the earth who claim to believe in the message of Jesus who they describe as the Prince of Peace show little of that belief in actual practice. *If even one great nation were unconditionally to perform the supreme act of renunciation, many of us would see in our lifetime visible peace established on earth.* ("Answer to *The Cosmopolitan*," *Harijan*, 6-18-38)

An Agenda for Peace after World War II

The San Francisco Conference[9] is announced to meet shortly. I do not know its agenda. Probably no outsider knows it. Whatever it may be, the Conference will have much to do with the world-to-be after the so-called end of the war.

Exploitation and domination of one nation over another can have no place in a world striving to put an end to all wars. It is only in such a world that the militarily weaker nations will be free from the fear of intimidation or exploitation.

(1) An indispensable preliminary to peace is the complete freedom of India from all foreign control, not merely because it is a classic example of imperialist domination but specially because it is a big, ancient and cultured country which has fought for its freedom since 1920 deliberately with Truth and Non-violence as its only weapon.

(2) Freedom of India will demonstrate to all the exploited races of the earth that their freedom is very near and that in no case will they henceforth be exploited.

(3) Peace must be just. In order to be that, it must neither be punitive nor vindictive. Germany and Japan should not be humiliated. The strong are never vindictive. Therefore, fruits of peace must be equally shared. The effort then will be to turn them into friends. The Allies can prove their democracy by no other means.

(4) It follows from the foregoing that there will be no armed peace imposed upon the forcibly disarmed. All will be disarmed. There will be an international police force to enforce the lightest terms of peace. Even this retention of an international police will be a concession to human weakness, not by any means an emblem of peace.

Thus the demand for Indian independence is in no way selfish. Its nationalism spells internationalism. (Statement to the Press, *Bombay Chronicle*, 4-18-45)

The Possibility of a World Federation Based on Nonviolence

Q. What about the war criminals?

A. What is a war criminal? Was not war itself a crime against God and humanity and, therefore, were not all those who sanctioned, engineered, and conducted wars, war criminals? War criminals are not confined to the Axis Powers alone. Roosevelt and Churchill are no less war criminals than Hitler and Mussolini.

Hitler was "Great Britain's sin." Hitler is only an answer to British imperialism, and this I say in spite of the fact that I hate Hitlerism and its anti-Semitism. England, America and Russia have all of them got their hands dyed more or less red—not merely Germany and Japan. The Japanese have only proved themselves to be apt pupils of the West. They have learnt at the feet of the West and beaten it at its own game.

Q. Would you have a world government?

A. Yes. I claim to be a practical idealist. I believe in compromise so long as it does not involve the sacrifice of principles. I may not get a world government that I want just now but if it is a government that would just touch my ideal, I would accept it as a compromise. Therefore, although I am not enamoured of a world federation, I shall be prepared to accept it if it is built on an essentially non-violent basis. (Interview with Ralph Coniston, *Mahatma Gandhi—The Last Phase*, I, Bk. I, before 4-25-45, cited in *MPW*, II, 501–2)

PERFECTION

Perfect Love Attainable on Earth

To say that perfection in not attainable on this earth is to deny God. We do see men becoming better under effort and discipline. There is no occasion for limiting the capacity for improvement. Life to me would lose all interest if I felt that I *could* not attain perfect love on earth. After all, what matters is that our capacity for loving ever expands. It is a slow process. How shall you love the men who thwart you even in well-doing? And yet that is the time of supreme test. (Letter to Esther Faering, *My Dear Child*, 1-13-18, cited in *EWMG*, 167)

POLITICS

Spiritualizing Political and Social Life

The masses came to know of Gokhale's[10] efficiency in work. All know Gokhale's life of action. But few know of his religious life. Truth was the spring of all his actions.

This was behind all his works, even his politics. This was the reason he founded the Servants of India Society, the ideal of which was to spiritualise the political as well as the social life of the nation. (Speech at Shantiniketan on Gokhale's Death, *The Ashram*, 6/7-15)

International Harmony Attained by Removing Exploitation

There can be no living harmony between races and nations unless the main cause is removed, namely, exploitation of the weak by the strong. We must revise the interpretation of the so-called doctrine of "the survival of the fittest." (Message to Marcelle Capy, SN 13117, 3-20-28)

Enlightened Anarchy, the Ideal State

Political power, in my opinion, cannot be our ultimate aim. It is one of the means used by men for their all-round advancement. The power to control national life through national representatives is called political power. Representatives will become unnecessary if the national life becomes so perfect as to be self-controlled. It will then be a state of enlightened anarchy in which each person will become his own ruler. He will conduct himself in such a way that his behaviour will not hamper the well-being of his neighbours. In an ideal State there will be no political institution and therefore no political power. That is why Thoreau has said in his classic statement that that government is the best which governs the least. ("Enlightened Anarchy—A Political Ideal," *Sarvodaya*, 1-39)

Social Revolution More Difficult than Political Revolution

Ever since I came to India I have felt that social revolution is a much more difficult thing to achieve than the political revolution, by which I mean ending our present slavery under the British rule. (Discussion with Workers and Staff Members, *Visva-Bharati News*, XIV, No. 9, 1220-45)

Independence and the Interdependence of Indian Village Republics

Independence must begin at the bottom. Thus, every village will be a republic or panchayat having full powers. It follows, therefore, that every village has to be self-sustained and capable of managing its affairs even to the extent of defending itself against the whole world. It will be trained and prepared to perish in the attempt to defend itself against any onslaught from without. Thus, ultimately, it is the individual who is the unit. This does not exclude dependence on and willing help from neighbours or from the world. It will be free and voluntary play of mutual forces. Such a society is necessarily highly cultured in which every man and woman knows what he or she wants and, what is more, knows that no one should want anything that others cannot have with equal labour.

In this structure composed of innumerable villages, there will be ever-widening, never-ascending circles. Life will not be a pyramid with the apex sustained by the bottom. But it will be an oceanic circle whose centre will be the individual always ready to perish for the village, the latter ready to perish for the circle of villages, till at last the whole becomes one life composed of individuals, never aggressive in their arrogance but ever humble, sharing the majesty of the oceanic circle of which they are integral units.

Therefore the outermost circumference will not wield power to crush the inner circle but will give strength to all within and derive its own strength from it. I may be taunted with the retort that this is all Utopian and, therefore, not worth a single thought. If Euclid's point, though incapable of being drawn by human agency, has an imperishable value, my picture has its own for mankind to live. Let India live for this true picture, though never realizable in its completeness. We must have a proper picture of what we want, before we can have something approaching it. If there ever is to be a republic of every village in India, then I claim verity for my picture in which the last is equal to the first or, in other words, no one is to be the first and none the last. ("Independence," *Harijan*, 7-28-46)

Separation of Religion and the State

If I were a dictator, religion and State would be separate. I swear by my religion. I will die for it. But it is my personal affair. The State has nothing to do with it. The State would look after your secular welfare, health, communications, foreign relations, currency and so on, but not your or my religion. That is everybody's personal concern!

You must watch my life, how I live, eat, sit, talk, behave in general. The sum total of all those in me is my religion. (Talk with a Christian Missionary, *Harijan*, 9-22-46)

Political Work Related to Social and Moral Progress

I feel that political work must be looked upon in terms of social and moral progress. In democracy no part of life is untouched by politics. (Talk with an American Journalist, *Harijan*, 10-6-46)

POVERTY

For the poor bread is their God. (Interview with Nirmal Kumar Bose, *The Hindustan Times*, 10-17-35)

PRINCIPLES

Drawing One's Own Corollaries from Principles

I do believe that it is a mistake, a dangerous thing, to get orders from me in every matter. My answer is bound to be only according to the way a question is put. I may make a mistake in giving my answer. Everyone should draw his own corollaries from general principles. (Letter to Mathuradas Trikumji, *Bapuni Prasadi*, 74, 8-13-24)

Living Moral Principles Necessary in All Spheres of Activity

If a person has violated a moral principle in any sphere of his life, his action will certainly have an effect in other spheres. In other words, the belief generally held that an immoral man may do no harm in the political sphere is quite wrong. And so is the other belief that a person who violates moral principles in his business may be moral in his private life or in his conduct in family affairs. Hence, whenever we do an evil we should overcome the tendency towards it. (Letter to Parasram Mehrotra, CW 9437, 4-22-32)

Conscious Striving to Live Principles

A principle is a principle, and in no case can it be watered down because of our incapacity to live it in practice. We have to strive to achieve it, and the striving should be conscious, deliberate and hard. (Discussion with Teacher, *Harijan*, 9-5-36)

RELIGION

True Religion Based on Morality

According to the Sufi point of view, no religion based on morality can be considered to be false. In reply to a question Jalaluddin[11] said, "The ways of God are as many as the number of souls of men." Elsewhere he says, "God's light is one but its rays are various in hue. We can worship God along any path, provided it be with a true and sincere heart." ("Jalaluddin Rumi," *Indian Opinion*, 6-15-07)

The Religion Which Transcends Religions

If I seem to take part in politics, it is only because politics encircle us today like the coil of a snake from which one cannot get out, no matter how much one tries.

I have been experimenting with myself and my friends by introducing religion into politics. Let me explain what I mean by religion. It is not the Hindu religion, which I certainly prize above all other religions, but the religion which transcends Hinduism, which changes one's very nature, which binds one indissolubly to the truth within and which ever purifies. It is the permanent element in human nature which counts no cost too great in order to find full expression and which leaves the soul utterly restless until it has found itself, known its Maker and appreciated the true correspondence between the Maker and itself. ("Neither a Saint nor a Politician," *Young India*, 5-12-20)

No True Politics Devoid of Religion

The confusion in the writer's mind has arisen because of his misconception of the work of the prophets he names [Buddha and Jesus] and of an awkward comparison between them and me.

I do not consider myself worthy to be mentioned in the same breath with the race of prophets. I am an humble seeker after truth. I am impatient to realize myself, to attain *moksha* in this very existence. My national service is part of my training for freeing my soul from the bondage of flesh. Thus considered, my service may be regarded as purely selfish. I have no desire for the perishable kingdom of earth. I am striving for the Kingdom of Heaven which is *moksha*. To attain my end it is not necessary for me to seek the shelter of a cave. I carry one about me, if I would but know it.

For me the road to salvation lies through incessant toil in the service of my country and there through of humanity. I want to identify myself with everything that lives. In the language of the *Gita* I want to live at peace with both friend and foe. Though, therefore, a Mussalman or a Christian or a Hindu may despise me and hate me, I want to love him and serve him even as I would love my wife or son though they hate me. So my patriotism is for me a stage in my journey to the land of eternal freedom and peace. Thus it will be seen that for me there are no politics devoid of religion. They subserve religion. Politics bereft of religion are a death-trap because they kill the soul. ("My Mission," *Young India*, 4-3-24)

God, All Things to All Men

God is that indefinable something which we all feel but which we do not know. Charles Bradlaugh described himself as an atheist no doubt but many a Christian declined to regard him as such. He recognized in Bradlaugh a greater kinship with himself than many a lip Christian. I had the privilege of attending the funeral of that good friend of India. I noticed several clergymen at the function. There were certainly several Mussalmans and many Hindus in the procession. They all believed in God. Bradlaugh's denial of God was a denial of Him as He was known to Bradlaugh to have been described. His was an eloquent and indignant protest against the then current theology and the terrible contrast between precept and practice.

To me God is truth and love; God is ethics and morality; God is fearlessness. God is the source of Light and Life and yet He is above and beyond all these. God is conscience. He is even the atheism of the atheist. For in His boundless love God permits the atheist to live. He is the searcher of hearts. He transcends speech and reason. He knows us and our hearts better than we do ourselves. He does not take us at our word for He knows that we often do not mean it, some knowingly and others unknowingly. He is a personal God to those who need His personal presence. He is embodied to those who need His touch. He is the purest essence. He simply Is to those who have faith, He is all things to all men. He is in us and yet above and beyond us. ("God and Congress," *Young India*, 3-5-25)

Essential Oneness of Souls

Souls seem to be many; but underneath the seeming variety, there is an essential oneness.

In its essence the soul is free from all evil, but torn from its source it partakes of evil and all other limitations even as a drop of water torn from its source and found as part of a dirty pool seems for the time being to partake of the pool's dirt. (Answers to Questions from Moolchand Agrawal, GN 765, 8-5-27)

Congregational Prayer, Supremest Social Obligation

Congregational prayer is an aid to being in tune with the Infinite. For man who is a social being cannot find God unless he discharges social obligations and the obligation of coming to a common prayer meeting is perhaps the supremest. It is a cleansing process for the whole congregation. But, like all human institutions, if one does not take care, such meetings do become formal and even hypocritical. (Letter to Mrs E. Bjerrum, SN 13221 & 15365, cited in *MPW*, I, 549, 6-10-28)

Faith Transcends Experience and Reason

He whose faith is pure always has a sharp wit. His reason tells him that faith is higher than experience, that it transcends experience, that it reaches where reason cannot. The seat of reason is the mind, that of faith is the heart. It has been the uniform experience of man that the heart is a thousand times more potent than the mind. That is why Krishna says in Chapter XVII of the *Gita*: A man is what his faith makes him. ("Reason v. Faith," *Hindi Navajivan*, 9-19-29)

All Religions Divinely Inspired but Imperfect

The question arises: why should there be so many different faiths? The soul is one, but the bodies which she animates are many. We cannot reduce the number of bodies; yet we recognize the unity of the soul. Even as a tree has a single trunk, but many branches and leaves, so is there one true and perfect Religion, but it becomes many as it passes through the human medium.

All religions are divinely inspired, but they are imperfect because they are products of the human mind and taught by human beings. (Letter to Narandas Gandhi, MMU, I, 9-23-30)

Inspiration through One's Inner Voice

For me the voice of God, of Conscience, of Truth, or the Inner Voice or 'the still small Voice' mean one and the same thing. I saw no form. I have never tried, for I have always believed God to be without form. One who realizes God is freed from sin for ever. He has no desire to be fulfilled. Not even in his thoughts will he suffer from faults, imperfections or impurities. Whatever he does will be perfect because he does nothing himself but the God within him does everything. He is completely merged in Him. Such realization comes to one among tens of millions. That it can come I have no doubt at all. I yearn to have such realization but I have not got it yet and I know that I am yet very far from it. The inspiration I had was quite a different thing. Moreover, many get such inspiration quite often or at some time.

The inspiration I got was this: The night I got the inspiration, I had a terrible inner struggle. My mind was restless. I could see no way. The burden of my responsibility was crushing me. But what I did hear was like a Voice from a far and yet quite near. It was as unmistakable as some human voice definitely speaking to me, and irresistible. I was not dreaming at the time I heard the Voice. The hearing of the Voice was preceded by a terrific struggle within me. Suddenly the Voice came upon me. I listened, made certain that it was the Voice, and the struggle ceased. I was calm. The determination was made accordingly, the date and the hour of the fast were fixed. Joy came over me. ("All About the Fast," *Harijan*, 7-8-33)

Equal Respect for All Religions

Q: In your autobiography you have said that you cannot think of politics apart from religion. Do you still hold that view? If so, how is it that in a country of many diverse religions like India you expect a common political policy to be adopted?

A: Yes, I still hold the view that I cannot conceive of politics divorced from religion. Indeed, religion should pervade every one of our actions. Here religion does not mean sectarianism. It means a belief in ordered moral government of the universe. It is not less real because it is unseen. This religion transcends Hinduism, Islam, Christianity, etc. It does not supersede them. It harmonizes them and gives them reality.

Q: By teaching respect for all religions you want to undermine the power of Islam. There can be no meeting ground between us and you.

A: I do maintain, in spite of you and others like you suspecting my motives, that mutual respect for one another's religions is inherent in a peaceful society. Free impact of ideas is impossible on any other condition. Religions are meant to tame our savage nature, not to let it loose. God is only one though He has countless names. Don't you expect me to respect your faith? You say Muslims have nothing in common with Hindus. In spite of your separatism, the world is moving towards universal brotherhood when mankind will be one nation. ("The Question Box," *Harijan*, 2-10-40)

God, the Life Force, Immanent and Transcendent

One ought always to remember, while dwelling on Him, that one is but a drop, the tiniest of creatures of the ocean that is God. One may experience Him by being in Him, but one can never describe Him. As Madame Blavatsky puts it, man in praying, worships the Great Power residing within. It is immaterial if some worship God as a Person and some others as a Great Power. Both are right, each in his own way. Nobody knows what is intrinsically right and nobody is likely ever to know. The ideal, to be an ideal, must forever remain out of reach. All the other forces are static, while God is the Life Force, immanent and at the same time transcendent. ("Is God a Person or a Principle?" *Harijan*, 8-18-46)

Gandhi, a Christian, a Sikh, a Jain, a Hindu

I think I am as much a Christian, a Sikh and a Jain as I am a Hindu. Religion does not teach one to kill one's brother however different his belief. (Speech at Prayer Meeting, *Hindustan*, 9-8-46)

SARVODAYA

Sarvodaya Depends upon *Satyagraha*

(Message for the first issue of *Sarvodaya*, a journal published by D. B. Kalelkar and Dada Dharmadhikari)

Sarvodaya is impossible without *satyagraha*. The word *satyagraha* should be understood here in its etymological sense. There can be no insistence on truth where there is no non-violence. Hence, the attainment of *sar-*

vodaya depends upon the attainment of non-violence. The attainment of non-violence in its turn depends upon *tapascharya*. *Tapascharya*, again, should be pure. Ceaseless effort, discretion, etc., should form part of it. Pure *tapascharya* leads to pure knowledge. Experience shows that although people talk of non-violence, many are mentally so lazy that they do not even take the trouble of familiarizing themselves with the facts. Take an example. India is a poor country. We wish to do away with poverty. But how many people have made a study of how this poverty came about, what its implications are, how it can be removed, etc.? A devotee of non-violence should be full of such knowledge.

It is the duty of *Sarvodaya* to create such means and not to enter into controversies. Editors of *Sarvodaya* should forget Gandhism. There is no such thing as Gandhism. I have not put anything new before India; I have only presented an ancient thing in a new way. I have tried to utilize it in a new field. Hence my ideas cannot be appropriately called Gandhism. We shall adopt truth wherever we find it, praise it wherever we see it, and pursue it. In other words, in every sentence of *Sarvodaya*, we should catch a glimpse of non-violence and knowledge. ("What is Sarvodaya?" GN 7680, 7-21-38)

The Well-Being of All Comes through Service and Renunciation

In the application of the method of non-violence one must believe in the possibility of every person, however depraved, being reformed under humane and skilled treatment. We must appeal to the good in human beings and expect response.

Is it not conducive to the well-being of society that every member uses all his talents, only not for personal aggrandisement but for the good of all? We do not want to produce dead equality where every person becomes or is rendered incapable of using his ability to the utmost possible extent. Such a society must ultimately perish. I therefore suggest that my advice that monied men may earn their crores (honestly only, of course) but so as to dedicate them to the service of all is perfectly sound. *Thena thyakthena bhunjithaha* [Having renounced, then enjoy] is a *mantra* based on uncommon knowledge. It is the surest method to evolve a new order of life of universal benefit in the place of the present one where each one lives for himself without regard to what happens to his neighbour. ("Not Necessarily Impure," *Harijan*, 2-22-42)

SATYAGRAHA

Satyagraha, Pure Soul-Force

It is said of "passive resistance" that it is the weapon of the weak, but the power which is the subject of this article can be used only by the strong. This power is not "passive" resistance; indeed it calls for intense activity. The movement in South Africa was not passive but active.

Satyagraha is pure soul-force. Truth is the very substance of the soul. That is why this force is called *satyagraha*. The soul is informed with knowledge. In it burns the flame of love. If someone gives us pain through ignorance, we shall win him through love. "Non-violence is the supreme *dharma*" is the proof of this power of love. Non-violence is a dormant state. In the waking state, it is love. (*"Satyagraha*—Not Passive Resistance," Ramchandra Varma, *Mahatma Gandhi*, 9-2-17)

Soul Force and Social Reform

Submission to the state law is the price a citizen pays for his personal liberty. Submission, therefore, to a state wholly or largely unjust is an immoral barter for liberty. A citizen who thus realizes the evil nature of a state is not satisfied to live on its sufferance, and therefore appears to the others who do not share his belief to be a nuisance to society whilst he is endeavouring to compel the state without committing a moral breach to arrest him. Thus considered, civil resistance is a most powerful expression of a soul's anguish and an eloquent protest against the continuance of an evil state. Is not this the history of all reform? Have not reformers, much to the disgust of their fellows, discarded even innocent symbols associated with an evil practice?

When a body of men disowns the state under which they have hitherto lived, they nearly establish their own government. I say nearly, for they do not go to the point of using force when they are resisted by the state. ("The Momentous Issue," *Young India*, 11-10-21)

Civil Disobedience: Transmuting Rage into Life-Saving Energy

When tyranny is rampant much rage is generated among the victims. It remains latent because of their weakness and bursts in all its fury on the slightest pretext. Civil disobedience is a sovereign method of transmuting this undisciplined life-destroying latent energy into disciplined life-saving energy whose use ensures absolute success. ("Duty of Disloyalty," *Young India*, 3-27-30)

Satyagraha, Touching the Hearts of Terrorists and Rulers

I am in dead earnest about this greatest of weapons at the disposal of mankind. It is claimed for *satyagraha* that it is a complete substitute for violence or war. It is designed, therefore, to reach the hearts both of the so-called "terrorists" and the rulers who seek to root out the "terrorists" by emasculating a whole nation. But the indifferent civil resistance of many, grand as it has been in its results, has not touched the hearts of either the "terrorists" or the rulers as a class. Unadulterated *satyagraha* must touch the hearts of both. (Statement to the Press, CW 9137, 4-2-34)

Soul Force More Powerful than Atomic Bombs

I want a *swaraj* in which the millions of illiterates in our country will realize its benefits. You have to cultivate the strength to achieve that. The government under *swaraj* should be such that people may clearly see the distinction between the arbitrary and autocratic British rule and the democratic government run on non-violent lines. I am an optimist. I maintain that once the reins of Government are transferred to us we will realize our responsibilities and all the artificial barriers existing at present will vanish.

My faith in non-violence and truth is being strengthened all the more in spite of the increasing number of atom bombs. I have not a shadow of doubt that there is no power superior to the power of truth and non-violence in the world. See what a great difference there is between the two: one is moral and spiritual force, and is motivated by infinite soul-force; the other is a product of physical and artificial power, which is perishable. The soul is imperishable. When soul-force awakens, it becomes irresistible and conquers the world. This power is inherent in every human being. But one can succeed only if one tries to realize this ideal in each and every act in one's life without being affected in the least by praise or censure. (Talk with Congress Workers, *Biharni Komi Agman,* 217, cited in *MPW,* II, 121, 4-17-47)

SERVICE

Perfection Attained through Service

We rise only by actual service and by taking the risk of making mistakes whilst we are serving. Not one of us is perfect. Not one of us is able to realize the whole of our spiritual ambition. All the same, in the humblest manner possible we have to continue to serve and hope that through that service we may some day realize that ambition. If we all refuse to serve, until we attain perfection, there will be no service. The fact is that perfection is attained through service. (Letter to K. Santanam, SN 19545, 5-11-26)

Boundless Service through the Heart

As I see women and observe their condition in the course of my tours, I think of the tasks before you and realize that real education is of the heart. If pure love springs in it, everything else will be added. The field of service is unlimited. Our capacity for service can also be made boundless, for there is no limit to the strength of the soul. (Letter to Ashram Women, GN 3704, 10-7-29)

Realizing God through Selfless Service

The purpose of life is undoubtedly to know oneself. We cannot do it unless we learn to identify ourselves with all that lives. The sum total of that life is God. Hence the necessity of realizing God living within every one of us. The instrument of this knowledge is boundless selfless service. (A Letter, *Mahadevbhaini Diary*, I, 243, 6-21-32)

Personal service when it merges into universal service is the only service worth doing. (Letter to Amrit Kaur, CW 3706, 7-31-47)

SILENCE

Through Silence Everything Can Be Achieved

Today is my day of silence. Therefore I am not able to speak to you. You must please excuse me. What a good thing is silence! I have personal experience of it. The joy one derives from silence is unique. How good it will be, if everyone observed silence for some time every day! Silence is not for some great men; I know that whatever one person is able to do can be done by everyone, given the effort. There is a saying amongst us that through silence everything can be achieved. There is much truth in this saying. (Speech Read Out at Prayer Meeting, Madras, *The Hindu*, 1-30-46)

SOCIALISM AND COMMUNISM

The Concept of Socialism in the *Bhagavad Gita*

Socialism is a term of the modern age but the concept of socialism is not a new discovery. Lord Krishna preaches the same thing in the *Gita*. One need have in one's possession only what one requires. It means that all men are created by God and therefore entitled to an equal share of food, clothing and housing. It does not require huge organizations for the realization of the ideal. Any individual can set about to realize it. First of all, in order to translate this ideal into our lives we should minimize our needs, keeping in mind the poorest of the poor in India. One should earn just enough to support oneself and one's family. To have a bank balance would thus be incompatible with this ideal. And whatever is earned should be earned with the utmost honesty. Strict restraint has to be kept over small matters in our lives. Even if a single individual enforces this ideal in his life, he is bound to influence others. Wealthy people should act as trustees of their wealth. But if they are robbed of this wealth through violent means, it would not be in the interest of the country. This is known as communism. Moreover, by adopting violent means we would be depriving society of capable individuals. (Talk with Manu Gandhi, *Biharni Komi Agman*, 201-2, 4-15-47)

Establishing Socialism through Constructive Work

I appreciate your desire to bring about equality of living standards in society. I want the same thing. But our first concern should be to come together, think what is in the best interest of the country and set the people to constructive work. Our people have lived in slavery for 150 years and need to be trained for a different way of life now. We shall have to do solid work among the people. Since you look upon me as an adviser and seek my advice of your own free will, I have only one advice to give, and that is that if you wish to establish socialism, there is only one way in which it can be done: go and live among the poor in the villages, live as they live, be one with the village people, work for eight hours daily, use only village-made goods and articles even in your personal lives, remove illiteracy among the village people, eradicate untouchability and uplift the women. Make your life an ideal one in this way; when the people see your transparent lives every minute of the day as clearly as we see pictures on a screen, their influence will be felt throughout the country and reform its life.

Take the village people and slum-dwellers in your hands and give them the benefit of your knowledge, skill, insight, constructive work and patriotic spirit. (Talk with Socialists, *Bihar Pachhi Dilhi*, 14–19, cited in *MPW*, 5-27-47)

The Common Practice of Communists Harms Workers

Hardly one man in a thousand can be found who practices communism in everyday life. Communists have come to consider it their supreme duty, their supreme service, to create disaffection, to generate discontent and to organize strikes. They do not see whom this discontent, these strikes, will ultimately harm. (Talk with Communists, *Dilhiman Gandhiji*, I, 142 10-25-47)

STRIVING

Victory lies in striving. (Letter to Nirmal Chandra Dey, SN 12653a, 12-21-27)

SUFFERING

Purification and Progress through Self-Suffering

No country has ever risen without being purified through the fire of suffering. Mother suffers so that her child may live. The condition of wheat-growing is that the seed grain should perish. Life comes out of Death. Will India rise out of her slavery without fulfilling this eternal law of purification through suffering? Progress is to be measured by the amount of suffering undergone by the sufferer. The purer the suffering, the greater is the progress. Hence did the sacrifice of Jesus suffice to free a sorrowing world. If India wishes to revive her ancient wisdom and to avoid the errors of Europe, if India wishes to see the Kingdom of God established on earth instead of that of Satan which has enveloped Europe, then I would urge her sons and daughters not to be deceived by fine phrases, the terrible subtleties that hedge us in, the fears of suffering that India may have to undergo, but to see what is happening today in Europe and from it understand that we *must* go through the suffering even as Europe has gone through, but not the process of making others suffer. ("The Law of Suffering," *Young India*, 6-16-20)

SWADESHI

Reliance on Our Own Strength through *Satyagraha*

We can easily attain happiness if we exert ourselves to that end during the year that has just commenced. *Swadeshi* carries a great and profound meaning. It does not mean merely the use of what is produced in one's own country. That meaning is certainly there in *swadeshi*. But there is another meaning implied in it which is far greater and much more important. *Swadeshi* means reliance on our own strength. We should also know what we mean by "reliance on our own strength." "Our strength" means the strength of our body, our mind and our soul. From among these, on which should we depend? The answer is brief. The soul is supreme, and therefore soul-force is the foundation on which man must build. Passive resistance or *satyagraha* is a mode of fighting which depends on such force. That, then, is the only real key to success for the Indians. ("New Year," *Indian Opinion*, 1-2-09)

Swadeshi in Religion, Politics and Economics

Swadeshi is that spirit in us which restricts us to the use and service of our immediate surroundings to the exclusion of the more remote. Thus, as for religion, in order to satisfy the requirements of the definition, I must restrict myself to my ancestral religion. That is the use of my immediate religious surroundings. If I find it defective, I should serve it by purging it of its defect. In the domain of politics, I should make use of the indigenous institutions and serve them by curing them of their proved defects. In that of economics, I should use only things that are produced by my immediate neighbours and serve those industries by making them efficient and complete where they might be found wanting. (Speech on *Swadeshi* at Missionary Conference, Madras, *The Hindu*, 2-28-16)

The *Swadeshi* Vow

With God as my witness, I solemnly declare that from today I shall confine myself, for my personal requirements, to the use of cloth manufactured in India from Indian cotton, silk or wool and I shall altogether abstain from using foreign cloth, and I shall destroy all foreign cloth in my possession.

I may add that covenanters to the restricted *swadeshi* referred to here will not rest satisfied with *swadeshi* clothing only. They will extend the vow to all other things as far as possible. ("The *Swadeshi* Vow—II," *The Bombay Chronicle*, 4-18-19)

TRUTH

"Path of Truth for the Brave Alone"

"The path of truth is for the brave alone, never for a coward." I realize the significance of this poem[12] more and more as days pass. I also see that it is not for grown-ups only to put the idea of this verse into practice; children and students, too, can do so. If we try to know and follow the path of truth right from childhood, then alone, on growing up, shall we be saved from following the path of untruth. Just as a disease, if neglected, becomes chronic and incurable, so also untruth, if permitted to take root in us from childhood, will later grow into a serious disease and, becoming incurable, gradually ruin our health. It is for this reason that we find untruth increasing in us.

So the highest lesson to be learnt during one's student-life is that one should know truth and act on it.

This path has always been for the brave because a much greater effort is required to go up the steep slope of truth than to climb the Himalayas. If at all, therefore, we want to work in this direction and serve ourselves, we should give the first place to truth and march forward with unshakeable faith in it. Truth is God. ("Path of Truth for the Brave Alone," *Madhpudo* [a manuscript magazine of the Ashram School, *Sabarmati*], I, ii, 7-20)

Following Nothing but Truth

Beyond limited truths there is one absolute Truth which is total and all-embracing. But it is indescribable, because it is God. Or say, rather, God is Truth. All else is unreal and false. Other things, therefore, can be true only in a relative sense.

He, therefore, who understands truth, follows nothing but truth in thought, speech and action, comes to know God and gains the seer's vision of the past, the present and the future. He attains *moksha* though still encased in the physical frame.

If we get one single person, before the 31st of December, who would practice truth to such perfection, *swaraj* should be ours this very day. Some of us are no more than *satya-agrahis* [non-followers of truth], those, in other words, who aspire to follow truth scrupulously, but they hardly succeed in doing so even in the limited sphere of speech. We thus see that observance of the vow of truth is no easy matter. ("What Is Truth?" *Navajivan*, 11-20-21)

Beauty in Truth

All true Art must help the soul to realize its inner self. In my own case, I find that I can do entirely without external forms in my soul's realization. I can claim, therefore, that there is truly sufficient Art in my life, though you might not see what you call works of Art about me. My room may have blank walls; and I may even dispense with the roof, so that I may gaze out upon the starry heavens overhead that stretch in an unending expanse of beauty. What conscious Art of man can give me the panoramic scenes that open out before me, when I look up to the sky above with all its shining stars? This, however, does not mean that I refuse to accept the value of productions of Art, generally accepted as such, but only that I personally feel how inadequate these are compared with the eternal symbols of beauty in Nature. These productions of man's Art have their value only so far as they help the soul onward towards self-realization.

I see and find Beauty in Truth or through Truth. All Truths, not merely true ideas, but truthful faces, truthful pictures, or songs, are highly beautiful. People generally fail to see Beauty in Truth, the ordinary man runs away from it and becomes blind to the beauty in it. Whenever men begin to see Beauty in Truth, then true Art will arise.

Truth is the first thing to be sought for, and Beauty and Goodness will then be added unto you. Jesus was, to my mind, a supreme artist, because he saw and expressed Truth; and so was Mohammed, the Koran being the most perfect composition in all Arabic literature—at any rate—that is what scholars say. It is because both of them strove first for Truth, that the grace of expression naturally came in; and yet neither Jesus nor Mohammed wrote on Art. That is the Truth and Beauty I crave for, live for, and would die for. (Discussion with G. Ramachandran, *Young India*, 11-13-24, 11-20-24)

Truth Not Simple

Truth is not so simple as it appears to you. You know the story of the elephant and seven blind men who actually touch him. They all touched him at different parts. Their descriptions therefore differed from one another. They were all true from their own points of view and yet each appeared to be untrue from the points of view of the rest. The truth was beyond all the seven. We are all, you will perhaps agree, in the position of these seven sincere observers. And we are blind as they were blind. We must therefore be content with believing the truth as it appears to us. (Letter to Mrs. R. Armstrong and Mrs. P. R. Howard, SN 10779, 7-9-26)

Cultivating Humility in the Pursuit of Truth

My message to Christians would be to cultivate humility instead of arrogating to themselves the exclusive possession of absolute truth. The only way I know of bringing about better understanding between different peoples is to treat all as of ourselves. (Letter to Allen Melton, SN, 15239, 9-14-29)

God as Truth, Knowledge, and Bliss

The word *satya* is derived from *sat*, which means that which is. *Satya* means a state of being. Nothing is or exists in reality except Truth. That is why *sat* or *satya* is the right name for God. In fact it is more correct to say that Truth is God than to say that God is Truth. But as we cannot do without a ruler or general, the name God is and will remain more current.

And where there is Truth, there also is knowledge which is true. Where there is no Truth, there can be no true knowledge. That is why the word *chit* or knowledge is associated with the name of God. And where there is true knowledge, there is always *ananda*, bliss. There sorrow has no place. And even as Truth is eternal, so is the bliss derived from it. Hence we know God as *Sat-chit-ananda*, one who combines in Himself Truth, knowledge and bliss. (Letter to Narandas Gandhi, MMU, I, 7-22-30)

Truth Is God

We believe—and I think it is the truth—that God has as many names as there are creatures and, therefore, we also say that God is nameless and since God has many forms we also consider him formless, and since he speaks to me through many tongues we consider him to be speechless and so on. And so when I came to study Islam, I found that Islam too had many names, but I had not come to recognize God for my personal satisfaction as Truth. I would say for those who say God is love, God is love. But deep down in me I say God may be love, but God is Truth. If it is possible for the human tongue to give the fullest description of God, for myself I have come to the conclusion that God is Truth. But two years ago I went a step further and said Truth is God.

Seeing that the human mind works through innumerable media and that evolution of the human mind is not the same for all, it follows that what may be truth for one may be untruth for another and hence those who have made these experiments have come to the conclusion that there are certain conditions to making experiments. Just as for science there is an indispensable course common for all, even so it is true for persons who would make experiments in the spiritual realm—they must submit to certain conditions. And since everybody says it is his inner voice which speaks, you must listen to the voice, and you will then find out your limitations as you go along the path. Therefore, we have the belief based upon uninterrupted experience that those who would make diligent search after Truth—God—must go through these vows: the vow of truth-speaking and thinking of truth, the vow of *brahmacharya*, of non-violence, poverty and non-possession. If you do not take these five vows you may not embark on the experiment. There are several other things which were prescribed, but I must not take you through all those. But those who have made these experiments know that it is not proper for everyone to claim to hear the voice of conscience and it is because we have at the present moment everybody claiming the right of conscience without going through any discipline whatsoever that there is so much untruth being delivered to a bewildered world. All therefore that I can in all humility present to you is that Truth is not to be found by anybody who has not got an abundant sense of humility. If you would swim on the bosom of the ocean of Truth, you must reduce yourself to a zero. Further than this I may not tonight go along this fascinating path. (Speech at a Meeting in Lausanne, *Mahadev Desai's Diary*, 12-8-31)

Truth Holds the Universe Together

Do you remember my definition of God? Instead of saying that God is Truth, I say that Truth is God. I did not always think thus. I realized this only four years ago. But without knowing it I always acted as if it was so. I have always known God as Truth. There was a time when I doubted the existence of God, but even at that time I did not doubt the existence of Truth. This Truth is not a material quality but is pure consciousness. That alone holds the universe together. It is God because it rules the whole universe. If you follow this idea, it contains the answer to all your questions. If you have any difficulty, however, put your question to me. For me this is almost a matter of direct experience. I say "almost" because I have not seen face to face God Who is Truth. I have had only a glimpse of Him. But my faith is unshakeable. (Letter to Boys and Girls, *Mahadevbhaini Diary*, I, 27, 3-21-32)

An Increasingly Clearer Vision of Truth

The *atman* dwelling in a body is imprisoned in it like the air in a jar, and, as that air cannot use its natural power so long as it believes itself unconnected with the air outside, so the *atman* imprisoned in a body remains cut off from the power of omnipotent God so long as it believes itself the doer of things. For this reason, too, it is only when we say that everything which happens is done by God that we speak the perfect truth as befits a *satya-grahi*. The desires of a votary of truth are good and, therefore, they are al-ways fulfilled.

The world is not separate from us or we from the world. All are connected with one another in their inmost essence and the actions of each have effects on all others. Actions here include thoughts also. Hence not a single thought is without its effect. That is why we must cultivate the habit of thinking good thoughts.

By regarding Truth as God, we save ourselves from many a pitfall. We no longer desire to see miracles or hear about them. We may find difficulty in understanding what "seeing God" means; there can be no difficulty in un-derstanding the meaning of "seeing Truth." Seeing Truth may itself be diffi-cult, it is so. But as we go nearer and nearer towards It, we can have an in-creasingly clearer vision of Truth that is God, and that strengthens our hope and faith that one day we shall have a full vision of It. (Letter to Purushottam Gandhi, *Mahadevbhaini Diary*, I, 106–7, 4-18-32)

Examining One's Behavior Daily to Overcome Shortcomings

If we follow truth today in solving the problems which confront us in our daily life, we shall know instinctively how to act in difficult situations when they arise. Each of us should examine only himself or herself from this point of view. Do I deceive anybody knowingly? If I believe that B is a bad person but show him that I believe him to be good, I deceive him. Do I try to show, in order to win people's respect or esteem, that I possess certain virtues which in fact I do not possess? Do I exaggerate in my speech? Do I hide my misdeeds from persons to whom I should confess them? If a superior or co-worker puts me any question, do I evade him? Do I keep back what I ought to declare? If I do any of these things, I am guilty of untruth. Everybody should examine his conduct daily in this manner and try to overcome his shortcomings. One to whom truth has become second nature and who has risen to a state so that he can never speak untruth may not do this. But everyone who has the least trace of untruth in him or who can follow truth only with effort should examine him-self daily as explained above and put to himself those or any other similar questions which may occur to him and reply to them. Anybody who follows this practice even for a month will clearly observe a change having taken place in himself. ("How to Observe Truth," MMU, II, 7-3-32)

Experiments in Truth Led to Method of Nonviolence

Without any elaborate scheme I have simply tried in my own way to apply the eternal principles of truth and non-violence to our daily life and problems.

Like a child I did whatever occurred to me on the spur of the moment during the course of events.

Then I realized that what I was doing were experiments in truth. In doing so I have sometimes erred and learnt by my errors. Life has thus become for me a series of experiments in truth. In my pursuit of truth I came across the method of non-violence. (Speech at Gandhi Seva Sangh Meeting—III, *Gandhi Seva Sanghke Divitiya Adhiveshan*, 50, 3-3-36)

Growing from Truth to Truth

At the time of writing I never think of what I have said before. My aim is not to be consistent with my previous statements on a given question, but to be consistent with truth as it may present itself to me at a given moment. The result has been that I have grown from truth to truth; I have saved my memory and undue strain; and what is more, whenever I have been obliged to compare my writing even of fifty years ago with the latest, I have discovered no inconsistency between the two. ("Conundrums," *Harijan*, 9-30-39)

Contrasting Absolute and Relative Truth

I write the truth as I personally see it. Absolute truth alone is God. It is beyond reach. At the most we can say it is *neti, neti* [not this, not this]. The truth that we see is relative, many-sided, plural and is the whole truth for a given time. There is no scope for vanity in it and the only way of reaching it is through *ahimsa*. Pure and absolute truth should be our ideal. We can reach the ideal by constantly meditating on it, and reaching it is attaining *moksha*. (Letter to Vamanrao Joshi, *Pyarelal Papers*, 11-7-45)

VOLUNTARY POVERTY

Voluntary Poverty Leads to Fuller Service to Others

I came definitely to the conclusion that, if I had to serve the people in whose midst my life was cast and of whose difficulties I was witness from day to day, I must discard all wealth, all possessions.

And now, as I recall those days of struggle, I remember that it was also painful in the beginning. But, as days went by, I saw that I had to throw overboard many other things which I used to consider as mine, and a time came when it became a matter of positive joy to give up those things. And one after another then, by almost geometric progression, the things slipped away from me. And, as I am describing my experiences, I can say a great burden fell off my shoulders, and I felt that I could now walk with ease and do my work also in the service of my fellowmen with great comfort and still greater joy. (Speech at Guildhouse Church, *The Guildhouse*, 9-23-31)

VOWS

Vows Strengthen Power of Will

If we resolve to do a thing, and are ready even to sacrifice our lives in the process, we are said to have taken a vow. It is essential for every person to train himself to keep such vows; one can strengthen one's power of will by doing so and fit oneself for greater tasks. One may take easy and simple vows to start with and follow them with more difficult ones. We shall find several examples in history of men undergoing great suffering for the sake of a pledge. To embrace *satyagraha* amounts to taking a great vow. ("Importance of Vows," *Indian Opinion*, 10-8-13)

Never Abandon a Vow

A vow serves the same purpose as a lighthouse does. If we keep our eyes fixed on it, we shall come safe through any storm. The lighthouse itself cannot quieten the storm, yet it guides sailors caught in a storm and helps them to fight it, even so a vow is a kind of powerful force which saves a human being from the innumerable waves raging in the heart.

There are many who do not mind risking their lives merely to be able to see a lifeless spot like the North Pole. Why should we, then, wonder or be unhappy if we have to put in a thousand times more difficult effort in order to conquer our powerful foes such as anger, malice and so on. Our success lies in the very struggle for this deathless glory. The effort itself is victory. If those who sail to the North Pole fail in their object, their effort may be considered to have been wasted, but every effort we make in our life to conquer these foes, attachment and aversion, will have taken us forward. Thus, no effort, however slight, towards such an end is ever wasted—that is the Lord's assurance.[13]

The only encouragement, therefore, which I can give this student is that he should go on striving and never lose heart. He should never abandon the vow. He should banish from his dictionary the word "impossible." If he forgets his vow at any time, he should do *prayaschitta*[14] and remind himself of the vow. Every time he violates it, he should start again, and have complete confidence that he is bound at last to succeed. No man of spiritual illumination has ever told us of his experience that untruth had ever triumphed; on the contrary, every such person has unanimously proclaimed most emphatically his experience that in the end truth triumphs. We should keep the experience of these persons in mind, and entertain no doubts of any kind when striving for a good end or be afraid to take a vow with a virtuous aim. Pandit Rambhuj Datt Chaudhari has left us a poem in Punjabi with the following refrain: "Never accept defeat, though you lose your life." ("Significance of Vows," *Navajivan*, 8-1-26)

The Sanctity of the Pledged Word

Being accustomed from very childhood to taking vows I confess I have a strong bias in favour of the practice. A vow imparts stability, ballast and firmness to one's character. What reliance can be placed on a person who lacks these essential qualities? An agreement is nothing but a mutual interchange of vows; simultaneously one enters into a pledge when one gives one's word to another. In old days, the word of mouth of illustrious persons was regarded as good as a bond. They concluded transactions involving millions by oral agreements. In fact our entire social fabric rests on the sanctity of the pledged word. ("The Efficacy of Vows," *Navajivan*, 8-11-29)

WAR

The Prolonged Torture of Economic War

The cry for peace will be a cry in the wilderness, so long as the spirit of non-violence does not dominate millions of men and women.

An armed conflict between nations horrifies us. But the economic war is no better than an armed conflict. This [armed conflict] is like a surgical operation. An economic war is prolonged torture. And its ravages are no less terrible than those depicted in the literature on war properly so called. We think nothing of the other because we are used to its deadly effects.

The movement against war is sound. I pray for its success. But I cannot help the gnawing fear that the movement will fail, if it does not touch the root of all evil—man's greed.

Will America, England and the other great nations of the West continue to exploit the so-called weaker or uncivilized races and hope to attain peace that the whole world is pining for? Or will Americans continue to prey upon one another, have commercial rivalries and yet expect to dictate peace to the world? Not till the spirit is changed can the form be altered. The form is merely an expression of the spirit within. ("Non-Violence—The Greatest Force," *The Hindu*, 11-8-26)

Support of Earlier Wars due to His Belief in British Empire

Q. In South Africa you supported an alien Government in its war against the Boers, although it was at that time oppressing the Indians; again in 1914 you supported the British Government in its War against Germany. How is the situation altered since then that you should refuse to support your own country in a war of independence?

A. The situation today is radically different for me from what it was at the time of the Boer War or the War in 1914. On both the occasions I was a believer in the Empire. I thought that in spite of its lapses the sum total of its activity was beneficial to the world. And though I was against war at that time as I am now, I had no status or strength to refuse to participate in war. I suppressed my private judgment in favour of the duty of an ordinary citizen. My position is wholly different now. I have become by force of circumstances a teacher of non-violence. I claim to enforce my teaching in my own life to the best of my ability and I feel that I have the strength to resist war in my own person. (Interview at Nagpur Station, *Young India*, 1-10-29)

WOMEN AND MEN

Men and Women Cultivating the Best in Themselves

My ideal is this: A man should remain man and yet should become woman; similarly a woman should remain woman and yet become man. This means that man should cultivate the gentleness and the discrimination of woman; and woman should cast off her timidity and become brave and courageous.

Both man and woman can become fearless. Man thinks that he can be fearless, but it is not always true; similarly, woman thinks she is weak and allows herself to be called so; this too is not right. Women have no need at all for fear.

Only the self can raise the self; the self is the help of the self. Only women can raise women. This requires *tapascharya* and hard work. It is true that women are more capable of it than men; but the *tapascharya* must be intelligent. Today women merely toil on in a helpless condition like drudges.

It may be agreed that no one can save woman except herself. But it may be · asked, "Can she be self-supporting?," My heart says that she can. If she learns *satyagraha*, she can be perfectly independent and self-supporting. She will not have to feel dependent upon anyone. This does not mean that she shall not take any help from others. She will certainly. But if such help be not forthcoming she will not feel destitute. If we are detached, even while we use the articles which we receive, we are self-dependent. ("Talks with Ashram Women," *Bapuna Patro—Ashramni Behnone*, 1926, cited in *MPW*, 391, 394)

Woman and Man, One in Soul, Different in Vocation

My own opinion is that, just as fundamentally man and woman are one, their problem must be one in essence. The soul in both is the same. The two live the same life, have the same feelings. Each is a complement of the other. The one cannot live without the other's active help.

But somehow or other man has dominated woman from ages past, and so woman has developed an inferiority complex. She has believed in the truth of man's interested teaching that she is inferior to him. But the seers among men have recognized her equal status.

Nevertheless, there is no doubt that at some point there is bifurcation. Whilst both are fundamentally one, it is also equally true that in the form there is a vital difference between the two. Hence the vocations of the two must also be different.

The division of the spheres of work being recognized, the general qualities and culture required are practically the same for both the sexes.

I have suggested in these columns that woman is the incarnation of *ahimsa*. *Ahimsa* means infinite love, which again means infinite capacity for suffering. Who but woman, the mother of man, shows this capacity in the largest measure? ("What Is Woman's Role?" *Harijan*, 2-24-40)

Women's Marvelous Power—Non-Violence—Lying Dormant

If only the women of the world would come together they could display such heroic non-violence as to kick away the atom bomb like a mere ball. Women have been so gifted by God. If an ancestral treasure lying buried in a corner of the house unknown to the members of the family were suddenly discovered, what a celebration it would occasion. Similarly, women's marvellous power is lying dormant. If the women of Asia wake up, they will dazzle the world. My experiment in non-violence would be instantly successful if I could secure women's help. ("Message to Chinese Women," *Bihar Pachhi Dilhi*, 354, 7-18-47)

GANDHI'S REFLECTIONS IN THE LAST MONTHS OF HIS LIFE

Agony over the Partition of India

The purity of my *yajna* will be put to the test only now. Today I find myself all alone. I see clearly that we are setting about this business the wrong way. We may not feel the full effect immediately, but I can see clearly that the future of independence gained at this price is going to be dark. I pray that God may not keep me alive to witness it.

People now ask me to retire to Kashi or go to the Himalayas. I laugh and tell them that the Himalayas of my penance are where there is misery to be alleviated, oppression to be relieved. There can be no rest for me so long as there is a single person in India whether man or woman, young or old, lacking the necessaries of life, by which I mean a sense of security, a life style worthy of human beings, i.e., clothing, education, food and shelter of a decent standard.

I shall perhaps not be alive to witness it, but should the evil I apprehend overtake India and her independence be imperiled, let posterity know what agony this old man went through thinking of it. Let not the coming generations curse Gandhi for being a party to India's vivisection. (Talk with Manu Gandhi, *Bihar Pachhi Dilhi*, 50-52, 6-1-47)

India's *Satyagraha* the Non-Violence of the Weak, Not of the Strong

I would love to attempt an answer to a question which has been addressed to me from more than one quarter of the globe. It is:

How can you account for the growing violence among your people on the part of political parties for the furtherance of political ends? Is this the result of the thirty years of non-violent practice for ending British rule? Does your message of non-violence still hold good for the world? I have condensed the sentiments of my correspondents in my own language.

In answer I must confess my bankruptcy, not that of non-violence. I have already said that the non-violence that was offered during the past thirty years was that of the weak. India has no experience of the non-violence of the strong. It serves no purpose for me to continue to repeat that the non-violence of the strong is the strongest force in the world. The truth requires constant and extensive demonstration. What if the best of my ability is very little? May I not be living in a fool's paradise? Why should I ask people to follow me in the fruitless search? These are pertinent questions. My answer is quite simple. I ask nobody to follow me. Everyone should follow his or her own inner voice. If he or she has no ears to listen to it, he or she should do the best he or she can. In no case should he or she imitate others sheep-like. ("Non-Violence," *Harijan*, 6-29-47)

India's Freedom Won by Passive Resistance

Some people ask me if what has happened and what is happening and the Dominion Status[15] that we are about to get will lead to *Ramarajya*.

What has come about cannot lead to *Ramarajya* or the Kingdom of God. Today I look around and find *Ramarajya* nowhere.

People ask me if the rule of the sword and the bullet that prevails today is not the result of my teaching of truth and non-violence for thirty-two years. But does this then mean that for thirty-two years I have prevailed through lies and hypocrisy? Does it mean that the millions of people who imbibed the lesson of *ahimsa* from me have after thirty-two years suddenly become liars and murderers? I have admitted that our *ahimsa* was the *ahimsa* of the weak. But in reality weakness and *ahimsa* cannot go together. It should therefore be described not as *ahimsa* but as passive resistance. But the *ahimsa* I advocated was not the *ahimsa* of the weak while passive resistance is only for the weak. Then passive resistance is a preparation for active and armed resistance. As a result the violence the people had been harbouring in their hearts has now suddenly erupted.

Our passive resistance has not been a complete failure. We have all but won our freedom. The violence we see today is the violence of cowards. There is also such a thing as the violence of the brave. If four or five men enter into a fight and die by the sword, there is violence in it but it is the violence of the brave. But when ten thousand armed men attack a village of unarmed people and slaughter them along with their wives and children it is the violence of cowards. America unleashed its atom bomb over Japan. That was the violence of the cowards. The non-violence of the brave is a thing worth seeing. I want to see that non-violence before I die. For this we should have inner strength. It is a unique weapon. If people had realized its beauty, all the life and property that have been lost would never have been lost. (Speech at Prayer Meeting, *Prarthana Pravachan*, I, 217–20, 7-4-47)

Gandhi's Talisman

I will give you a talisman. Whenever you are in doubt, or when the self becomes too much with you, apply the following test. Recall the face of the poorest and the weakest man whom you may have seen, and ask yourself if the step you contemplate is going to be of any use to him. Will he gain anything by it? Will it restore him to a control over his own life and destiny? In other words, will it lead to *swaraj* for the hungry and spiritually starving millions?

Then you will find your doubts and yourself melting away. ("A Note," *Mahatma*, VIII, 89, 8-47)

Gandhi's "Last Will and Testament," his Proposal to Transform the Indian National Congress into an Organization Dedicated to the Constructive Programme

Though split into two, India having attained political Independence through means devised by the Indian National Congress, the Congress in its present shape and form, i.e., as a propaganda vehicle and parliamentary machine, has outlived its use. India has still to attain social, moral and economic independence in terms of its seven hundred thousand villages as distinguished from its cities and towns. The struggle for the ascendency of civil over military power is bound to take place in India's progress towards its democratic goal. It must be kept out of unhealthy competition with political parties and communal bodies. For these and other similar reasons, the A.I.C.C.[16] resolves to disband the existing Congress organization and flower into a Lok Sevak Sangh.[17] ("His Last Will and Testament," *Harijan*, 1-29-48)

NOTES

1. Guru Nanak was the founder of Sikhism; Kabir, a poet and sage, sought to bring Hinduism and Islam together; Chaitanya was a Hindu saint; Shankara, a philosopher and ascetic, developed *Advaita* Vedanta Hinduism; Dayanand was a great Hindu reformer; Ramkrishna was a nineteenth-century sage who taught universal brotherhood.
2. Gujarat Vidyapith, an institution of higher learning founded by Gandhi
3. Teacher or spiritual guide
4. A Hindu sage, author of the *Yoga Sutra*
5. Those who have renounced the world
6. Tens of millions
7. Pure, harmonious
8. General Reginald Dyer ordered the massacre in Amritsar April 13, 1919.
9. Conference where the Charter of the United Nations was adopted
10. G. K. Gokhale, a strong advocate of home rule in India, Gandhi's "political guru"
11. Jalaluddin Rumi, Muslim poet and sage
12. Poem by eighteenth-century Gujarati poet Pritamdas
13. *Bhagavad Gita*, II, 40
14. Atonement
15. On 7-15-47, India and Pakistan would become independent nations, dominions associated with the British Empire, free to terminate this association if they chose.
16. A.I.C.C., All-India Congress Committee
17. Lok Savak Sangh, Servants of the People

III

WRITINGS ABOUT GANDHI— PART A: GANDHI'S PRACTICE AND THEORY OF *SATYAGRAHA*

8

The Birth of Gandhian *Satyagraha:* Nonviolent Resistance and Soul Force

Michael W. Sonnleitner

In early January 1908, birth was given to a revolutionary new concept.[1] For the last forty years of his life Mohandas K. Gandhi would use "*satyagraha*" to describe the nonviolent action approach he first developed in South Africa (1908–1914) and then applied to his homeland of India (1915–1948). His *satyagraha* campaigns would eventually inspire social change activists throughout the world, including such leaders as Vinoba Bhave in India, Danilo Dolci in Sicily, Dom Helder Camera in Brazil, and Martin Luther King, Jr., in the United States. Yet even as the historical importance of *satyagraha* has been widely discussed, the environmental context in which the concept was created has not been well examined. As a result, analyses of the term frequently fail to convey the depth the concept deserves.[2]

This essay should serve to clarify the meaning of *satyagraha* even as the political and personal contexts out of which it emerged are explored. These efforts help to explain why Gandhi's opinions regarding the rule of law and coercion in promoting social change underwent a radical transformation as he formulated the concept of *satyagraha*. Although important ramifications of the analysis can hardly be examined at length here, it is hoped that the improved understanding of *satyagraha* that emerges may spark others to conduct research in areas too briefly mentioned.

THE CONCEPT OF *SATYAGRAHA*

The birth of *satyagraha* as a concept was announced in a newsletter Gandhi wrote before January 10, 1908 and published in *Indian Opinion* on January 11. Gandhi had invited readers to participate in a contest for suggesting a Gujarati language counterpart to "passive resistance." Maganlal Gandhi, second son of

.ushalchand Gandhi (a cousin of Mohandas), proposed "sadagraha"—which can be roughly translated as "firmness in deeds for a good cause." Even as he gave the prize to Maganlal, however, Gandhi announced his conclusion that *satyagraha* was better than the external deeds emphasis of *sadagraha*.[3]

Joan V. Bondurant correctly translates *satyagraha* as literally "holding firm to truth."[4] Moreover, Gandhi wrote that "Truth (*satya*) implies love and firmness (*agraha*) engenders and therefore serves as a synonym for force."[5] This logic led him to use the terms "truth force" and "love force" interchangeably—a practice which has deep religious significance due to Gandhi's views that "Truth is God" and "Where love is, there God is also."[6] When, in this context, it is understood that Gandhi also equated God with the Supreme *Atman* (Soul), which we are all equally a part of, it becomes understandable how Gandhian *satyagraha* also becomes synonymous with "soul force."[7] When it is further recognized that the Sanskrit "*Sat*" also means "Is" or "Being," the metaphysical importance of *satyagraha* becomes apparent since, in effect, it can be translated as holding firm to that which ultimately is—the soul of a thing that partakes of God.[8]

While the metaphysical/theological analysis of Gandhi's views could be examined in greater detail,[9] the purpose here is better served by allowing Gandhi to elaborate upon his *satyagraha* concept himself and one of its most crucial ramifications: "Satyagraha is soul force pure and simple, and whenever and to whatever extent there is room for the use of arms or physical force, there and to that extent is there so much less possibility for soul force. These are purely antagonistic forces in my view, and I had full realization of this antagonism even at the advent of Satyagraha."[10]

The sweeping scope of Gandhi's denunciation of physical force, consistent in his writings after 1908, is somewhat moderated by his Hindu hierarchical perspective in which one looks at things as undergoing degrees of development. The use of the word "extent" in the statement quoted above serves to reflect Gandhi's view that degrees of physical force will be an inherent aspect of any political action. Nevertheless, any coercive element should be minimized. If "coercion" is defined as force which makes a being act contrary to its own will and in accordance with the will of another, Gandhi clearly came to disfavor it. It was his conclusion that "To use brute force, to use gunpowder, is contrary to satyagraha for it means that we want our opponents to do by force that which we desire but he does not. And if such a use of force is justifiable, surely he is entitled to do likewise to us. And so we should never come to an agreement."[11]

Coercion is rejected in principle, in other words, because a kind of categorical imperative required Gandhi to grant the same prerogatives to others as he would grant to himself. In addition, the *satyagraha* objective of attaining to agreement—being open to progressively improved visions of what is true in a situation—would be sacrificed. Thus Gandhi's frequent admission that all human views of Absolute Truth are necessarily incomplete, relative, and therefore (to that extent) false, draws him to conclude that nonviolence including noncoercion is the only way to promote the communication necessary for the learning process to continue.[12]

The concrete ramifications of Gandhi's noncoercion position are substantial. A short time after the birth of *satyagraha*, for example, he wrote in *Hind Swaraj* how law is another form of the exhibition of brute force and should not be enforced against public opinion.[13] By late in 1909 Gandhi announced that no future appeals would be made to the British Crown for legal enforcement of the rights of British Indian subjects in South Africa.[14] He even went beyond his advice to people to settle their quarrels out of court and in 1910 ended his own career as a lawyer. As Gandhi wrote to one of his political opponents in 1910, it had become his position that "The function of violence is to obtain reform by external means; the function of soul force is to obtain it by growth from within which, in its turn, is obtained by self-suffering, self-purification."[15]

By 1910, therefore, Gandhi had evolved a faith in the reality of a nonphysical force which, with a requisite willingness to undergo suffering, could prompt his opponents to "see the error of their ways and cease to harass us by trying to impose their will on us."[16] In an attempt to help explain how Gandhi came to hold such an unusual perspective, it may now be useful to analyze the context in which the concept of *satyagraha* was formulated. As will become quickly apparent, Gandhi's pre-*satyagraha* thinking included a primary reliance upon physical force and law enforcement as a means of pursuing political ends. How this came to change will become part of the focus for analysis.

PRE-*SATYAGRAHA* CONTEXT

While representing South African Indians on a deputation to London in 1906, Gandhi told the British secretary of state for India that "I do think the Government ought to protect those who are voteless, and not merely in a haphazard way, but *that protection ought to be a* real force, and we look to you, sir, as our advocate and trustee, to give us the protection we are entitled to."[17] Such an appeal by Gandhi was consistent with his actions prior to the formulation of "*satyagraha*" as a concept. As early as 1894 Gandhi had appealed to the British to disallow a legislative move by whites in Natal to disenfranchise the few Asians there entitled to vote.[18] Later he had complained about laws prohibiting Indians from walking along designated footpaths, preventing them from traveling either first or second class on the railways, and making them liable to arrest for being out of their homes without a pass after nine o'clock at night.[19] Gandhi knew that as long as he lived in British South Africa, the government in London had veto power to void any law which ran contrary to the rights of non-white British citizens of the Empire.

According to the Charter of 1833 and the Proclamation of 1858, all Indians were guaranteed the same rights and privileges enjoyed by His Majesty's other subjects. These guarantees were strengthened by assurances made to the Indian community in Article 26 of the Pretoria Convention of 1881 and in Article 14 of the London Convention of 1884. Indeed, there was a long-standing dispute between the government in Britain and those in South Africa as to whether or not the apartheid Law 3 of 1885 contravened these conventions.[20] Law 3 of 1885, which provided for legal segregation of all business and living facilities owned by nonwhites, was thus not systematically implemented with regards to Indians until well after the Boer War (1899–1902).

During the Boer War (1899–1902) the Indian community hoped to bargain with its loyalty for increased protection by the British government. At the end of the war, however, the position of the British Indian citizen remained obscure. Article 39a of the New Transvaal Constitution, for example, required any disability to be borne by "Europeans and non-Europeans alike" even though Law 3 of 1885 was *not* removed from the statute books.[21] After the war Gandhi continued to make his appeals for physical protection even as the fears of the white South African (of being outnumbered and outcompeted by Indian businesspeople) grew in intensity. These fears were well-reflected in a letter mailed to a prominent Natal politician in late 1906 by Jan Smuts, Gandhi's future adversary in the Transvaal Government. It was Smuts' feeling that "The Asiatic cancer, which has already eaten so deeply into the vitals of South Africa, ought to be resolutely eradicated."[22]

As a primary means of eradicating the alleged Indian threat, the Crown Colony of the Transvaal passed the Asiatic Law Amendment Ordinance No. 29 on September 20, 1906. Among other things, that law provided for compulsory registration (including humiliating fingerprints) of all Asian males above the age of eight. It also stipulated that the only Indians who could remain in the Transvaal were those who were lawfully resident there prior to May 31, 1902 (the end of the Boer War). Those who could remain under the new Ordinance, moreover, were to become subject to a systematically enforced Law of 1885. Accordingly, those who were not subject to deportation under the 1906 Ordinance could be forced out of business and thus encouraged to return to India through astute manipulations of the segregation statute.

Using words which described the Ordinance as a "Black Act," Gandhi requested the *active intervention* of the secretary of state for the Colonies, the secretary of state for India, and the viceroy of India.[23] In addition, on September 11, 1906, Gandhi led an Indian mass meeting to take the famous pledge of Resolution IV. The pledge called upon its adherents to submit to repeated imprisonment "until it shall please His Most Gracious Majesty the King-Emperor to grant relief."[24] No doubt it was to Gandhi's very pleasant surprise that the British Government, in fact, disallowed (vetoed) the Black Act on December 3, 1906.

The Indians' elation in South Africa was short-lived. On December 6, 1906, the former Crown Colony of the Transvaal was granted a new status as Self-Governing Colony. Rule from London would henceforth be more indirect, with a greater predisposition to allow colonial ordinances to stand according to the will of local legislatures. On March 22, 1907, the Ordinance of 1906 was exactly replicated in the Asiatic Registration Act which passed through the Transvaal parliament. The Liberal Party then in power in Britain refused to listen to the Conservative opposition of those like Lords Ampthill and Curzon and gave approval to the new law on May 9, 1907. Thus it was that the British "sacrificed Indian interest on the altar of Anglo-Africaner reconciliation."[25]

As it became clear that the Black Act would become law, a revolutionary new Gandhi began to emerge. On May 11, 1907, he announced to the world that "We will not submit to the Act, no matter what relief is granted."[26] The pledge of Resolution IV, taken ten months before, was reaffirmed—but with a difference. The difference is soon reflected in a spiritual emphasis throughout Gandhi's writings. We are told that "God protects" those who choose to obey "divine law" and "defy this murderous law."[27] While Gandhi had previously placed his hopes for relief on London, he now declared that "God is the only judge who will redress our grievances."[28]

To say that the granting of Royal Assent to the Black Act was the only factor contributing to Gandhi's increasingly spiritual emphasis, however, would be misleading. Religious experimentation in his own life had already taken the committed paths of voluntary poverty (1905), celibacy (1906), and the renunciation of such worldly protection as is implied in abandoning his life insurance policy (1906). The Royal Assent, therefore, seems to have acted as a prime encouragement for Gandhi to continue developing reliance upon God which had already begun.

Neither royal assent nor Gandhi's increasing faith in God, however, appears adequate to explain the noncoercive emphasis which would soon be a part of the *satyagraha* concept. Indeed, to expect God to redress grievances might merely imply a greater faith in the coercive power of the deity than in that of the state. It is at this point that two major nonreligious thinkers serve to have interacted with Gandhi's emerging views.[29] These two thinkers were the Americans William MacIntyre Salter and Henry David Thoreau. Both Salter's *Ethical Religion* and Thoreau's *An Essay on Civil Disobedience* were approvingly summarized by Gandhi in his *Indian Opinion* newspaper. Gandhi was much taken by Salter's tripartite analysis of actions as immoral, nonmoral, and moral. Immoral actions are those which are done willfully even though the doer knows them to be wrong. Nonmoral actions are those, regardless of consequences, which are more rooted in habit or in fear than in one's own will. Moral actions are distinguished by Salter as reflecting conscious and willful action undertaken for good (meaning unselfish) purposes. The relevance of this to the coercion issue is apparent as we note that Gandhi approvingly quoted Salter: "So long as we act like machines (out of habit), there can be no question of morality. If we want to call an action moral, it should be done consciously and as a matter of duty (out of will). Any action that is dictated by fear, or by coercion of any kind, ceases to be moral."[30]

At a time when Gandhi wanted a basis for calling his actions moral, as opposed to those of the state, he became open to Salter's noncoercion framework. This orientation was reinforced by his interpretation of Thoreau, to whom he introduced his readers in September 1906. It was Gandhi's view that Thoreau's "writings are at present exactly applicable to the Indians in the Transvaal" insofar as "that government is best which governs least" and "law never made a man a whit more just."[31] Forced by historical circumstances to rely upon his own resources, Gandhi thus formed the opinion that it was positively beneficial for people to exercise direction over the course of their own lives. Justice, in this context, would be seen not as a result of the coercive enforcement of legal safeguards but as a by-product of people acting morally according to what they believe to be right.

At this point we can see that a functional definition of *satyagraha* had emerged even before the concept was given birth. Gandhi had, by late 1907, come to believe that moral people must hold firm to (and act upon) their view of what is true at any point in time, allowing for their views to change over time. As a part of this process, coercion was to be minimized, out of respect for the duty of opponents to hold firm to (and act upon) their own view of what is true at any point in time. Rather than coerce others to agree with a particular position, the new concept would aim to compel them to reflect upon their position and thus encourage new positions to develop in a creative dialectical interaction.

On December 27, 1907, Gandhi was arrested for having refused to take out the registration certificate required under the Asiatic Registration Act. Between the time of his arrest and the time of his trial and sentencing (January 10, 1908), Gandhi was freed on bail. It was during this period, and in the context of his thinking as it had evolved by then, that Gandhi conceived of *satyagraha* as the best term to use in describing his nonviolent action approach.

Later, in India, Gandhi elaborated upon the noncoercive intent of *satyagraha*: "When satyagraha is aimed at a wicked government, its concern must not be so much with paralyzing government as with being proof against wickedness. In general, it must not aim at destruction but at construction and deal with causes rather than symptoms."[32]

To be sure, by 1914 Gandhi was well aware of the political side of his new approach as "based upon the immutable maxim that government of the people is possible only so long as they consent either consciously or unconsciously to be governed."[33] Yet it was also his view that people can exercise coercive power over one another only if the other cooperates out of fear or conditioned habit. While the oppressor may be able to kill one's body, in other words, one could deny the ability of the oppressor to make one act contrary to one's own will and in accordance with the will of another. Far from being intentionally coercive, therefore, the civil disobedience which may be used in *satyagraha* Gandhi regarded as "disobedience to untruth," designed to undermine the very basis upon which coercion rests.[34]

Consistent with his do-unto-others as you would have them do-unto-you philosophy, Gandhi ceased to call for coercive assistance from the British in the struggle of Indians in South Africa. Utilizing some of his influential friends in Parliament, for example, he could have sought to make the guarantee of a £5,000,000 loan to the Transvaal in the spring of 1907 contingent upon the alleviation of Indian grievances. He could have continued to urge that the veto be used on newly oppressive legislation like the Immigrants Restriction Act. Ratification of the proposed Union Constitution could have been linked with an insistence upon the removal of Indian disabilities. Indeed, it should be remembered that British troops were garrisoned in South Africa and could have been forced to intervene if Gandhi had acted to escalate the tensions and maximize the coercive resources at his disposal.[35] Instead, Gandhi undertook none of the intentionally coercive options which were open to him.

When the Self-Governing Colonies in South Africa became the independent Union of South Africa on May 31, 1910, Gandhi felt no sadness that his opponents were then legally out from under the imperial thumb. From 1908 and to the end of his life he would declare that "It is with our tried weapon of satyagraha that we are to fight."[36]

IN THE LIGHT OF EXPERIENCE

The analysis of the birth of *satyagraha* could be concluded at this point but for additional considerations which may grant us a deeper understanding of Gandhi's faith in *satyagraha*. Certainly Gandhi's faith was bolstered after the imprisonment of him and two hundred others successfully forced the Transvaal government to negotiate a settlement. Gandhi was released from prison on January 30 after having agreed with Jan Smuts to voluntary registration (and fingerprinting) on condition that the Asian Registration Act would thereafter be repealed. Although this was a victory in the eyes of all who believed the white-dominated Transvaal government might be trusted to fulfill such an agreement, a significant group of militant Indians thought Gandhi had betrayed them. Responding to a threat of death to the first Indian attempting to register, Gandhi declared publicly that he would, himself, be the first to so register.

On February 10, 1908, Gandhi was assaulted by Mir Alam Kham and others as he sought to register in conformity with the Gandhi-Smuts agreement. He was struck with a lead pipe and a wooden stick and kicked, thereby sustaining injuries above the left eye, on the forehead, to the upper lip (and three teeth), as well as to his left-side ribs, knee, and hand.[37] Upon regaining consciousness, Gandhi reportedly asked about his assailants and then requested that no charges be brought against them (noncoercion emphasis).[38] Yet the most remarkable observations associated with this near-death experience were made by Gandhi in an article written in English and printed in *Indian Opinion* on February 22, 1908: "I have grown more fearless after this incident. If I had not regained consciousness, I would not have felt the suffering that I went through later. We can thus see that there is suffering only as long as the soul is in intimate union with the body. I became aware of the suffering only when the soul's union with the body was restored."[39] In the same newspaper issue, Gandhi summarizes the "secret of satyagraha" by observing how "A Satyagrahi enjoys a degree of freedom not possible for others, for he is a truly fearless person. Once his mind is rid of fear, he will never agrée to be another's slave. He who has attained to the satyagraha state of mind will remain ever victorious, at all times and places and under all conditions irrespective of whether it is a government or a people he opposes, whether they be strangers, friends, or relatives."[40]

From the two lengthy quotations just cited we can conclude several things. First, as a result of his near-death experience, Gandhi became more fearless. Second, Gandhi believed that a truly fearless person could not be defeated. Implicitly, at least, there is a third conclusion based on an assumption that fear is based upon fear of pain and suffering: A fearless person is one who becomes aware of the fact that *there is suffering only when the soul is in union with the body.*[41] In other words, after Gandhi's near-death experience he clearly came to believe that the soul is immortally separate and distinct from the body, and that a mental awareness of this fact is somehow related to the capacity for being victorious under all circumstances.[42]

The invincibility of a sufficiently developed *satyagrahi* was concretely elaborated upon by Gandhi in a later newspaper article in which he cites numerous examples of *satyagrahis* in history, including Daniel who, after being caged into the lion's den, was left unharmed by the lions. Indeed, in a letter addressed to Jamnadas Gandhi in 1913, Gandhi claims that "the exercise of the purest soul-force, in its perfect form, brings about instantaneous relief."[43] Although Gandhi never claimed to exercise *satyagraha* (soul force) in its perfect form, the noncoercive powers he claimed for it are quite significant. Indeed, this would be particularly so as Gandhi conceived of Daniel not coercing the lions to peacefulness—but compelling them to so reflect upon their lives as to voluntarily choose to be peaceful!

Precisely what Gandhi's vision of *satyagraha* as soul force was may remain beyond analysis and approach the mystical. Yet it is true that only after the near-death experience of February 10, 1908, does Gandhi begin describing an "all embracing living light" which is "greater than a million suns put together" and "radiates life and light and peace and happiness."[44] This light, which Gandhi claimed was "ever forgiving" and "all loving,"[45] he further identified with the Supreme *Atman* (God) within each of us which, he believed, could communicate to us through a "still small voice within."[46] That this voice from the light within compels reflection in all those whom it touches would, in this context, explain how Gandhi might believe Daniel's lions to have been pacified.[47]

Whatever may be the metaphysical framework through which each of us views reality, it is clear that Gandhi believed in "an undefinable mysterious Power that pervades everything . . . a Living Power" that (after 1908) was beyond dispute.[48] Toward the end of his life, Gandhi would continue to hold firm to a faith in the Living Force of his God, as he observed: "Our life is of that Force. That Force resides in but is not of the body. He who denies the existence of that great Force denies to himself the use of that inexhaustible Power and thus remains impotent."[49]

SATYAGRAHA IN PERSPECTIVE

It has here been shown how the birth of Gandhi's *satyagraha* concept was concurrent with a radical transformation in his ideas regarding the roles of law and coercion in promoting social change. Having compared Gandhi's *satyagraha* views with those enunciated by him prior to 1908, it is clear that Gandhi came to intentionally minimize any reliance upon physical force even as he grew in his faith concerning soul force. That historical developments within the colonial context of South Africa influenced the course of Gandhi's thinking is also clear. In the very least, his disillusionment with the British government after royal assent was granted to the Black Act in 1907 prompted him to consider more seriously the thinking of writers like Salter and Thoreau even as he became more consciously dependent upon God.

Precisely how much of his new concept can be explained in terms of historical events and intellectual influences remains uncertain in the context of his near-death experience of February 10, 1908. While the importance of this experience may remain in dispute, it is nevertheless clear that Gandhi's faith in the existence of "soul" and in the power of "soul force" was reinforced by it.[50] It is also true that Gandhi makes reference to the inner Light of one's soul only after 1908, complete with the illustration of Daniel as one who might reflect that Light in the presence of lions. Regardless of whether Gandhi was correct in his perception of *satyagraha* as soul force, the analysis of his views in this context render his positions with respect to coercion and law more understandable. To physically enforce one's own point of view, after all, becomes quite unnecessary if one may embody the power to force others to so reflect on themselves as to voluntarily admit the error of their ways.

Whether due more to the physical force inherent in a mass movement, or to the soul force that inspired him, Gandhi did emerge victorious in South Africa. After Jan Smuts broke the agreement of 1908, resistance was renewed against the Transvaal government. Eventually the last of the Black Act would be repealed, along with several other causes for grievance, in July 1914.[51] During the nine-year period of resistance activity (1906–1914), well over six thousand Indians had suffered imprisonment and a new concept representing Gandhi's nonviolent approach had been formed. As he prepared to leave South Africa in 1914, Gandhi shared his view that "We did not want to be governed by the Asiatic Act of 1907 of the Transvaal, and it had to go before this mighty force. . . . [We had] thus to draw out and exhibit the force of the soul with us for a period long enough to appeal to the sympathetic cord in the governors as the lawmakers."[52]

Born in the context of South Africa, Gandhian *satyagraha* would later be applied against British rule in India. Throughout the successful India independence movement and thereafter this key concept would be mostly understood on superficial levels, when at all. It is hoped that the analysis presented in this essay will encourage a depth of understanding upon which future research may improve.

172 *Michael W. Sonnleitner*

NOTES

Acknowledgement: Special appreciation is due to the following persons who offered valuable advice in my research for and preparation of this article: Mulford Q. Sibley (former Professor of Political Science, University of Minnesota) and James D. Hunt (Professor of Religion and Philosophy, Shaw University).

1. My dating of the *satyagraha* concept to January of 1908 refers to the formulation of the word itself. (See: *Indian Opinion*, 1-11-08, in *The Collected Works of Mahatma Gandhi* [*CWMG*] (New Delhi: Publication Division, Ministry of Information and Broadcasting, 1958–1994), 8:23. Writing nearly twenty years later, Gandhi described the advent of the idea of *satyagraha*—involving nonviolent resistance—as occurring at a mass meeting on 9-11-06. (See: *Satyagraha in South Africa* [Madras, 1928], 86–93.) For the purposes of the present paper, it is most accurate to cite the 1908 date both because, in 1906, Gandhi was still describing his method as that of "passive resistance" and because *satyagraha*, as later conceived, would clearly depart from the more coercive emphasis that is integral to "passive resistance."

2. Even that scholarship, which may be able to examine the political environment of South Africa (1895–1914) more meticulously than is possible in such a brief essay as this, generally fails to focus on the concept of *satyagraha* as such and thus provides a more superficial understanding of the concept than is here provided. See, for example: P. D. Pillai, "Gandhi in South Africa: The Origin of his Philosophy of Nonviolent Protest," *Dalhousie Review*, 1969, 244–53; Frene M. Ginwala, *Class Consciousness and Control: Indian South Africans, 1860–1946* (Oxford University Ph.D. dissertation, 1974); Maureen Jean Tayal, *Gandhi: The South African Experience* (Oxford University Ph.D. dissertation, 1980); and Maureen Swan, *Gandhi: The South African Experience* (Ohio University Press, 1985).

3. *Indian Opinion*, 1-11-08, in *CWMG*, 8:23.

4. Joan V. Bondurant, *Conquest of Violence: The Gandhian Philosophy of Conflict* (Berkeley: University of California Press, 1971), 16.

5. *Satyagraha in South Africa*, 177.

6. *Indian Opinion*, 2-8-08, in *CWMG*, 8:61. Gandhi elaborated upon this in greater detail in a letter to P. G. Matthew on 7-9-32, in *Harijan*, 3-27-47, and is quoted in Bondurant, *Conquest of Violence*, 19. See also: *Satyagraha in South Africa*, 360.

7. Gandhi describes God as Supreme *Atman* in a letter fragment just after 11-27-11, *CWMG*, 11:189. He declares that "we are part and parcel of the great universal whole" in the famous Registration Burning Speech, 8-16-08, *CWMG*, 8:459. That "all souls have the same attributes" was mentioned in a letter to Maganlal Gandhi, 2-18-13, *CWMG*, 11:437. As further documentation of the fact that Gandhi saw the "same soul" residing in every person see: *Young India*, 9-25-24, in Raghavan Iyer, *The Moral and Political Thought of Mahatma Gandhi* (New York, 1973), 8. Gandhi also reflects the *Advaita Vedantan* analogy of the drop of water and the ocean in *Indian Opinion*, 4-29-14, *CWMG*, 12:412.

8. This conclusion can be substantiated by reading the account in O. P. Dhiman, *Gandhian Philosophy* (Amabala, 1972), 23.

9. Cf. Michael W. Johnson (Johnson was my last name prior to adopting Sonnleitner just prior to my marriage in 1983), *The Roles of Law and Coercion (or Soul Force and Social Change) according to M. K. Gandhi and M. L. King Jr.* (University of Minnesota Ph.D. dissertation, March 1979), ch. 1–3.

10. *Satyagraha in South Africa,* 177.

11. *Hind Swaraj or Indian Home Rule* (Ahmedabad: Navajivan, 1938), 81, originally published in 1909.

12. These conclusions follow from Gandhi's acceptance of the Jain doctrine of *anekantavada* (the manysidedness of truth). See Gandhi in *An Autobiography or the Story of My Experiments with Truth* (Ahmedabad: Navajivan, 1970), and in *CWMG,* 39. Also note the discussions by Erik H. Erikson, *Gandhi's Truth: On the Origins of Militant Nonviolence* (New York: Norton, 1969), 181, and Bondurant, *Conquest of Violence,* 16.

13. *Hind Swaraj,* 78–79.

14. Speech at the Farewell Meeting in London, 11-12-09, *Indian Opinion,* 12-11-09, *CWMG,* 9:543.

15. Letter to W. F. Wybergh, 5-10-10, *Indian Opinion,* 5-21-10, *CWMG,* 10:246–50.

16. *Indian Opinion,* 1-8-10, *CWMG,* 10:121.

17. Interview with Lord Morley, 11-22-06, *CWMG,* 6:212. Similar appeals were made to Lord Elgin, Secretary of State for the Colonies, 11-8-06, *CWMG,* 6:110–12, and to members of the British Parliament, *CWMG,* 6:105. Note: the deputation was sent in opposition to the Asiatic Law Amendment Ordinance and was in London from 10-21-06 to 12-1-06.

18. Petition to Lord Ripon against the Franchise Law Amendment Bill in Natal, 7/1894, *CWMG,* 1:124–27.

19. Interview to *The Statesman,* 11-10-1896, *CWMG,* 2:126–27.

20. Cf. Robert A. Huttenback, *Gandhi in South Africa* (Ithaca, 1971), 102–22.

21. Cf. Benjamin Sacks, *South Africa: An Imperial Dilemma* (Albuquerque, 1967), 225.

22. Quoted by Henry Polak, *Mahatma Gandhi,* 56.

23. Cables sent on 9-8-06, *CWMG,* 5:416. See also *Indian Opinion,* 9-1-06, *CWMG,* 5:404, and *Indian Opinion,* 9-8-06, *CWMG,* 5:411.

24. Johannesburg Mass Meeting, 9-11-06, *Indian Opinion,* 9-15-06, *CWMG,* 5:423.

25. G. B. Pyrah, *Imperial Policy and South Africa: 1902-1910* (Oxford, 1955), 105.

26. *Indian Opinion,* 5-11-06, *CWMG,* 6:471.

27. Cf. *Indian Opinion,* 7-13-07, *CWMG,* 7:97, and *Indian Opinion,* 7-27-07, *CWMG,* 7:121.

28. *Indian Opinion,* 8-24-07, *CWMG,* 7:189.

29. Due to space limitations, analyses of the intellectual influences of Leo Tolstoy, John Ruskin, and others have not been included in this essay. Such influences (primarily prior to 1906) do not have much impact upon Gandhi's perceptions with regards to the role of coercion that is so central to his *satyagraha* concept. The influence of Salter (who has been neglected in the literature) and of Thoreau did occur during the crucial 1907–1911 time frame which, in the context of this essay, makes them more relevant.

30. *Ethical Religion,* 43, in Raghavan Iyer, *Moral and Political Thought,* 64. Iyer goes on to note how, for Gandhi, exploitation and injustice are seen as directly related to "*akrasia,*" or weakness of will, 69. For further reference to Salter, cf. *Indian Opinion,* 1-19-07, in *CWMG,* 6:284-87. Note: Gandhi ran his series of articles on Salter, the founder of the Society for Ethical Culture in Chicago, in *Indian Opinion* between 1-5-07 and 2-23-07.

31. *Indian Opinion,* 9-7-07, *CWMG,* 7:217–18.

32. *Young India,* 12/21, in Iyer, *Moral and Political Thought,* 314.

33. "Golden Number" before 7-11-14, *CWMG,* 12:461.

34. *Indian Opinion*, 3-7-08, *CWMG*, 8:131. Civil disobedience would also be described by Gandhi as "a powerful expression of a soul's anguish," *Young India*, 11-10-21, Bondurant, *Conquest of Violence*, 166; reflected in disciplined action, *Young India*, 8-25-21, *Non-Violent Resistance*, ed. Bharatan Jumerappa (Ahmedabad, 1951), 56; in accordance with what one believes to be the moral law, *Indian Opinion*, 1-26-07, *CWMG*, 7:298–300; when that moral law is transgressed by government, *Satyagraha in South Africa*, 342; with a full willingness of the resister to accept the consequences/punishment prescribed for the action, *Indian Opinion*, 11-27-07, *CWMG*, 9:507, and *Navajivan*, 2-10-29, *CWMG*, 39:443.

35. Sacks, *South Africa*, 180-262.

36. *Indian Opinion*, 7-31-09, *CWMG*, 9:269. It should be noted that Gandhi maintains that his views changed very little after 1909. Cf. Preface, 7-14-38, *Hind Swaraj*, 18. Prominent scholars of Gandhi also agree with this assessment. Cf. Iyer, *Moral and Political Thought*, 9, and Bondurant, *Conquest of Violence*, 8, etc.

37. *Indian Opinion*, 2-22-08, *CWMG*, 13:92–97.

38. *Satyagraha in South Africa*, 154.

39. *Indian Opinion*, 2-22-08, *CWMG*, 13:92–97.

40. *CWMG*, 13:91–92.

41. Cf. *Indian Opinion*, 6/09, Iyer, *Moral and Political Thought*, 291. Note: while Gandhi had faith in reincarnation prior to 2-10-08, he seems willing to emphasize it on an experiential basis only after this point.

42. *Indian Opinion*, 6-5-09, *CWMG*, 9:236. Note: this might have been his view before, but it clearly was after.

43. Letter of 7-2-13, *CWMG*, 9:50.

44. Cf. *Young India*, 2-7-29, 42, *The Mind of Mahatma Gandhi*, ed. R. K. Prabhu and U. R. Rao (Ahmedabad, 1967), 44. Also: *Young India*, 4-18-29, *CWMG*, 9:174.

45. *Young India*, 3-5-25, 81, *CWMG*, 9:50.

46. *Harijan*, 5-6-33, 4, *CWMG*, 9:50.

47. The similarities between Gandhi's description of the near-death experience if compared with accounts documented in Raymond Moody's *Life After Life* (New York, 1975) are astonishing. In particular, see the description of the Being of Light which forces a reflective quality to emerge in all it touches: 58–64.

48. *Young India*, 10-11-28, *The Mind of Mahatma Gandhi*, 47-48.

49. *Harijan*, 7-20-47, *The Mind of Mahatma Gandhi*, 249.

50. It should be recognized, for example, that one could build a persuasive case debunking the argued importance of the near-death experience. After all, if Gandhi had actually had an experience fitting the descriptions of Elizabeth Kübler-Ross, Raymond Moody and others, why did he not quite explicitly and meticulously say so? Unfortunately, perhaps, Gandhi cannot be credited with having publicly shared absolutely everything about himself. As Erik Erikson shows in *Gandhi's Truth*, scholars may need to interpret events and suggest hypotheses to explain why apparent changes have taken place. If Gandhi had clearly revealed everything about himself and the development of his thinking, there would be little need for researchers like myself to write articles about him and his nonviolent approach.

51. Huttenback, *Gandhi in South Africa*, 326–32. As this author elaborates, the plight of Indians in South Africa was not completely alleviated by Gandhi's *satyagraha* successes. Law 3 of 1885 remained on the statute books and the voting franchise was virtually denied in most regions.

52. "Golden Number," before 7-11-14, *CWMG*, 12:461.

9

Gandhian Freedoms and Self-Rule

Anthony J. Parel

Swaraj is a state of being of individuals and nations.[1]

Swaraj is a basic concept of Gandhi's political philosophy. This concept is more basic than is even nonviolence, a concept with which his name is universally associated. There is no question that he made an original contribution to the theory and practice of nonviolence and that the world is grateful to him for it. The fact remains, however, that nonviolence, for all its importance, is only a means to *swaraj*, whereas *swaraj*, according to Gandhi, is "a state of being"—of individuals and of nations.

Gandhi used the concept of *swaraj* in different senses and in different contexts. For purposes of analysis I group these senses under four headings—national independence; political freedom of the individual; economic freedom of the individual; and spiritual freedom of the individual, or self-rule. Of these, the first three, in some respects, are negative in character. Thus national independence is freedom from alien rule; political freedom of the individual is freedom from oppression by other individuals, groups, or the state; and economic freedom of the individual is freedom from poverty. Freedom as self-rule, in contrast, is positive in character. It is a state of being to which everyone, especially those who are politically and economically free, ought to aspire.

As will presently become apparent, Gandhi's concept of *swaraj* is a complex one. There are several reasons for this. We have already referred to the first, which is that it has four distinct aspects. The second reason has to do with his sources, for he drew from both Indian and Western sources. From the Indian sources he derived the all-important notion of self-rule. Almost all of the classical systems of Indian philosophy—the Vedanta and the Yoga systems, for example—deal with the ways and means of attaining self-rule, known also as self-realization, or *moksha*. No matter how strongly committed he was to political and economic freedoms, he never lost sight of the fact that humans, by their destiny, also have the duty to strive for self-rule. And one of the important things he sought to achieve was to find ways and means of harmonizing self-rule with political and economic freedoms.

Western sources supplied Gandhi with the starting points of his notions of independence and political and economic freedoms. And there is good reason for this. Classical Indian political philosophy, being a theory of monarchy, lacked a tradition of political freedom and a notion that people are the repository of power and authority. In India's ancient and medieval past we do not find anything comparable to the democratic tradition of ancient Athens or the republican tradition of ancient Rome. In classical India the king and his entourage alone were thought of as being politically free, while the people were treated as the passive element of the monarchical regime. This was true also of the Islamic political tradition of medieval India. It was only in the nineteenth century that India awoke to the idea that the people, not kings or emperors, were the legitimate source of power and authority. Likewise, both under the Hindu and the Muslim regimes, there was no notion of the political freedom of the individual. This notion, too, entered India in the nineteenth century. The Indian National Congress, from its very inception in 1885, gave this concept formal recognition. And Gandhi in his turn adopted it as part of his own philosophy. His training in London as a lawyer and his later readings and activities both in South Africa and India made him a staunch advocate of national as well as individual freedoms.

The fact that Gandhi derived the notions of political and economic freedoms from the West does not mean that he accepted them without making significant modifications. Indeed, a good deal of his creative thought went into the process of introducing into the Western notions of freedom the elements he selected from Indian thought. Thus, in his hands the notions of national independence and political and economic freedoms of the individual underwent a subtle conceptual transformation. That is to say, notwithstanding the fact that initially he borrowed these ideas from the West, in the end he managed to imprint on each of them a recognizably Gandhian stamp.

Those who are nurtured in only one philosophical tradition will find Gandhi's mixing of ideas taken from East and West rather difficult to follow. If that understandable difficulty is to be overcome, and if they are to derive some moral and intellectual benefits from his thought, they will do well to make an effort to expand their own intellectual horizons. For it is through the mixing of ideas that political philosophies evolve and civilizations change for the better. Speaking in very broad historical terms, I am inclined to see Gandhi as being instrumental in bringing closer together Western and Indian conceptions of freedom, the way, for example, St. Augustine or St. Thomas Aquinas is said to have been instrumental in bringing biblical and classical thought closer together. From the point of view of the idea of freedom, the nineteenth century and early twentieth century were crucial periods for India. For the first time the Indian idea of freedom was placed side by side with the Western idea of political and economic freedom. And no one made a greater contribution to formulating a compound idea from these two concepts than did Mahatma Gandhi.

The third factor that adds complexity to Gandhi's meanings of freedom arises from the languages in which he expressed them—Gujarati and English. He wrote his major works—*Hind Swaraj*, the *Autobiography*, *History of Satyagraha in South Africa, Commentaries on the Gita*—in Gujarati. Of these, he himself translated only one into English, *Hind Swaraj*, which for that reason alone remains an irreplaceable source for deciphering Gandhi's meanings.

In addition to the major works mentioned above, Gandhi, over a period of four decades, wrote editorials on a regular basis for his three weekly journals, *Indian Opinion, Young India*, and *Harijan*. These editorials, written in English, remain excellent sources of information on how he used the English language to express his ideas of freedom. A close reading of these editorials remains indispensable for getting a sound grasp of Gandhi's meanings.

To the above categories of writings must be added his important correspondence with such figures as Jawaharlal Nehru, Rajaji, Tagore, and others, and the numerous reports, constitutions, declarations, resolutions, and so on that he wrote on behalf of the Indian National Congress. They too were composed in English, and the spectacle of how he effortlessly mixed concepts from the East and the West is something that no student of Gandhi can afford to miss.

Consulting the dual linguistic sources of his ideas, then, is part of any serious study of Gandhi's political philosophy. Thus, in Gujarati he normally used the same word, *swaraj*, to express all four aspects of freedom. In his English writings, however, he freely used such different words as "home-rule," "self-rule," "independence," "freedom of the individual," "liberty," "rights," "fundamental rights," and "economic freedom," as well as *swaraj*, which is now used as an English word. The context in which the terms occur is often important.

A fourth factor that adds to the complexity of Gandhi's conception of freedom is the fact that he was not a philosopher in any formal sense of the term. He was primarily an activist who used philosophical language to express his thought. Certainly a philosophy underlies his thought and actions, but that does not make him a philosopher. The task of giving a philosophical account of his thought and actions he wisely left to the philosophers themselves.

Finally, there is the question of the historical context in which he lived and acted. Almost to the end of his life, he lived as a colonial in a colonial country. This fact alone should explain why he was so preoccupied with the idea of national independence. We may compare this preoccupation of his with Hobbes' preoccupation with sovereignty and political obligation. Hobbes did not live in an England under alien rule, but he did live in an England torn by civil war. This had something to do with his special concern for the notion of sovereignty in the *Leviathan*.

The same holds true for Gandhi's preoccupation with political freedom or rights of the individual. India is a multiethnic, multicaste, multireligious, multilinguistic country, and if independence was to have the beneficial effects he thought it should have, it had to manifest itself from the start in the freedoms that individuals enjoyed—regardless of their various differences. That is why, in his view, the freedom of the individual had to be the hallmark of an independent India.

Gandhi's concern with economic freedom also had a contextual explanation. When he spoke of economic freedom he spoke primarily of the poor and of freedom from poverty. Historically, Indian poverty remained a function of the caste system. The lower one's caste, the poorer one's station in life. The rich in India did not have to seek economic freedom since they already enjoyed it. Neither was he thinking in terms of economic freedom in the laissez-faire sense. He had in mind not so much the free enterpriser as the poorest of India's poor.

Finally, his reinterpretation of the meaning of self-rule also had a historical context. In the nineteenth and early twentieth centuries, the traditional notion of self-rule met with a serious crisis, the like of which it had never faced. At the heart of the crisis was the question of whether self-rule was compatible with political and economic activities. For according to the ancient and medieval traditions of India, self-rule was an apolitical and an asocial state of affairs. A self-ruling person was supposed to remain indifferent to any political oppression or poverty that may be around him or her. Those who aspired to self-rule tended to seek it outside the paths of politics and economics. Self-rule was thought to require world-renunciation if not world-negation—a point made rather powerfully by Albert Schweitzer in his *Indian Thought and Its Development*. As notions of political and economic freedoms began to impinge on modern India, the question of whether the pursuit of self-rule could be made compatible with political activity became a thorny one. Swami Vivekananda, for instance, was opposed to taking any part in politics whereas Sarvepalli Radhakrishnan actively, if judiciously, engaged in politics.[2] But no one spoke more fervently of the need to harmonize political action with self-rule, nor did any one demonstrate a more practical way of meeting that need, than did Mahatma Gandhi.

I have made these preliminary remarks to emphasize the point that two streams of thought met in Gandhi. They did so at a time when the world was passing from the colonial period to the period of national independence. The idea of independence, a modern idea, underwent a gradual transformation when it reached India's ancient culture. Fortunately, modern India did not see any radical opposition between the ancient and the modern. Gandhi's celebrated criticism of modern civilization was constructive, not wholly negative. His treatment of the modern idea of freedom should be studied not on the basis of the supposition of a radical opposition between the ancient and the modern, the way, for example, Leo Strauss supposes with respect to modern Western political philosophy. It should be studied instead with the supposition of room for reasonable accommodation between the ancient and the modern.

In what follows I shall give a brief account of each of the four aspects of Gandhi's notion of *swaraj*.

NATIONAL INDEPENDENCE

National independence is the first aspect of Gandhi's notion of *swaraj*. By independence he means collective freedom from alien rule. The enjoyment of sovereign independence is a basic human need. In modern times, however, collective freedom often means *national* independence, since the nation is taken by many to be the legitimate political community. There is nothing original in Gandhi's adoption of national independence as an aspect of his philosophy of freedom. What is original is the qualification he attaches to the means of attaining it. Historically wars of one kind or another were thought to be the normal means of attaining independence. Gandhi does not accept this view. In place of wars and violence, he introduces nonviolence as the more desirable means of attaining independence. And therein lies one of the reasons for his claim to originality. To him the means by which independence is achieved is almost as important as independence itself.

Gandhi's ideas of independence are set out in a number of different texts—in speeches, reports, memorandums, resolutions, declarations, and the like. I shall make brief comments on three of these. The first is, of course, *Hind Swaraj*, his most basic work. Its overall aim was to clarify the meaning of *swaraj*. The notion of *swaraj* was a much-debated notion when Gandhi wrote his book. The moderate wing of the nationalist movement had identified independence with autonomous status for India within the British Empire, a status to be attained through constitutional means, i.e., with the goodwill and consent of the imperial power. The extremist wing, on the other hand, had identified independence as replacing alien rule with Indian rule, brought about by any means available, including the use of terror and armed rebellion. In either case, independence meant a change in the nationality of the rulers: the British were to be replaced by Indians. Anything more fundamental was neither sought nor required.

Gandhi rejected the above mentioned views, arguing that independence should mean more than replacing British rule with Indian rule. It should mean replacing British rule with genuine *swaraj*. Otherwise, there would be only a replacement of one form of coercive rule by another, or as he put it, "English rule without the Englishman." "You want the tiger's nature, but not the tiger; that is to say, you would make India English, and, when it becomes English, it will be called not Hindustan but Englistan. This is not the *swaraj* that I want."[3]

The *swaraj* that Gandhi wanted linked independence with self-rule. What self-rule means I shall explain in a subsection below. For the present it is sufficient to note that according to Gandhi, independence without a capacity for self-rule would mean nothing more than the rule of the strong—the economically and politically strong—over the economically and politically weak. It would not mean the rule of equals by equals. The fact that the strong are of the same nationality as the weak did not make the rule by the strong any better than colonial rule. Self-rule would give independence a new meaning. This is one of the major teachings of *Hind Swaraj.*

The meaning of independence is further articulated in *Constructive Programme,* a nineteen-point essay that Gandhi published in 1941.[4] Its main argument was that without a strong civil society independence would benefit mainly the upper castes, and would lack a positive content beneficial to the people as a whole. Historically national independence was seen as a matter of right. While granting that it was a matter of right, he insisted that more than asserting a right was required for independence. Independence required a collective capacity for building and maintaining a strong civil society. The *Constructive Programme* gave a brief outline of what civil society in India urgently needed. It needed peace between Hindus and India's minorities; removal of the caste system and untouchability; small-scale industries; village sanitation; adult education and literacy; emancipation of women; education in health and hygiene; and improvement of the lot of students, peasants, industrial laborers, and tribals. Strengthening civil society was the way to attain "*poorna swaraj* or complete independence by truthful and nonviolent means."[5]

The third text that articulates Gandhi's concept of independence is "The Declaration of Independence," which he wrote in 1930 on behalf of the Indian National Congress, and which drew on the more famous American Declaration of Independence. He had two main purposes in drawing up the Declaration. The first was to state "the why and wherefore" of independence; and the second, to impress upon the people the need to use only nonviolent means to attain it.[6]

Gandhi's Declaration is divided into three parts. The first part sets out the philosophical reasons why India should be independent: As a people, Indians have an inalienable right to it. To this collective right are attached certain individual rights, such as the right to the fruits of one's toil, to the necessities of life, and to the opportunities for individual growth.

The right to independence included the additional collective right to alter or abolish existing government. The terminology of "alter or abolish" resembles that found in the American Declaration. The underlying assumption is that legitimacy of any government depends not only on the will of the people but also on the ability of the government to provide protection for the rights of its citizens. The first part of Gandhi's Declaration reads as follows:

> We believe that it is the inalienable right of the Indian people, as of any other people, to have freedom and to enjoy the fruits of their toil and have the necessities of life, so that they may have full opportunities for growth. We believe also that if any government deprive a people of these rights and oppresses them, the people have a further right to alter or to abolish it.[7]

The second part of the Declaration lists India's grievances against Britain. It speaks of the "fourfold disaster" that colonialism had visited upon India. In this regard, too, Gandhi's text bears comparison with the text of the American Declaration, which also contains the American colonies' long list of the complaints against Britain. Gandhi's list is shorter than the American list. The grievances are grouped under four headings: economic, political, cultural, and spiritual.

Economically India has been ruined in several ways. The revenue derived from the Indian people is out of all proportion to their income; village industries have been destroyed; customs and currency have been so manipulated as to heap further burden on the people; and the import policy so favored British goods as to bring about the general economic ruination of the country.

Politically India has been ruined because the people have no power to shape the laws that govern them. "All administrative talent" has been killed and people have to be satisfied with petty village offices and clerkships.

Culturally the new system of education has torn Indians away from their cultural moorings. They have been made to "hug the very chains" that bind them.

Spiritually, compulsive disarmament has made Indians "unmanly." The presence of an alien army of occupation has made Indians believe that they are unable to defend themselves against external aggression and internal disorder.

The list of grievances ends with a call on Indians to refuse to submit to colonial rule. "We hold it to be a crime against men and God to submit any longer to a rule that has caused this fourfold disaster to our country."[8]

Whereas the first two parts of Gandhi's Declaration bear some similarity to the American Declaration of Independence, the third part bears no such similarity. Indeed it marks a sharp departure with respect to the means to be used for attaining independence. There is no question of any use of violence. And there will be no Indian war of independence. Noncooperation with the colonial government is the recommended means. "We recognize that the most effective way of gaining our freedom is not through violence."[9] The alternative means suggested include withdrawal of voluntary association with the colonial government, civil disobedience, and nonpayment of taxes.

I conclude this brief account of Gandhi's notion of national independence with two general observations. The first is that according to him independence is necessary but not sufficient for full human flourishing, whether at the national or at the individual level. There is no question of subordinating the political freedom of the individual to the interests of any national myth. "Mere withdrawal of the English is not independence. It means the consciousness in the average villager that he is the maker of his own destiny, [that] he is his own legislator through his chosen representatives."[10]

The second observation has to do with the distinction between independence and self-rule. Independence is negative freedom while self-rule is positive freedom. The latter requires "self-restraint" or "disciplined rule from within." *Swaraj* for Gandhi is a "sacred" or "Vedic" word coming from the very origins of Indian civilization. "Independence," on the other hand, is a modern concept; it does not require any "disciplined rule from within." It often means "license to do as you like."[11] There is no question that Indians should embrace the modern notion of independence, but in doing so they should also try to link it with the ancient notion of self-rule.

POLITICAL FREEDOM OF THE INDIVIDUAL

Political freedom of the individual is the second aspect of Gandhi's notion of *swaraj*. In modern political thought individual political freedom is often spoken of as a "right" or "rights." In so far as this is the case, Gandhi also defends freedom in the sense of "rights"—although, as we shall see presently, that does not make him a "rights theorist," in the Western sense of that phrase. (The point is elaborated further by Judith Brown in her essay in this volume.)

The transmutation of the concept of right into that of individual liberty has had a long history, going back at least to Thomas Hobbes. As John Finnis has pointed out, Hobbes stipulated that "a right" (*jus*) was paradigmatically a liberty.[12]

The process of change in the meaning of rights did not end with Hobbes. According to Finnis the notion of rights underwent further changes. Thus there are now a "choice" theory of rights and a "benefit" theory of rights. The first sees rights as the freedom to choose what one wants, whereas the second sees rights as something beneficial that a person has.[13]

Gandhi taught that in the modern world, life worthy of a human being would not be possible without the benefits of rights. He learned this salutary lesson early in his career: to be without rights in the modern world was to be treated as something less than human. He found out in South Africa that "as a man and as an Indian," he had no rights. "More correctly, I discovered that I had no rights as a man because I was an Indian."[14] That is to say, the application of modern rights was subject to imperialist and racially based restrictions. The reason for this, he inferred, was the more that rights were aligned to interests (rather than to natural justice), the less universal they tended to become.

Gandhi took very seriously the program of modifying the received notion of rights. In fact one of his major contributions to political philosophy—*satyagraha*—was meant to be a new method of defending rights. Much has been written on the subject of *satyagraha*, but the original idea often gets buried under a mountain of secondary literature. It will do no harm therefore to go back to Gandhi's original definition of *satyagraha*. "Passive resistance [*satyagraha*] is a method of securing rights by personal suffering; it is the reverse of resistance by arms."[15] It is no exaggeration to say that all his *satyagraha* campaigns, both in South Africa and in India, had the purpose of securing rights in a new way.

The crowning achievement of his defense of individual freedoms and rights was the passing of the famous Resolution on Fundamental Rights and Economic Changes at the 1931 session of the Indian National Congress.[16] He codrafted this resolution with Jawaharlal Nehru and presented it himself to the full assembly of the Congress. In historical terms the importance of this resolution is comparable to his Declaration of Independence, discussed above.

From the Western point of view, there is nothing very original in the list of rights included in the Resolution. All the basic rights commonly found in Western constitutions are mentioned: the right to freedom of association, conscience, religion, speech, and a free press; rights of minorities to their culture, language, and religion; the right to private property, to keep and bear arms, to be treated equally without regard to differences of gender, caste, creed, or physical disability; the right to form labor unions, to adult suffrage, to a living wage, to old age benefits, and to maternity leave. The Resolution also provided for the religious neutrality of the state. As the preamble to the Resolution declared, one of the chief aims of the Resolution was "to enable the masses to appreciate what *swaraj* . . . will mean to them." That is to say, political independence would mean nothing unless it guaranteed the rights of the individual.[17]

Though Gandhi is a defender of rights, he defends them in his own way. There are two reasons for this: the first is that he does not accept the theory of human nature on which much of modern Western theory is based, and the second is that he does not subscribe to the epistemology underlying much of modern Western theorizing.

The modern Western theory of human nature on which rights are based presupposes that humans are basically bodily creatures, led by their imagination, appetites, aversions, and instrumental reason. They are not by nature social beings. They are radical individualists, distrustful of one another. Rights are the means by which they can protect their individual interests from the interference of others.

As for its epistemology, much of modern Western theory of rights is based on dogmatic empiricism. That which cannot be empirically verified or demonstrated has no cognitive status. This discounts any spiritual insights humans may have. This is not surprising since modern rights theory has no use for a theory of the soul that claims to be spiritual and immortal.

Gandhi's defense of freedoms and rights is based on his view of human nature, which he borrows from Indian sources. Humans are body-soul composites. They are by nature social beings: "Man is not born to live in isolation but is essentially a social animal independent and interdependent."[18] As bodily beings, each tends to claim things as "mine."[19] This is reasonable so long as such claims remain within the bounds of natural sociability and the principles of self-rule, and so long as the principles of self-rule have their source in the spiritual soul. That is to say, whereas bodily existence justifies rights, spiritual powers make it possible for humans to keep the pursuit of rights within the bounds of natural ethics.

As for epistemology, Gandhi assumes that humans live by truths established by empiricism, reason, and spiritual insights. Here he relies on the epistemology and the anthropology underlying the *Bhagavad Gita*. There is a hierarchy of powers and faculties within humans: body; senses; the mind; intelligence *(buddhi)*; and a spiritual, immortal spirit *(atman)*.

Given Gandhi's anthropology and epistemology, it is not surprising that he introduced two significant modifications into the theory of rights. The first had to do with duty, and the second, as noted already, with *satyagraha*.

Rights by themselves, Gandhi felt, were not enough to secure the peaceful political well-being of humans. Beneficial and necessary though rights were to such well-being, they needed to be complemented by duty *(dharma)*. Given the basic unity of human nature, Gandhi saw no reasonable basis for positing a fundamental opposition between rights and duties. In his view, the opposition that modern Western theory of rights posits between rights and duties is owed to the particular anthropology and epistemology it chose to adopt rather than to any self-evident truths about human beings. And thanks to his philosophical anthropology and epistemology, he is able to give an explanation of what *dharma* is, and how we can know its first principles. "*Dharma* does not mean any particular creed or dogma. Nor does it mean reading or learning by rote books known as *Shastras* [the traditional treatises on *dharma*] or even believing all that they say. *Dharma* is a quality of the soul and is present, visibly or invisibly, in every human being. Through it we know our duty in human life and our true relations with other souls. It is evident that we cannot do so till we have known the self in us. Hence *dharma* is the means by which we can know ourselves."[20]

The distinction that is implicit in the above passage between *dharma* as a "quality of the soul" and *dharma* as it is found in books, customs, and codes is an important one. The first type of *dharma* I call "natural *dharma*." Through this *dharma* humans have access to basic moral insights about what is right and wrong, good and evil. Such access is available to anyone who has true self-knowledge. The second type of *dharma*—the *dharma* of books, and so forth—I prefer to call positive, sociolegal codes. They are the products of history and social organizations, designed to govern the social and political relations of individuals and communities. They have the force of moral duty only insofar as they are in conformity with natural *dharma*. Accordingly, if any existing sociolegal code is found to be wanting in the light of new moral reflections, it would have to be modified or even abandoned altogether.

In the case of India, the codes governing caste, for example, had to be seen in light of the new moral insights that Indians had gained as a result of their contact with Western thought. This explains why the old caste codes were gradually replaced by the new code of individual rights and freedoms. Although this was a welcome change, it did not follow that the new code of rights and freedoms ought to stand outside the domain of natural *dharma*. Indeed the new code had to be in conformity with natural *dharma*, if it were to have the force of moral duty behind it. That is why in Gandhi's view modern rights and duties could and ought to be explained in relational, rather than in oppositional terms.

We can now understand why Gandhi was never tired of saying that duty came before rights. He was willing to defend rights only on this supposition: "Real rights are a result of performance of duty."[21] "No one will have any right but what are inherent in the willing performance of one's duties.[22] He was quite unwilling to endorse schemes of elevating modern rights over duty. There was the well-known case of his refusal to endorse the scheme put forward by H. G. Wells, an English writer, to draw up a charter of "rights of man." He advised Wells that he ought to spend his talents on better causes like drawing up a charter of "duties of man."[23] Gandhi's response to the 1948 United Nations committee engaged in drafting the Universal Declaration of Human Rights also reflects a similar attitude. This was Gandhi's response to the committee: "All rights to be deserved and preserved come from duty well done. Thus the very right to live accrues to us only when we do the duty of citizenship of the world. From this fundamental statement perhaps it is easy enough to define the duties of man and woman and correlate every right to some corresponding duty to be first performed. Every other right can be shown to be a usurpation hardly worth fighting for."[24] The same view was expressed to the framers of India's new constitution: "Fundamental rights can only be those rights the exercise of which is not only in the interest of the citizens but that of the whole world. . . . Rights cannot be divorced from duties. This is how *satyagraha* was born, for I was always striving to decide what my duty was."[25]

Gandhi claimed that the assertion of rights without due regard for corresponding duties would in the long run turn liberty into license. "Liberty cannot be secured merely by proclaiming it. An atmosphere of liberty must be created within us. Liberty is one thing, and license another. Many a time we confuse license for liberty and lose the latter. License leads one to selfishness whereas liberty guides one to supreme good. License destroys society, liberty gives it life. In license propriety is sacrificed; in liberty it is fully cherished."[26]

So much for the first modification that Gandhi introduced into the theory of modern rights and freedoms. Turning now to the second modification, namely that entailed in the techniques of *satyagraha*, we see how the securing of rights takes on a new direction. *Satyagraha* helped to focus attention on a crucial question, namely the relationship of rights to violence. That there was a historical relationship between the two was undeniable. The French Revolution and the *Rights of Man and the Citizen* bore witness to this. The question was whether this relationship was necessary or only historical. Gandhi saw no reason to suppose that it should be necessary. That is why he ventured to introduce "personal suffering" as one mode of securing rights.

As the Gujarati text makes clear, "personal suffering" meant accepting voluntarily the *penalties* attached to the active resistance to unjust laws. Acceptance of penalties implied acceptance of the rule of law. *Satyagraha* therefore was not a threat to the rule of law. Indeed it was meant to be one way of making law more just than it actually would be at any given time.

By introducing the element of "personal suffering," Gandhi made the process of securing rights less violent and more peaceful. This is what *satyagraha* is all about. Historically, the securing of rights took place in an atmosphere of mutual antagonism, which often spilled into civil wars, wars of liberation, revolutions, riots, and the like. *Satyagraha* sought to improve the moral and the psychological atmosphere in which disputes about rights were approached. It called for self-examination on the part of both parties to the conflict. Self-examination was to bring them to reflect on what the truth of the matter was and what their respective duties were toward that truth. Out of such reflection each party would find areas of honorable compromise. But for the whole process to work rights and duties had to be taken together: what are my rights and my duties, and how do they stand in relation to the truth of the matter, and to the rights and duties of my opponent? The closer rights were brought to duties, the greater the chances of resolving disputes without resort to violence. To this extent *satyagraha* introduced something new into the theory of rights and freedoms.[27]

As Jan Christian Smuts, one of Gandhi's early adversaries and later one of his great admirers, had remarked, *satyagraha* "is Gandhi's distinctive contribution to political method."[28] It had its roots in Indian spiritual tradition, and as such, it represented one instance of Gandhi bringing Eastern and Western ideas closer together. And as Jacques Maritain has pointed out, *satyagraha* produced a resonance in Western political philosophy. According to Maritain, *satyagraha* was a form of the virtue of courage applied to politics. There were two kinds of courage, he wrote, "the courage that attacks and the courage that endures suffering inflicted on oneself." The first opposed evil through attack and coercion, which might lead to the shedding of blood; the second opposed evil by "suffering and enduring," which ultimately might lead to "the sacrifice of one's own life." Gandhi's own "work of genius has been the systematic organization of patience and voluntary suffering as a special method or technique of political activity."[29]

For reasons of space, I do not go into the critical question of the degree of success that Gandhi achieved by introducing a twofold modification in the modern theory of rights. However, I would like to close this discussion by pointing out that, irrespective of his success or failure in this particular issue, he has made a major contribution to political thinking. That contribution consists in giving currency to a new pattern of political thinking, namely the comparative pattern. Out of ideas taken from the East and the West he was able to develop a new political praxis, which had sound philosophical justification. His defense of rights and freedoms suggests that there are different and valid ways of defending them. The current Western way of defending rights and freedoms is not the only way they can be defended. How one defends them will depend, among other things, on the style of philosophizing that one employs, and on the theory of human nature and the theory of knowledge one adopts. There is no reason to think that the current Western style of philosophizing and the current Western conception of human nature and epistemology are the only valid ones.

In this context it is not inopportune to refer to a related issue, the drafting of the 1948 Universal Declaration of Human Rights. The framers of that declaration were drawn from the major philosophical traditions of the world. As Mary Ann Glendon has pointed out, the framers discovered that the lists of basic rights and values they received from their constituencies were "essentially similar." But they justified their respective lists on the basis of their own philosophical traditions. The views were similar, but the explanations different. As Jacques Maritain, one of the most active members of the drafting committee, famously remarked, "Yes, we agree about the rights, but on condition no one asks why."[30]

Gandhi too agreed that rights were necessary for and beneficial to human beings. However, he gave his own explanation of how and why they could be so.

ECONOMIC FREEDOM OF THE INDIVIDUAL

Economic freedom of the individual is the third aspect of Gandhi's notion of *swaraj*. By economic freedom Gandhi meant freedom from poverty. Poverty is a phenomenon relative to given societies. But the Mahatma had his own criteria of judging whether a given society suffered from freedom-denying poverty. The criteria were the availability of the necessities of life (decent food, clothing, and dwelling), the ability to enjoy the fruits of one's toils, and the opportunity for growth of the individual. All three of these, as we have seen above, were mentioned in his Declaration of Independence. The resolution on fundamental rights and economic change had also stipulated, as we have seen, that political freedom must include real economic freedom of the poor.[31]

Gandhi's attack on poverty as an obstacle to freedom needs highlighting, especially since in his personal life he was given to practicing voluntary poverty. How could one practice voluntary poverty and at the same time be against poverty? The answer to this apparent inconsistency can be found in his religious psychology: his voluntary poverty was an act of penance, even of spiritual protest against the involuntary poverty of the Indian masses. It was not an approval, much less a glorification of involuntary poverty. However, misunderstandings exist. Even so perceptive an observer of India as the late Octavio Paz, the Nobel laureate, was moved to remark that Gandhi thought of poverty as "a solution to injustice or excess."[32] Gandhi did not think of poverty in this way. He voluntarily accepted the lifestyle of the poor in order to demonstrate his solidarity with them. Poverty was no more natural to him than it was to them. It was a product of an unjust social order, removable by human effort.

He firmly believed that economic freedom had to come pari passu with political freedom. In *Hind Swaraj*, for example, he had taken as "understood that anything that helped India to get rid of the grinding poverty of her masses would in the same process establish *swaraj*."[33]

Given Gandhi's criteria of economic freedom, it is hardly surprising that he did not identify it with the freedom that laissez-faire theorists speak of. His notion of economic freedom was consistent with his position that humans had no *absolute right* to private property. No doubt he defended a certain type of right to private property, but that right was conditional to the wellbeing of the community in which one lived. His defense of the conditional right to private property was consistent with his notion of the trusteeship of property. Going back to a teaching of the "Ishopanishad," he held the view that only the Lord had absolute dominion over the goods of the earth, and that those goods were given to humans as a trust. While each person had a right to the necessities of life, the fruits of his or her toil, and to what was needed for his or her full growth, the right to the surplus was governed by the principle of trusteeship and the needs of the community.[34]

The economic freedom that Gandhi defended could be realized only if a certain kind of economic arrangement of society was available. We have already referred to the ideal disposition of the right to property. There were other ideas equally important. Some of these he derived from John Ruskin, the nineteenth-century friendly critic of British capitalism. Two of his works, *Unto This Last* and the *Political Economy of Art,* influenced him greatly.

Three of Ruskin's ideas Gandhi found basic to his own thought. The first had to do with the motivations at work in economic activity, and the role that the soul plays in them. Modern political economy, according to Ruskin, had limited these motivations to enlightened self-interest. It chose to treat humans as if the soul did not play a role in the economic life of an individual. Accordingly it tended to treat "social affections" as only "accidental and disturbing elements in human nature." Ruskin rejected the soulless approach of modern political economy. He argued that humans were engines "whose motive power [was] a Soul," whose operations could falsify every calculation of the political economist. The largest quantity of work will be done, he claimed, not for pay or under pressure. "It will be done only when the motive force, that is to say, the will or spirit of the creature, is brought to its greatest strength by its own proper fuel, namely by the [social] affections."[35]

The second idea taken from Ruskin was that modern political economy popularized a wrong understanding of what wealth was: wealth as possessions accumulated by a certain arrangement of capital and labor. The right notion of wealth, Ruskin argued, was that it was a means to life. "There is no wealth but life, including all its powers of love, of joy, and of admiration. That country is the richest which nourishes the greatest number of noble and happy human beings; and that man is richest who, having perfected the functions of his own life to the utmost, has also the widest helpful influence, both personal, and by means of his possessions, over the lives of others."[36]

The third idea from Ruskin was that every human being deserved decent conditions of life, even the last and the least. The idea was derived from the Parable of the Vineyard, in the Gospel of St. Matthew 20:1–14. The Gospel also gave Ruskin the title of his book *Unto This Last.* According to the parable, the workers in the vineyard received a decent wage, irrespective of the number of hours they had worked. That is to say everyone, even the workers who came in the last hour, deserved a decent wage. Gandhi adapted this idea to his Indian audience by use of the term *sarvodaya*, meaning the welfare of all. *Sarvodaya* later became the name he gave to his economic philosophy.

To Ruskin's ideas Gandhi added Timofei Bondaref's idea of bread labor—labor that every able-bodied person had to do simply because they were bodily creatures. Whether rich or poor, every human had to engage, if only for a few hours, in some form of bread labor. To the notion of bread labor, he added the idea that work was a sacrament, a *yajna*, a spiritually healthy activity—an idea taken from the *Bhagavad Gita.*

In addition to the ideas that were to go into the economic arrangement of society, Gandhi had also paid special attention to certain economic institutions. In doing so, he kept in mind the economic condition of India's poor. What India needed, he argued famously, was not mass production but production by the masses. The latter option had a better chance of success if villagers were encouraged to be small agricultural proprietors, and village industries and other small-scale industries were promoted. He was skeptical of the capacity of modern corporations to promote economic freedom as he understood it. He was equally skeptical of the modern industrial technology that favored the well educated and those who had access to vast capital. The preference of modern political economy for mass production tends to inhibit local initiatives, and to increase the gap between rich and poor both domestically and internationally.

Gandhi was not opposed to "machinery" (his nineteenth-century terminology for industrial technology). What he was opposed to was "the craze" for it. As supplement to human labor, technology could bring about beneficial conditions of labor, and thereby expand the scope of economic freedom. "Machine power can make a valuable contribution towards economic progress." But those who have control over the machinery tend not to pay adequate attention to the freedom of "the common man."[37] "[T]he machinery method" is harmful when the same thing could be done easily by millions of hands not otherwise occupied.[38] "Machinery is a grand yet awful invention. It is possible to visualize a stage at which the machines invented by man may finally engulf civilization. If man controls the machines, then they will not; but should man lose his control over the machines and allow them to control him, then they will certainly engulf civilization and everything."[39]

Gandhi identified two specific threats to freedom arising from a civilization driven by technology. The first was imperialistic aggression in the search of markets, and the second was domestic exploitation of the masses by those who had control over technology. He saw the possibility of a dangerous connection developing between industrial economy as it functions today and imperial expansionism. He wondered how long an industrialized India could resist embarking upon imperialistic ventures. "We cannot industrialize ourselves," he warned Indians, "unless we make up our mind to enslave humanity."[40] What was true of an industrialized India would be equally true of any other major industrialized country. The fault lay not so much in the countries themselves but in the pattern of control that modern industrial economy seems to demand. Nuclear weapons only highlighted the potential danger to freedom that this pattern contains. "Those who have atom bombs are feared even by their friends. If we take a wise view, we shall be saved from the working of machinery."[41]

To remove the threat to freedom from modern large-scale economic enterprises was one of Gandhi's main concerns. His promotion of the spinning wheel and production of *khadi*, cloth made through hand spinning and hand weaving, is best seen in light of this concern. The historical significance of Gandhi's spinning wheel lies in its metaphor as appropriate technology. Its practical economic uses—as a means of training the poorest of the poor of India in the habits of economic discipline and cooperation, in acquiring a minimum capability for economic activity under conditions actually available to the poor—did not extend beyond the 1920s and 1930s. But its moral and symbolic uses did have a lasting influence: it tended to awaken the rich of India to the plight of India's poor, and to instill in the poor a belief that even in the most economically hopeless situations they could help themselves. The desire for economic freedom could be fulfilled only if the poor could acquire capabilities that they could translate into economically beneficial activities. The spinning wheel did not require much capital and technology. It was within the reach of the poor. They could learn of economic freedom by using the spinning wheel as a start. It is in its symbolism that its significance lies today. If technology is to safeguard economic freedom, it had to be easily available to even the poor.

But beyond theories of property, notions of work, small, decentralized economic ventures, and appropriate technology, there was still the problem of the side-by-side existence of the rich and the poor in society. How could this phenomenon tally with the idea of economic freedom? Gandhi seemed willing to tolerate this phenomenon so long as the poor enjoyed economic freedom as he defined it. Even so the existence of excessive difference between the rich and the poor did bother him. Interestingly enough he wanted the rich themselves to be aware of the differences that separated them from the poor. He wanted a spiritual dialogue to take place in the soul of the rich, a dialogue in which they would have to justify their wealth morally to themselves. This idea was expressed in what has come to be known as Gandhi's "talisman." Written in August 1947, the year in which India attained independence, it was addressed to India's wealthy. It brings together the interconnectedness of the questions of poverty and wealth, conscience, economic freedom, and *swaraj*:

> Whenever you are in doubt, or when the self becomes too much with you, apply the following test. Recall the face of the poorest and the weakest man whom you may have seen, and ask yourself if the step you contemplate is going to be of any use to him. Will he gain anything by it? Will it restore him to a control over his own life and destiny? In other words, will it lead to *swaraj* for the hungry and spiritually starving millions?
> Then you will find your doubts and yourself melting away.[42]

SELF-RULE

Self-rule is the fourth and the most important aspect of Gandhi's idea of *swaraj*. Self-rule is the process of removing the internal obstacles to freedom. When achieved it is nothing other than spiritual freedom. According to Gandhi the capacity of self-rule, more than any other capacity, distinguishes humans from brutes: "the essential difference between man and brute is that the former can respond to the call of spirit in him and rise superior to the passions that he owns in common with the brute."[43] Self-rule presupposes the agency of the spirit (individual *atman*). The spirit exerts its influence on the empirical ego, on emotions, mind, and intelligence. Under the influence of the spirit, the inner powers of the moral agent become integrated, such that he or she becomes a spiritually aware person, guided by true self-knowledge. The process by which the spirit integrates inner faculties has a dynamic quality, which is suitably expressed by the concept of "ruling." Hence the terminology of self-rule, *swaraj*. The spirit or the higher self "rules" the lower self or the empirical ego.

Self-rule is a self-achieved state of affairs, not something "granted" by others. It "could not be granted even by God. We would have to earn it ourselves. *Swaraj* from its very nature is not in the giving of anybody."[44] It depends entirely on our internal strength.[45] For a person to be fully free, it is not enough to have the external obstacles to freedom removed; it is equally necessary to have the internal obstacles removed as well.

Gandhi derived the idea of self-rule and spiritual freedom from the *Bhagavad Gita*. Nineteen verses of the second chapter of this work (vv. 54–72) draw the celebrated portrait of "the person of steady wisdom," the *sthitha-prajna*. The *sthitha-prajna*, for Gandhi, was the model of a self-ruling, spiritually free person. He sought to model his own life on that basis. Therefore he included those nineteen verses of the *Gita* as part of his daily prayers, and recited them every day for at least the last forty years of his life.

There can be no self-rule without the practice of virtue—virtue being the directing of the inner powers of a person to their proper purposes. Here, too, Gandhi draws from the Indian tradition, in this case from Patanjali's *Yogasutra* II.30. Patanjali lists five virtues necessary for anyone contemplating the attainment of spiritual freedom. They are nonviolence, truthfulness, nonstealing, chastity, and greedlessness. But Gandhi expands the list. He is not satisfied with tradition. He modifies it, so that spiritual freedom can become relevant to life in a modern society. Thus, on his own initiative, he adds six more virtues: *swadeshi* (concern for what pertains to one's own country), removal of untouchability, bodily labor, control of the palate, fearlessness, and respect for all religions.[46] There is no question that Gandhi is drawing out the civic potential inherent in spiritual freedom.

Self-rule is also a self-transformative activity. A spiritually integrated person is no longer a slave of the passions, but is able to go about his or her daily affairs in the light of true self-knowledge. Gandhi speaks of "self-conversion"[47] and "mental revolution,"[48] and of the experience of inner freedom. "*Swaraj* is a state of mind to be experienced by us. We've to win it by our own strength . . . . *Swaraj* consists in our efforts to win it."[49]

The self-rule that Gandhi defends was not an empty, utopian dream, but a real state of affairs of which a person can have experiential evidence. Experience of self-rule would make one aware of one's duties toward others, and above all, it would make one sensitive to social injustice. That is to say, self-rule leads to deeper self-knowledge, which in turn awakens one's social and political conscience. The exercise of freedom within has consequences for freedom without. Self-rule bridges the internal world of spiritual freedom and the external world of political and economic freedoms. "It is *swaraj* when we learn to rule ourselves. It is, therefore, in the palm of our hands. Do not consider this *swaraj* is like a dream. Here there is no idea of sitting still. The *swaraj* that I wish to picture before you and me is such that, after we have once realized it, we will endeavor to the end of our lifetime to persuade others to do likewise. But *swaraj* has to be experienced by each one for himself. One drowning man will never save another. Slaves ourselves, it would be a mere pretension to think of freeing others."[50]

Although Gandhi derived the idea of self-rule from the Indian tradition, one must remember that he at the same time sought to innovate the traditional notion of self-rule. That is to say, he sought to make self-rule compatible with the modern ideas of independence, individual freedom, and economic freedom. The experience of self-rule brought with it a moral concern to *persuade* others to become fully free: "after we have once realized it, we will endeavor to the end of our lifetime to persuade others to do likewise."[51]

Without doubt Gandhi brought about a major conceptual change in the Indian notion of spiritual freedom. For according to Indian tradition, spiritual freedom was supposed to be an apolitical and an asocial state of affairs, requiring withdrawal from the sociopolitical world. But he reinterprets self-rule in such a way as to give spiritual freedom a social, political, and economic profile. A seeker of spiritual freedom need no longer leave the world. The addition of the six new modern virtues to the five traditional ones was part of Gandhi's innovative strategy.

Gandhi's own life was an experiment in making spiritual freedom socially, politically, and economically dynamic. As the introduction to his autobiography famously stated, his life goal was the attainment of spiritual freedom, which he felt he could not attain unless he entered the world of social, political, and economic action. "All that I do by way of speaking and writing, and all my ventures in the political field, are directed to this same end."[52] Its concluding chapter returns to the same idea: a person who aspires after spiritual freedom and self-rule "cannot afford to keep out of any field of life. That is why my devotion to Truth has drawn me into the field of politics."[53]

The principle that underlies Gandhi's notion of self-rule, then, is that self-rule ought to find expression in appropriate political and economic activities. The ability to act well in the socio-economic-political arena is the test of the new meaning of self-rule. Self-rule, and the inner transformation and integration that go with it, prepare one to lead the life of an active citizen. That is why, in his view, spiritual freedom cannot remain an asocial nor an apolitical nor an atemporal condition.

Persuasive though Gandhi was with most people on the question of the new meaning of spiritual freedom, some had difficulty in seeing things his way—at least initially. They included Mahadev Desai, his faithful secretary, who in his early years agreed to disagree with him on this issue. A little-known debate between them, recorded in his diary, *Day-to-Day with Gandhi*, is indicative of the sway that the old notion of spiritual freedom had on some.

The basic issue was this: Could one attain spiritual freedom regardless of the political and economic conditions of the society under which one lived? Would the absence of political independence impede the process of attaining spiritual freedom? Can a seeker after spiritual freedom remain indifferent to political bondage?

As we saw above Gandhi really believed that the experience of spiritual freedom necessarily brought with it a strong social and political awareness. That being the case he could not see how a spiritually free person could remain indifferent to political and economic bondage. There was something wrong with the traditional conception of spiritual freedom that tolerated indifference toward political and economic bondage. Spiritual freedom, to be truly human, had to be socially and politically active.[54] The defense of this view constitutes one of his major contributions to political philosophy.

To bring the foregoing brief survey to a conclusion, *swaraj* for Gandhi was "an all-satisfying goal for all time." He wanted India "to come to her own," and he believed India could do so only if it realized *swaraj* in all its four aspects.[55]

Why did Gandhi feel compelled to bring the four disparate aspects of freedom together? For one thing, there was the context of history. History placed before him two traditions, modern Western and ancient Indian. There was also a moral imperative. For he felt that the modern West had ignored the truth that humans were body/spirit composites, and as such the desire for freedom could be fully satisfied only by means of self-rule. He strongly believed that bearing witness to this ignored truth was his life mission. Full human development, he insisted, called for the development of all aspects of freedom. To pursue one aspect of freedom without simultaneously pursuing the other aspects was to distort the meaning of freedom and to interfere with the process of human development.

In the final analysis, the question of why there should be harmony between freedom and self-rule revolves around the deeper question of whether humans should be treated as beings endowed with an immortal spirit. Gandhi believed that they should be so treated. What is more, he was able to develop a theory and a practice that corresponded to that belief.

NOTES

1. M. K. Gandhi, *The Collected Works of Mahatma Gandhi* [hereafter *CWMG*] (New Delhi: Publications Division, Ministry of Information and Broadcasting, 1958–1994), 20:99. *Swaraj*, a Sanskrit word, compounded of *swa* and *raj*, "self" and "rule," has the first meaning of "self-ruling," and the secondary meanings of "self-resplendent" or "self-luminous." *Swarajya* means "independent dominion" or "sovereignty." Monier Monier-Williams, *A Sanskrit-English Dictionary* (Oxford: Oxford University Press, 1899), 1276.

2. "Let no political significance be ever attached falsely to any of my writings or sayings. What nonsense! . . . I will have nothing to do with nonsense. I do not believe in politics. God and Truth are the only policy in the world. Everything else is trash." Cited in Romain Rolland, *The Life of Vivekananda* (Almora, India: Advaita Ashram, 1965), n.1, 103–4; "India is immortal if she persists in her search for God. But if she goes for politics and social conflict, she will die." Ibid., 168. For Radhakrishnan's response to Albert Schweitzer, see S. Radhakrishnan, *Eastern Religions and Western Thought* (New York: Oxford University Press, 1959), ch. 3.

3. M. K. Gandhi, *Hind Swaraj and Other Writings* [hereafter *HS*], ed. Anthony J. Parel (Cambridge: Cambridge University Press, 1997), 28.

4. *CWMG,* 75:146–66.

5. *CWMG,* 75:146.

6. *CWMG,* 71:116.

7. *CWMG,* 42:384.

8. *CWMG,* 42:385.

9. *CWMG,* 42:385.

10. *CWMG,* 42:469.

11. *CWMG,* 45:263–64.

12. John Finnis, *Natural Law and Natural Rights* (Oxford: Clarendon Press, 1980), 208.

13. Finnis, *Natural Law and Natural Rights,* 208–9.

14. *CWMG,* 23:115.

15. *HS,* 90.

16. *CWMG,* 45:370–72; see also J. Nehru, *An Autobiography* (London: The Bodley Head, [1936] 1958) 267–68, where Nehru speaks of the codrafting of the Resolution with Gandhi.

17. *CWMG,* 45:370.

18. *HS,* 155.

19. *The Bhagavad Gita,* ed. R. C. Zaehner (Oxford: Oxford University Press, 1973), ch. 2., v. 71.

20. *CWMG,* 32:11.

21. *HS,* 82.

22. *CWMG,* 73:89.

23. *CWMG,* 71:430.

24. *CWMG,* 88:100.

25. *CWMG,* 88:230.

26. *CWMG,* 42:380.

27. This point is well made by Joan V. Bondurant's classic study, *Conquest of Violence: The Gandhian Philosophy of Conflict* (Berkeley and Los Angeles: University of California Press, 1967).

28. Jan C. Smuts, "Gandhi's Political Method," in *Mahatma Gandhi: Essays and Reflections on His Life and Work,* ed. S. Radhakrishnan (Bombay: Jaico Publishing House, 1995), 229.

29. Jacques Maritain, *Man and the State* (Chicago: The University of Chicago Press, 1951), 69–70.

30. Quoted by Mary Ann Glendon, "Reflections on UDHR," *First Things,* no. 82 (April 1998), 23.

31. *CWMG,* 45:370.

32. Octavio Paz, *In Light of India* (New York: Harcourt Brace, 1997), 114.

33. *CWMG*, 39:389.

34. "By the Lord (*isa*) enveloped must this all be/Whatever moving thing there is in the moving world/With this renounced, thou mayst enjoy/Covet not the wealth of anyone at all." "Ishopanishad" 1, in *The Thirteen Principal Upanishads*, trans. by Robert E. Hume (Oxford: Oxford University Press, 1931), 362.

35. John Ruskin, *Unto This Last and Other Writings*, ed. Clive Wilmer (London: Penguin Books, 1985), 167–70. Gandhi paraphrased *Unto This Last* in 1908 and published it under the title *Sarvodaya* (the welfare of all).

36. Ruskin, *Unto This Last*, 222.

37. *CWMG*, 87:249.

38. *CWMG*, 47:89–90.

39. *CWMG*, 48:353.

40. *CWMG*, 58:400.

41. *CWMG*, 82:132–33.

42. *CWMG*, 89:125.

43. *CWMG*, 58:248.

44. *CWMG*, 20:133.

45. *CWMG*, 35:294.

46. *CWMG*, 59:335.

47. *CWMG*, 35:212.

48. *CWMG*, 36:47.

49. *CWMG*, 23:71–72.

50. *HS*, 73.

51. *HS*, 73.

52. *CWMG*, 39:3.

53. *CWMG*, 39: 01.

54. The following debate between Gandhi and Desai, as recorded by the latter, reveals Gandhi's radical views on the relationship of self-rule to political and economic action.

Desai: Would the man who understands that the Indweller is apart from the body and who lives a life consistent with this knowledge, ever be swept off his feet by the infatuation of driving back the invading hordes of foreigners?

Gandhi: No, he would not. But he would certainly possess the power to do so. It's a different matter whether he uses it or abstains.

Desai: Do you mean to say that in this climate of foreign domination there is no individual in the whole of India who has realized the Self? If that is your belief, the old quarrel between us raises its head again. I for one have a deep-rooted conviction that there are such men. They are entirely indifferent about these mundane matters. They don't care a rap whether there is an invasion of India or a conflagration that burns it up.

Gandhi: There may be, I don't know. But I have my doubts.

Desai: Am I then to understand you to mean that political serfdom blocks the way of Self-realization? You know you have asserted that you have entered the political arena to reach that goal?

Gandhi: Yes, that's true in my case. I am prepared however to say that there may be individuals here and there in whose case political subjection may not come in the way of Self-realization. But what about people at large?

Desai: I am speaking for stray individuals only. The public is never going to win spiritual freedom *en masse*.

Gandhi: I agree. About the masses you are right. I hold, at the same time, the firm belief that it is impossible that even such a self-realized Master *(jnyani)*, who has taken a vow of silence, can remain an unaffected witness and refuse to influence the atmosphere even with his thought, if he be in Ahmedabad in the midst of a revolution so ablaze as this one. I don't think there can exist men who remain so indifferent.

Desai: Let us drop the subject and agree to differ. Mahadev Desai, *Day-to-Day with Gandhi*, vol. 1, 11/17 to 3/19 (Varanasi: Sarva Seva Sangh, 1968), 181–82.

55. *CWMG*, 35: 456.

10

Gandhi's Politics

Ronald J. Terchek

Today, in politics, democracy is the name for what we cannot have—yet cannot cease to want.[1]

Politics is unavoidably about power and people, about how power can enable or disable people. With this in mind, Gandhi observes that "political power is not an end but one of the means of enabling people to better their condition in every department of life."[2] Working with this perspective, he seeks to understand the nature of power, how it is expressed in rhetoric and practice, and the ways, if any, it might be legitimated and limited. In unfolding his answers, Gandhi shares and departs from liberal-democratic views on politics as well as blends political realism and idealism to his view of what a good polity should be all about. He insistently challenges standard conceptions of power and invites his readers to question familiar approaches to the subject. To do this, Gandhi denies the conventional liberal distinction between civil society and the state and liberal claims to neutrality in order to disclose the many sites of power in both the public and private realms and how power often favors some at the expense of others. He sees power residing not only in the state but also in social practices (such as untouchability), ideology (the authority of modernity), the structure of the economy, and the myriad ways that ideas and people are organized. All the while, he challenges an activist state, finding it pretentious in what it thinks it can accomplish and dangerous in the way it uses people to achieve its objectives.

The problems of political power are lessened but not solved by democratizing it, according to Gandhi. Distrusting the adequacy of standard ideas about democracy, he denies that voting and elections are sufficient either to assure a government based on popular consent or to safeguard the autonomy of everyone. Representative democracy is important to Gandhi, but he argues that popular rule requires even more.[3] Holding that any state reflects the configurations of power that exist in society, he wants to promote a regime where significant economic, social, and political inequalities have been reduced and where all forms of power are dispersed. For him, the ideal democracy protects and reflects plurality, most especially responding to those who have been excluded in the past. In this spirit, Gandhi sees that "This age of awakening of the poorest of the poor" is the "age of democracy."[4] To make it a reality, he urges democrats to struggle to make government simple and avoid hierarchy and domination. Even should this succeed, Gandhi finds an ideal democracy can make mistakes, and he invests his citizens with civil disobedience to confront injustice that might arise there.

Gandhi's conception of power is intimately tied to his radical views of freedom and autonomy.[5] For him, individuals not only carry duties and deserve freedom but also are the ultimate source of power. In locating power in individuals, Gandhi wants them to know that they can govern themselves. Attempting to be self-governing, of course, can bring harsh penalties and we typically say that someone who is punished lacks power. Gandhi denies this, holding that defiant persons no longer allow fatalism or fear to be their governors. He sees people surrendering their power when they refuse to assert their convictions, leading him to claim that "no man loses his freedom except through his own weakness."[6]

HIND SWARAJ

The way that the cosmos, duties, power and autonomy come together for Gandhi can be seen in his view of *Hind Swaraj* or Indian self-rule. Gandhi seeks to make *swaraj* a concept that not only brings self-rule to the country and its people but also unites Indians to one another. For Gandhi, India once enjoyed self-rule, but that was before the advent of colonialism and "modern civilization."[7] To regain its freedom, Gandhi insists, requires all Indians to resist domination and to rule themselves. For him, this means not only empowerment but also "self-control."[8] This will occur, on his account, not because India has its own flag, army, and centralized state which exercises an unlimited sovereignty over citizens but because all Indians treat each other with equal regard and respect, are able to subdue necessity, and see themselves related in a cosmos.

In this respect, Gandhi's sense of Indian independence diametrically differs from conventional understandings of national self-determination. As nationalism develops, claims of territorial sovereignty are extended not only to control the resident population but to everything under its jurisdiction. On this view, the sovereign determines which policies enhance its understanding of the security, well-being, and development of the nation. With modern sovereignty, constitutionally designated officials claim the right to arrange and rearrange their priorities at will, constrained only by competing centers of power and by technology (with the idea that with less political opposition and more sophisticated technology, they can rearrange more). This is what characterizes most anticolonial movements whose goal is to wrest sovereign control from alien hands and place it under indigenous control.[9]

Gandhi disputes this view, finding that such movements unwittingly trap themselves when they accept the definition of victory set by their former colonial masters, namely that the winner exercises unhindered sovereign control. From Gandhi's perspective, such a victory not only severs the harmony of the community, it also permits officials to ignore autonomy, tradition, and the environment. He sees claims to modern sovereignty consigning these latter goods, now remainders, to a subordinate and expendable position. From Gandhi's perspective, if national independence is exercised apart from a cosmological outlook, the very purpose of Indian independence is defeated. National independence is no improvement for him if Indians replace colonial officials who dominate their fellow citizens or destroy their own civilization, society, and environment.

Gandhi's *Hind Swaraj* is about the ability of ordinary Indians to rule themselves. For this reason, Gandhi holds that an India independent of imperial rule but steeped in internal domination and poverty has no real self-governance.[10] For him, both the whole and the parts must be free, and each must reflect a sense of interdependence and cooperation. Among other things, this means to Gandhi that citizens ought not have their lives scripted and directed by others. The vision Gandhi holds for an independent India of self-governing men and women is not only about goals but also about the ways those goals are pursued. For this reason, he insists that politics must be primarily about means; change must come nonviolently, and he warns that "if our political condition undergoes a change, irrespective of the manner in which it is brought about . . . the change will not be in the direction of progress but very likely the opposite."[11]

GANDHI'S MULTIPLE MEANINGS OF POWER

Gandhi finds conventional meanings of power are incomplete. In the standard account, power is the ability of one actor to cause others to behave in ways they would not have otherwise chosen. On this account, power can be either positive or negative. With the former, powerholders promise some good to induce others to act in particular ways. For example, parents promise a treat to their children, interest groups offer contributions to political candidates, or governments offer subsidies to businesses to get the recipients to act in a particular way. The inducements are negative when some harm is threatened, as when parents threaten to punish their children, interest groups oppose a candidate, or governments penalize certain conduct.

Whether positively or negatively expressed, such expressions of power are usually directed at overt behavior.

Gandhi recognizes that these are palpable, consequential expressions of power that cannot be ignored. But he has several complaints about the adequacy of such constructions of power. In the first place, the emphasis is on active rather than latent power; as a consequence, power that is quiet is disregarded, and Gandhi wants to rouse quiet Indians to express their power. Conventional expressions also disregard the potential power that lies with the quiet and complacent. Moreover, the empirical emphasis of power frequently loses sight of the often unexpected and unwelcome consequences of applied power which can harm not only others but also the powerholders. Gandhi also finds that standard views of power tend to be static and take current power arrangements to be natural and settled.

Another problem he has with much contemporary political analyses is that the state is the focus of power and little attention is given to sites of power in civil society. What is overlooked is the way that nonpolitical institutions and practices enlarge, shift, contract, or close the choices of individuals and define, redefine, locate, and relocate meanings of the good, necessity, success, and harm. Moreover, a state-focused view of power ignores how private power invades the public realm to use public power for private purposes. For this reason, Gandhi wants to confront not only the state but the other locations of power that he finds hierarchical, asymmetrical, and dominating.

Especially unusual in the literature, Gandhi invests individuals with extraordinary power. He does this in two very different ways. First, he argues that what individuals accept or tolerate serves to perpetuate institutions and practices that would otherwise languish and disappear. He holds that individuals, having transferred their power, can recover it when they wish, with civil disobedience if necessary.[12] In reclaiming their power, people "nearly establish their own government" and rule themselves.[13] If agents are to be autonomous and remain loyal to their moral commitments, Gandhi wants them to see they cannot transfer responsibility to institutions that act in their name but in ways that deny their own moral commitments. On his account, most people do not understand the complicated machinery of the government. They do not realize that every citizen silently but none the less certainly sustains the government of the day in ways of which he has no knowledge. Every citizen therefore renders himself responsible for every act of his government. And it is quite proper to support it so long as the actions of the government are bearable. But when they hurt him and his nation, it becomes his duty to withdraw his support.[14]

With this in mind, Gandhi insists that no government exists independently of what the people accept. They may accede to their government because they genuinely support it. Or they may disagree with the state's conduct but nevertheless acquiesce because the costs of dissent are high, because they are fatalistic, or because they are preoccupied with their own individual concerns. Whatever the reason, Gandhi argues, government rests on their sufferance, even though the state or individuals might deny the relationship. By making power visible and by teaching people they are the basis of power, he thinks he can domesticate it and make it accountable to clear-sighted citizens.

The second way Gandhi credits individuals with power appears in his call for the individual to stand alone, if necessary, to reclaim power. On his account, lonely assertions of power can have a powerful demonstration effect as others come to see their complicity in their own domination and understand that they can recover the power they ceded to others.[15] One reason he pushes this argument is that he wants to empower those on the periphery who are told they have no power and believe it.

In what follows in this essay, I will be using the varied understandings Gandhi credits to power, some conventional and some uniquely his. In doing so, I mean to show that he broadens standard meanings of power to include more phenomena than is usually the case and that part of his reconstruction of power involves positions that are ordinarily thought to be contrary to power, such as Gandhi's view of the power of love.

THE POWER OF LOVE

Gandhi claims he can change attitudes and behavior over the long term by mobilizing the power of love. Because he seeks to alter both attitudes and behavior, he asks how people who are committed to particular ideas about what is real, possible, and good can voluntarily come to a different understanding. If individuals are ambivalent or unsatisfied about their current views, then they are open to solid, rational arguments to change. But Gandhi recognizes that those he wants to convert usually carry their own strong convictions and are not readily open to alternative, particularly conflicting, standards. Therefore, he reasons, he must appeal to their "heart," and he does this through love. Then, he believes, his opponents are open to the possibility of seeing the world in a different way. Once this happens, he thinks they are ready to hear rational appeals and conversion is possible.

Gandhi knows that conventional applications of power have incredible abilities to change behavior because of the rewards and penalties they carry. But such inducements do not necessarily convince people to genuinely want what they are commanded to do. Moreover, when the inducements are lifted, many return to their earlier ways of thinking and acting, making the effects of power only temporary. Gandhi holds that love is different; it is a force for lasting change which breaks down resistances. For him, love creates the basis for trust rather than the suspicion that accompanies conventional uses of power. It does this by speaking to a transcendent, rather than to an instrumental self, and disclosing what people share.

Holding that everyone has the capacity to love and everyone can respond to love, he argues that it is love that holds people together, not their interests. Moving as it does beyond particularities, love is said to appeal to what is best in persons, and when love is operative, bonds of friendship and community can thrive. Although others have called for strong civic attachments to form a national bond, Gandhi wants to do much more. He intends to universalize love, roaming beyond conventional boundaries and reaching for those who have significantly different ways of looking at the world. Moreover, Gandhian love is expressed nonviolently and, in this way, treats everyone as worthy of respect. Finally, Gandhi holds that because love can melt hatred and anger, it is possible to forge agreements and evolve outlooks that enable different men and women to live together amicably.

By asking people to love their opponents, and even suffer for their commitments, Gandhi wants to avoid what Nietzsche calls resentment.[16] Resentment is born out of the hatred and fear we have of those we think are responsible for harming us. It rests on the assumption that if the other is conquered, we are released from its torment and now free to make our own choices. Gandhi sees this as a delusion. Recognizing that others are often a source of injustice and need to be resisted, he wants such resistance to avoid two common mistakes embedded in a politics of resentment. One is the idea that the contest must be fought on the terrain defined by others because such a move means that any victory will mimic the standards of success predetermined by the other. For Gandhi, part of the struggle is to locate the field that speaks to our needs and is not hostile to our autonomy. The second mistake Gandhi wants to avoid is the idea that once we have defeated the other, the task of liberation is complete and all good things will follow.[17] This ignores the fact that in accepting the terms of the other, we repress our own aspirations which have now become remainders as we adopt the terms defined by the other to describe us and what is important. Gandhian love seeks to defeat resentment and open new ways of thinking of how we can live harmoniously with the other.

HOW DOES GANDHI UNDERSTAND POLITICS?

There once was a time, Gandhi argues, when politics were relatively unimportant. Life was simple and people led coherent lives.[18] On his account, politics seldom intruded into the lives of ordinary people and demanded little from them. At most, rulers exacted some tribute, but this imposition did not disturb the lives of ordinary people. What transpired in palaces or on battlefields little affected stable self-understandings and routines. Satisfied with their tribute, rulers did not generally disturb the rhythm of everyday life, and the traditions of local communities guided conduct rather than the state. This, Gandhi contends, changes in the modern age.

Today, he finds that it matters to ordinary people what happens in the corridors of power; it affects how they meet their multiple needs and the identity they are assigned. On Gandhi's reading, the modern state penetrates into basic, ordinary routines and invades what was once private. It does this not only by coercively extending state power into private space but also by legitimizing new institutional practices which, he believes, redefine the good, diminish the need for cooperation, and alter the ways men and women make a living. As Gandhi sees it, we have not asked to become political; rather politics compels our attention because it continually and profoundly intrudes into our lives today. In the modern "age, our degradation reveals itself through our political condition. . . . In the olden days, our peasants, though ignorant of who ruled them, led their simple lives free from fear. They can no longer afford to be unconcerned."[19]

For Gandhi, politics is unavoidable in the modern age and state power is seen as particularly dangerous. In some important ways, Gandhi's argument corresponds to St. Augustine's. Sharing the view that power cannot justify itself, both part company with efforts to legitimate power on substantive or procedural grounds.[20] For Augustine and Gandhi, there is no legitimate reason why some people should force their will on others or why some should use the violence of the state to choose what others may choose. For each, no person or state has an inherent right to compel others to do what they would not have freely chosen for themselves. Augustine sees the state appropriating a power that is properly God's and making legitimacy into a secular principle born out of the necessity for order. Although Gandhi does not share Augustine's preoccupation about order, he agrees that necessity cannot be converted into morality. Power is important to both Augustine and Gandhi, who see individuals drawn in two very different directions. Augustine sees the choice between virtue and sin and finds that the latter has an unshakable presence, tied as it is to human pride. For Gandhi, people can develop morally or regress to the state of the "brute," and individuals "must choose" which course they will take.[21]

Augustine and Gandhi see pride at work in our various efforts to graft our conceptions of justice to political power and, in doing so, to justify the coercion of some over others. The search for secular justice is sometimes a well-intentioned effort to move beyond the contingent and pursue a conception of the good, and partly a reflection of pride. However, Augustine finds efforts to legitimize coercive power as the great human conceit, mimicking the divine in claiming knowledge about what constitutes the good and the ability to achieve it. Armed with these deceptions, the proud believe they can exonerate their use of power over others. With similar arguments, Gandhi finds that any claim to the truth is, at best, partial and unavoidably tainted with our pride, and he seeks to disable arguments that exonerate political coercion for the sake of a higher good.

Although Gandhi's critique of politics parallels much of Augustine's, their views rest on very different premises. Even though both believe that human reason is frail and can never fully understand a comprehensive truth, Augustine confidently concludes that we can approach the truth through Christian faith. For his part, Gandhi believes that essential elements of the truth are captured only incompletely by any particular religious or secular position; at best, each embodies a slice of the truth but holds none can claim a comprehensive understanding of the truth because each is partial. More than that, Gandhi places much more emphasis on the autonomy of individuals and the power of love as a brake on political power than Augustine, who emphasizes eternal salvation. While Augustine believes we are at our best when we follow God's word through a life of prayer and devotion, Gandhi argues that we are at our most religious when we actively confront injustice in the world.

Gandhi's reading of politics is based on his understanding of the pervasiveness and unavoidability of power, and he seeks to confront, diffuse, and challenge it and expose the pride that often drives it. On his account, pride is always ready to assert itself, whether in the state or civil society, and always ready to hunt for more power to implement its plans. For this reason, Gandhi reasons, politics in the modern era especially must be about clear-sightedness and nonviolent struggle.

CIVIC EDUCATION

Gandhi finds that most people commonly misunderstand the nature of power and politics, limiting their political attention to formal institutions, laws, and rituals and usually taking little notice of how power pervades society.[22] He seeks to educate his fellow citizens about the nature of power, its myriad sites, its dangers, and how it enables or disables them. Armed with such an understanding, he believes that people are better equipped to detect and challenge abuses of power and make it responsible.[23]

Popular conceptions of power and politics typically reflect the civic education and socialization of citizens. This education covers not only what is taught at home and in schools but also the lessons attached to political activities and rituals, such as with elections or civic commemorations. When this kind of civic education takes hold, it serves to legitimize both political power as constituted and the basic laws governing behavior and property. The lessons citizens learn usually give an important place to the goodness, legitimacy, and appropriateness of their regime and its ideas of fairness and equity. However, the focus of conventional civic education on governmental arrangements and rules has the effect of concealing other sites and practices of power located throughout society. In the process, it conceals the ways that many forms of power direct choice and assess costs.

Gandhi is particularly concerned about the hidden character of much contemporary power. For him, conventional political education is misleading not only because its formalism conceals much power but also because individuals do not understand they are the basis of political power and are implicated in its uses. Learning about the formal obligations and rights allotted to them, they also typically accept the limits assigned to them and the need to defer and acquiesce. For Gandhi, most of what we learn about power and politics is incomplete and unrealistic. To talk, as he does, about our "hallucination about titles, law courts, schools, and councils"[24] means that people invest an aura in them that is unreal. Titles are said to bring authority, courts justice, schools a neutral education, and councils fair laws. For his part, Gandhi wants to problematize these practices and make them observable sites of power.[25]

THE NEW IDOL

Gandhi finds that many place an unwarranted faith in the state, either the current or a reformed one. They fail to see the causes of their discontents often lie elsewhere as they call on the state to strike out at the objects of their resentment. In doing so, he thinks they elevate the state to a position that is based on a dangerous deception that it represents the people, acts on their behalf, and can cure what ails them. In this respect, Gandhi's concerns parallel Nietzsche's observation that "coldly [the state] tells lies too; and this lie crawls out of its mouth: 'I, the state, am the people.' That is a lie!"[26]

With Nietzsche, Gandhi sees the pretentiousness of the modern state as menacing. Rising out of the ashes of religion and tradition that aimed at the good, the modern state fills a vacuum, promising to replace neglected gods and discarded traditions. For his part, Nietzsche finds that the modern state "lures them, the all-to-many—and . . . devours them, chews them, and ruminates! 'On earth there is nothing greater than I: the ordering finger of God am I'—thus roars the monster."[27] Nietzsche laments that today, even "great souls" are prey to its seductive claims. Those with "rich hearts" believe they have no recourse but to turn to the state; in doing so, they become its creatures and not their own masters. Again Nietzsche: "It will give you everything if you will adore it, this new idol: thus it buys the splendor of your virtue and the look of your proud eyes."[28]

To explore Gandhi's critique of the pretentiousness of the modern state, including those that are democratic, I take up several themes in his work which question the necessity and desirability of a superintending state as well as what passes for the legitimacy of the democratic state.[29] When Gandhi initially raises questions about the adequacy of democracy, both fascism and communism are threatening political movements and his criticisms are taken at the time as wrongheaded and beside the point. Since the destruction of fascism and the collapse of Soviet communism, democracy has become the nominal legitimizing principle of government. At the same time, many who are highly committed to democracy have argued that the actual practices of Western politics are pale copies of what democracies should look like in practice.[30] In many ways, their criticisms reflect elements of Gandhi's earlier challenge to Western democratic theories and practices, and I will scan some of their critiques in order to situate Gandhi's own position. In what follows, I concentrate on Gandhi's arguments with the democratic state as we have come to know it.

PROBLEMATIZING DEMOCRATIC POLITICS

Gandhi attempts to decenter claims that a universal franchise and majoritarian procedures are sufficient to legitimize power. He thinks the extension of the franchise is necessary but insufficient for a robust democracy, particularly in the face of countertendencies in complex, modern societies to dedemocratize the polity. One of the major impediments to democratizing any regime is the tendency of public officials simultaneously to display and hide their power.[31] By concentrating on the ceremonial, the monumental, and the martial, they seek to invest themselves as the carriers of the nation's best interests and security and to legitimize their use of power and the political institutions they manage. At the same time, those with power rarely bargain publicly about who is to get and who is to pay. The public debates in which they engage seldom reflect the rational, dispassionate search for solutions that is celebrated in classical conceptions of democracy but serve instead as rhetorical devices to reinforce supporters and embarrass opponents. Moreover, the debates that appear open and spontaneous often mask prior decisions that are made by oligarchs, far from the gaze of the public.[32]

The tendency of power to hide itself behind the ceremonial, to become hierarchical and concentrated, and to avoid accountability are the very things Gandhi wants India to avoid in its construction of democracy. In his search for a responsive, nonviolent mode of popular government, he insists India must move beyond the competitive elections and pluralism that mark Western democracies, and he urges participatory, decentralized modes of politics.[33] Even with these reforms, he sees future dangers because of the inherent dangers of power and the unavoidability of pride. To domesticate power in order to make it fit for human society requires that power be continually exposed and scrutinized. Otherwise, it has a tendency to hide and become dangerous, not hospitable, to democracy.

Gandhi is also concerned with the tendency in modern democracy to be satisfied with the proposition that formal political equality assures everyone the same voice in public space and ensures popular accountability. He wants a more expansive sense of equality, one that enables all to stand on the same solid footing when they face their government. A democracy that is built on steep economic and social inequalities is one that is apt to be more responsive to those with more and indifferent to those with less. As Gandhi sees matters, this cannot qualify as a real democracy.[34]

THE ISSUE OF MAJORITARIANISM

In contemporary democracies, competitive elections provide an accepted way of determining the will of the majority and investing government with legitimacy. However, it is not always clear what is meant by the term "majority" or how it operates in democratic practice. Contemporary democratic theorists have discussed how the term is fungible, how different decision rules reveal very different outcomes, how some are included in the democratic process but others are not, how the scale and complexity of modern society reduces citizen control, and how other institutions—such as bureaucracies, interest groups, and corporations—undermine democratic accountability.[35]

Even when democratic decision making represents the majority, Gandhi asks about the status of the minority. Sometimes, losing affects matters of convenience or issues of marginal concern. Gandhi is not particularly interested in these losses because the essential autonomy of individuals is not affected. However, he finds that if human beings are degraded by the rules of the majority, losing is something quite different than with the earlier case. Here we encounter Gandhi's suspicions of claims that democratic governance is an adequate check on the abuse of power. Unlike William Jennings Bryan, who thinks the voice of the people is the voice of God, Gandhi holds the voice of the people is the voice of voters, a fallible collection of often well-meaning (but sometimes indifferent or self-interested) people who constitute something over fifty percent of the population. While the democratic process eliminates the tyrannical rule of one or a few over the majority, Gandhi believes that it cannot overcome human fallibility and, he concludes, cannot legitimately coerce a minority to obey laws contrary to its deepest principles.[36] Not surprisingly, he readily concludes that "In matters of conscience, the law of majority has no place."[37] With this in mind, he observes "the majority vote . . . does not cancel the minority vote. It stands. Where there is no principle involved and there is a programme to be carried out, the minority has got to follow the majority. But where there is a principle involved, the dissent stands, and it is bound to express itself in practice when the occasion arises."[38]

Gandhi does not expect his position will lead to a flood of objections to majority decisions. However deeply suspicious he is of government, he grants that it is necessary to provide a minimal order in social life and thinks most citizens accept this position. In assigning a duty to citizens to be vigilant about abuses of power, he does not want them to inflate every grievance into a matter of conscience and claim an exemption from any rule that is inconvenient or disagreeable. In this regard, Gandhi writes, he would "be deeply distressed, if on every conceivable occasion every one of us were to be a law unto one-self and to scrutinize in golden scales every action of our future National Assembly."[39] For him, mistakes might be made by the government, and the issue is whether these errors rob persons of their autonomy. Gandhi finds it just as repugnant to be apathetic about serious injustices coming from the majority as it is to elevate personal interests over democratically enacted rules.

POLITICAL INTEREST

Gandhi recognizes that most people do not shake their concerns about themselves. The way they make a living, raise a family, and interact with others, and the way their background empowers or degrades them are important to ordinary people and, Gandhi thinks, they should be. The perennial danger for Gandhi is that people frequently make their own interests their primary standard for judging politics. For many, politics becomes a means to enhance their well-being, even if that means others must pay for their benefits or others are injured by their claims. For this reason, Gandhi wants to make politics safe from interests, not hospitable to them.[40]

In the modern world, Gandhi believes, interests have assumed unwelcome dimensions. Most obviously, they have multiplied, and many have little or nothing to do with exercising a person's autonomy or meeting necessity. For this reason, Gandhi challenges the pluralist position that no interest should count for more than another interest and everyone should be free to advance his or her interest, however defined.[41] Gandhi wants to rank interests, making the well-being of the most destitute the highest one. On his account, "every [other] interest, therefore that is hostile to their interest, must be revised or must subside if it is not capable of revision."[42]

Gandhi denies the pluralist view that politics is a vast market, with candidates and parties acting like firms, seeking to win votes (or customers) for their product. In the pluralist account, winning is what counts, and it becomes necessary to build a coalition with promises of individual advantage. In this setting, any coalition that is formed may or may not be coherent, may or may not interfere with the minority, and may or may not endanger the group's or the community's long-term welfare.[43] With its emphasis on constructing a winning coalition with promises of short-term gains, the market model of politics does not and (according to such defenders as Anthony Downs and Robert Dahl) cannot speak to a common good or general welfare.[44] The foundation of this form of politics is not the citizen but the organized interest group.[45] This Gandhi rejects as vigorously as he can.[46] For him, "ultimately, it is the individual who is the unit."[47]

For Gandhi, we need a different conceptual language to think about democracy than can be supplied by political pluralism. One reason is its penchant to concentrate on immediate benefits for strategic publics. With this in mind, he criticizes the narrow, short-term focus he detects in British parliamentary politics in his time. While it hardly resembles the vote-trading and coalition building that has come to characterize modern political pluralism, Gandhi sees the British model as unable to speak to a general good. Political favors are widely dispersed, not in the forms of "what are generally known as bribes," but as a "subtler influence" that steers elected officials away from a search for the common good.[48] He also fears that speech is distorted in pluralist democracy; it has become primarily cathartic and not communicative. But if voters can only hear how something affects their interests, they will be deaf to the concerns and needs of others. As he understands it, the evolution of democracy is not possible if we are "not prepared to hear the other side. We shut the doors of reason when we refuse to listen to our opponents, or having listened make fun of them. If intolerance becomes a habit, we run the risk of missing the truth."[49]

Gandhi attempts to secure a different kind of pluralism in India, one that is attentive to and protective of the multiple traditions and practices that mark the country. He sees different local customs providing people with their own particular modes of understanding, making a living, raising a family, and meeting their multiple needs. To assume that out of the welter of differences, one state-imposed solution should crowd out all alternatives denies standing to other practices and logics. Distinguishing between political and cultural pluralism, he finds that in pursuing the former, the latter is discounted and becomes lost.[50] One reason Gandhi continually returns to the villages of India is that he considers them to be havens for the diverse moral practices and traditions that demonstrate the mutual dependence of ordinary men and women on one another.[51]

CHALLENGING BUREAUCRACY

Bureaucracies in the modern democratic polity commonly develop in response to popular pressures for state action. Today, the public expects government to provide public education and health services, assure safe drinking water and sanitation, and license health professionals, to name just a few of the tasks citizens routinely assign to the modern state. But modern democracies appear unable to tame the administrative and regulatory organizations they have created to perform these tasks. One reason is that citizens want efficiency in the delivery of services, and bureaucracies take on hierarchical forms that promise to increase both control and efficiency.[52] This drive for the timely, efficient delivery of services masks the high price that Max Weber has shown bureaucracy to charge for its services: the more it is "dehumanized," the more completely it succeeds in eliminating from official business love, hatred, and all purely personal, irrational, and emotional elements which escape calculation.[53]

For Weber, the rule-governed nature of bureaucracies that are said to assure the fair and neutral application of law comes with a heavy cost. One reason is that bureaucratic neutrality emphasizes that officials set aside personal or partisan considerations when they regulate or administer. This means not playing favorites and speaking in an impartial voice. However, the bureaucratic process is marked with all sorts of assumptions that are far from impartial. For Foucault, it "ceaselessly characterizes, classifies, and specializes" and engages in "surveillance, continuous registration, perpetual assessment and classification" in ways that are "both immense and minute."[54] From this perspective, the modern bureaucratic state is not neutral when it assigns identities to others who are now known by the requirements of state policy and not by their character or needs. Because bureaucratic classifications are not benign but carry power that can affect individuals in the most profound ways, Gandhi is suspicious of claims to neutrality that sanction the use of power over others. For him, the partiality of any truth and the criticality of autonomy mitigate against the bureaucratic impulse to classify and categorize individuals. Moreover, Gandhi finds the bureaucratic proclivity to rest on expertise means it does not have to listen but merely applies its version of the truth; for this reason, he wants specialists to stop, listen, and be accountable.[55]

With its claims to neutrality, instrumental reason, and efficiency, bureaucracy depoliticizes the world, and we encounter fewer sites of contested power and more locations for problem solving. This Gandhi wants to resist, not because he equates the good life and the good community with continued conflict but because he sees that claims that promise to settle issues through technical solutions frequently mask configurations of power that shape social relationships and, thereby, leave steep inequalities and institutionalized indignities undisturbed.

POLITICAL COMPLEXITY AND CONTROL

One of the sharpest differences separating Gandhi's view of democracy and most contemporary accounts fixes on the way we respond to the complexity of modern society and government. However much we may want to return to a more simple time, the modern argument runs, the realities of our era compel us to take complexity into account when we design and manage public institutions. This means that earlier conceptions of a simple accountability need to be reassessed and replaced by new ones that respond to a world that has greatly changed.

Several critics have noticed a tendency to respond to complexity by seeking to simplify popular ideas of politics and to approach politics symbolically and not substantively. Indeed, with growing complexity, the need for ritual, thought by some to be an outmoded relic of the past, intensifies in the late modern world as the basis for understanding politics. In discussing the re-placement of substance with symbolism, Murray Edleman warns that politi-cal ritual "involves its participants symbolically in a common enterprise," and he goes on to argue that it "promotes conformity and evokes . . . joy in con-formity."[56]

For his part, Gandhi argues that manipulation and democracy are contra-dictory terms. As he sees matters, "Democracy is not a state in which people act like sheep. Under democracy individual liberty of opinion and action is jealously guarded."[57] He fears that complex institutions threaten to over-whelm individuals caught in legitimizing rituals. How the potency of politi-cal ritualism works in modern democracies can be seen in the observations of David Kertzer: "Through participation in the rites [of voting], the citizen of the modern state identifies with larger political forces that can only be seen in symbolic form. And through political ritual, we are given a way to under-stand what is going on in the world, for we live in a world that must be dras-tically simplified if it is to be understood at all."[58]

Kertzer finds that the invisible state "must be personified before it can be seen, symbolized before it can be loved, imagined before it can be con-ceived."[59] Gandhi recoils at the personification and symbolization of the state. Should this come to pass, people no longer judge but acquiesce, and obedience becomes the automatic response to the benevolent state. Then, citizens forget that the state never escapes its coercive properties.[60] Gandhi wants to remind people that "The State represents violence in a concentrated and organized form. The individual has a soul, but as the State is a soulless machine, it can never be weaned from violence to which it owes its very ex-istence."[61]

To humanize the state and make it the object of love is to put people off guard. To address this problem, Gandhi calls for a comprehensive education in politics, not just a formal one, and he wants to exchange symbolic simpli-fication for real simplification by radically decentralizing government and dispersing power to local communities.[62] There, he expects people to en-counter a government they can understand and control. The language they use to judge government comes from their own experiences and is not man-ufactured for them elsewhere.

GANDHI'S IDEAL DEMOCRACY: THE *PANCHAYAT RAJ*

In developing his theories of popular government, Gandhi returns to the vil-lages of India where, he believes, people are less vulnerable to the control of others and better positioned to challenge abuses of power. Gandhi's ideal political arrangement for the village is the *panchayat,* an ancient form of governance with a five-member assembly elected by the villagers.[63] There, he expects power to flow from the base. This is possible, Gandhi thinks, because the social and economic conditions that favor autonomy are in place: every citizen is able to earn a living and steep inequalities have been eliminated.[64]

Gandhi assigns the *panchayat raj* a limited but what he considers an important list of duties it can readily accomplish and which cannot be adequately addressed by individuals on their own: "the education of the boys and girls in its village; its sanitation; its medical needs; the upkeep and cleanliness of village wells or ponds; and the uplift of and daily wants of the so-called untouchables."[65] Given his abhorrence of violence, Gandhi deprives the *panchayat raj* of the authority to punish; rather it is expected to rely on "its moral authority, strict impartiality, and the willing obedience of the parties concerned" to assure its smooth operation.[66] As he sees it, the success of the *panchayat* leadership comes not in solving disputes, but in avoiding them.[67] When conflict does occur, he calls on public opinion to "do what violence can never do."[68]

In Gandhi's version of democracy, "the weakest should have the same opportunity as the strongest."[69] To achieve his vision, he calls for economic floors and ceilings to assure that the range of inequalities is narrow.[70] For him, steep inequalities make it difficult for citizens to understand each other and thereby reduce the chances of finding mutually satisfying agreements.[71] On his account, the ideal village republic will be a structure on sand if it is not built on the solid foundation of economic equality. Economic equality must never be supposed to mean possession of an equal amount of worldly goods for everyone. It does mean, however, that everyone will have a proper house to live in, sufficient and balanced food to eat, and sufficient *Khadi* with which to cover himself. It also means that the cruel inequality that obtains today will be removed by purely nonviolent means.[72]

Gandhi's "perfect democracy [is] based upon individual freedom. The individual is the architect of his own government. The law of non-violence rules him and his government."[73] Acknowledging that many see his goal as "utopian," he insists that politics needs standards, and he offers the highest standard he can imagine. Even though he knows his "picture" of India is not completely "realizable," the country "must have a proper picture of what we want before we can have something approaching it."[74] Gandhi's effort to restore the *panchayat raj* can be read as another of his morality tales, this one designed to show the importance of decentralized government.[75] As with his other tales, he seeks to disclose the importance of people taking charge of their lives, and for this to happen, they must be part of a cooperative, participatory community.[76] Gandhi's democracy is not primarily about a set of procedures or institutions but about sites of self-conscious action. In constructing his political ideal, he offers not another interest to pluralist politics but a different way of thinking and talking about politics and the state and, in this way, of recalling what are becoming remainders in modern politics.

POLITICS AND RELIGION

Gandhi is intensely spiritual and, he claims, reluctantly political.[77] He participates in politics, "only because politics encircle us today like the coil of a snake from which one cannot get out, no matter how much one tries. I wish, therefore, to wrestle with the snake."[78] In his wrestling match, he calls on religion to animate him and seeks to join it with politics.[79] However, his fusion of the two departs from either of the forms familiar in the West. In one, the state retains sovereignty and favors one religion over others or approves a particular church as the official religion as with the Orthodox Church of Imperial Russia. The other is where the church determines some public policies or the state and church are combined under the jurisdiction of religious officials, as with the Papal States. Gandhi's linkage of politics and religion has a radically different character. He does not want the state to become involved in what he calls "denominationalism."[80] Paralleling the liberal effort to separate church and state, Gandhi writes that "The State has nothing to do with [religion]. The State would look after your secular welfare, health, communications, foreign relations, currency, and so on, but not your or my religion. That is everybody's personal concern."[81]

What then does Gandhi mean when he says he wants to join politics and religion?[82] From his perspective, we do not make civic institutions spiritual by making them holy (which puts them beyond criticism) or having them enforce a particular religious ideal (which makes them coercive). On his view, institutions have a spiritual dimension when their own internal practices and external effects enhance, rather than demean, the dignity of persons.[83] For this reason, Gandhi thinks that if the internal practices of an institution diminish autonomy, it is "irreligious."

Emphasizing that politics should be driven by moral principles, he strenuously objects to views of politics that hold moral principles and virtues are appropriate to private but not public life. This position is epitomized by Niccolo Machiavelli's famous aphorism that the prince must learn how not to be good if he is to remain a prince.[84] Gandhi fears that when private and public life have their own distinct and sometimes contradictory moral foundations, there is the constant danger that public officials, however selected, treat citizens as means to political ends. Arguing that "political life must be an echo of private life and there cannot be any divorce between the two," Gandhi wants each to be morally directed.[85] He maintains that citizenship depends on a morally coherent life, that no good citizen fails to practice the ordinary virtues, and that politics must be informed by moral standards, not by interests.[86]

This line of thinking leads Gandhi to insist that an individual's religion must be expressed in "service to the helpless."[87] Although meditation and prayer are important to him, if this is all that describes a person's religious commitments, Gandhi finds them woefully inadequate.[88] For this reason, he insists that "religion which takes no account of practical affairs and does not help to solve them, is no religion."[89] Insisting that religion is more than talk, ritual, and meditation, he observes that it is good enough to talk of God whilst we are sitting here "after a nice breakfast and look forward to a nicer luncheon, but how am I to talk of God to millions who go without two meals a day. To them God can only appear as bread and butter."[90]

For Gandhi, the destitute need work, and the highest spiritual exercise in India is to promote the conditions which enable everyone to work for a living.[91] For him, the spiritual life is not concentrated on the future and the far-off but on the present and the local.[92] His reformulations of service touch many realms, and what he says about service not only undermines traditional, particularly Brahminic, views of religion but also conventional ideas about political participation, the topic of the next section.[93]

REDEFINING POLITICAL PARTICIPATION

In thinking about an ideal mode of politics, Gandhi seeks to empower citizens rather than the state. He goes about this by radically redefining political participation in ways that not only depart from minimalist modes, such as voting, but also from more energetic modes, such as participatory democracy where citizens are active in more sites.[94] Gandhi finds these modes are important but inadequate, and he offers three new understandings of participation. One involves politicizing ordinary Indians and showing them politics continually intrudes into their everyday lives. Second, Gandhi believes people act politically when they engage in service, such as working to eliminate untouchability. Each activity is democratic in the broadest sense because, Gandhi insists, everyone can participate in them, with different people deciding which is the best expression for them. Gandhi's third form of participation concerns leaders who dedicate their lives to the well-being of their communities and express their politics through service.

Gandhi wants Indians to understand that their everyday decisions ought to reflect their political and ethical commitments. This is what lies behind his call to Indians to resign from the British civil service and leave British schools. The issue for Gandhi is not so much about hurting the British as it is keeping Indians from contributing to their own domination.[95]

Gandhi's effort to politicize what had been taken to be nonpolitical can be seen in his championing of *khadi*, or spinning homemade cloth.[96] *Khadi* is so important to Gandhi that, at one point, he makes it a requirement for the franchise, a move that seems bizarre.[97] Its prominence reflects Gandhi's view of full citizenship as a broad, participatory identity rather than one which is procedurally designed to be inclusive. Spinning for Gandhi is not simply a manual activity but a moral, political, and economic project. He credits it with contributing to full employment, diminishing dependencies on other nations, enabling people to take responsibility for themselves (because they now have a living income that they have earned), and promoting a sense of self-worth.[98] From his perspective, those who think spinning is irrelevant or beneath them reject their responsibility to their community and their duties to the most vulnerable members of society. For Gandhi, this kind of detachment disqualifies someone from full citizenship; here and elsewhere, he denies citizenship is adequately conceptualized as a universal entitlement and insists that it must always be tied to concrete responsibilities.

Gandhian service is based on the premise that people are able to "renounce self-interest" and act on behalf of the good of the community.[99] This can be seen in the advice he offers a group of male students at Pachaiyappas College regarding the "hardships of child widows."[100] Because of the heavy hand of superstition, child widows are destined to remain unmarried and become destitute and lonely. To challenge this injustice, he asks the students "to make this sacred resolve that you are not going to marry a girl who is not a widow, you will seek out a widow girl."[101] For Gandhi, this is not an act of charity by the students; rather, it is an act of their humanity and stems from the duties they owe others in an interconnected cosmos. And it is political because it challenges patterns of power and practices that disable some in the most degrading ways. Moreover, he is telling the students that it is not good enough for them to condemn unjust, hurtful practices; they are responsible for alleviating suffering now, not just criticizing it and waiting for others to challenge it actively.

Gandhi's reconceptualized political participation is also addressed to those who aspire to be leaders and dedicate their lives to service to the public.[102] Unlike professional politicians who make laws, Gandhi's political leaders are to be "Servants of the People" who teach people how to become autonomous rather than legislating for them. They are expected to engage in education, economic self-help, social work, and political mobilization and, in these ways, assist members of their communities to take charge of their own lives.[103]

Gandhi's views of service and leadership appear in his Constructive Programme in 1922, and he repeats them frequently. In addition to calling for communal unity between Hindus and Moslems, the abolition of untouchability, and the establishment of *khadi*, his Constructive Programme is meant to foster local industries, improve sanitation, educate all children as well as adults, promote provincial languages as well as Hindi, and emancipate women. As independence approaches, he calls on the Congress Party to disband and its members to become "Servants of the People" and promote the Constructive Programme.[104] Because of its prominent role in the independence movement, Gandhi thinks Congress is uniquely fitted for the tasks of moral regeneration and voluntary social reconstruction.[105] If his supporters become preoccupied with power and office in New Delhi, he fears they will misunderstand the nature of democratic leadership and neglect their obligations to their fellow citizens.[106]

In his reconstructed meaning of political leadership, Gandhi's ideal leaders abandon conventional power and are said to gain or rather earn their authority within their local communities through sacrifice, work, and disinterest about their own situations. Because this occurs in a local setting, the actions and intentions of any potential leader can be judged more accurately and confidently by prospective followers than when aspirants to leadership are distant and removed. For this reason, Gandhi holds that the authority of the ideal leader voluntarily flows from citizens who have not been manipulated.

On his reading, legitimate leadership is more likely to evolve in a community where men and women can reliably test the sincerity of the leader. Partha Chatterjee has argued that this amounts to replacing politics with morality, but it is more apt to say that Gandhi cannot conceptualize politics without morality. His version of the ideal servant can be seen in his own life. He is someone who owns no private property, possesses few personal possessions,[107] spins *khadi* daily, and spends time working and living with ordinary Indians to empower them.[108]

FROM A MINIMAL STATE TO A LIMITED STATE

Gandhi sees the state unavoidably relying on coercion, including violent coercion. And he finds the modern state embodying centralized, hierarchical, bureaucratized structures that are particularly dangerous to individual self-governance. Not surprisingly, he attacks the state as a "soulless machine."[109] However, Parekh shows that from the 1930s onward, Gandhi alters his view of the state, increasingly seeing it as a vehicle for change, better equipped than public opinion to right deep-seated, institutionalized injustices, such as untouchability.[110] While still of great value to Gandhi, public opinion and other nonstate remedies sometimes seem too halting and unreliable to serve as the only means to affect the changes he considers most essential. His move to accept state action discloses a Gandhi who is willing to tolerate coercion for limited, specific goals; his circumscribed endorsement of state power is not meant to promote justice but to dismantle injustice.[111]

Injustice can be understood as the reverse of justice. In many ways it is. Standards of justice are highly specific: we can think of Aristotle's conception of distributive justice, a Lockean conception of rights as a reflection of justice, or Marx's classless society as the just society. With each standard, injustice is the negation of a positive theory of justice. Each conception of justice comes with its own construction of injustice. The Lockean liberal, for example, finds that state expropriation of private property is unjust and a Marxist sees private property, particularly concentrated capital, is unjust. At this point, identifying injustices becomes an extension of the question, "What is justice?"

Gandhi wants to reverse the way we talk about justice and injustice and make injustice the primary basis for judgment and action.[112] He thinks diverse men and women can agree that particular forms of domination and suffering are unjust, whether they are liberals or Marxists, Indians or British, even though they share little understanding of what the just society might look like.[113] Emphasizing injustice also keeps us in the present and localizes our concerns. Gandhi sees people preoccupied with justice fixing their gaze on the future where they imagine the final conquest of good over evil. Fortified with their perfectionist ends, there is the danger that they find little need to consider the harms they cause others in their march to a future good.[114] An opposite danger in focusing on future justice is that people do nothing about correcting the injustices of the present because they are unprepared to settle for anything less than a perfectionist outcome.[115] Gandhi constantly challenges this kind of political lethargy just as he complains about Indian nationalists who are so focused on national independence that they do not recognize and respond to the other injustices in their own society. In placing his politics firmly in the present, Gandhi continually asks about such costs and insists people are responsible for the pain they tolerate or cause today in their quest for a better tomorrow. Concentrating on injustice introduces urgency and constraint on the use of power and lays the basis for his support for limited state action. For Gandhi, injustice is tangible and observable and not imagined (as future justice is), and he offers support for state action to relieve suffering and subordination but seldom for more.

For his part, Gandhi does not believe the state *qua* state can overcome its reliance on violence and therefore he continues to approach it skeptically. When he calls for state action, he holds that it must be always accompanied with a "minimum of violence" and he assigns it limited tasks.[116] Gandhi's discussion of an enlarged state is usually tied to eliminating untouchability, encouraging employment, and providing an equitable distribution of land for the peasants.

Even though Gandhi gives the state a wider role to play as India approaches independence, he continues to rely primarily on public opinion and never repudiates his observation of 1927 that "Government cannot afford to lead in matters of reform. By their very nature Governments are but interpreters and executors of the expressed will of the people whom they govern."[117] For all of his cautious acceptance of the state, Gandhi continues to work for decentralization, warn about political abuses, and offer his "Servants" as a way of addressing local problems without having to rely on the state. In sanctioning limited state power, Gandhi means to narrow its scope of action to combat the most severe forms of injustice that are visited on the most vulnerable members of society. And he attempts to bring it under the same unconventional methods he mobilizes against British colonial rule: popular pressure and civil disobedience.

EXPERIMENTAL POLITICS

Gandhi offers a view of politics that is local, simple, and participatory, and many criticize his vision as distracting. For them, his theory of politics misses the mark.[118] This is the case if we focus on how we can specifically apply his various theories in the late modern world with all of its complexity. However, the real issue ought to be about his aspirations for a politics dedicated to enhancing the autonomy of everyone. For Gandhi, politics and the state are unavoidable in the modern world; he never presents his idealized regime as one where power has disappeared or the state has withered away. He acknowledges that even in the best political arrangement, power can be abused and must be resisted.[119] To achieve his goals, Gandhi weaves together several requirements for the good polity. One concerns decentralizing and simplifying government and rendering it accountable. The second theme focuses on a civic education that recognizes the various, often opaque, locations of power and the ways it can be abused and the ways people can expose and challenge power. Third, he wants individuals to escape acute dependencies in order to govern themselves. Fourth, he expects citizens to become active in their society, often as an alternative to state action. Finally, he offers nonviolence as a way of proceeding politically.

Set at this level of generality, Gandhi's ideal politics retains its utopian flavor and also carries a sense that this is the kind of politics that many desire. They do not want to live in a regime where power is hidden except when it is abused, and they want to be autonomous rather than frightened or fatalistic. For Gandhi, claims such as order, efficiency, growth, and productivity carry insufficient purchase to override the claims for individual self-governance. He wants to rob such claims of their self-importance and show they ought not routinely trump a politics that aspires to be open and accountable. Popular control of government is always elusive, but it is surely not enhanced when efforts to undermine it are ignored or when the friends of democracy decline to acknowledge that contemporary democracy can generate its own abuses of power.[120]

In mounting his attack on the centralized, bureaucratic state and interest group politics, Gandhi seeks both to problematize the modern state and politics and to experiment with alternatives. His formulation of politics is not meant to settle political questions but to keep them alive, and his experiments are not meant to discover perfectionist solutions but to be resilient to diversity and openness. In this way, Gandhi hopes to protect the goods that he fears are becoming lost in modern, mass, complex democracy. The problematizing impulse that Gandhi carries to his discussions of violence and to economics also finds a place in his view of politics. Holding that we cannot escape state power, he wants us to tether it because, even with its limited capacity to do good, it has an extraordinary aptitude to do great harm.[121]

Gandhi says he enters politics because it has become unavoidable, and he does not expect to retreat to some quiet, tranquil place where politics can be ignored. Efforts to return to a mythic past that bypasses politics are a dangerous stance to Gandhi because they leave power unattended except by those who would use it for their own advantage. For him, the danger in contemporary politics is a new fatalism which denies that people can either control the institutions of modern society or recover what is valuable from the past and states that they ought not to try. To be political, on Gandhi's reading, means that people come equipped with a broad understanding of power, judge the uses of power with the materials of their own reformed tradition, demonstrate the courage to act nonviolently to remove injustice, and engage in service.

In the end, Gandhian politics is about struggle. The very goals he offers cannot fit comfortably in the modern world, and from a Gandhian perspective, they ought not be expected to. His goals serve as reminders about what is important but in danger of being lost. Gandhian struggle is not only against the entrenched power of the state; it is also a struggle with concentrations of private power in civil society. Each of these struggles precludes discovering a new, harmonious cosmos because Gandhi wants constantly to disturb any arrangement that fosters its own forms of domination and humiliation.

NOTES

1. John Dunn, *Western Political Theory in the Face of the Future* (Cambridge: Cambridge University Press, 1979), 27.

2. *Young India*, 7-2-31; see also Bondurant, *Conquest of Violence* (Berkeley: University of California Press, 1967), 184.

3. See *Nonviolence in Peace and War*, ed. Bharatan Kumarappa, vol. 1, 22–23.

4. *Democracy: Real and Deceptive*, ed. R. K. Prabhu (Ahmedabad: Navajivan, 1961).

5. For a further discussion of Gandhi's views on democracy and autonomy, see Ronald Terchek, "Gandhian Politics," in *New Dimensions and Perspectives in Gandhism*, ed. V. T. Patil (New Delhi: Inter-India Publications, 1988).

6. Cited in Nirmal Bose, ed. *Selections from Gandhi* (Ahmedabad: Navajivan, 1957), 122.

7. *Hind Swaraj*, ch. 8.

8. *Hind Swaraj*, ch. 20.

9. In responding to those who want to wrest sovereignty from the British and place it in Indian hands, Gandhi retorts, "you want English rule without the Englishman. You want the tiger's nature, but not the tiger, that is to say, you would make India English. . . . This is not the *swaraj* that I want." *Hind Swaraj*, ch. 4.

10. If independence means "a change from white military rule to a brown [one], we hardly need make any fuss. At any rate, the masses then do not count. They will be subject to the same spoliation as now if not even worse." *Young India*, 12-19-29.

11. Foreword, *Gokhale's Speeches*, Iyer, Raghavan, ed. *The Moral and Political Writings of Mahatma Gandhi* (Oxford: Clarendon Press), vol. 1: 138.

12. "Submission to the State law is the price a citizen pays for his personal liberty. Submission, therefore, to a State wholly or largely unjust is an immoral barter for liberty." *Young India*, 11-10-21.

13. *Young India*, 11-10-21.

14. *Young India*, 7-28-20.

15. See his justification to engage in civil disobedience on his own during World War II after the Working Committee of the Congress Party rejects his appeal to support a nationwide campaign of civil disobedience. *Harijan*, 6-19-40.

16. Nietzsche holds that "every sufferer instinctively seeks a cause for his suffering. . . . The suffering are one and all dreadfully eager and inventive in discovering occasions for painful affects," *On the Genealogy of Morals*, trans. Walter Kaufmann and R. I. Hollingdale (New York: Vintage, 1989), 127.

17. This is one of the central arguments of *Hind Swaraj*. Gandhi argues against accepting British terms of engagement and offers his own mode of response politically, economically, and socially.

18. Gandhi acknowledges that prior periods carry their own forms of subordination, as in the case of untouchability, and they must be resisted. However, he thinks the rhythm of life is not greatly altered when one prince replaces another in the premodern era.

19. "Foreword," Gokhale's Speeches, in Iyer, *Writings*, vol. 1: 137–38.

20. This stands in opposition to Aristotle's ideal state as pursuing the common good, Locke's assignment to the state to act as an "impartial umpire" to protect rights, or Rousseau's social contract as embodying the general will. For Augustine and Gandhi, each of these goods represents an inadequate justification of power. None of them, by itself or in tandem with other principled standards, can vindicate the use of force by some over others.

21. *Harijan*, 6-7-40.

22. Gandhi also thinks that a proper understanding of politics is stymied by the tendency of people to concentrate on the formal institutions of government or for them to assume a fatalistic view that nothing can be done to effect change. Another obstacle to a Gandhian conception of power comes with a narrow conception of what politics can accomplish. He continually complains that many think that if India gains its independence from Britain, the great task of politics is finished. However, he insists, this is based on a misunderstanding of what politics can and cannot accomplish. See *Hind Swaraj*.

23. In this vein, he writes, "Swaraj is to be attained by educating the masses to a sense of their capacity to regulate and control authority." *Young India*, 1-29-25.

24. *Young India*, 4-20-21.

25. In the modern world, much that we see is filtered through the mass media. What they choose to ignore and what to emphasize structure our own sight and understanding of politics. See Gandhi, *An Autobiography or the Story of My Experiments with Truth* (Ahmedabad: Navajivan Publishing House, 1972), Part II, ch. 28.

Gandhi fears that the mass media are replacing reliable sources of knowledge. "Unfortunately, the newspapers had become more important to the average man than the scriptures . . . and other good literature" (*Harijan*, 4-27-47). His own view of what constitutes an editor's responsibility comes in the opening pages of *Hind Swaraj*. "One of the objects of a newspaper is to understand popular feeling and to give expression to it; another is to arouse among the people certain desirable sentiments; and the third is fearlessly to expose popular defects. . . . To the extent the people's will has to be expressed, certain sentiments will need to be fostered, and defects will have to be brought to light" (*Hind Swaraj*, ch. 1). Also see Sailendr Bhattacharyya, *Mahatma Gandhi: The Journalist* (Bombay: Times of India Press, 1962).

26. Friedrich Nietzsche, *Thus Spake Zarathustra*, in *Portable Nietzsche*, ed. Walter Kaufmann (New York: Penguin, 1976), 161.

27. *Zarathustra*, 161. Compare with Hobbes's Leviathan who is called the "mortal God."

28. *Zarathustra*, 161–62.

29. See Thomas Pantham, "Thinking with Mahatma Gandhi: Beyond Liberal Democracy," *Political Theory* 11, no. 2 (7/83): 165–88.

30. See Norberto Bobbio, *Future of Democracy* (London: Polity Press. 1987); and Danilo Zolo, *Democracy and Complexity* (University Park: Pennsylvania State University Press, 1993). Similar criticisms come from other quarters as well. See Bhikhu Parekh, *Gandhi's Political Philosophy* (Notre Dame: University of Notre Dame Press, 1989); Nandy, *Traditions, Tyranny, Utopias* (Delhi: Oxford University Press, 1987); Jurgen Habermas, *Legitimation Crisis* (Boston: Beacon Press, 1976); and Claus Offe, *Contradictions of the Welfare State* (Cambridge: MIT Press, 1984).

31. Bobbio finds that "one of the cliches heard in all past and present debates on democracy is the assertion that it is 'open government' by a 'visible power.'" But he discovers an "invisible power" lurks in the background, unnoticed by many commentators who insist that what they see (rather than what is hidden) is what counts. *Future*, 79.

32. See Friedrich Hayek, *Political Order of a Free People* (Chicago: University of Chicago Press, 1973), for a conservative critique along these lines; for a neorealist critique, see Bobbio, *Future*; for a similar critique from the left, see Offe, *Contradictions*.

33. See Gandhi, *Democracy: Real and Deceptive* (Ahmedabad: Navajivan, 1961).

34. See *Democracy: Real and Deceptive*.

35. On the fungibility of majorities, see Kenneth Arrow, *Social Choice and Individual Values* (New Haven: Yale University Press, 1951); on the role of decision rules, see E. E. Schattschneider, *The Semisovereign People* (New York: Harcourt Brace, Jovanovich, 1975); on complexity, see Zolo, *Democracy and Complexity*; and for a discussion of accountability, see Robert Dahl, *Dilemmas of Pluralist Democracy* (New Haven: Yale University Press, 1982); Theodore Lowi, *The End of Liberalism* (New York: Norton, 1969); and Charles Lindbloom, *Politics and Markets* (New York: Basic Books, 1977).

36. "I do not believe in the doctrine of the greatest good for the greatest number. It means in its nakedness that in order to achieve the supposed good of fifty-one percent, the interest of forty-nine per cent may be, or rather should be, sacrificed." "Letter to an Indian Friend," 7-4-32 in Mahadev Desai, *The Diary of Mahadev Desai* (Ahmedabad: Navajivan, 1953), 149.

37. *Young India*, 8-4-20.

38. *Harijan*, 8-11-40, in Iyer, *Writings*, vol. 2, 248. From Gandhi's perspective, "The rule of the majority has a narrow application, i.e., one should yield to the majority in matters of detail. But it is slavery to be amenable to the majority, no matter what its decisions are" (*Young India*, 3-2-22).

39. *Nonviolence in Peace and War,* vol. 1, 22–23.

40. In this regard, Gandhi echoes the concerns of many different democratic theorists who often disagree among themselves about other matters. See, for example, Rousseau's apprehension about particular wills crowding out the general will in *The Social Contract* as well as Madison's distrust of factions dominating government in *Federalist No. 10*.

41. See Arthur Bentley, *The Process of Government* (Evanston: Principia Press, 1908) for the classical formulation of pluralism; for two of the most influential accounts, see David Truman, *The Governmental Process* (New York: Knopf, 1951), and Dahl, *Who Governs* (New Haven: Yale University Press, 1961).

42. *Young India*, 9-17-31.

43. For a critique along these lines that remains highly influential in American democratic theory, see Joseph Schumpeter, *Capitalism, Socialism, and Democracy* (New York: Harper & Brothers, 1942).

44. Anthony Downs, *An Economic Theory of Democracy* (New York: Harper and Row, 1957), and Dahl, *Who Governs?*

45. Bobbio reflects a common observation when he writes that in "democratic states . . . it is less and less the individual who is the most influential factor in politics and more and more it is the group: large organizations," *Future*, 28.

46. Consider Gandhi's opposition to a separate electoral list for the untouchables in legislative bodies. He wants them represented as individuals, not as members of a group. See Gandhi, *The Nation's Voice* (Ahmedabad: Navajivan Press, 1932), 40.

47. *Harijan*, 7-28-46.

48. *Hind Swaraj*, ch. 5.

49. *Harijan*, 5-31-42.

50. Gandhi appreciates that India is a mosaic of diverse cultures, languages, and religions. No centralized formula can respect this plurality, and to try to impose one means destroying what is distinctive in each. To make universalizing binding rules is to rob the world of its diverse groundings.

51. For a further discussion of the contrast between Gandhi's democratic politics and pluralism, see Ronald Terchek, "Gandhi's Democratic Theory," in *Political Thought of Modern India*, ed. Thomas Pantham and Kenneth Deutsch (New Delhi: Sage of India, 1986).

52. Max Weber observes that "in its most rational development, [the bureaucratic state] is precisely characteristic of the modern state," *From Max Weber*, ed. H. H. Gerth and C. Wright Mills (New York: Oxford University Press, 1958), 82.

53. *Economy and Society* (Berkeley: University of California Press, 1978), 975.

54. Michel Foucault, *Discipline and Punish: The Birth of the Prison*, trans. A. Sheridan (New York: Vintage, 1979), 209, 212.

55. See *Young India*, 8-11-21.

56. Murray Edleman, *The Symbolic Uses of Politics* (Urbana: University of Illinois Press, 1967), 16. Edleman extends this argument in a later book, arguing that "everyone who grows up in our society is bound to become aware, at some level of consciousness, that an individual vote is more nearly a form of self-expression and of legitimation than of influence," *Constructing the Political Spectacle* (Chicago: University of Chicago Press, 1988), 97.

57. *Young India*, 3-2-22.

58. David Kertzer, *Ritual, Politics, and Power* (New Haven: Yale University Press, 1988), 1–2.

59. Kertzer, *Ritual, Politics, and Power*, 6.

60. For Gandhi, conventional politics is about power and coercion, and the phenomena Kertzer describes mask these realities.

61. Nirmal K. Bose, *Selections from Gandhi* (Ahmedabad: Navajivan, 1957), 41.

62. Gandhi also wants individuals to develop more "simple tastes" and move away from a "multiplicity of material wants" which add to the complexity of contemporary society. See *Young India*, 9-3-25.

63. *Harijan*, 7-26-42.

64. *Harijan*, 1-18-48.

65. *Young India*, 6-5-31.

66. *Young India*, 6-5-31.

67. *Harijan*, 6-4-48.

68. *Harijan*, 6-1-47.

69. Gandhi, *Nonviolence in Peace and War*, vol. 2, 269.

70. He holds that his version of a democracy "is clearly an impossibility so long as the wide gulf between the rich and the hungry millions persist," *Democracy, Real and Deceptive*, 68.

71. In societies where there are great disparities of wealth, the rich and poor assign different meanings to common words. What the rich mean by justice or rights is not what the poor mean by these terms. The meanings are not only disparate but often discordant.

72. *Harijan*, 8-18-46.

73. *Harijan*, 7-26-42.

74. *Harijan*, 7-28-46.

75. On Gandhi's reading, "True democracy cannot be worked by twenty men sitting at the centre. It has to be worked from below by the people of every village," *Harijan*, 1-18-48.

76. For him, politics is best approached in a circular rather than linear or hierarchical way. Gandhi sees a united India "composed of innumerable villages [where] there will be ever-widening, never-ascending circles. Life will not be a pyramid and the apex sustained by the bottom," *Harijan*, 7-28-46.

77. It is helpful to notice that Gandhi is not particularly religious. Although he attended temple as a child out of respect for his mother, he is not a templegoer as an adult and he never builds a temple in any of his ashrams. Nevertheless, he is deeply spiritual.

78. *Young India*, 5-23-20.

79. "Quite selfishly, as I wish to live in peace in the midst of a bellowing storm howling round me, I have been experimenting with myself and my friends by introducing religion into politics," *Young India*, 5-12-20.

80. "I do not believe that the State can concern itself or cope with religious instruction. I believe that religious education must be the sole concern of religious associations. . . . We have suffered enough from State-aided religion and a State Church. A society or a group, which depends partly or wholly on State aid for the existence of its religion . . . does not have any religion worth the name," *Harijan*, 3-23-47.

81. *Harijan*, 9-22-46. Compare with Locke's *Letter on Toleration*. Gandhi also observes that even if "the whole community had one religion," it is a mistake for the state to become involved because there are "as many religions as minds. Each mind had a different conception of God from that of the other," *Harijan*, 3-16-47.

82. For a further discussion of the relation Gandhi draws between politics and religion, see *Young India*, 6-18-25. Also see V. T. Patil, "Gandhi and His Ideas on Reli-

gion and Politics," in *New Dimensions and Perspectives in Gandhism,* ed. V. T. Patil (New Delhi: Inter-India Publications, 1988), 169–80; Chatterjee, *Gandhi's Religious Thought* (Notre Dame: University of Notre Dame Press, 1983); Iyer, *Moral and Political Thought,* 38–51; and Parekh, *Gandhi's Political Philosophy,* 65–109. Also see Thomas Pantham, "Indian Secularism and Its Critics," *Review of Politics* 59, no. 3 (Summer 1997): 523–40.

83. Gandhi's understanding of spirituality does not carry the transcendent character conventionally attributed to the term. Margaret Chatterjee remarks that "Gandhi drew no distinction between spirituality and social involvement," *Gandhi's Religious Thought,* 175. Earlier in her book, she observes that "Gandhi made no distinction between the sacred and the profane," 149.

84. "It is necessary for a prince, who wishes to maintain himself, to learn how not to be good, and use this knowledge or not use it, according to the necessity of the case," *The Prince* (New York: Modern Library, 1950), 58. What Machiavelli says to the prince can be applied to ambitious state officials, interest groups, and citizens as well.

85. Speech, 5-8-15, in Iyer, *Writings,* vol. 1: 375.

86. See speech, 4-27-15, in Iyer, *Writings,* vol. 1: 373–76.

87. *Young India,* 8-14-24.

88. On Gandhi's account, "The Brahman who has understood the religion of today will certainly give Vedic learning a secondary place and propagate the religion of the spinning wheel, relieve the hunger of the millions of his starving countrymen, and only then . . . lose himself in Vedic studies." "If I have to make the choice between counting beads or turning the wheel, I would certainly decide in favor of the wheel, making it my rosary, so long as I found poverty and starvation stalking the land," *Young India,* 8-14-24.

89. *Young India,* 6-7-29.

90. *Young India,* 10-15-31.

91. In emphasizing service, Gandhi is replacing, according to Parekh, "the traditional repertoire of spiritual exercises with a wholly new set of his own, including cleaning latrines, living and working among the untouchables and nursing the sick," *Gandhi's Political Philosophy,* 106–7.

92. One of the highest forms of religious activity for Christians comes with the work of missionaries Christianizing unbelievers. Gandhi, for one, does "not believe in people telling others of their faith, especially with a view to conversion. Faith does not admit of telling. It has to be lived and then it becomes self-propagating," *Young India,* 10-29-27. For Gandhi, religion becomes "self-propagating" when its members continually apply their ideals in their own local community, addressing the suffering of its most vulnerable members, and responding to the injustices that reside in their own society. For Gandhi, people who are sincerely religious should address injustice at home.

93. See Gandhi, *Constructive Programme* (Ahmedabad: Navajivan, 1941), 58.

94. There are several kinds of participatory models in democratic theory. The developmental approach claims citizens are extended by participation, learning not only about issues but how much they depend on others and others depend on them in their common projects. Another model concentrates on how community effectiveness is enhanced through widespread, intense activity. In these renditions, the participatory democrat stands in sharp contrast to the interest-carrying citizen who sees democratic politics as a competitive game and not a cooperative activity.

95. See *Hind Swaraj.*

96. See *Harijan*, 4-10-37.

97. *Young India*, 10-27-24.

98. For a selected collection of Gandhi's writings on spinning, see *Spinning and Khadi* (Lahore: Gandhi Publications League, 1943).

99. *Harijan*, 6-29-35. In the same piece, Gandhi holds that "service, like virtue, is its own reward and [the person engaging in service] will rest content with it."

100. In some areas of India during Gandhi's lifetime, marriages are arranged between children, to be consummated years later. In the meantime, each child lives with his or her parents. If the boy dies under this arrangement, the girl is considered a child widow.

101. *Young India*, 9-15-27.

102. "I felt compelled to come into the political field because I found that I could not do even social work without touching politics. I felt that political work must be looked upon in terms of social and moral progress." On his reading, "No part of life is untouched by politics" in the modern era and one "cannot sit still while the people are being ravaged," *Harijan*, 10-6-46.

103. "The *Gandhi Seva Sangh* [Gandhi's voluntary service organization] has come into existence for the purpose of carrying on the constructive programme. That alone is real politics. . . . What do we care if they do not call it politics? We shall remain within the Congress fold, but keep ourselves away from power and elections," Gandhi, Speech at Gandhi Seva Sangh, 2-22-40, in Iyer, *Writings*, vol. 1: 425.

104. He admits that he and his supporters "used politics to put our principles into practice. Now, after some experience, we are renouncing politics," Speech, 2-22-40, in Iyer, *Writings*, vol. 1, 423. Also see Gandhi, *Constructive Programme*. However, Gandhi does not advocate disbanding the state. Rather, he wants a parallel structure in place which carries political functions and is close to and controlled by local publics.

105. Throughout his career in India, Gandhi's relationship with Indian politicians in the Congress was often uneasy. He was suspicious of efforts to socialize the economy, build up the military forces, and create a strong central state; yet this is the direction of the Congress leadership. Whatever the practical, political consequences of his call for the disbanding of Congress, Gandhi's theoretical position is unmistakable. The political parties and the state are simply unable and incompetent to accomplish certain tasks, and when it tries, it often injures.

106. Gandhi grows increasingly impatient with many office-holders in the Congress. He finds it is "fast becoming an organization of selfish power-seekers and job-holders. Instead of remaining the servants of the public, Congressmen had become its lords and masters. The Congress was, moreover, torn by petty intrigues and group rivalries," *Harijan*, 6-1-47.

107. The personal belongings consist of his clothes, eyeglasses, books, a watch, and a few other assorted items.

108. See Gandhi, "The Village Worker," in *Rebuilding Our Villages* (Ahmedabad: Navajivan, 1952). Also see Dennis Dalton, *Mahatma Gandhi: Nonviolent Power in Action* (New York: Columbia University Press, 1993), 191. On one occasion, Gandhi talks about the way he would conduct himself as a "Servant." He expects the village families to ask him to teach their children, but he thinks he will be otherwise busy with other local projects and unable to devote the time to this request. He will offer to find a teacher and the families to bear the expense. Later, they will learn "the importance of hygiene and sanitation, and when they come and ask for

a sweeper, I will tell them: 'I will be your sweeper and I will train you all in the job,'" *Harijan*, 3-17-46.

109. Bose, *Selections from Gandhi*, 41. Earlier, Gandhi observes that people "cannot be made good by law. . . . I would prevent people from drinking and smoking. . . . But to regulate these things by law . . . would be a remedy probably worse than the diseases. . . . There is no law against using kitchens as closets or drawing rooms as stables. But public opinion, that is, public tastes will not tolerate such a combination. The evolution of public opinion is at times a tardy process but it is the only effective one," *Young India*, 7-9-25. Even after he gives the state more room for action than he did in the 1920s, he continues to have doubts about how far it can reconstruct attitudes and never leaves the idea that widescale conversion is necessary in India if the untouchables are to be free.

110. Parekh, *Gandhi's Political Philosophy*, 118–21.

111. Service, always important to Gandhi's views of politics, assumes a larger presence in his writings after he gives the state more room to act. If citizens rely only on the state to address injustice, then it is the state that becomes autonomous, and not citizens. His version of service extends to personal activities aimed at relieving and eliminating the suffering of the most vulnerable members in society.

112. See Judith Shklar's *The Faces of Injustice* (New Haven: Yale University Press, 1990) for an extended discussion of the different phenomenologies attached to justice and injustice.

113. Gandhi does not expect everyone simultaneously to discover that a particular practice is unjust. However, he believes that over time, everyone will respond to voluntary suffering.

114. This is one of Gandhi's major objections to state socialism. See *Harijan*, 7-14-47.

115. *Young India*, 6-28-28.

116. When he occasionally talks about the government owning industry and land, he insists that this will be accomplished nonviolently. However, he is vague and laconic as to how this will be done. See Jayantanuja Bandyopadhyaya, *Social and Political Theory of Gandhi* (Bombay: Allied Publishers, 1969), 114–15.

117. *Young India*, 10-20-27.

118. These are the objections of Parekh, *Gandhi's Political Philosophy,* and Partha Chatterjee, *Nationalist Thought and the Colonial World: A Derivative Discourse* (Delhi: Oxford University Press, 1986).

119. This is why he wants the Servants to teach civil disobedience.

120. Gandhi claims that power always reappears and can never be completely restrained by liberal constitutionalism. At this point, the issue for Gandhi is how individuals confront power they take to be used for an unjust purpose: "I look upon the power of the State with the greatest fear, because, although while apparently doing good by minimizing exploitation, it does the greatest harm to mankind by destroying individuality," Interview, 1934, in D. G. Tendulkar, *Mahatma: The Life of M. K. Gandhi* (New Delhi: Ministry of Information and Broadcasting, 1951–1954), vol. IV, 15.

121. "I look upon the power of the State with the greatest fear, because, although while apparently doing good by minimizing exploitation, it does the greatest harm to mankind by destroying individuality." Interview, 1934, in Tendulkar, *Mahatma*, vol. IV, 15.

11

"*Satyagraha*: The Only Way to Stop Terrorism"

Richard L. Johnson

Mohandas K. Gandhi developed a trenchant analysis of the violent nature of modern civilization and of violent Indian opposition to Western imperialism, as well as nonviolent alternatives to both forms of violence. In 1909 he met with all known Indian terrorists in London and wrote on his way back to South Africa his programmatic statement, *Hind Swaraj* (*Indian Home Rule*), a dialog between an Editor, Gandhi's mouthpiece, and a Reader, an Indian who advocated terrorism against the British Raj. Gandhi understood that British imperialism was rooted in the pervasive violence of modern civilization and that its opponents unwittingly bought into the underlying violence of that civilization, even as they thought they would destroy it. In the Subject Index to the *Collected Works of Mahatma Gandhi* (*CWMG*), there are thirty references to terrorism and terrorists—generally called extremists, anarchists, or revolutionaries—from 1909 to 1945.

Gandhi described the terrorism of anti-imperialists and of imperialists and examined their interrelationship from the vantage point of *satyagraha* (clinging to Divine Truth), an experimental nonviolent alternative to all forms of violence. *Satyagraha* involved practical, spiritually and morally based responses to the sociopolitical conditions created by direct and structural violence. Gandhi believed that "satyagraha is the only way . . . to stop terrorism."[1]

He went from South Africa to London in 1909 to garner support for his nonviolent campaign to end the repressive laws promulgated by the South African government against the Indian minority. Many prominent British leaders seemed sympathetic to Gandhi's campaign, but he discovered in London that their sympathy did not translate into concrete forms of assistance. At the same time, he talked with a wide range of Indians in London, seeking a unified nonviolent response to British imperialism. He found little more support for *satyagraha* from Indians than he found from the British. In fact, a few days before his arrival, the Indian terrorist Madanlal Dhingra assassinated Sir Curzon Wyllie, the former viceroy of India, in London.

Gandhi was able to enter into dialogue with his opponents, both imperialists and their violent opponents. While he was in London in 1909 he wrote a letter to Lord Ampthill, a former acting viceroy of India and one of the leading British imperialists he hoped to influence: "Opposed as I am to violence in any shape or form, I have endeavored specially to come in contact with the so-called extremists who may be better described as the party of violence. This I have done in order if possible to convince them of the error of their ways."[2] He did not simply write them off but rather observed them carefully, finding that "some of the members of this party are earnest spirits, possessing a high degree of morality, great intellectual ability and lofty self-sacrifice."[3] Over the years—from these early conversations in London up to the end of his life—Gandhi listened to and spoke with Indian terrorists. He agreed with their desire to end British rule and with their idealism but understood that their methods would actually hurt the cause of Indian independence. He converted many to nonviolent resistance to the British.[4]

From Gandhi's perspective, anti-imperialist terrorists were violent, but so were the imperialists. By forging a third path between these forms of violence, Gandhi could see clearly how similar they were. The origin of imperialist and anti-imperialist violence was their belief in modern civilization. As a young man, Gandhi had also believed in modern civilization, and now that he had turned against it, he was warning his compatriots that believing in it would destroy their own civilization:

> The British Government in India constitutes a struggle between the Modern Civilization, which is the Kingdom of Satan, and the Ancient Civilization, which is the Kingdom of God. The one is the God of War, the other is the God of Love. My countrymen impute the evils of modern civilization to the English people and, therefore, believe that the English people are bad, and not the civilization they represent. My countrymen, therefore, believe that they should adopt modern civilization and modern methods of violence to drive out the English. *Hind Swaraj* has been written in order to show that they are following a suicidal policy, and that, if they would but revert to their own glorious civilization, either the English would adopt the latter and become Indianised or find their occupation in India gone.[5]

Gandhi understood that modern civilization is at its core what Elise Boulding calls a "war culture."[6] Anyone who accepted modern civilization accepted war, consciously or unconsciously. In their assassinations of British officials, the extremists were accepting the underlying violence of modern civilization. These assassinations, though at times successful, led inevitably to political failure, according to Gandhi. The English tyrant "refuses to be killed. . . . He is a multi-headed monster."[7] The English people were not the issue. It was the ideology, the way of life, the fundamental assumptions having to do with an acceptance of violence as necessary in statecraft. To Gandhi, that violence was related to the belief in materialism and immorality or irreligion, masquerading in the name of morality and religion. He clearly differentiated between the Christianity of Christ, which he saw as compatible with ancient Indian religions, and the Christianity of imperialism, imperialism cloaked in a Christian garb and subversive to the Christianity of Christ. Gandhi believed that Indian culture, by contrast, was essentially spiritual and nonviolent.

With this fundamental critique of modern civilization, known in the Gandhi literature as his critique of modernity, it is not surprising that he was able to understand how closely linked the Indian terrorists were to modern civilization. Many in Great Britain and India saw the terrorists' methods as different from those of the British, who seemed so "civilized." Many thought that the British imprisoned, even executed, their opponents, but reluctantly, for strictly moral reasons; the terrorists killed wantonly, without regard to basic norms of morality. Gandhi saw behind the façade. Both sides killed because they believed in violence, no matter how reluctant or wanton they may have seemed to be. Whether one killed in the name of imperialism or in the name of Indian independence, the fundamental ideology was, according to Gandhi, based on the violence inherent in modernity.

Gandhi had his Reader state in *Hind Swaraj*: "We will assassinate a few Englishmen and strike terror; then a few men who will have been armed will fight openly. . . . We will undertake guerrilla warfare, and defeat the English." The Editor replied, "It is a cowardly thought, that of killing others. Whom do you suppose to free of assassination. The millions of India do not desire it. Those who are intoxicated by the wretched modern civilization think these things."[8] Gandhi asserted that the extremists were "intoxicated by the wretched modern civilization" not only because they used similar methods to their Western opponents but also because most were adherents of various Western ideologies. Two of the most important were Shyamji Krishnavarma and Vinayak Savarkar. Krishnavarma was an avid follower of Herbert Spencer, whom he quoted on the masthead of his journal, *The Indian Sociologist*: "Resistance to aggression is not simply justifiable but imperative. Non-resistance hurts both altruism and egoism." He believed that violent resistance was necessary and that "non-resistance," a widely used term at the time for nonviolence, hurt oneself and others. He wrote in 1909 that Gandhi's philosophy of nonviolence was "utterly subversive of all ethical, political and social ideals."[9] Savarkar agreed, and Nathuram Godse, who assassinated Gandhi in 1948, was an ardent supporter of Savarkar.

The imperialists asserted the moral superiority of imperialism, backed by violence; the extremists asserted the moral superiority of their independence movement, backed by violence. As James Fitzjames Stephen, a prominent imperialist, wrote, "the English in India are the representative of peace compelled by force."[10] Most in the West and many, especially middle-class, Indians thought that the British were morally superior to the Indians. Gandhi agreed with the extremist position that Indian independence was superior to *Pax Britannica*, but he called them on the means by which they intended to achieve that independence. In *Hind Swaraj*, Gandhi argued that means and ends are convertible terms. "Only fair means can produce fair results."[11] In his critique of the extremists' approach, Gandhi wrote, "by using similar means [brute force] we can only get the same thing that they [the British] get."[12]

Gandhi's analysis of the violent underpinnings of imperialism and its opponents would warrant our attention, but of course he did not limit himself to analysis. In fact he developed his analysis in the crucible of nonviolent resistance to imperialists and anti-imperialists. He believed that Western civilization was a terrible disease, but "not an incurable" one, and that the English people were "not bad at heart."[13] He believed that *satyagraha* was a way to redeem both the English and the Indians, oppressors and oppressed. He appreciated and learned from a number of Western writers from Plato to Thoreau and Tolstoy, and he accepted certain Western ideas, although he often re-interpreted them in the light of Eastern thought. He loved the British constitution. He was trained as a lawyer and used his legal skills to analyze British actions not in line with their constitution.

The essence of *Hind Swaraj* is in Gandhi's interpretation of *swaraj*, which can mean parliamentary home rule in the sense of Indian independence or it can mean self-rule, self-restraint, self-realization (*moksha*) which to Gandhi was the spiritual and moral duty to develop oneself. *Swaraj* as self-rule is generally seen as the primary focus of the individual Hindu's duty; *swaraj* as political home rule is more generally seen as a Western idea. Gandhi's genius was his lifelong attempt to combine the two, bridging and thereby transforming Western and Eastern thought. As he wrote, "if we become free India is free. And in this thought you have a definition of Swaraj. It is Swaraj when we learn to rule ourselves. . . . Such Swaraj has to be experienced by each one himself."[14] His belief was that when enough Indians experienced *swaraj* in the sense of self-rule, then the British would not be able to rule them. Their parliamentary home rule would take place as the natural result of their inner self-rule.

Satyagraha is a theory and practice that blended the inner and outer forms of *swaraj*. For Gandhi, *satyagraha* was soul force, truth force, love force, all combined in the long-term dedication to service of others. Gandhi's Religion of Service was using soul force to uplift others, especially the poor. He certainly related *satyagraha* to religion, but not religion in the narrow sense of one faith over against another. "Here I am not thinking of the Hindu, the Mohamedan, or the Zorastrian religion, but of that religion that underlies all religions."[15] It is the spiritual essence of a person, expressed by many within their religions; but as Gandhi recognized, that essence was expressed as well in those activists who did not necessary accept organized religion.[16] He sought to follow a path in which his own liberation and the liberation of the nation became one. As he wrote in South Africa, "nobility of soul consists in realizing that you are yourself India. In your emancipation is the emancipation of India. All else is make-believe."[17]

For Gandhi the spiritual and the moral were the same, or we may say that the spiritual was for him the inner capacity to live a moral life. The definition of true civilization, in opposition to modern civilization, demonstrates this congruence of the moral and the spiritual: "Civilization is the mode of conduct which points out to man the path of duty. Performance of duty and observation of morality are convertible terms. To observe morality is to attain mastery over our mind and our passions. So doing we know ourselves. The Gujarati equivalent for civilization is good conduct."[18] For Gandhi, attaining mastery over our mind and passions was a spiritual capacity, and it was observing morality. He saw the immorality, the irreligion, the violence of Western civilization and its violent opponents, and he posited *satyagraha* as the spiritual/moral path out of both violent ideologies.

Hind Swaraj was the first time Gandhi laid out his theory of *satyagraha*. He continued to work on it the rest of his life, to try out over and over what he called his "experiments with Truth." He meditated, seeking to apply spiritual/moral principles to each new challenge, and he then acted to the best of his ability according to these principles. Whether a given experiment succeeded or failed in the moment was less important to him than the ongoing effort to test out *satyagraha*. *Hind Swaraj* marked a major shift in his thinking away from relying on the British to help in his effort to end the racist laws against his Indian compatriots in South Africa. Gandhi argued that only Indians themselves could use *satyagraha* to transform themselves—self-rule—to create then parliamentary home rule. But he still believed he was a part of the British Empire, and even though he disagreed with many British practices, he thought that the Empire was essentially sound.

After he returned to India, Gandhi made a final break with the Empire. It was at that time, as the British stepped up their violence to quell his countrywide Rowlatt *Satyagraha*, that Gandhi understood for the first time not only that violence was a foundation of modern civilization but also that the British acted against the Indians in the "spirit of terrorism," an expression he used three times in early April 1919.[19] Gandhi saw the terrorism of the British at that time less than two weeks before they unleashed their greatest violence against unarmed Indians gathered at the Jallianwalla Bagh in Amritsar. No warning was given, over 1650 were wounded, with 379 dead. Brigadier General Reginald Dyer had ordered the shootings because he had prohibited public meetings, although it later emerged that a town crier had been told to announce the prohibition at times and places where no one was likely to hear him. During the Hunter Commission that investigated the massacre, a judge asked General Dyer, "was it not a form of frightfulness?" He answered, "No, it was not. . . . It was a horrible duty I had to perform. I think it was a merciful thing. I thought that I should shoot well and shoot strong, so that I or anybody else should not have to shoot again. I think it is quite possible that I could have dispersed the crowd without firing, but they would have come back again and laughed, and I would have made what I consider to be a fool of myself."[20] General Dyer was released from his position, but many of the British, in India and back at home, believed that he was merely doing his "horrible duty."

To a certain extent he was right in the logic of imperialism, which rested on two pillars. Imperialism, at least in part, needed military force, one of its pillars of power over colonials. The other pillar, equally important, was the ideology of imperialism. As long as Indians thought that British imperialists were morally superior to them, it would continue, for they would have no reason as inferiors to oppose it. Taken together, especially when the ideology is widely accepted and military force is rarely used, they reinforced the legitimacy of the Raj.

But for the first time ever, a countrywide nonviolent civil disobedience campaign challenged both the ideological pillar and the military pillar of British rule. If they used "too much" force, as they did in Amritsar, then their ideological pillar would begin to crumble. Many questioned the moral superiority of General Dyer's massacre of Indians, given that they did not even know they were breaking a curfew. But if the British did not use the military force, they could not maintain control. Unarmed protesters did not seem morally inferior to the British, especially when General Dyer believed that the only way to maintain British rule was with a display of massive force. The only danger to political *swaraj* was a lack of inner *swaraj*, either by the terrorists, who discredited Indian efforts to win independence by nonviolent means, or even worse, by those who committed violence in the name of nonviolence.

Gandhi believed that Indian independence would have been won in 1922 had it not been for the massacre at Chauri Chaura, a massacre in which Indian police supporting the Raj were burned and hacked to death by violence on the part of so-called *satyagrahis*. In a long, thoughtful article in *Young India* of 4-9-25, "My Friend, the Revolutionary," Gandhi looked at the role of violence by Indian revolutionaries.

> I respectfully contend that their sacrifice, nobility and love are not only a waste of effort, but being ignorant and misguided, do and have done more harm to the country than any other activity. For, the revolutionaries have retarded the progress of the country. Their reckless disregard of the lives of their opponents has brought on repression that has made those that do not take part in their warfare more cowardly than they were before. . . . The masses are not prepared for the repression that follows in the trail of revolutionary activities and unwittingly strengthen the hand of the very Government which the revolutionaries are seeking to destroy. It is my certain conviction that had the Chauri Chaura murder not

taken place the movement attempted at Bardoli [a major *satyagraha* campaign in Gujarat] would have resulted in the establishment of swaraj.[21]

The violence by revolutionaries and by those who claim to be *satyagrahis* damaged the Indian independence movement because, I would submit, it left in place the twin pillars of imperialism, the ideological and the military justifications for continued power over the Indians. If there had been no violence in Chauri Chaura, Gandhi would not have needed to call off *satyagraha*. If the revolutionaries did not assassinate the British, then the Raj's ideology of moral superiority and their counterviolence would not be justifiable. True *satyagrahis* would not give the British the excuse of self-defense. Anti-imperialist terrorists gave the British ideological and military legitimacy in the eyes of many. In a battle of violence against violence, in Gandhi's terms Satan against Satan, only violence multiplies. As he wrote, "Armed conspiracy against something satanic is like matching satans against Satan. But since one Satan is one too many for me, I would not multiply them."[22] Most Indians and the British themselves could not see the Raj as Satanic unless the Indians were, by contrast, morally superior to the British. If they could carry off a major *satyagraha* campaign without violence, they could give "an ocular demonstration," as Gandhi wrote, that British military force would be used unjustifiably and therefore immorally.

That is exactly what happened eight years later in the Salt Campaign, the most brilliant and successful *satyagraha* campaign in the Indian independence movement. This 240-mile march to the sea by Gandhi and 78 members of his ashram unleashed a tidal wave of Indian support for *satyagraha*. The nonviolent raid on the Dharasana Salt Works was one of the most impressive actions in the campaign. White-clad *satyagrahis* came up line by line for hours, only to be beaten to the ground by Indian soldiers under British command. Many in the world understood for the first time that the British had no moral superiority in India. The higher morality lay with the *satyagrahis*. Over eighty thousand Indians were jailed in the Salt *Satyagraha*, and millions participated in some way during the campaign. Even though it took another seventeen years for the British to grant independence, it is widely believed that the Salt Campaign turned the tide in India. All the violence was committed by the British and their Indian soldiers and police. The legitimacy of the Raj was never reestablished for the majority of Indians and an ever increasing number of British subjects.

Gandhi proved with the Salt *Satyagraha* that nonviolent resistance to the violence of an oppressive regime could be effective. Terrorism by the government or the opponents of that government could not: "It is an ever-growing belief with me that truth cannot be found by violent means. The attainment of national independence is to be a search for truth. Terrorist methods, whether adopted by an oppressor or his victim, can, I am convinced, never be effectively answered by violent resistance, but by only civil resistance."[23] He asserted that terrorism existed on both sides of the political struggle and that violence on one side can never answer violence on the other side. To be sure, as Gandhi recognized, violent resistance can overthrow a repressive regime, but for him true independence involved a revolution of thinking and acting not found when one violent regime follows another: "when, as in Europe, the people have gained their freedom by being able to use greater violence than the enthroned authority, it is at least doubtful if they, not excluding the English, have got real freedom. The masses there still feel ground down by the moneyed classes who have the reins of government in their hands."[24] Regime change through violent means does not involve real freedoms because those who win power by violence tend to maintain it by violence.

Terrorism on either side does not bring true independence, and it makes matters worse, especially the counterterrorism by a government: "I know that terrorism is taking deeper root owing to the counter-terrorism of the [British] Government. The counter-terrorism is much more mischievous in its effects, because it is organized and corrupts a whole people. Instead of rooting out terrorism it creates an atmosphere for the approval of terrorist methods and gives them artificial stimulus."[25] It makes sense that the counterterrorism of a government is even more pernicious than that of a nongovernmental terrorist group. Both forms of terrorism bring about the loss of life, but only the terrorist activities of a government damage a people. Counterterrorism is carried out in the name of the people and to the extent that they continue to support that government, they become coresponsible for the state-sponsored terrorism. Counterterrorism stimulates terrorism, as Gandhi stated. Each side justifies their violence as a necessary response to the terrorism of the other side.

At the beginning of the twenty-first century, especially since the attacks on New York and Washington on September 11, 2001, there is a danger of an unending spiral of terrorism and counterterrorism. Gandhi's *satyagraha* could provide us with a workable alternative to the dilemma because he developed it over time in response to similar circumstances. *Satyagrahis* were able to end the cycle of Indian terrorism and British counterterrorism on the subcontinent. To be sure, Gandhi and his coworkers did not solve the problem of communal violence and other severe problems in India. However, he was fully aware that it would take much effort and many more *satyagrahis* to create the nonviolent society he wished to achieve. Nonviolent movements in the second half of the twentieth century and the beginning of the twenty-first century have been successful in many different cultures. It is true that new forms of terrorism and counterterrorism are likely to require new forms of nonviolent action. But considering the challenges to international security today, Gandhi's insight that "satyagraha is the only way . . . to stop terrorism" appears as valid now as it was in his lifetime.

NOTES

1. *The Collected Works of Mahatma Gandhi (CWMG)* (New Delhi: Publication Division, Ministry of Information and Broadcasting, 1958-1994), 15:107.

2. *CWMG*, 9:508.

3. *CWMG*, 9:509.

4. Dennis Dalton mentions for example that D. R. Harkare, a member of Gandhi's *Satyagraha* Ashram and one of the select group of ashramites who participated in the complete Salt March of 1930, began before his work with Gandhi "with a youthful involvement in terrorism and contempt for nonviolence," *Mahatma Gandhi: Nonviolent Power in Action* (New York: Columbia University Press, 1993), 103.

5. Mohandas K. Gandhi, Preface to the English translation, *Hind Swaraj and Other Writings*, ed. Anthony J. Parel (Cambridge: Cambridge University Press, 1997), 7.

6. Cf. ch. 1, "History at Sword's Point? The War-Nurtured Identity of Western Civilization," *Cultures of Peace: The Hidden Side of History* (Syracuse: Syracuse University Press, 2000), 13–28.

7. *CWMG*, 27:134.

8. *Hind Swaraj and Other Writings*, 77.

9. Parel's Introduction to *Hind Swaraj and Other Writings*, xxv–xxvi.

10. Parel's Introduction to *Hind Swaraj and Other Writings*, xix.

11. *Hind Swaraj and Other Writings*, 84.

12. *Hind Swaraj and Other Writings*, 81.

13. *Hind Swaraj and Other Writings*, 34.

14. *Hind Swaraj and Other Writings*, 72.

15. *Hind Swaraj and Other Writings*, 43.

16. According to Douglas Allen, "Gandhi states that atheists may deny the existence of God, but they still have a passion for discovering truth. Therefore, 'rather than say that God is Truth, I should say that Truth is God.' This often allows those who have rejected theistic or other traditional religious formulations to relate to Gandhi's concept of Truth," ch. 16, 317.

17. *CWMG*, 10:206–7.

18. *Hind Swaraj and Other Writings*, 67.

19. *CWMG*, 15:164, 172, 174–75.

20. Cited in Robert Payne, *The Life and Death of Mahatma Gandhi* (New York: E. P. Dutton, 1969), 340.

21. *CWMG*, 26:486–87.

22. *CWMG*, 26:489.

23. *CWMG*, 55:426.

24. *CWMG*, 46:2.

25. *CWMG*, 56:34.

12

Gandhi and Human Rights: In Search of True Humanity

Judith M. Brown

To historians one of the most interesting aspects of the career of Mahatma Gandhi is the way he was, and is, continuously "reinvented." In his lifetime people made and remade Gandhi, the image and myth, finding in him a resource for the project on which they were engaged.[1] After his death he was made into the Father of the Indian Nation, despite the fact that India was departing radically from his vision of what true *Hind Swaraj*[2] should be. Since then Western admirers have turned him into an apostle of nonviolence and an activist for human rights. It is not surprising that he should be seen as one of the most outstanding protagonists of human rights in South Asia in this century. He was the leader of a movement for a people's right to self-rule. He was tireless in his work for India's poorest, most deprived and oppressed. Moreover, he was an innovative thinker and strategist in relation to the means of achieving change in society and polity. However, when one enquires more closely into Gandhi's thought and work, this clear image of a theorist and champion of human rights fades. He was a much more complex figure, and his thinking was not embedded in the human rights discourse of the Western liberal world. The subtitle to this chapter is a hint in the direction of this ambiguity. For the central issue he was constantly addressing was that of discovering and enabling an authentic humanity, and the practical implications of this search in the lives of women and men in community.

GANDHI AND HUMAN RIGHTS THEORY

Before we explore Gandhi's understanding of the true nature of humanity, and of the idea of human rights, we should remind ourselves of the historical evolution of modern thinking about human rights—in contrast to the

237

philosophical background from which he came. Theories of human rights in a recognizably modern form emerged in the very specific historical circumstances of Europe and North America, and were powerfully shaped by Western philosophical assumptions and concerns.[3] The political background to this was the emergence of nation-states and sociopolitical struggles to wrest power from small groups who were entrenched in power. Rights theories originated in the thinking of Hobbes and Locke, and then began to expand and to become central to Western liberal thought. They have since flowered in the mid- and late twentieth century in a range of international declarations of human rights, most famously the 1948 Universal Declaration of Human Rights. The Indian Constitution, which came into being after lengthy discussion late in 1949 and reflects this wider trend, contains a section guaranteeing a range of Fundamental Rights such as rights to freedom, equality, freedom of religion, freedom from exploitation.[4]

There are several aspects of this philosophical development that are particularly significant in comparison to Gandhi's stance. In the particular historical juncture in which human rights thinking emerged in the West, and of course in India in the context of the nationalist movement, the primary concern was with the rights of the individual in relation to the state, and to a lesser extent in relation to the rest of society. Rights theory was not only fundamentally protective of the individual vis-à-vis the state; but was also deeply skeptical about society and humanity itself. It was thus also a bulwark for the individual against the malign and threatening forces within society and human collectivities. Rights theory also reflects contemporary understandings of what is essential to being human, and is a way of marking out and protecting those attributes that are seen as essential not only for human existence but for human flourishing and development. As such it gives immense importance and indeed priority to the individual. It is also flexible— capable of expanding as understanding changes of what it is to be a flourishing human. Hence it has extended from ideas about liberty and freedom of thought and speech to include rights to health and education, and has also incorporated ideas of group rights—groups ranging from nations to ethnic groups, to women and children.

Gandhi came from a very different philosophical background. The tradition of Hindu political thinking was highly developed and sophisticated.[5] But it had no rights discourse and did not place major emphasis on the value of the individual and his or her protection and development. Its concerns were far more with communities than individuals; it saw no problem with basic inequalities between individuals, and did not address issues of social change and conflict. The core of its concern was the creation and preservation of a social and political community based on the two ideals of *danda* or force, and *dharma* or duty. It is the latter which is particularly relevant in understanding Gandhi. *Dharma* meant not just the religious duty of the individual but also that of the status group: its objective was making a human society that would conform to an underlying order and balance in the universe (*rta*). This led to a stress on duties rather than on rights, and on the mutual interdependence of individuals and groups if the whole was to function morally. (This tradition could produce something that superficially looks like a "right," such as the apparent right to resist an unjust king. On deeper exploration it is clear that this resistance is not a right but application of duty, the duty of subjects to remove a ruler who is failing in his particular duty to guard his people and uphold the moral order.)

Gandhi was not a trained philosopher, in either the Hindu or the Western tradition. However, he became an avid reader as well as being a trained lawyer after his studies in London, and he was well aware of the thrust of Western political thought. But he was adamant that he could not accept the rights discourse within Western tradition, and refused to ground his campaigns in it. In 1940 he was in touch with the English writer H. G. Wells, who had drawn up a list of human rights, and Gandhi told Wells robustly that he would do better by drawing up a list of the duties of man.

> Begin with a charter of Duties of Man . . . and I promise the rights will follow as spring follows winter. I write from experience. As a young man I began life by seeking to assert my rights and I soon discovered I had none not even over my wife. So I began by discovering performing my duty by my wife, my children, friends, companions and society and I find today that I have greater rights, perhaps than any living man I know.[6]

In July 1947 he expounded this theme even more directly in an article in his paper, *Harijan*, which he entitled "Rights or Duties?"[7] He was addressing what he saw as a "great evil that is afflicting our society today"—the prevailing talk by capitalist, zamindar, laborer, and prince alike of his rights. With independence imminent he warned, "If all simply insist on rights and no duties, there will be utter confusion and chaos." He went on to say, "If instead of insisting on rights everyone does his duty, there will immediately be the rule of order established among mankind. . . . I venture to suggest that rights that do not flow directly from duty well performed are not worth having. They will be usurpations sooner discarded the better." A few days earlier in one of his regular prayer discourses he had spoken of the constitution-making work of the Constituent Assembly, which was currently discussing what the rights of citizens should be in independent India. His own thinking was very different: "the proper question is not what the rights of a citizen are, but rather what constitutes the duties of a citizen. Fundamental rights can only be those the exercise of which is not only in the interest of the citizen but that of the whole world."[8] Clearly Gandhi was not a Western liberal. He was working from quite a different set of presuppositions about the nature of humanity and the social order and of the interrelationships of humans in society. In this he was closer to the traditions of Hindu political thinking on *dharma* and *rta*. Yet he was deeply concerned for the poor and disadvantaged, in what seems like a very modern and liberal way. So we must explore more deeply Gandhi's vision of an authentic human existence, and the roots of his concern for the disadvantaged and his commitment to nonviolence as a method of change.

GANDHI'S VISION OF AUTHENTIC HUMANITY

Gandhi did not build his vision of humanity and the good society on the idea of rights; yet ironically he was in one sense supremely individualistic in his thinking. For him the individual man, woman, and child were of supreme importance, for if individuals were true to their deepest moral nature then this was the foundation for a healthy and moral social, economic, and political order. It was this that lay behind his concern for the minutiae of people's lives—a concern deeply appealing to people who felt encompassed by his radiating compassion, and was the reason why they affectionately called him *Bapu* (diminutive of father). To take just one example, Jawaharlal Nehru told his sister, "Nan" (Vijaylakshmi Pandit), how even during the great 1932 fast on the issue of untouchability Gandhi had sent Nehru a telegram in jail, telling him that he had seen his daughter and reassuring him. "How extraordinarily considerate he is and how he thinks of others."[9] To his contemporaries it sometimes seemed bizarre that a political leader should concern himself with such intimate personal questions as his colleagues' health or their marital problems, or more broadly with the mundane problems of village people's diet, health, and sanitation. But he believed that all aspects of an individual's life reflected their degree of spiritual growth and therefore deserved attention if one was concerned with the roots of society.

Gandhi believed (in the tradition of *advaita*) that each individual partook of, and had latent and inherent within, the divine that lies at the heart of the cosmos. Each individual was designed and destined to pursue and foster this divinity, which he called Truth, internally and externally. A life lived in ignorance or deliberate defiance of ultimate Truth was a subhuman and inauthentic life. It was this belief that lay behind the subtitle he gave to his autobiography—"The Story of My Experiments with Truth." He believed that this essential search for Truth could only be through the pursuit of duty or *dharma:* and *dharma* was learned through tradition modified by reason and conscience. But for him spiritual searching and striving were not pietistic and inward looking, but robust and outgoing, leading one to social and political activism. In a famous passage at the end of his autobiography he wrote:

> To see the universal and all-pervading Spirit of Truth face to face one must be able to love the meanest of creation as oneself. And a man who aspires after that cannot afford to keep out of any field of life. That is why my devotion to Truth has drawn me into the field of politics; and I can say without the slightest hesi-

tation, and yet in all humility, that those who say that religion has nothing to do with politics do not know what religion means.[10]

For Gandhi the goal of the authentic human person was thus the search for Truth: to put anything before that search, such as possessions, power, or success, was to be subhuman. The search for Truth was man's fundamental duty.

A further assumption inherent in Gandhi's vision of authentic humanity was that men and women were perfectible. He was a supreme optimist about individuals and what might be called "the human condition." (It was for this reason that when writing about his life I called it *Gandhi: Prisoner of Hope,* adapting a biblical phrase that seemed to encapsulate him so well.[11]) Examples of this optimism about people were his tolerance of his son, Harilal, or his hope during the Second World War that even Hitler could be radically changed if exposed to the force of nonviolence. It lay also behind his concern for British people as individuals, though he thought their imperial system "satanic." For Gandhi, therefore, people and the social order were fundamentally benign if only people could realize (both in the sense of to understand and to make real) their humanity, and recognize the truth about themselves and their neighbors. This was in stark contrast to the skepticism of rights discourse that saw a need for a protective device against society at large as well as organized power structures.

Gandhi's understanding of the individual in relation to society was also undergirded by the assumption that all are linked to each other in an underlying unity inherent in the moral order of the universe. From this it flowed that all deeds, both good and bad, had wide-ranging implications, like ripples radiating out in water from the place where a stone has been thrown. This also meant that for Gandhi ends could never justify evil means, for good and bad means alike yielded fruit as surely as a seed is the source of an eventual and inevitable type of tree. Further, there could be no divorce between public and private standards of morality, for in a real sense nothing was ever morally private because all actions affected not only the subject but all those around in widening circles. He argued that people must in thinking about their actions and their possessions recognize their fundamental interdependence with others. In the prayer discourse on rights flowing from duties on June 28, 1947 he put this graphically: "we are born debtors in the world to which we owe a debt and we are dependent on others right from birth. Man becomes man only by recognizing his dependence on others."[12]

From Gandhi's vision of what it meant to be truly human flowed a vision of and commitment to the creation of a social and political order in which human interdependence would be recognized, and people's spiritual core would be fostered, and in which individuals could seek after Truth for themselves and for their neighbors in India and in the world at large. In this vision there was little place for notions of human "rights." Gandhi's vision of the good society for Indians had taken its basic shape by the time he wrote *Hind Swaraj* in 1909. He believed it should be organized on lines he presumed to be those of India's "traditional" society and civilization in contrast to those that underpinned modern, Western social structure. In this envisaging of India's past he was no historian (either of India or of Western societies). Indeed his image of "the real India" was strikingly similar to that perceived by colonial rulers—an India that was rural and small-scale, based on the village community, where people earned their living through agriculture and domestic "industry" to provide for basic needs. This was a world where social relations were structured by primordial ties of kinship and patterns of deference and patronage that ensured cohesive local communities that provided for the needs of all their members. Gandhi's rationale in deploying this vision was very different from that of the British. They were anxious to describe India as the "other" of British society, and so to justify their rule and the changes it was working in India. Gandhi, however, used it as the basis for his vision of a true *swaraj* society, in contrast to what he condemned as modern industrial society (regardless of its national variants in the West). He saw this as violent and coercive, encouraging false values of gain, wealth, and power, and therefore making almost inevitable false social divisions and confrontations. His moral vision was reinforced by his personal experience of Europe at the turn of the century, when a visit to England convinced him that Western civilization was destroying itself by its crazy grasping of material possessions.[13] By contrast he argued that a moral society's goals should be sufficiency for all rather than accumulation of excess for some (which amounted to theft from others). Its social and economic arrangements and relationships should be small-scale and rural, since this would allow people to recognize their essentially common humanity shared with their neighbors and their interdependence on their neighbors, and would encourage people to be content with simplicity and sufficiency rather than hankering after accumulated goods and power, and lavish display of individual "achievement." At the heart of this vision of the moral society were two key concepts that were to become the hallmarks of Gandhi's personal life and his teaching about the future shape of a free India. One was *ahimsa*, the Hindu notion of not harming, or nonviolence, which he reconstructed as a result of his interactions with other religious traditions, particularly in South Africa, to mean a broad compassion and charity toward all living creatures. The other was *sarvodaya* or the welfare and greater good of all, a concept he began to use and refine after reading Ruskin's *Unto This Last*, and paraphrasing it for his Indian readers in South Africa in 1908.[14] This is often referred to as Gandhi's "nonviolent socialism." As with his use of *ahimsa*, here also he took a Hindu notion—in this case of social order underpinned by morality—and infused it with ideas gained from his contacts with a wider world of thought and belief.

Gandhi recognized that changing the social order could not be divorced from changing the political order and required serious consideration of the nature of the polity, as well as practical political involvement. He argued that a people's political arrangements should be designed to recognize, sustain, and promote their moral core and capacity for self-control and self-regulation. In contrast he saw the modern state as essentially dehumanizing rather than promoting an authentic humanity. Its monopolization of decision making and force took away from individuals their duty (and therefore their "right") of spiritual self-realization and self-regulation. Moreover, it was inherently violent, depending on fear and force, and therefore was essentially immoral.[15] Such an opposition to the modern state inevitably caused misunderstandings and friction between Gandhi and his colleagues in India's nationalist movement, such as Jawaharlal Nehru.[16] Not only did they in a sense wish to inherit the *raj* after their long struggle for self-determination, they also recognized that a modern, centralized state was vital for their vision of a strong India with a vibrant economy, the capacity to defend itself, and the ability to raise taxes that would in turn enable social investment in the country of which an alien government had proved incapable. It was their view that eventually triumphed when India attained *swaraj*, and for this they were prepared to pay the price of partition.

In contrast Gandhi envisaged for India an ideal that was the opposite of a modern, centralized state monopolizing decision making and buttressing itself and its decisions with varieties of coercion. He hoped for a loose confederation of decentralized local polities, in which as far as possible small-scale communities would regulate their own affairs without the use of force.[17] He called this ideal "Enlightened Anarchy," writing in 1939:

> Political power, in my opinion, cannot be our ultimate aim. It is one of the means used by men for their all-round advancement. The power to control national life through national representative is called political power. Representatives will become unnecessary if the national life becomes so perfect as to be self-controlled. It will then be a state of enlightened anarchy in which each person will become his own ruler. He will conduct himself in such a way that his behavior will not hamper the well-being of his neighbors. In an ideal state there will be no political institution and therefore no political power. That is why Thoreau has said in his classic statement that that government is the best which governs the least.[18]

This exposition suggests that Gandhi gave little value to his nationalist colleagues' understanding of democracy and the democratic relationship between the citizens and the state, just as his criticism of the British parliament did thirty years earlier in *Hind Swaraj*. Yet Gandhi believed there was an intimate moral connection between individuals and the political order, for each person was implicated in and therefore responsible for that order. From this it followed that individuals were obliged by their duty to pursue Truth, to withdraw cooperation from a state that became immoral, and to refuse to obey laws that were clearly wrong and immoral. "Satanic" was the worst, most profoundly critical adjective he used of the British *raj*, and the reason he gave for noncooperation with it from 1920 onwards.

A THEORY AND PRACTICE OF MORAL GROWTH

Gandhi recognized from his time in South Africa that the articulation of ideals was not enough. Some way had to be found of practical coping when things went "wrong." The situation of migrant Indians there forced him into an unlooked-for political and social involvement. He began to experiment with responses to the practical world of daily existence in situations where clearly the social and political order did not sustain what he perceived as authentic humanity, and did not nurture the individual's pilgrimage after Truth. Such responses were painfully worked out over his whole adult lifetime, and he never stopped "experimenting with Truth," even in the dark days of communal violence that preceded independence and partition. (The bizarre experiment in sleeping naked with a young female relative in 1946 that confused and embarrassed many of his political colleagues was totally explicable in terms of Gandhi's understanding of the link between an individual's inner purity of life and his ability to influence the outer situation.) Although he went on refining and experimenting throughout his time in India as a mature thinker and activist, by the time he finally left South Africa in 1914 he had clarified the core of an ideal of nonviolent opposition to wrongs of various kinds, what he came to call *satyagraha*, or truth force. However, he was adamant that this was not merely a convenient political strategy for weak people and groups who had little or no access to political or physical power, which were the connotations of the English phrase "passive resistance" that he refused to use as a description of his action. Much more profoundly, *satyagraha* was a theory and practice of moral growth that enabled Truth-seekers to deal with situations where clearly his ideals for individuals, for society, and for the operation of political power were not being followed.

In Gandhi's ideal of *satyagraha* came together many of his core beliefs and assumptions. Here were the ideals of the primacy of the spiritual in authentic human existence, the interdependence of all life, the need to discern moral modes of action, and above all the essential principle of *ahimsa*, nonviolent compassion in action. It was this bundle of mutually reinforcing ideals that was the foundation for Gandhi's commitment to *satyagraha* as the only moral means of following Truth in practical situations and combating perceived wrong or un-Truth, which would in their operation safeguard the moral integrity and authentic humanity of all concerned in any situation of conflict. The *satyagrahi* was, therefore, in Gandhi's eyes, one who set as his goal the pursuit of Truth for himself and those around him, who had prepared himself for the arduous and often dangerous path of nonviolent resistance to wrong by a disciplined lifestyle. Right through his active political life, from his early days in South Africa to the final tumultuous months of his life, he insisted that people could not just adopt *satyagraha* as a convenient strategy in a particular situation. The true practice of *satyagraha* demanded hard and prolonged practice in self-discipline, indeed the adoption of a lifestyle marked by simplicity and self-abnegation, which was designed to cultivate moral and physical courage, fearlessness in the face of evil and violent opposition, and detachment from the consequences of one's actions. Such a life he attempted to put into practice personally in South Africa as an individual and then in his two communities of Phoenix and Tolstoy Farm, which were the precursors of his Indian *ashrams*. Simple food, spartan living conditions, regular manual labor, sexual restraint and for him personally the discipline of celibacy, and daily prayer were designed to generate a clarity of spiritual vision and a tranquillity of spirit in the absence of many of the worldly ties of affection and possession that make ordinary people so reluctant to take risks in the service of Truth.

But how did Gandhi expect this mode of conflict resolution to work? What were the intended dynamics of *satyagraha*? Firstly, he saw *satyagraha* not in terms of a right to resist but rather as the fulfillment of a duty to resist perceived wrong. It was designed at a deep moral and spiritual level to set in motion radical processes of moral transformation—not by coercion but by conversion, by changing the moral perceptions of all those involved in the conflict concerned. It was thus aimed at altering the total dynamics of a situation, and at opening the way to a broader vision of right and wrong, to the possibility of compromise on nonessentials, and to an attitude of mutual understanding and forgiveness between former opponents.[19] It was in part for this reason that Gandhi was always anxious for "talks" with officials of the *raj* before contemplated civil disobedience movements and at strategic points during them. Most notable were his famous talks with the then-current viceroy, Lord Irwin, in 1931, which ended civil disobedience temporarily and paved the way for Gandhi's presence at the Round Table Conference in London in 1931. (This is certainly not to deny that there were also more obviously "political" considerations at work in Gandhi's strategic planning: "talking" with a viceroy, for example, gave Congress considerable legitimacy and standing as "the spokesman" for the nationalist movement.) It was also because of this sense of *satyagraha* as means to enable mutual moral growth that Gandhi was not greatly concerned with the numbers of *satyagrahis*. His intention was never to make the life and work of the opponent impossible, or in the case of the *raj* to bring government to a halt: in this way again *satyagraha* was very different from passive resistance. He was much more concerned with the quality of the *satyagrahis* and their reliability in the face of temptations to abandon nonviolence—hence his emphasis on strict discipline, as in the case of the 1930 march to Dandi to make salt on the seashore, or in that most Gandhian of *satyagrahas*, the "individual civil disobedience" movement of protest against the war in 1940–1941. In this movement he quite literally handpicked those individuals and categories of people who would be permitted to make the protest, gave detailed instructions on protesters' appropriate behavior, and was evidently conscious that he was making a unique experiment in nonviolent action.[20] His belief was that even one genuine *satyagrahi* could begin the process of moral transformation that *satyagraha* would inevitably bring about, if properly undertaken. Large numbers of untrained and uncontrollable activists were worse than useless and would indeed negate the moral dynamic of any campaign. This was the reasoning behind his abandonment of the first great all-India noncooperation campaign in 1922 after the massacre of policemen at Chauri Chaura, and behind his disillusion with the "Quit India" campaign of 1942. It was also the rationale behind his attempts in 1946 to prove that his personal purity and self-control in sexual matters was such that he at least had the strength to be a sole *satyagrahi* in the situation of escalating communal violence.

The historian of Indian politics has of course to weigh the political "efficacy" of Gandhi's nonviolent campaigns, in ways that would have been quite alien to Gandhi himself. To him the action of true *satyagraha* on circumstances of conflict was a matter of theological faith, and he was only making an affirmation of its inevitable moral consequence, given his understanding of it and of human nature. Even when confronted in 1938 by the plight of the Jews in Nazi Germany he argued that true *satyagraha* would transform the situation: to him even their death in large numbers would not be a sign of *satyagraha*'s defeat. Moreover, when confronted by the "failure" of the 1942 "Quit India" movement and the subsequent outbreak of internecine violence within the subcontinent, he asserted that his compatriots had never offered true *satyagraha*.[21] This is not the place to discuss such philosophical and political issues. But an understanding of *satyagraha* as a theory and practice of moral growth (rather than as a strategy for exerting pressure on the opponent) does suggest that Gandhi placed it in the context of an understanding of human duties and the duty to follow after Truth rather than in the context of human rights and the grasping of such rights.

SOME PRACTICAL OUTCOMES

The concluding part of this discussion of Gandhi and human rights deals with some practical outcomes of Gandhi's vision of authentic humanity and his evolution of *satyagraha* as a mode of change, deliberately focusing on examples where Gandhi may superficially look like a human rights thinker and activist. In each case we shall find his thinking much more complex, and his goals often more circumscribed.

Gandhi is most notable as the leader of the Indian nationalist movement, and thus presumed to be a champion of the rights, individually and as a national group, of people to liberty and self-determination. Gandhi, however, rarely used the English word "independence" in his discourse, but preferred to use the Hindi word *swaraj*. At its most basic it means self-rule: but for him it also carried all the moral implications of self-control and self-regulation. By 1920 he had come to feel that British rule was, as he put it, "satanic." But its evil lay not primarily, if at all, in the rule of one national group over another. He believed that it was wrong because it was morally destructive of India's ancient, traditional, and spiritual civilization that had enabled its people to journey after Truth in the context of a small-scale and rural society whose socioeconomic arrangements for their common life were compatible with Truth-seeking.

He had come to these conclusions in 1909 when he wrote *Hind Swaraj*, which was a devastating critique of the *raj* as the importer of the destructive forces of Western civilization into India, and of those Westernized Indians such as doctors and lawyers who gladly collaborated in the enterprise of the "modernization" of their country. Writing a few weeks earlier he had given his friend, Henry Polak, a preview of his views, what he called humorously "a terrible dose." He said his views were "not new but they have only now assumed such a concrete form and taken a violent possession of me." From the perspective of Gandhi as a possible protagonist of Indians' rights to freedom, what was most significant was his assertion that it was not the British who were ruling India but "modern civilization"; and that "If British rule was replaced tomorrow by Indian rule based on modern methods, India would be no better, except that she would be able then to retain some of the money that is drained away to England." In his view India's "salvation" lay not in political independence but in undoing what she had learned over the last half century of modern civilization, while her educated people would have to learn again to live the simple peasant life. Most startlingly he asserted, "England can help India to do this, and then she will have justified her hold of India."[22] To Gandhi continuing British rule over India was also evil because it destroyed Indians' duty to regulate their own affairs, and in so doing to grow morally. He thus formulated a vision of *swaraj* that was to be markedly at odds with the vision of political independence held by most of his colleagues in the Indian National Congress and in the country at large. For him *swaraj* was not a matter of Indians ejecting the British and stepping into their shoes and seats of power, running what was still essentially a colonial state. It was a great enterprise of moral regeneration of a whole people and a transformation of their society, a righting of the wrongs and weaknesses that had made colonial rule possible, and ultimately a transformation of the processes of governance.

Gandhi's speeches and writings are full of this understanding of true *swaraj*. Apart from *Hind Swaraj* itself, which he refused to retract in later years, despite the difference of opinion it caused with valued colleagues, there are two key texts that elaborate how he saw India's future, and how this vision was located in a discourse on radical social change reflecting human duty rather than on human rights to freedom. One was an extended description of his envisaged Constructive Programme for India.[23] Its main thrust was a program of social reconstruction and transformation, including unity between religious groups, removal of the practice of untouchability, prohibition, the promotion of hand-spun cloth, village sanitation, new forms of education for children and adults, changes in the position of women, and greater economic equality. As he said in the introduction, these were the means by which he thought complete independence could be created. In contrast overtly political means, including civil disobedience, had virtually no place in this broad vision of the way to create true *swaraj*. He specifically said that civil disobedience could only be used to right a specific "wrong" or on a symbolic issue, but never for a general cause such as independence. *Swaraj* could not be "won" in the sense of wresting it from the British: it had to be created from below. He returned to this theme just before his death, with a draft constitution for a much-changed Congress after the withdrawal of the British in 1947.[24] He urged Congressmen to turn their backs on political action and party organization and turn themselves into a society to serve the people, for "the Congress in its present shape and form, i.e., as a propaganda vehicle and parliamentary machine, has outlived its use. India has still to attain social, moral and economic independence." The failure of his people to attain true *swaraj* in 1947 was one of the great sadnesses of the final months of his life: the violence between different religious groups and the way politicians and administrators happily took over British patterns of exercising power alike convinced him that India had not achieved the real *swaraj* he had expounded all his life. This showed how his priority was never a "right" to freedom but a duty to create the sort of society and polity in which Indians could become genuinely human.

Gandhi's wide-ranging campaigns on behalf of some of the most deprived in Indian society, and against some of its grossest inequalities have also contributed to the popular later view of him as a rights activist. (It is no coincidence that he and Martin Luther King, Jr., are so often bracketed together in this respect.) However, on closer inspection Gandhi was clearly not engaged in the definition and protection of human rights: rather, he was endeavoring to eliminate wrongs or evils in society that harmed the whole as well as the individuals and groups who were ill-treated or discriminated against. He was aiming far more for the moral awakening and deepening of insight among the powerful and the oppressors than among the weak and deprived. His hope was that the powerful and privileged could be brought to see their moral duty as inherently spiritual people who could only become authentically human if they followed after Truth. He was definitely not attempting to organize movements for the pursuit of "rights" or the forcible reordering of the distribution of power and resources. This stance of course in political terms made him very attractive to the bulk of conservative Congressmen who had no wish for independence to include a socioeconomic revolution.

It also infuriated those who were genuinely committed to radical change and found offensive his preempting of the epithet of "socialist."

One example of Gandhi's stance on privilege was the way he fashioned a doctrine of "trusteeship" as an answer to the problem of economic inequality in India. He argued that there was no place for class conflict or for claiming workers' "rights" in the construction of a new India and in the context of the nationalist movement. Instead the rich and well endowed with any kind of resource should be converted to seeing that they were not the owners of these resources but their trustees, holding them in trust so that they could be used for the welfare of all. In his 1941 Constructive Programme he was clear that there had to be a leveling down of the few rich and a lifting up of "the starved naked millions on the other," and that there could be no nonviolent polity while there was the gulf between the rich and the "hungry millions." But even while acknowledging the ridicule that had been poured on his doctrine of trusteeship, he insisted on its rightness and eventual efficacy.[25] Just before independence he warned against the persistent talk of "rights"—by capitalists and zamindars, by princes, by laborers and peasants. "If all simply insist on rights and no duties, there will be utter confusion and chaos." By contrast, if people did their duty there would "immediately be the rule of order established among mankind." He was clearly primarily concerned about a society based on order, where the priority should be not the pursuit of rights but the rooting out of evil that threatened the totality of the social order and the interdependence of its component parts. "While it is true that these hereditary inequalities must go as being injurious to the well-being of society, the unabashed assertion of rights of the hitherto down-trodden millions is equally injurious, if not more so to the same well-being."[26]

Even in Gandhi's lifelong campaign against untouchability the same line of reasoning was clear. He was adamant from his time in South Africa that the practice of treating certain groups at the base of Hindu society as untouchable and polluting on ritual grounds had to go; though he never advocated the destruction of caste as a mode of social organization. His reasoning was not that untouchables had rights as individuals and citizens not to be discriminated against, though this was the argument of the independent Indian state in the Fundamental Rights laid down in the constitution, and when in 1955 it attempted to abolish the practice by law. Gandhi believed that untouchability was a religious matter, that it had no religious basis but was a late accretion to Hindu tradition, and that it was deeply destructive of Hinduism. It denied the status of untouchables as humans and therefore potential Truth-seekers, and in the particular circumstances of imperial rule threatened to play into British hands and divide the Indian body politic even more than it was already divided by communal divisions. The aim of his campaign against the practice was primarily to awaken caste Hindus to their responsibilities toward their fellow humans and brother Hindus. Only secondarily did he hope to rouse untouchables themselves, to perceive their true religious status and to begin to reform their lifestyles, to make themselves more acceptable to wider Hindu society. His strategy was accordingly fashioned to touch the consciences of the higher castes—by example, for he permitted no distinctions on grounds of caste in his personal life and in his *ashrams*, by speaking and writing, and ultimately by fasting. He never encouraged the use of organized mass *satyagraha* by untouchables themselves, and he opposed the protection of the group's "rights" and the pursuit of their social advancement by any special protection or positive discrimination, as in his fast against separate electorates for untouchables in 1932.

Gandhi also paid considerable attention to the diverse problems associated with the position of Indian women and asserted that they had a vital role in the nationalist movement and in the making of a new India. Whether he was a champion of women's "rights" is another matter. He acknowledged, for example, in his 1941 Constructive Programme, that women had "been suppressed under custom and law for which man was responsible and in the shaping of which she had no hand."[27] He went on to argue that in a truly *swaraj* society women would have as much right to shape their own destinies as did men, but at once he tied that right to a duty. "But as every right in a nonviolent society proceeds from the previous performance of a duty, it follows that rules of social conduct must be framed by mutual co-operation and consultation." Although Gandhi was no radical feminist insisting on the definition and pursuit of women's rights, and although in some respects his preferred image of the strong Indian woman was located in Hindu tradition, his stance was highly significant, for he was insisting that women should be their own transformers rather than being the objects of male projects of reform for men's own reasons. But again his reasoning lay in his understanding of a society undergirded by and reflecting a moral order, in which all were interdependent, and wrong done to one would harm the whole. In the particular context of India in the early twentieth century he argued that the treatment of women hurt the common welfare of the nation and denied to the whole what women had to offer—as wives, mothers, and activists in the public arena. As in the case of untouchables, his strategy was not organized resistance to male attitudes and habits, nor women's concerted campaigns on their own behalf. He took the route of personal example and of persistent teaching, and of welcoming women into nationalist activities to prove their equal status and value. Thousands of Indian women in their turn were to recognize how contact with Gandhi and his campaigns had transformed their vision of themselves, their family lives, their public activities, and perhaps most significantly the way they brought up their daughters.

CONCLUSION

The Gandhi "invented" by those concerned with human rights and their pursuit in the later twentieth century turns out, on closer study, to be as much of a myth as the varieties of Mahatma conjured up by his countrymen in his lifetime. He was a deeply complex figure, both as an activist and a thinker, and his own complexities were deepened by the ways in which he was used by his colleagues and supporters. He is not an easy exemplar or hero for the end of the century unless his teaching is grossly simplified, and his life is lifted out of the complexities and compromises of Indian politics. Those who would appropriate him for the cause of human rights fail to understand that his goal for humanity was very different from theirs, as was his perception of what was of most value in human existence. For them rights are the device for protecting core values and attributes of individual and group life, vis-à-vis the forces of state and society. For him recognition of individual duty and social and moral interdependence were the foundation of an authentic human existence. But that is not to say that Gandhi's teaching and painful experiments with Truth have nothing to say to other times and places. Among the many messages of his life are the problem of marrying ideals and action, which involves the issue of ends and means and the degree to which compromise is essential in practical life; the need to explore practical varieties of nonviolence as part of men's repertoire of resolving conflict unfettered by Gandhi's theologically dogmatic understanding of its dynamic; and a renewed appreciation of the fact and significance of human interdependence as a counterbalance to the atomistic individualism that has been central to Western philosophical and political traditions. It is surely because of unease on such issues in the contemporary world that people have turned to Gandhi, however simplistically they have subsequently refashioned him as an icon and mentor in their search for inspiration.

NOTES

1. For a study of this process see S. Amin, "Gandhi as Mahatma: Gorakhpur District, Eastern UP, 1921–1922," in *Subaltern Studies 111. Writings on South Asian History and Society,* ed. R. Guha (New Delhi: Oxford University Press, 1986), 1–61.

2. This was the title of his most significant piece of extended writing on the nature of Indian freedom, written in 1909. See *Gandhi: Hind Swaraj and Other Writings,* ed. A. J. Parel (Cambridge: Cambridge University Press, 1997).

3. An excellent introduction to these issues is M. Freeden, *Rights* (Milton Keynes: Open University Press, 1991).

4. See G. Austin, *The Indian Constitution. Cornerstone of a Nation* (Oxford: Oxford University Press, 1966).

5. B. Parekh, "Some Reflections on the Hindu Tradition of Political Thought," *Political Thought in Modern India,* eds. T. Pantham and K. L. Deutsch (New Delhi, Beverly Hills, London: Sage Publication, 1986), ch. 2.

6. Gandhi to H. G. Wells, cable, 7/40, *The Collected Works of Mahatma Gandhi* [*CWMG*] (New Delhi: Publications Division, Ministry of Information and Broadcasting, 1958–1994), 71:430.

7. *Harijan*, 7-6-47, in *The Moral and Political Writings of Mahatma Gandhi*. Vol. 3, *Non-Violent Resistance and Social Transformation*, ed. R. Iyer (Oxford: The Clarendon Press, 1987), 496–98.

8. 6-28-47, *CWMG*, 88:230.

9. J. Nehru to Nan, 10-4-32, Nehru Memorial Museum & Library, New Delhi, Vijaylakshmi Pandit Papers.

10. M. K. Gandhi, *An Autobiography* (London: Jonathan Cape [1927] 1966), 420.

11. Judith M. Brown, *Gandhi. Prisoner of Hope* (New Haven, CT: Yale University Press, 1989).

12. *CWMG*, 88:231–32.

13. *Indian Opinion* (10-2-09), *CWMG*, 9:389.

14. *Indian Opinion*, 9 articles in 5-7/08, *CWMG*, 8.

15. An excellent discussion of this is ch. 5, "Theory of the State," of B. Parekh, *Gandhi's Political Philosophy: A Critical Examination* (Notre Dame, IN: Notre Dame University Press, 1991).

16. Gandhi's painful awareness of this is clear in a letter to J. Nehru (10-5-45), *CWMG*, 81:319–21.

17. Interview, 7-28-46, *CWMG*, 85:32–34.

18. *Sarvodaya* (January 1939), in *Moral and Political Writings*, vol. 3, 602.

19. See D. Dalton, *Mahatma Gandhi. Nonviolent Power in Action* (New York: Columbia University Press, 1993).

20. This episode is deeply reflective of Gandhi's understanding of *satyagraha* although it tends to receive little attention from historians. See Brown, *Gandhi. Prisoner of Hope*, 329–32.

21. For a discussion of these issues see Judith M. Brown, "The Vision of Non-Violence and the Reality," in *Gandhi and South Africa. Principles and Politics,* 7, eds. Judith M. Brown and Martin Prosesky (Pietermaritzburg: University of Natal Press, 1996).

22. Gandhi to H. Polak (10-14-09), *CWMG*, 9:477–82. Also partially quoted in *Gandhi: Hind Swaraj*, 129–33.

23. 12/41, *CWMG*, 75:146–66. Also partially quoted in *Gandhi: Hind Swaraj,* 170–81.

24. 1-29-48, *CWMG*, 90:526–28. Also quoted in *Gandhi, Hind Swaraj,* 191–93.

25. 12/41, *CWMG*, 75:158.

26. *Harijan* (7-6-47), in *Moral and Political Writings*, vol. 3, 496.

27. *Constructive Programme* (7/41), *CWMG*, 75:155.

13

The Constructive Programme

Michael Nagler

MAKING OMELETTES: THE THEORY OF THE CONSTRUCTIVE PROGRAMME

Although Gandhi would describe himself in a British court as a "professional resister," and we tend to think of him as such, that was not the only string to his bow. Even *as* a resister, he preferred to work on constructive alternatives and "cooperate with good" (as Martin Luther King, Jr., would put it), rather than to confront wrongful authority and "non-cooperate with evil." From the very beginning—in 1894—"the question of internal improvement was also taken up" alongside agitation for the Indian community's basic rights in South Africa. As time went on, Gandhi placed more and more emphasis on this inward-looking dimension of the struggle. By the time of the major *satyagraha*s, it was not "also" but "primarily" a question of self-help on which he relied for the struggle. Eventually he formed the belief that the Constructive Programme alone would be the finest and most efficient way to *swaraj*. In the real world, things are rarely this ideal; but it was the ultimate conclusion toward which nonviolence tends: why be confrontational, conflictual, when you didn't need to?

Accordingly, when active resistance (what we might call the "obstructive programme") was stymied, he turned the bulk of his attention to the constructive (and proactive) dimension, drawing up an ambitious set of schemes for the complete reconstruction of Indian society—her final liberation from the "fourfold ruin" worked on her by foreign domination: economic, political, cultural, and religious.

In 1941, Gandhi published *Constructive Programme, Its Meaning and Place*. In this pamphlet he outlines eighteen projects suited to India's social, economic and other needs. These eighteen programs are—along with *satyagraha* itself,

253

the method for bringing them about—Gandhi's lasting contribution to a sustainable future.

The basic reasoning behind the Constructive Programme was not very complicated. Intuitively, we all feel that it's easier to change than to make others change; it's better to improve things than break things. In the long run, the net effect of constructive work is always constructive. "Obstruction" may be necessary in some cases, but at best it's only half the battle: something positive can only be achieved by positive—constructive—means.

All this is obvious, but when we get into a conflict, intuition doesn't always work. The Constructive Programme was designed to correct this vision and "put intuition back in business." *In so doing* it would loosen Indians' dependency on the British for protection, for income, for prestige, for security. Given human nature (on both sides of the conflict), some amount of showdown, of self-suffering and defiant disobedience would be necessary to bring freedom; but with strong Constructive Programme you could choose your own occasions and offer *satyagraha* from positions of strength.

There were significant strategic advantages also. The Constructive Programme was *nonconfrontational*; what could the British do about some villagers spinning in their homes, or making friends with the untouchables down the road, or fraternizing with local Muslims? Indeed in some cases *satyagrahis* were only doing what a real government was supposed to do for its people anyway, like combatting the "drink evil" and promoting adult education.

Also, with a robust Constructive Programme humming along in the background, you were never at a loss for something to do in between clashes—which is when most movements fall apart.

Naturally, cranking a spinning wheel is not as "exciting" as going to jail or facing a *lathi* charge; but nonviolence, after all, is about getting things done. Gandhi's way of putting it was, there is more Truth in patient, constructive work than in political ballyhoo or letting off steam:

> In violence, truth is the first and the greatest sufferer; in non-violence, it is ever triumphant. . . . If this preliminary observation has gone home with the reader, he [or she] will find the constructive programme to be full of deep interest. It should prove as absorbing as politics so-called and platform oratory, and certainly more important and useful.[1]

He had made this point as early as *Hind Swaraj:* even to liberate India from foreign rule, she would first have to be liberated from her own weaknesses. In fact, if she somehow got free of British control without doing so, those shortcomings and weaknesses would only drag her down again.

TOWARD "THE BELOVED COMMUNITY"

One of those weaknesses, perhaps the most dangerous, was the lack of harmony among India's astonishingly varied communities. In ancient times India had been a model of unity-in-diversity, maintaining harmony and mutual respect, for the most part, among her many different ethnic groups, religions, and independent villages (seven hundred thousand of them). But under British rule—as with any foreign rule—it had become increasingly difficult to practice the indigenous ways of accommodation, or even remember how unity-in-diversity was supposed to work. As the pressure on the Raj increased, the British increasingly resorted to the old "divide and conquer" policy of imperialism. At the Round Table Conference, the "communal issue" was thrown in Gandhi's face again and again, thwarting every suggestion he made that India be granted dominion status.

While Gandhi came to feel that there are natural differences among individuals and peoples, including the natural aptitudes that suited them for one role or another in society, the caste system of India, which had originally simply codified these differences for the sake of efficiency, had at some time in the past been corrupted into a horrible system of exploitation. This was blatant structural violence, an "excrescence" on his beloved Hinduism. Ever since South Africa, he had felt painfully the contradiction in Indians demanding of the Afrikaners and British what they would not grant to one-fifth of their own population at home: "Thus the Indians became the Panchamas [outcastes, untouchables] of the Transvaal."[2] Probably nothing occupied more of his energy than the full reintegration into Indian society of the casteless rejects, renamed by him *Harijans*, "children of God." Major campaigns, like the Temple Road *Satyagraha* at Vykom in 1925–1926, won important concessions for *Harijans*, and his greatest fast would be undertaken against Government's attempt to enshrine the segregation of the *Harijans* in a separate electorate.

Once, in the 1920s, Gandhi went to give some talks in the orthodox South. When he arrived to address the gathering, he saw that the "untouchables" had all been directed to sit in a segregated area. What was he to do? He decided to have his seat moved over to the *Harijan* side and addressed everyone from there! When he came back to speak the next day, the barriers had been removed and everyone was seated together.

But there was an even more fateful division. The trauma of the Muslim invasions, dating back to the tenth century, had never completely healed. Hostility alternated with periods of relative toleration, and the age-old process of assimilation that may have led to some eventual harmony—India's way of dealing with invasions throughout her long history—was disrupted by the British presence. When Gandhi returned to India in triumph and began his work at home, there was a "golden age" of cooperation between the two communities, as the Empire was perceived as a common enemy: but as pressure mounted on the Raj, it increasingly resorted to the old imperial strategy of divide-and-conquer and deliberately set the one-quarter of the population that was Muslim against the Hindu majority. Gandhi pressed for Hindu-Muslim unity wherever possible, but at times, he "dared not speak" to the issue, so explosive were the tensions.

Still, he was not tempted to rely on legislative remedies, any more than with the *Harijan* cause. Out of all these divisions, Gandhi insisted that his countrymen could create a diverse, harmonious "extended family," not by laws or slogans—by what he called *heart unity*. "Heart unity" means that no matter how different you are from me—in religion, outlook, caste, level of affluence, culture, race, or sex—I identify with your well-being: I want you to be happy. Not to be like me, but to thrive in your own way. If I really feel you're doing something wrong (as the Hindus felt the Muslims were doing by killing cows), I can try to persuade you. Ultimately, I can offer *satyagraha*. But as long as there's heart unity underneath, even our active disagreement by nonviolent means will not cause us to feel hostility to one another; on the contrary, it should bring us closer together in our joint search for truth. Without heart unity, the slightest difference can precipitate hostility; with heart unity, no amount of diversity on the surface can cause alienation, even disagreements, about religion.

Heart unity and *swadeshi* (in many ways a complementary principle) pervade Constructive Programme, as they do all of Gandhi's thinking. They explain, for example, why Gandhi wanted Indians to make their own cloth (*swadeshi*) but he was able to win over to his cause even the Lancashire mill workers whom he had idled by his boycott of their faraway manufacturers (heart unity). They explain, similarly, why he worked year in and year out to unite all the communities of India, but resisted attempts to divert their attention to other oppressed communities in the world (*swadeshi*)—not because he lacked compassion but because he firmly believed that by solving India's problems in India he would be making his best contribution to their problems in Africa or America (heart unity). In 1939, for example, he explained why the Congress should not add a resolution about black South Africans to its important declarations on the Indian community there:

> "I yield to no one in my regard for the Zulus, the Bantus and the other races of South Africa. I used to enjoy intimate relations with many of them. I had the privilege of often advising them. . . . But it was not possible to amalgamate the two causes. The rights and privileges—if any could be so called—of the indigenous inhabitants, are different from those of the Indians. So are their disabilities and their causes." This despite the fact that: "India has great regard and sympathy for all the exploited races of the earth and . . . would not have a single benefit at the expense of the vital interest of any of them. Indeed, the war against imperialism cannot wholly succeed, unless all exploitation ceases.[3]

We shall see how this careful balance played out in the American civil rights struggle years later. Heart unity would lead in time to what Martin Luther King, Jr., called "The Beloved Community."

Communal unity was the first plank of Constructive Programme, *Removal of untouchability* the second. No less than six other planks addressed communal unity: 9, Women; 14, Kisans (farmers); 15, Labour; 16, Adivasis (indigenous peoples); 17, Lepers; and 18, Students.

While communal tensions were the main problem addressed by the Constructive Programme, and "heart unity" the basic answer, there were many others; it was in all the most comprehensive program of social reconstruction ever undertaken by someone who was not an emperor or plenipotentiary. The thrust of several others, as we can well appreciate today, was economic.

THE HUB OF FREEDOM

Today the symbol of the modern Indian nation, emblazoned on her flag, is the spinning wheel. People tend to forget that for Gandhi the spinning wheel, or *charkha*, was no symbol but a very real tool to create affordable cloth, needed income, meaningful work, a wide-reaching infrastructure of individuals and cooperatives, and out of all this economic self-sufficiency for India: the key to *swaraj*.

Before the arrival of the British, Indian textiles had been the pride of Asia. Spinners and weavers were integrated into every community, along with fullers and other textile workers. Just before the British arrived much of that work was done in some communities by the Muslims. Thus when colonialism—bringing in its wake the disruption of social networks and the commoditization of work—came to India, it created poverty, idleness, and communal tensions on a vast scale. That, Gandhi saw, was in many ways the heart of the Raj—and its vulnerability. Since agricultural work was largely seasonal on the subcontinent, "cottage industry" like weaving and spinning was the perfect way to supplement farmers' meager incomes. This work restored pride in their work and a sense of connection with many others who would be involved in cloth, from the grower of the cotton to the buyer of the waistcloth (*dhoti*) or the world-famous sari worn by women for every occasion in almost every locality of the country—a sense of connectedness one could never have with a factory worker in Lancashire, *or* in Ahmedabad. Gandhi was adamant that Indian industrialization was no improvement over the English variety.

Charkha therefore (the word is used for the spinning wheel or the campaign) was the obvious answer to the whole exploitive structure of the Raj. And as mentioned above, it had a special Gandhian "spin": wearing *khadi* (homespun cotton cloth) would go far toward eliminating status symbols and showing off from people's wardrobes. Clothes serve a basic need (along with food and shelter), but when we can't stop at the human "need" that unites us and go on to the "greed" that divides us, we sew the seeds of discord. *Khadi* wearing would once again strike colonialism at its root, which is always its ability to divide. Under Gandhi's influence, even the fabulously wealthy Nehrus, at a family wedding, turned out in homespun.

If wearing *khadi* was a great democratizer, making it was even more so. At the heart of Gandhi's economic thinking was the concept of *bread labour.* Everyone, regardless of social rank or wealth—which in the Indian context was codified in the intricate network of caste—should be involved "hands on" in producing basic necessities of life on a daily basis. If you were a laborer, of course, no problem; but even if you were a Nehru or a college professor, you were asked to do your one hour of spinning, farming, building— but especially spinning—every day as your contribution to the healing of India's splintered society *and* drained economy. The idea was not to turn an intellectual into a farmer or vice versa, but to close the gap between intellectual and peasant or politician and laborer by shared experience and purpose. Working together (as modern sociologists have documented) reunites even those sundered by conflict.

And besides, as Tara Bhattacharjee (Gandhi's granddaughter) has said: "most of us, at some time in our lives, have rolled out a *chapati* (flat Indian bread). Similarly, every Indian should at some time in his life, feel and touch the *charkha*, for that is the *praan* or soul in all of us. We need cloth next to food."[4]

PUTTING IT ALL TO WORK

This comprehensive program addressed the "fourfold ruin" foreign rule had intensified or imposed upon the country: some of the efforts were cultural (7, 8, 11, 12), some economic (4, 5, 13, 15), some tackled health (3, 6, 10), while all taken together would give people an uplifting purpose and reground India's destiny on her ancient spiritual heritage—and common sense. On such foundations the country would be unconquerable, almost as a by-product.

In the first flush of his enthusiasm for the giddying possibilities of *satyagraha*, Gandhi had made the nation a glittering promise of what they could have if they gave him complete cooperation in the Constructive Programme. It became his rallying cry for that era: "Swaraj in one year." That did not happen—either the full cooperation or the *swaraj.* Quite unfazed, two decades later, when the bonds of colonialism were strained to the bursting point in 1941 and someone asked him what it would take to break them for good he affirmed, "Phenomenal progress in spinning."

We shall never know if he was right, since the near-total cooperation he asked for wasn't forthcoming, impressive as it was to see the village *maidans* (fields) filled with men, women, and youngsters turning the wheel. But Gandhi never wavered in his conviction that to attempt civil disobedience without the wholehearted backing of the masses, shown by their participation in the Constructive Programme, would be "mere bravado and worse than useless." If Congress expected him to do that, it would be "like a paralyzed hand attempting to lift a spoon."[5] He never stopped believing what he did in the early twenties, perhaps even earlier: with enough participation in the Constructive Programme, *satyagraha* and civil disobedience would be unnecessary.

In retrospect, the Constructive Programme, like much of Gandhi's life and work, was far ahead of its time: this may be the major reason it did not catch on strongly enough to continue after his death. If we look at the main problems facing us today, whether in India (which did a U-turn on most of Gandhi's ideas from the fifties onwards) or in the industrialized West, we will see that every one of the problems he addressed corresponds, *mutatis mutandis*, to our dilemmas:

Communal Unity	our biggest problem, worldwide!
Khadi	sustainable, decentralized industry
New Education	education in decline
Provincial Languages	"English only" controversy in North America
Economic Equality	four hundred billionaires now own one-half the world's material wealth!
Prohibition	substance abuse, etc.

The struggle to solve these grievous problems piecemeal, through violence, he would have pointed out, has not succeeded, nor can it. Instead, he worked tirelessly to institutionalize the Constructive Programme and revive the taste for meaningful, basic work in the hearts of the masses. Here his influence has been incalculable, possibly even greater than his "sister" discovery of *satyagraha* itself. For the world he envisioned was nothing less than the opposite and the cure of the industrial life of tension, corporatization, hurry, and money that has swept the world, including India, since 1948. E. F. Schumacher, the author of *Small Is Beautiful* and guru of the intermediate technology movement, once stated that everything he had done "grew out of Gandhi's spinning wheel." Some 1250 schools, clinics, hospitals, and community organizations that Gandhi founded with the help of his coworker Vinoba Bhave are still functioning today. As he said quite truly, "My real politics is constructive work."

NOTES

1. M. K. Gandhi, Preface to 2nd ed., *Constructive Programme: Its Meaning and Place* (Ahmedabad: Navajivan, 1945), 4.

2. M. K. Gandhi, *Satyagraha in South Africa, CWMG* (New Delhi: Publications Division, Ministry of Information and Broadcasting, 1958–1994, CD-ROM edition), 75:32.

3. D. G. Tendulkar, *Mahatma: The Life of M. K. Gandhi* (New Delhi: Ministry of Information and Broadcasting, 1951–1954), Vol. 5, 139.

4. "Conversation with Tara Bhattacharjee, East Bay Newsletter" *Gandhi Mela*, no. 7 (1995):19.

5. *Constructive Programme, CWMG*, 75:166.

III

WRITINGS ABOUT GANDHI—
PART B: GANDHI'S IMPACT
ON THE WORLD

14

Gandhi in the Mind of America

Lloyd I. Rudolph

My title is figurative, not literal; Gandhi never set foot on American soil. His presence is the result of American responses to his person, ideas, and practice. For most Americans, they were exotic, often alien, fascinating for some, threatening or subversive to others. This chapter analyzes America's reception and understanding of Gandhi by pursuing two questions: Is he credible? Is he intelligible?

To be credible, it must be possible to believe that his seemingly queer, quixotic person is someone like "us," someone who makes sense in terms of America's cultural paradigms and historical experience. From the beginning many thought that Gandhi was putting "us" on, that he was fooling us while fooling around. Was he for real or was he a fraud?

Even if "we" are prepared to accept an alien "other" like Gandhi as believable and authentic, the problem of intelligibility remains. What language, what images, what metaphors, what myths can be used to talk about him? How can we think about and talk about an alien other? In thinking and talking about Gandhi in America we are faced with an epistemological as well as an ontological problem.

Americans have been conscious of Gandhi since about 1920, when his first noncooperation campaign almost toppled British rule in India. He has been revered and reviled since then. In 1921, John Haynes Holmes told his Community Church congregation in New York that Gandhi was "the greatest man in the world," greater than even Lenin and Woodrow Wilson. "When I think of Mahatma Gandhi, I think of Jesus Christ." In 1930, the year of Gandhi's second great noncooperation campaign against the British Empire in India. Winston Churchill, the empire's great exponent, coined the epithet "the half-naked fakir," a phrase that spoke for Americans and Britons who identified Gandhi with India's self-inflicted poverty and with fraudulent spirituality.

Gandhi's presence in American consciousness has varied with historical circumstance and his public image. There is the anti-imperialist, a nationalist leader who challenged the British empire in India; the *guru*, a world-historical teacher whose ethic of nonviolent collective action in pursuit of truth and justice offers a new way to think, believe, and live; the *mahatma*, the greatest soul, saint, and *homo religiosus*, whose meaning is translated in terms commensurable with or found in America's religious perceptions and beliefs; and the fraud, an oriental "other" whose alien and subversive ideas and practices threaten American religion, morality, and politics. Each of these Gandhis, the anti-imperialist, the *guru*, the *mahatma*, and the fraud, provide text and context for a roughly chronological examination of Gandhi's meaning in and for America.

Gandhi's first public career in South Africa (1893–14), although not visible in America, became an important part of the Gandhi myth.[1] A failure in India as an England-returned barrister-at-law, he left at twenty-four to try again in a distant, alien country whose oppressed and exploited Indian minority of indentured laborers and poor cultivators needed him. In time, he found an answer to his search for himself and their needs in a method of collective action, *satyagraha*, nonviolent noncooperation and civil disobedience. By the time he returned to India in 1915, "The Story of My Experiments with Truth" (the title of his 1927 autobiography) had preceded him. Rabindranath Tagore, Nobel laureate in 1913, welcomed him as a "mahatma" and Gopal Krishna Gokhale, leader of Indian nationalism, as his political heir. Four years later, in 1919 at forty-six, he assumed the leadership of the national movement against British rule. The stage was set for Gandhi's reception in America.

In his invaluable *The Americanization of Gandhi: Images of the Mahatma*, Charles Chatfield identifies four periods when national attention to Gandhi was most intense: 1919–24, the period of Gandhi's first and most momentous noncooperation campaign against British rule; 1929–34, when Gandhi led a march to the sea to make salt, launched the second noncooperation campaign, and traveled to London as the sole representative of the Indian National Congress at the second Round Table Conference; 1939–44, the era of the Second World War when Gandhi attempted to secure Indian independence while not opposing the war against fascism; and 1947, the year of partition, communal violence and independence.[2]

Chatfield described Gandhi as "our lens on India." What Americans saw was his "enigmatic personality, his ideas on religious and economic questions, and his tactical and philosophic meaning of nonviolence."[3] He first appears on the American horizon in 1919, in the immediate aftermath of World War I. The war had dealt a devastating blow to the promise of technological and moral progress in the Western world. American consciousness was radically transformed. The fervid patriotism and lofty idealism that led millions to offer their lives for their country faded from view. For a time, war was discredited as a test of national greatness and as an instrument of policy. In the new antiwar climate, pacifism achieved a greater measure of credibility and public standing, a circumstance that helped to open the way to Gandhi's ideas and practice.

THE ANTI-IMPERIALIST LEADER

The transformations that followed World War I helped to focus attention on Gandhi. His success in using nonviolent collective action to challenge the mighty British empire in India intersected with political and ideological currents in America. Gandhi's successful use of nonviolence justified pacifists, some of whom opposed the great war. Woodrow Wilson, a broken man after the paralytic stroke on October 2, 1919, had failed to convince the Senate to ratify the League of Nations treaty. His vision of America's allies and of idealistic internationalism lay shattered after Warren Harding's election returned the country to "normalcy" in 1920. Varieties of pro- and anti-imperialism now shaped American notions of national interest. One variety opposed British but affirmed American imperialism; another embraced imperialism understood as the white man's burden and world order politics; a third opposed imperialism as such, condemning both British and American imperialism.

In 1922, press baron William Randolph Hearst became an early advocate of Gandhi's cause. Seizing the opportunity to twist the lion's tail that Gandhi's challenge to the British Empire offered, he authored a signed article in the *Washington Times* that inveighed against British rule in India. "On what basis of justice, or general good will, or public benefit, or individual advantage, or liberty, or democracy, or self-determination, or anything that is recognized as right, is India kept in Bondage by England?" America should scrap the "unnatural alliance" with England that "stultifies all our principles of liberty and nullifies the whole inspiring spirit of our history."[4]

It is ironic that it was the jingoist voice of America's "manifest destiny," the voice of a supporter of the expansion of American power not only across the North American continent but also into South America, the Pacific, and Asia, that brought Gandhi to the attention of America's public opinion. Colonel Robert R. McCormick, publisher of the *Chicago Tribune*, soon joined Hearst in publicizing Gandhi's challenge to British rule in India. It suited both publishers' purposes to use Gandhi's nationalist challenge to British rule in India to discredit and attack those who benefited from and admired Britain and its empire.

Hearst and McCormick spoke for an American nationalism and expansionist imperialism that had taken shape in the generations preceding the great war. By 1890 Americans had conquered the continent, closed the frontier, and begun to build a navy. It was the year in which the last armed conflict between Indians and whites took place at Wounded Knee, the Census

Bureau declared there was no longer a land frontier, and Congress authorized the building of America's first three battleships that would provide the
global military reach of a world power. It was in 1890 too that Alfred Thayer
Mahan launched his career as the preeminent theorist of American imperialism with the publication of his immensely influential *The Influence of Sea
Power on History.* He told his fellow Americans that "whether they will or no
Americans must begin to look outward," a theme that Rudyard Kipling em-
bellished for America's reading public with his poetic call to "Take up the
White man's burden/Send forth the best ye breed/Go bind your sons to ex-
ile/To serve your captives' need." By 1898, America had joined the competition for empire, going to war with Spain, annexing the Philippines, Puerto
Rico, and Hawaii, "liberating" Cuba, and, in 1900, sending five thousand
troops to China ostensibly to help put down the Boxer rebellion.

Pro-British imperialists believed it was the mission of the white races,
Britain and America, to bring order and civilization to the benighted. Admirers of the British empire in America included Presidents Theodore Roosevelt
and William Howard Taft. In 1908, Roosevelt was concerned with Britain's
ability to deal with Indian unrest and "hold down any revolt,"[5] and in 1909
he described the British role in India as "the greatest feat of the kind that has
been performed since the break up of the Roman empire . . . [and] one of the
most notable and the most admirable achievements of the white race during
the past centuries."[6] Echoing Roosevelt's sentiments, Taft in 1914 told the
Toronto Empire Club that "the debt the world owes England ought to be
acknowledged in a grudging manner." And President Woodrow Wilson, an
admirer and emulator of the English form of government as well as an advocate of self-determination, resisted the demands of Indian nationalists that
the Government of India be represented in the League of Nations. "Under no
circumstances," he told Colonel House, "would he consent to the admission
of a delegate from India because it was not self-governing."[7]

Like nationalist imperialists such as Hearst, those opposed to imperialism,
American as well as British, and sympathetic to the ordinary persons oppressed by colonial masters, also contributed to Gandhi's positive reception
in America after World War I. Their first manifestation was the Anti-
Imperialist League. Led by Harvard luminaries Charles Eliot Norton and
William James, ex-president Grover Cleveland, presidents Jordan of Stanford
and Angell of Michigan, Andrew Carnegie for capital and Samuel Gompers
for labor, and spoken for by E. L. Godkin's *Evening Post* and *Nation* and
Mark Twain, the League was founded in Boston at Faneuil Hall in June 1898.
The League tried—unsuccessfully—to ensure that the Spanish-American war
would result in liberation, not conquest.

Culturally, the ground for Gandhi in America was prepared by America's
version of an "oriental renaissance." Emerson's India-inspired transcenden-
talism ("The Oversoul," "Brahma") influenced Whitman's orientalism (most
evident in his poem "Passage to India"). Emerson's lavish praise for Whit-

man's *Leaves of Grass*, when it first appeared in 1855, helped Whitman on his way to becoming America's greatest poet. The orientalism of Emerson's Concord friend, Henry David Thoreau, took several forms. For a time he shared with Emerson the editorship of the transcendentalist magazine, *The Dial*. His meditative withdrawal to the Walden Pond and subsequent de facto renunciation of society and celebration of nature and solitude owed much to familiarity with the ideas and practice of Indian ascetics. Conversely, Gandhi's positive reception in America owes something to his multifaceted occidentalism; reading Thoreau's essay on "Civil Disobedience" helped in Gandhi's formulation and practice of *satyagraha* and its use by Martin Luther King, Jr.

Later, from an entirely different quarter of America's cultural landscape and without benefit of oriental texts, the outspokenly anti-imperialist Mark Twain helped translate India to America. After visiting that distant and exotic land in 1893 he wrote the widely read and frequently reprinted *Following the Equator: A Journey Around the World* (1897). Twenty-four chapters were devoted to "the most extraordinary country on earth." The master of fantastic realism and "the tall tale" about fabulous doings and beings, and the satirist and critic of middle-class pieties and conventions, found in India a land to his liking.

William Jennings Bryan, who visited India in 1905–1906, spoke and wrote against British imperialism. After his return Bryan is more often pictured as a yokel than a statesman. As a boy orator his speeches were said to be like the great Platte River, a thousand miles long and three inches deep. He stood three times for president, and these images should not obscure his role as the spokesman for Populism and Progressivism and a tribune of the people. Bryan was a forceful opponent of what he perceived as imperialist wars and the standing armies, big navies, and European entanglements they seemed to entail. When Woodrow Wilson broke his campaign pledge to keep America out of Europe's war, Bryan resigned his post as secretary of state in Wilson's cabinet.

In challenging his contemporary political adversaries and apologists for British rule in India, Theodore Roosevelt and William Howard Taft, Bryan contributed to the anti-imperialist ideological context in which Gandhi was perceived after World War I. "Let no one," Bryan wrote after his visit to India, "cite India as an argument in defense of colonialism." The Briton "has conferred some benefits upon India, but he has extorted a tremendous price for them. . . . [He] has demonstrated, as many before, man's inability to exercise, with wisdom and justice, irresponsible power over the helpless people."[8]

The sea change that occurred after World War I in America's outlook toward war, imperialism and orientalism helped make the *dhoti*-clad, wizened Gandhi a hero of pacifists whose opposition to the war now seemed justified. It also made him a hero of those opposed to British imperialism in India and to America's special relationship with England. American opinion was ready to celebrate a nationalist leader who was Asian, nonviolent, and "spiritual" if he was capable of challenging the British empire. In the early 1920s, Gandhi became a celebrity in American consciousness. What manner of person was he? Were Americans to admire, learn from, even believe in him, or had they let a spiritual and political Trojan horse into their midst?

THE GURU

Although it is a Hindu word, I use *guru* rather than "teacher" to discuss Gandhi's influence on important public figures in America. The English word "teacher" strongly suggests the Hindu word *adhyapak*, a teacher in a school or college, and only weakly if at all *guru*. A *guru* is a mentor and a master with respect or knowledge or skill and a spiritual guide, often but not always in a religious sense. A *guru* is not only at a higher plane of accomplishment but also at a higher plane of being than those who recognize or learn form him or her.

Gandhi was a *guru* for two prominent Americans, John Haynes Holmes and Martin Luther King, Jr., for most of their adult lives. He was a *guru* too for a third prominent American, Reinhold Niebuhr, but only for a short but important period (1930–1932) when, in the face of economic collapse, rising fascism, and aggressive war, he was seeking moral, nonviolent forms of collective action to realize "equal justice."

John Haynes Holmes

John Haynes Holmes was the earliest, the longest-serving, and arguably the most loyal and zealous of Gandhi's followers in America. Minister of the Community Church of New York from 1919 until 1949, editor of *Unity*, which spoke for a liberal Christianity that was pacifist, internationally and socially concerned, and politically radical, Holmes announced his "discovery" of Gandhi in 1921 and remained until his death in 1964, his most ardent admirer and advocate in America.[9] Between the wars particularly, Holmes' voice from the pulpit, the press (he wrote frequently for the *New York Herald Tribune*), and his and other journals of opinion was heard in New York, the East Coast, and beyond in support of radical reform at home and peace and anticolonialism abroad.

When, in 1927, Gandhi became correspondent from India for Holmes' journal, *Unity*, it published his autobiography (*The Story of My Experiments with Truth*) in the serial form in which it had recently appeared in India. This was the autobiography's first publication abroad. Holmes corresponded with Gandhi over many years and met him twice, once in England when Gandhi traveled to London from India to attend the second Round Table Conference in 1931 and a second time, more briefly, soon after Indian independence on August 15, 1947, when Holmes and his son Roger traveled to India by air to meet Gandhi at Delhi.[10] Gandhi was seventy-eight and would be murdered a few months later, on January 30, 1948.

Holmes announced in April 1921 that he would deliver a sermon on "Who is the Greatest Man in the World?" By his own retrospective account, "I climbed tremulously into my pulpit on Sunday morning. . . . To answer my own question." The answer he gave was M. K. Gandhi. "In the light of what was known, and not known, at that time about Gandhi here in our Western world," the audacity of his declaration, Holmes tells us thirty-two years later in *My Gandhi*, "seems now incredible."[11]

Holmes found Gandhi credible as a "mahatma" (translated to his attentive congregation as "the saint") and intelligible in Christian terms. "When I think of Lenin, I think of Napoleon. But when I think of Gandhi," Holmes told his congregation, "I think of Jesus Christ. He lives his life; he speaks his word; he suffers, strives, and will some day nobly die, for his kingdom upon earth."[12] Holmes had prepared his audience for this encomium by considering but rejecting several other contemporary great men and by telling what he knew of Gandhi's life and views. ("I wonder how many of you . . . know the story of his life. Listen while I tell this story, and see if I am right in calling its hero the greatest man in the world today!") It was a novel assertion but one that Holmes remained committed to for the rest of his life.

"The drama of this experience of discovery," Holmes wrote looking back to 1921 from 1953, "was terrific. Here was our world rent to ruin by mad resort to force and violence. Out of this vast convulsion (following World War I) there emerged this single man who put all his trust in truth and love. While the world gave itself over to self-destruction, Gandhi found the way of life and triumphantly walked therein. History has known nothing like it since Christ and Caesar."[13]

Holmes' sermon in April 1921 seems to have affected the formation of public opinion. Until mid-1921, news about India in American papers relied on Reuters, the British-owned news service whose imperial bias was evident from its failure to provide copy to America about the Jallianwalla Bagh massacre at Amritsar in 1919 and Gandhi's first noncooperation campaign. It did provide extensive coverage of the visit of the Prince of Wales in 1921 without mention of the hostility, boycotts, and violence with which it was met. Soon after Holmes' sermon, by mid-1921, news about India and Gandhi independent of British sources and views improved markedly. On March 13, 1922, when Holmes gave a second sermon about Gandhi, "Gandhi, His World Significance," it was reported in the *New York Times*. So too was a luncheon meeting a day earlier of the Foreign Press Association that discussed Gandhi's arrest on March 10, 1922. These were the first news reports about Gandhi that originated in the United States. By the spring of 1922, Gandhi had become news inside as well as outside the United States.

A decade after John Holmes had declared Gandhi to be "the greatest man in the world today," *Time* featured him on its cover as "Man of the Year" for

1930. It was the year of the Salt March, Gandhi's most effective challenge to the legitimacy of British rule in India. World attention and concern had moved from the prospect of prosperity and peace in 1921 to deepening depression and intimations of war in 1931. Gandhi's ingenious strategy and dramatic execution of the Salt March in March and April of 1930 had revitalized Indian nationalism and led Britain's new Labor government to the call for negotiations at the second Round Table Conference in London in September 1931. Gandhi was to be the sole representative of the Indian National Congress.

The prospect of Gandhi, now the Mahatma for some and for many a world-historical figure, leaving for London stirred John Haynes Holmes and Reinhold Niebuhr to dash to London in the hope of a meeting with the man who both believed held the key to Christian conduct on behalf of social justice. Holmes was then a leading figure in the East Coast liberal reform establishment, Niebuhr on the verge of becoming one.[14] Despite the resemblance between their causes and their commitments and their ostensible friendship, by 1931 the younger, ambitious Niebuhr had come to regard the more senior and established Holmes not only as "the faithful publicist for Gandhi in the United States" but also as the "ultimate symbol of the sentimental liberal pacifist,"[15] who failed to recognize that "the human capacity for love is always tainted by the inclination to be self-serving and even destructive."[16] Willy-nilly, in late August 1931 Holmes and Niebuhr embarked on a competitive mission to meet, learn from, and speak for Gandhi in America.

Holmes of course had every advantage, not least a personal invitation for Gandhi to meet him in London should he attend a conference there. Nevertheless, twenty-two years later, in the 1953 book, *My Gandhi*, Holmes adopts a tone of great humility and self-effacement; he tells the story of his encounter with Gandhi as if he was nobody who became somebody by virtue of Gandhi's grace.

As Holmes tells the story, he was touring in Switzerland when he happened to see a newspaper with a dispatch from Bombay telling of Gandhi's embarkation for the Round Table Conference.

> I was appalled at the spectacle of my own audacity in seeking intrusion upon so important, even historic occasion . . . would not [the Mahatma] . . . be troubled by my unheralded appearance and my insistent expectation of an interview? . . . When I reached London, the first thing I did was to hunt out Miss Lester [Murial Lester, head of Kingsley Hall, the East End settlement house, at which Gandhi would stay] and state my case. "I will be a busboy," I said, "a dishwasher, a garbage man, if only you let me in to see and talk with Gandhi." She not only gave me entrance, but managed, in kind and clever ways, to bring the Mahatma and me together. So I hoped I was not overreaching myself, nor exacting attention to which I was not entitled.[17]

Gandhi, of course, expected to see Holmes; he had corresponded with him for a decade and on July 30, 1931, wrote to Holmes from the Sabarmati

ashram that "if I do succeed in going to London we must meet."[18] Gandhi
was not surprised to find Holmes among those who greeted him at Folke-
stone when his boat-train arrived from Boulogne on September 12, 1931.
They met on four subsequent occasions over the next five days, the last time
being Thursday, September 17, when Holmes advised Gandhi not to accept
any of the several invitations he had to visit America.

This proved to be the most significant aspect of Holmes' encounter with
Gandhi. Holmes was determined to prevent Gandhi from being exposed to
what he believed would be an exploitative and uncomprehending America.
The preliminary to one of the invitations was to be an interview with Jimmy
Walker, the Mayor of New York, who was then in London. Webb Miller, a
well-known correspondent who had covered Gandhi's Salt March and was
currently representing the United Press, tried to arrange the interview. According to Holmes' account of his five days in London, he not only prevented Webb Miller from arranging for an interview between Gandhi and the
charming but corrupt Mayor of New York but also dissuaded him from accepting any invitations to visit America.

Miller's report of Gandhi's Salt March (March 12 to April 6) had caught
world attention at the time, subsequently became a classical account of the
practice of nonviolent resistance, and was seen by millions in 1982 and 1983
as recreated in the film *Gandhi*.[19] Miller apparently wanted to capitalize on
the world personality that he had had a hand, he thought, in creating.[20]
Holmes was "disgusted, even frightened" by "such tricks for making news"
and by "a deliberate attempt to exploit [Gandhi] . . . for cheap and vulgar
ends." Later, when Gandhi asked Holmes, "Do you know Mayor Walker?"
Holmes told him that "I am acquainted with [his] . . . record because I helped
to write it. . . . Mr. Walker is . . . now under serious charges of misconduct in
office, and is pretty certain to be removed. His administration had become a
municipal scandal. I should hate to see you in company with the Mayor, and
my sober judgement is that you should not receive him." The meeting did
not take place, nor did Gandhi, after consultation with Holmes, accept any
of several invitations to visit America.

Invitations for Gandhi to visit America at the conclusion of the Round
Table Conference were at hand when he arrived in London. Many of them,
according to Holmes, were from "more or less designing persons" who
"counted shrewdly on the prestige which he would bring to movements or
interests they represented." At least one, Holmes conceded, "was signed by
more or less influential names [Holmes did not give them but they included
Adolph Ochs, publisher of the *New York Times*, Alfred P. Sloan, chairman of
the General Motors corporation, Robert M. Hutchins, president of the University of Chicago, John Dewey, the philosopher, Jane Addams, the social
worker, the Rabbi Stephen S. Wise], and showed some appreciation . . . of
the problems involved." On October 9, 1931, under a two-column headline
on page one that read "Gandhi to visit US if we take him seriously; Holmes'

warning of ridicule deters him," the *New York Times* quotes Gandhi as saying "If [the invitors] . . . can convince Holmes I ought to go to America I shall be glad to reconsider my decision." But Holmes was not satisfied; he could see no real "evidence of preparation for Gandhi's coming." A reception, committee, itinerary, speaking engagements, care for the Mahatma's comfort and safety, an informed and sympathetic press, and interviews with the President and other leading citizens were all required. Yet "so far as I could see, no responsible organization was at hand or in prospect to take over as difficult and important a piece of business as the people of this country have ever attempted."

Holmes' objections, it turned out, were more fundamental than the inadequacy of preparations for the visit. From the beginning, Holmes writes, "I was opposed to the whole proposition." Gandhi's place after the conference was India "in this hour of counting crisis."

"Finally," Holmes confesses, "there was the question . . . as to whether the American people as a whole were ready to receive the Mahatma in true appreciation of his character and work." He had not yet won independence for India from Britain. "His policies were regarded as fantastic, and his personality as queer. . . . What I dreaded in 1931 . . . was a vast explosion of vulgar curiosity and ribald jesting."

Having said this much, Holmes recoiled: "I was perhaps ignoring Gandhi's supreme power and influence over men. His simplicity and grace, to say nothing of his courage, were passports to human favor." Had not Gandhi been "rapturously received and applauded" by the Lancashire weavers who had been all but ruined by his noncooperation boycott in India of cotton goods imported from England? Yet looking back in 1953, Holmes concluded, "as I thought then, that I was right in disfavoring the whole American proposal."[21]

Before rushing to judgment on Holmes' advice, we should bear in mind the circumstances surrounding Gandhi's reception in Britain. London in September 1931 was at the epicenter of a worldwide economic disturbance that began with the October 1929 stock market crash in America; the world and domestic economies were collapsing. Ramsay MacDonald's first national coalition government, formed on August 25, 1931, to deal with the "national emergency" just two weeks before the Round Table Conference opened, was already on its last legs, and was in no position to bargain about independence for India, the issue that Gandhi insisted had to be settled before the problem of India's minorities could be tackled. A hostile British press mocked and belittled him. When Gandhi made his opening remarks at the Round Table Conference, a speech *Chicago Tribune* correspondent William L. Shirer considered "the greatest of his long political life," the conference secretariat refused to make a verbatim record, the popular press largely ignored it, and *The Times* buried it. Most papers reveled in the prospect that the Conference would fail and Gandhi with it.[22]

The mood of uncertainty and fear generated by Britain's economic and political disintegration deepened Holmes' doubts. Unsettled by Webb Miller's scheme to link Gandhi with the corrupt and failing mayor of New York and worried that Americans would find Gandhi's ideas "fantastic" and his personality "queer," Holmes may have asked himself if a reception similar to the British establishment's hostile and uncomprehending one awaited Gandhi on the other side of the Atlantic. On balance, Gandhi's most ardent and most forceful advocate in America seemed to fear that, once on American soil, Gandhi would lose credibility and find it difficult to explain to himself in terms that Americans would understand. Did Holmes, Gandhi's self-appointed vicar in America, underestimate the Mahatma and misread American opinion? Reinhold Niebuhr's response to Gandhi suggested that he may have.

Reinhold Niebuhr

Holmes, when faced with the prospect of an earthly Gandhi on American soil, was overcome by doubts about Gandhi's credibility and intelligibility. Reinhold Niebuhr seems to have come to opposite conclusions. True, he did not have to advise Gandhi about a trip to America. But his account of "seeing" Gandhi in London suggests a different conclusion than Holmes. Gandhi's "innate dignity" did not allow the charge of being a "ridiculous figure." By declaring Gandhi a "prophet" and "statesman," Niebuhr, "the prophet to politicians," "father of us all" (liberal cold warriors, neorealists and, perhaps, neoconservatives), "establishment theologian," and aspiring politician, seemed to reveal that Gandhi in 1931 may have been what he hoped to become in America.[23]

When Niebuhr sailed for England in August 1931, his head was full of questions he wanted to put to Gandhi. They were the key questions for his book on social change: What was the difference between violent and non-violent resistance to evil and between nonresistance and any form of resistance?

Niebuhr at this time was still in his pacifist and socialist phase. He had helped to establish the pacifist Fellowship of Reconciliation, supported in 1928 the non-Marxist Socialist Party led by ex-Presbyterian minister Norman Thomas, and had visited the Soviet Union in the summer of 1930. Niebuhr spoke of the centrality of "social intelligence" for social action but linked it, in an article on "The Religion of Communism" in the *Atlantic* (April 1931), to "some kind of religion" which is "the basis of every potent social program. Those who fear too much fanaticism which is the inevitable by-product of religiously created energy are consigned to social impotence by the multitude of their scruples." Religious energy was dangerous—it bordered on fanaticism—but essential. This was the Niebuhr who hastened to London to meet Gandhi, a man who seemed to be providing the religious energy needed for national and social liberation.

Unlike Holmes, Niebuhr did not meet and talk to Gandhi in London. Along with a bevy of supporters he was left standing outside Kingsley Hall while John Haynes Holmes, Niebuhr's "ultimate symbol of the sentimental liberal pacifist . . . went inside for a personal appointment."[24] Niebuhr, the budding political realist, did not find Gandhi bizarre or absurd: "Since it is Gandhi's day of silence, the crowd outside and several dozen of us inside the hall who hope for an interview get no more than a smile from him. It is a very engaging and charming smile and one begins to regret the charges of sentimentality one has brought against friends [could Niebuhr have John Haynes Holmes in mind?] who have insisted that the homeliness of the man is soon forgotten, once he reveals his personality. Nor is there anything ridiculous about him, in spite of the loincloth (that article of apparel looks like what boys call track pants) and the homespun Indian shawl. There is too much innate dignity about the man to allow the impression of a ridiculous figure, which London newspapers try so assiduously to cultivate, to remain."[25]

In the key chapter of *Moral Man and Immoral Society*, "The Preservation of Moral Values in Politics," Niebuhr elaborates and refines his interpretations of Gandhi in "What Chance Has Gandhi?," the article he wrote soon after his return from London. The 1931 article and the 1932 chapter constitute Niebuhr's considered estimate of Gandhi. It was of a world-historical, even transcendent, figure. In the decaying and desperate world of failed capitalism and failing democracy, Gandhi's ideas and practices as Niebuhr interpreted them provided a religiously meaningful and politically effective way to pursue "equal justice, the most rational ultimate objective in society." He wondered "whether there has ever been a more historical moment in the centuries than this visit of Gandhi to London."[26]

After this almost hagiographic estimate of December 1931, Niebuhr clearly became more ambivalent about Gandhi as he proceeded to write *Moral Man and Immoral Society*, "a conscious declaration of independence from the pacifistic circle—liberal and Socialistic—in which he had worked in the previous decade."[27] In his December 1931 article Gandhi, the unique "prophet" and "statesman," combined "translucent honesty" and "spiritual self-discipline" with "necessary opportunism" and "patient application of general principles to detailed situations."[28]

In *Moral Man and Immoral Society* Niebuhr arrived at the view that the responsible Christian should accept the use of force and that the use of force implied the use of violence in certain situations. He came to this position in part through an at best superficial and at worst perverse interpretation of Gandhi's use of nonviolent resistance or *satyagraha* (soul-force). Gandhi, according to Niebuhr, used nonviolence as a pragmatist; he was not committed to nonviolence absolutely. "Beginning with the idea that social justice could be resisted by . . . truth force and soul force . . . [Gandhi] came finally to realize the necessity of some type of physical coercion upon the foes of his people's freedom, as every political leader must."[29] For weak collectives such as Indian nationalists or weak minorities such as American Negroes, nonviolence was the best tactic. Having made Gandhi intelligible in realist terms, Niebuhr held that he, not Gandhi's self-appointed champion in the United States, John Haynes Holmes, was "a true Gandhian."[30]

Niebuhr broke with his liberal Protestant and political reformist past in *Moral Man* by arguing that coercion, even violent coercion, that liberates "oppressed nationalities" or the "working classes" in the name of equal justice is "placed in a different moral category from the use of power for the perpetuation of imperial rule or class dominance." Conflicts involving oppressed nationalities and classes were not resolved through nonviolence that made mutual understanding and accommodation possible but by force that eventuated in victory for one side and defeat for the other. In 1932, Niebuhr believed that victory over imperialists, capitalists, and fascists required physical force, not truth force.

But Niebuhr could not so easily repudiate his past self, a self which Gandhi captured and enhanced and to which, in modified form, he gradually returned. Towards the end of chapter IX of *Moral Man*, "The Preservation of Moral Values in Politics," he presented another Gandhi, one more in keeping with the Gandhi both Niebuhr and John Haynes Holmes saw in London at Kingsley Hall.

"The advantage of nonviolence as a method of expressing good will," he wrote, "lies in the fact, that it protects the agent against the resentments which violent conflict always creates in both parties to a conflict, and that it proves this freedom of resentment and ill-will to the contending party in the dispute by enduring more suffering than it causes." Again affirming Gandhi's view of conflict resolution based on nonviolence and the mutual pursuit of truth, he observed that "One of the most important results of the spiritual discipline against resentment in the social dispute is that it leads to an effort to discriminate between the evils of a social system and situation and the individuals who are involved in it. . . . Mr. Gandhi never tires of making a distinction between individual Englishmen and the system of imperialism which they maintain."

Niebuhr concludes his chapter on Gandhi in *Moral Man* with a powerful endorsement of Gandhi's perspective. "There is no problem of political life to which religious imagination can make a larger contribution than this problem of developing nonviolent resistance. The discovery of elements of common human frailty in the foe and, concommitantly, the appreciation of all human life as possessing transcendent worth, creates attitudes which transcend social conflict and thus mitigate its cruelties. . . . These attitudes . . . require a sublime madness which disregards immediate appearances and emphasizes profound and ultimate unities."

Niebuhr then turns orientalism on its head: "It is no accident of history that the spirit of nonviolence has been introduced into contemporary politics by a religious leader of the orient." Because occidental man lacks the spirit of nonviolence he is "incapable of engaging in nonviolent social conflict." Western man's spiritual bankruptcy is the result of being "deprived of religion." Lacking a meaningful religious life "the white man" has become a "beast of prey." Niebuhr is particularly concerned about the disappearance of the religious inheritance of the disinherited, for whom the spirit required for nonviolent resistance is most important. "Even if," he concludes, "justice should be achieved by social conflicts which lack the spiritual elements of nonviolence, something will be lacking in the character of the society so constructed."[31]

In the final paragraph of "The Preservation of Moral Values in Politics," Niebuhr attempts to save his "realistic" account of "moral man and immoral society" by denying the Gandhi he has just so eloquently affirmed. "The perennial tragedy of human history," he alleges, "is that those who cultivate the spiritual elements usually do so by divorcing themselves from or misunderstanding the problem of collective man where the brutal elements are most obvious. . . . [T]o the end of history the peace of the world, as Augustine observed, must be gained by strife."[32]

Niebuhr's pacifist, liberal (both secular and Christian), and socialist friends and allies were shocked, dismayed, and for some, betrayed by *Moral Man's* "cynicism" and "unrelieved pessimism." Niebuhr answered his critics, who included Norman Thomas and John Haynes Holmes, by charging them with being "immersed in the sentimentalities of a dying culture."[33] Addressing his critics from the columns of his own *World Tomorrow*, Niebuhr "for the first time labeled himself a 'Marxian as well as a 'Christian'"—the better to distinguish himself from the likes of John Haynes Holmes, with whom he had now come to verbal blows and who was "now his chief nemesis on the religious left."[34]

Yet, as Richard Fox put it in his recent distinguished biography, Niebuhr was trying to have it both ways: idealism and realism. Coercion, even force, had to be used, to oppose and defeat immoral "collectives" in the domestic and international arenas. Unlike his brother, Richard, Reinhold's faith did not involve abandoning himself to God's will. Rather, "he held to the old liberal dream of transforming human society. . . . Despite his fulminations against sentimental liberalism, against complacent faith in the redemptive character of human goodwill, Reinhold remained a thoroughgoing liberal."[35] It was the liberal Niebuhr, the Niebuhr who dreamt of transforming human society, who so admired and identified with Gandhi the prophet and statesman in his ability to command a nation and humble an empire.

Martin Luther King, Jr.

Gandhi's greatest and most enduring success as a *guru* in America was the influence he had on Martin Luther King, Jr. Through King, Gandhi affected the conduct of the civil rights movements that began in the mid-1950s and crested in the mid-1960s. King discovered Gandhi early in his career, made Gandhi's ideas and practice his own, and remained faithful to them when, in what turned out to be the last years of his life, many of those whom he had previously influenced and led abandoned *satyagraha* and nonviolence.

King, the preeminent leader of the civil rights movement in America, played a central role in moving the country toward a resolution of what Gunnar Myrdal called "An American Dilemma," the contradiction between the equality promised in the Declaration of Independence and the reality of inequality found in slavery, segregation, discrimination, and poverty.

In 1950, King had heard Dr. Mordecai Johnson, then president of Howard University, speak about Gandhi. Johnson, who admired Gandhi, had just returned from India. King found Johnson's account of Gandhi "so profound and electrifying that I left the meeting and bought a half-dozen books on Gandhi's life and works."[36]

King began reading about *ahimsa* (nonviolence) and *satyagraha* (collective action in pursuit of truth), terms that have been subject to extensive interpretation in American scholarly, intellectual, and religious circles.[37] "I came to see," King wrote, "that the Christian doctrine of love operating through the Gandhian method of nonviolence was one of the most potent weapons available to the Negro in his struggle for freedom. . . . Gandhi was probably the first person in history to lift the love ethic of Jesus above mere interaction between individuals to a powerful and effective social force on a large scale."[38]

In the dozen years between King's launching the civil rights movement in 1956 and his murder in 1968, the mood and vocabulary of the country changed. Negroes became "blacks" and blacks called for black power. Some advocated violent means to achieve liberation and ethnic identity. Frantz Fanon replaced Jesus and Gandhi as the teacher of black power extremists. King objected less to the idea of black power than he did to two ideas frequently associated with it: retaliatory violence and separation. Both violated his Gandhian values.[39] *i agree*

Other disappointments and failures followed. Like Gandhi, who near the end of his life faced the carnage of partition riots, King towards the end of his life faced the violence of city riots and the escalation of the war in Vietnam. King and Gandhi were despised and opposed from "within," Gandhi by militant Hindu fundamentalists, King by extremist blacks; and from "without," Gandhi by "two nation" Muslims, King by J. Edgar Hoover and white racists and segregationists. Both were murdered and martyred. These affinities and parallels between King's and Gandhi's life made Gandhi a familiar figure in otherwise unlikely American households.[40]

Gandhi's presence in American popular consciousness as a person to respect or to vilify is partially linked to Martin Luther King, Jr.'s reputation and standing. They were at their nadir in the years immediately following King's death in 1968. His growing significance for Americans, whites as well as blacks, was evident when a King bust joined representatives of other American statesmen and heroes in the rotunda of the Capitol on January 20, 1986, and the United States for the first time celebrated the birthday of Martin Luther King, Jr., as a national holiday.

THE *MAHATMA*

One of Gandhi's images in America was that of the *mahatma*. Its meaning was determined in part by long-standing attitudes and beliefs about India and the Orient and about Christianity that structured perceptions and evaluations.

Since the late renaissance and certainly since the mid-eighteenth century the Occident has found it difficult to regard the Orient in any other light than backward, inferior, and benighted. Gandhi, the *homo religiosus*, the man of religion, whether as a *mahatma*, a saint, or a teacher of a way of life like Buddha or Jesus, quickly became a source of controversy and inspiration.

Until Gandhi became America's "lens on India," American views on Indian religion, society, and politics were largely filtered through British sources. They include those of the missionary Alexander Duff, who held that "of all the systems of false religion ever fabricated by the perverse ingenuity of fallen men, Hinduism is surely the most stupendous." Charles Grant could not "avoid recognizing in the people of Indosian a race of men lamentably degenerate and base," and John Stuart Mill, echoing the view of his father, James Mill, regretted that "in truth, the Hindu, like the eunuch, excels in the qualities of the slave."[41] More generally, the West's cultural hegemony and superiority made it difficult to accept an Indian, an oriental such as Gandhi, as a teacher of the good life.[42] The conquering West equated the superiority of its power and wealth with the superiority of its civilization and beliefs. Gandhi made a dent in this sense of superiority. The notion that the East could teach the West, that America had something to learn from Gandhi's reception as a religious figure reveals a great deal about how American attitudes about India and the Orient structured his presence in America.

"Charlie" Andrews, the Anglican missionary who early on became one of the principal interpreters of Gandhi to the West, first met Gandhi in Durban on January 1, 1914.[43] He bent to touch his feet. It was an act of canonization. Mark Juergensmeyer, a leading contemporary interpreter of Gandhi in America, traces the origins of the Western propensity to construct Gandhi as a saint to C. F. Andrews' accounts of his initial encounters with Gandhi and to Rabindranath Tagore's use of the term "mahatma" in 1915 when Gandhi returned to India.[44]

"Saint," a culturally available category for an otherwise anomalous being, was not an Indian term.[45] Saint in Western parlance can refer to persons canonized by the Church for preeminent holiness (official saints) or to one of a

Christian God's chosen people, a person in whom grace had triumphed and who was, as a consequence, eminent for piety or virtue. The aura of Christian holiness and transcendent power associated with the term "saint" quickly melded with English versions of Indian terms loosely translated as saint. In 1915, Rabindranath Tagore, the recent Nobel laureate, used an Indian term, *mahatma* (great soul), to welcome Gandhi on his return to India from South Africa. Mahatma was taken to be an Indian version of a saint and the two terms became hard to distinguish in Western usage. Mohandas Gandhi came to be referred to and known as Mahatma Gandhi (as if this were his proper name), a designation that nevertheless suggested his saintly meaning and provenance. But was Gandhi a "saint" by his own lights? Could he have meant to be a saint in India, much less in America? What does his construction as a saint tell us about Gandhi in America?

Mark Juergensmeyer argues that although Gandhi's canonization as a saint was largely at the initiative of his English and American admirers, he collaborated in the result: "What made Gandhi truly a Christ figure for Westerners from Andrews through Attenborough . . . was not just that he looked the part. He acted the part too—or at least his actions were amenable to that interpretation. He was regarded as a man who exhibited saintly qualities." Gandhi it seems wanted it that way, wanted his Western admirers to believe he was a saint. His capabilities, Juergensmeyer reasons, revealed his intentions. "The fact that he . . . appeared unclad but for a loincloth made him look like what many Americans expected in a Messiah. . . . [B]ehind his wizened appearance was the awesome cultural backdrop of India, which seemed to Gandhi's American admirers as distant from the modern age as Jesus' Galilee."

Ultimately Gandhi himself becomes responsible for the cultural noise that accompanied his translation from the world of the Indian orient, the world of *sannyasis, sadhus, gurus, rishis*, and *swamis*, to the world of the American occident, the world of saints. It begs the question to hold that "saintliness, like beauty, exists largely in the eye of the beholder" if Gandhi *meant* to play the saint to his occidental admirers. They may have "extravagantly revered" him but Gandhi becomes culpable if they were gullible. An authentic modern saint has a powerful appeal. Gandhi became a *homo religiosus*, more "adequate" than Jesus to the "global, rational, modern point of view. . . . Gandhi, the English speaking, London trained, Hindu is intercultural in his appeal—'a universal saint' as [John Haynes] Holmes put it. . . . Many Christians, especially those of a liberal theological bent who shy away from an other worldly view of Christ, feel that Gandhi fills the role as adequately as Jesus did."

According to Juergensmeyer, "the point of view is as interesting as the object of attention." It is the authenticity of the believers, not the authenticity of the saint that "shows that sainthood is far from dead, even in the present day." For Juergensmeyer there seems to be a touch of manipulation and a hint of fraud in the emergence of Gandhi the saint.[46]

Gandhi himself had trouble coping with his "saintly" image, what he called his "*darshan* dilemma." Soon after Gandhi returned from South Africa in1915 he attended the Kumbha Mela, a vast religious assemblage of pilgrims and sadhus. Darshan seekers did not allow him a minute to call his own. "The *dharshanvalas*' blind love has often made me angry, and . . . sore at heart." At the same time, "the unique faith of India and the frankness and generosity of our people enchant me." Yet the people do not "profit in any way by having *darshan*"; he knew nothing in himself, he said, that made him "worthy of giving *darshan.*" It is not possible," he said, "simultaneously to work and to give *darshan.*" "I do," he protested, "make every effort to extricate myself from this dilemma." His solution ultimately was not to choose between *darshan* and work but to try to do it both: "At present, even when people come from *darshan,* I continue to write and do other work."[47]

The second difficulty that Juergensmeyer encounters with "St. Gandhi" is one endemic to saints. Those who bracket Gandhi with Jesus as a saint can encounter the same difficulty with respect to Jesus. We ordinary mortals cannot be like such saints. According to Juergensmeyer, Gandhi "is portrayed as essentially different from us, endowed with a spiritual power to which ordinary mortals are not privy. . . . We can laud his moral achievements without feeling the necessity to live up to all of them ourselves." Reinhold Niebuhr, Juergensmeyer's teacher, found Jesus' virtues "dazzling precisely because they are not emulable: they are extremes of selfless love that provide ordinary Christains with a noble but ultimately unobtainable goal." For Juergensmeyer Gandhi's saintliness is similar: "We cannot live up to the standard that he achieved."[48] Saint Gandhi may be a credible construction for some like John Haynes Holmes; but for grudging admirers like Niebuhr and Juergensmeyer his sainthood did not provide a satisfactory guide to the religious life.

Gandhi neither wanted to be nor claimed to be a saint. A *guru*, yes, perhaps a *sannyasi* or *sadhu*, even a *mahatma*, but not a saint. The lives of saints are indeed unlike those of ordinary mortals. Gandhi's confessional autobiography, "The Story of My Experiments with Truth," was meant to show just how ordinary and mortal a creature he was. It showed too that Gandhi managed to realize in his daily life and his public actions cultural ideals that many Indians honored in their own lives and actions but found difficult but not necessarily impossible to enact. Gandhi did not, like a saint is said to do, mean to mediate for or empower others. If he meant to be anything, he meant to be a *guru*, to teach through example, action, and precept. Margaret Chatterjee, in her superb book on *Gandhi's Religious Thought,* observes that "The guru idea has been exploited in recent years by Christian theologians in India, but not too successfully, for the guru in Hindu traditions is a preceptor, not a mediator. The tables can be turned and guru and disciple reverse their roles."[49]

If I am right in believing that those who for good or ill assimilated Gandhi to the essentially Christian concept of saint misread the historical text they confronted, their "mistake" does not remove the image of "St. Gandhi" from the meaning of Gandhi in America. It continues to play an important and controversial role.

Beyond the image of Gandhi, the universal saint, and incorporating it lay the possibility that Gandhi was a *homo religiosus*, a world-historical teacher of transcendent ethics comparable to Buddha, Mohammed, and, particularly for Christians, Jesus. During Pope John Paul II's widely reported visit to India in February, 1986, he told inquiring reporters on his return to Rome, "I was there to evangelize. . . . I have evangelized the Indian people through the works of Mahatma Gandhi." "Gandhi," according to the Pope, "was much more of a Christian than many people who say they are Christians."[50] Other Christians than Pope John Paul II have viewed Gandhi in this framework. Kenneth Scott Latourette in his 1953 *A History of Christianity* argued that through Gandhi "the influence of Christ . . . became more dominant in . . . [India] than at any previous time. Through Gandhi the teaching and example of Jesus made for nonviolent resistance, greater opportunity to the depressed classes, and the positive meanings of unselfish service." Jaroslav Pelikan, another distinguished Yale historian of Christianity, in his 1985 *Jesus Through the Centuries: His Place in the History of Culture*, links Gandhi to Jesus in his chapter on "The Liberator."[51] John Haynes Holmes, a Protestant, and Thomas Merton, the Catholic, treat Gandhi as a redeemer and a liberator.[52]

Pope John Paul II's "recognition" of Gandhi in 1986 was foreshadowed by Pope John XXIII in *Pacem in Terris* and by the Church's *Declaration on the Relationship of the Church to Non-Christian Religions (Nostra Aetate)* of the Second Vatican Council, October 28, 1965. This *Declaration* recognized Hinduism, Buddhism, Islam, and other faiths as religions and said of them, "The Catholic Church rejects nothing which is true and holy in these religions. . . . [They] often reflect a ray of that Truth which enlightens all men (John 1:9)."

Gandhi, the *homo religiosus*, revived issues first raised in the fifth century by the English (or Irish) theologian Pelagius, in his dispute with Augustine of Hippo over Adam's fall, original sin, and God's grace. Pelagius disputed Augustine's doctrine that the consequence of Adam's fall entailed original sin and restricted to Christians only the possibility of knowing God and of God's grace. Pelagians took the view that God's grace gave man free will, that subsequently it was "helpful but not necessary and that the heirs of Adam were not stained with original sin." Consequently, non-Christians could act righteously and know God. Pelagius' dispute with Augustine did not end in the fifth century.[53] It is the mentality that made it possible to write *Nostra Aetate* in 1965 and for Pope John Paul II to evangelize in Gandhi's name in 1986.

We have seen that "Saint Gandhi," while an image of Gandhi in America, was not an image Gandhi meant to convey. At the same time, Gandhi thought about Christianity in terms not unlike those used by liberal Protestants and neo-Pelagian Catholics about him. There was, at this level but not at others, mutual admiration and an elective affinity that facilitated Gandhi's reception in America. In words that might have pleased Pelagius and no doubt did please John Haynes Holmes, Gandhi in 1941 said that "because the life of Jesus has the significance and the transcendency to which I have alluded, I believe he belongs not solely to Christianity, but to the entire world, to all races and people."[54] "But this is not to say," Margaret Chatterjee adds to her gloss of Gandhi's views, "that those who have not heard the name of Christ Jesus cannot do the will of the Lord." For Gandhi, Jesus was "a great world teacher among others." "Jesus," Gandhi continued, "preached not a new religion but a new life."[55]

Catholic Christians were not as quick to respond to Gandhi, the *homo religiosus*, as were some liberal Protestant Christians. Pope Pius XI twice refused Gandhi's requests to call on him when, in his only trip abroad as India's national leader, he passed through Rome in December 1931 on his way back from the second Round Table Conference. Pope John Paul's first act on his visit to India fifty-five years later was to visit the site of Gandhi's cremation on the bank of the Jumna River. Removing his shoes, the Pope knelt in silent prayer at the memorial to the "apostle of nonviolence" and then spoke of humanity's debt to "this man so marked by his noble devotion to God and his respect for every living being. . . . It is entirely fitting," he said, "that this pilgrimage should begin here. Today we still hear him pleading with the world 'Conquer hate by love, untruth by truth, violence by suffering.'"[56]

The Pope's ten-day tour of India was widely reported in America's electronic and print media. His tasks were manifold, complex, and delicate. Unlike his visits to other third world countries, in India he was a Christian pontiff appealing to a predominantly Hindu country.

The Pope prepared for his trip to India by immersing himself in the teachings of Gandhi. In India he quoted Gandhi often and at length. In Rome on his return he told reporters, "I have evangelized the Indian people through the words of Mahatma Gandhi."[57] Was this good tactics in a poor, Hindu country, or the revitalized neo-Pelagianism and the ecumenism of Vatican II's *Nostra Aetate?* At the beginning of his tour, the Pope appealed to Gandhi when he said that "I want to show respect, esteem, and encouragement to all those who search for God, who commit themselves to search for perfection, who work in the services of their brothers to construct peace and justice." Joaquin Navarro Valls, the chief Vatican spokesman accompanying the Pope, characterized the Pope's invocation of Gandhi as part of a "broader effort to link Roman Catholic teaching to Gandhi's objectives."[58]

Gandhi the "saint," mahatma, and *homo religiosus* had been heard and seen in America for three decades to mixed reviews, contested evaluations, and ambiguous understandings. His presence in American consciousness was mediated by shifting and intersecting historical currents and by metathought, the mentality that selects and colors contemporary events and experience.

THE FRAUD

Gandhi, Charles Chatfield found, was America's lens on India. He was also its lightning rod for images of India and the Orient, a particularly powerful, pervasive, and intrusive version of the "other." Xenophiles find themselves attracted by the other, xenophobes repelled; but what comes first, the experience of thinking and feeling about the other or the cultural paradigms, the metaideas, that distinguish "them" and "us?"

The British images of India depicted earlier, the India of "false religion," a "lamentably degenerate" people, and a "slave" mentality, were common in an America that, until after World War I, got most of its news and views from British sources. Just as there were exceptions to the European and British image of India and the orient, contributors to the integral humanism of the "oriental renaissance" who learned in India as well as about India, such as the Frenchman Anquetil-Duperron and the Englishman Sir William Jones, so too were there American exceptions, Ralph Waldo Emerson, Henry David Thoreau, Walt Whitman, and Mark Twain. But when Gandhi, the Indian and the oriental, appears in the press and quarterlies of the early 1920s, he is constructed and interpreted not only in terms of the imperialist politics of that era, but also in terms of deep-rooted metaideas and cultural paradigms about India and the East.

The film *Gandhi* provided a particularly effective lightning rod for the view of Gandhi as fraud. Released in 1982 but seen for the most part in 1983, it won an unprecedented eight academy awards, topped the list for viewers, and made a lot of money. It presented Gandhi as an epic hero: a myth for our time, perhaps for all time. In a world in which entertainment and news construct each other and history is made as well as represented on the screen, illusion and reality can merge. *Gandhi* was great entertainment and great box office, but it was also a message and a worldview. An Indian saint became a transcendent figure. Although America was neither seen nor mentioned in the film, the visual language of the film—the film as text—was taken by some to legitimize and justify ideas and actions at issue in America. More than ever before, Gandhi became a popular concept in America.

The film generated a neoconservative backlash, what Hendrick Hertzberg in a brilliant riposte to two such attacks labeled "a nasty outbreak of Mahatma-bashing."[59] Its principal spokesperson was Richard Grenier, film critic for *Commentary* and sometime novelist. In the March, 1983 number of *Commentary* Grenier engaged in "Deflating the Gandhi Myth" by depicting "The Gandhi Nobody Knows" as a fraud. In particular, he asserts the "St. Gandhi" presented in the film was really a lecher, racist, hypocrite, fool, and faddist. The film's director, Sir Richard Attenborough, "Dickie" to Grenier, is depicted as a paid political propagandist for the Government of India (it financed one-third of the film's cost) who surreptitiously, even subliminally, slipped in his pacifist, socialist, environmentalist, and anti-imperialist views.[60]

We are dealing, Grenier says, "with two strangenesses here, Indians and Gandhi himself." His principal authority for the claim of strangeness is V. S. Naipaul, "a Hindu and a Brahmin, born in Trinidad" and the author of two "quite brilliant" books, *An Area of Darkness* and *India: A Wounded Civilization*. It is not the literary quality of Naipaul's books that Grenier admires but their depiction of Indian orientalism, the alien other that Grenier feels is so repellent.

India, according to the Naipaul quoted in Grenier, "has little to offer the world except its Gandhian concept of holy poverty and the recurring crooked comedy of its holy men." Hinduism as Naipaul understands it "has given men no idea of a contract with other men. . . . It has enslaved one-quarter of the populations [the untouchables] and has left the whole fragmented and vulnerable. . . . Through centuries of conquest the civilization declined into an apparatus for survival, turning away from the mind . . . and creativity . . . stripping itself down, like all decaying civilizations, to its magical practices and imprisoning social forms."

Naipaul says that Gandhi's autobiography reveals that he was headed for "lunacy." He was rescued by his response to external events, a response—presumably *satyagraha*—that was determined in part by "his experience of the democratic ways of South Africa." It was in South Africa that Gandhi caught a glimmer of that strange institution, i.e., democracy, "of which he would never have seen even a reflection within Hindu society." Gandhi, like India more generally, is "dependent in every practical way on other, imperfectly understood civilizations." Grenier and Naipaul are building not only on nineteenth-century British orientalist views of India but also on more recent orientalist constructions of India and Gandhi, among which Katherine Mayo's *Mother India* is paradigmatic.

First published in 1927, *Mother India* was written in the context of official and unofficial British efforts to generate support in America for British rule in India. It added contemporary and lurid detail to the image of Hindu India as irredeemably and hopelessly impoverished, degraded, depraved, and corrupt. Mayo's *Mother India* echoed not only the views of men like Alexander Duff, Charles Grant, and John Stuart Mill but also those of Theodore Roosevelt, who glorified in bearing the white man's burden in Asia and celebrated the accomplishments of imperialiam.[61]

Mayo took special aim at Gandhi, whose success in challenging British rule deeply troubled her British friends and patrons. They took special pains to provide information, facilitate her travel and interviews in India, and publicize her book after its publication. Gandhi agreed to her request for an interview and spent a good deal of time answering her queries about the state of India and giving his views about the causes of, and remedies for, India's ills. Her selective and truncated account of Gandhi's views made them appear "thoroughly ridiculous."[62]

Katherine Mayo was obsessed with two evils, Hinduism and disease. The two seemed to be linked in some kind of ontological nexus. In an article in the *Atlantic Monthly* soon after Gandhi's widely reported Salt March in 1930, she returned to the task of denigrating Gandhi's image in America. After charging him with sedition, she alleged that a smallpox epidemic in an area where Gandhi had walked on his way to Dandi was due to the contagion carried by his followers. They in turn had been contaminated before their departure on March 12, 1930, because Gandhi's ashram was a "smallpox pest center." Mayo succeeded in adding a new dimension to the litany of the ills of Hindu India. Many years later Daniel Patrick Moynihan, who served as United States ambassador to India under Presidents Nixon and Ford, echoed Katherine Mayo when he publicly remarked that the only thing India had to export was communicable diseases.

Katherine Mayo made sense to Americans: health was better than disease; monotheist Muslims better than idolatrous Hindus; enslaved, dehumanized, but underdog and potentially Christian untouchables better than their upper-caste Hindu oppressors who were in any case incapacitated physically and morally by their horror of pollution. The obvious and moral conclusion was that British rule, which helped and protected Muslims, untouchables, and Christians, must and should continue. Gandhi's teaching that all religions approached truth and his doctrinal and practical efforts to realize national and religious brotherhood and to purify Hinduism by ridding it of untouchability were spurious, politically inspired deceptions designed to unite India behind his demand for independence.

WHO GOES THERE, FRIEND OR FOE?

Gandhi first entered American public consciousness in 1921 after John Haynes Holmes declared him to be the greatest man in the world. He is still present and is likely to remain so.

Gandhi began as an anti-imperialist, an intrepid opponent of the British empire in India who appealed to William Randolph Hearst, an American press baron virulently opposed to British power and prestige. Gandhi's meaning quickly moved from the realm of history, of factuality and positive truth, to encompass the realm of myth, of belief and imaginative truth. He became a *guru* for some and a *mahatma* for others, a world-historical figure whose life and message could teach a new way of living and acting.

But there was a powerful countercurrent that challenged the view that America had anything to learn from Gandhi. Some held that Americans were being deceived; Gandhi was a fraud, not saint. As Franky A. Schaefer, the evangelical fundamentalist who introduced Richard Grenier's Gandhi-bashing book, *The Gandhi Nobody Knows*, put it, "it is the time that Westerners—Christians and Jews—adopt a little more self-confidence in answering the challenge of Hinduism. Christians in particular need to affirm the fact that there is only one Christ and Savior and his name is Jesus, not Gandhi."[63] The persistence and intensity of efforts to denigrate and unmask Gandhi are measures of the threat that some feel from his growing acceptance in the West as a world figure whose nonviolent pursuit of truth advanced the meaning and practice of civilized living.

NOTES

1. See Mohanda K. Gandhi, *Satyagraha in South Africa* (Ahmedabad: Navajivan, 1950; 1928), and Robert A. Huttenback, *Gandhi in South Africa; British Imperialism and the Indian Question* (Ithaca: Cornell University Press, 1971).

2. Charles Chatfield, ed., *The Americanization of Gandhi: Images of the Mahatma* (New York and London: Garland Publishing, 1976).

3. Chatfield, 24–25.

4. Reproduced in the *Hindu* (Madras), 2-27-22, as quoted in Manoranjan Jha, *Civil Disobedience and After: The American Reaction* (Meerut and Delhi: Meenakshi Prakashan, 1973).

5. Roosevelt to Whitlaw Reid, Ambassador to London, 11-26-08, in Elting E. Morrison, *The Letters of Theodore Roosevelt* (Cambridge: Harvard University Press, 1952), vol. 6, 1383–84.

6. *Some American Opinions on the Indian Empire*, London, nd., 1–2, as quoted in Jha, *Civil Disobedience*, 10.

7. David Miller, *The Drafting of the Covenant* (New York: G. P. Putnam's Sons, 1982), vol. 492, no. 56, and Charles Seymour, *The Intimate Papers of Colonel House: The Ending of the War* (Boston: Houghton Mifflin Co., 1928), 311. Only after General Smuts pointed out that India as a signatory power would automatically have a right to a delegate did Wilson "acquiesce" to Government of India membership.

8. *The Old World and Its Ways* (St. Louis: The Thompson Publishing Co., 1907), ch. XXVI, "British Rule in India," 308.

9. The Holmes papers are in the library of Congress, Washington, D.C. Holmes left his extensive collection of books by and about Gandhi to Harvard where they are now housed in the University library.

10. He was a professor of philosophy at Mount Holyoke College for most of his career.

11. John Haynes Holmes, *My Gandhi* (New York: Harper and Brothers, 1953), 29. The sermon was delivered on 4-10-21 at the Lyric theatre to an overflow congregation "who expected to hear Woodrow Wilson or Sun Yat-Sen, Lloyd George, or Lenin." Carl Hermann Voss, "John Haynes Holmes: Discover of Gandhi," *Christian Century*, 5-6-64, in Chatfield, *Americanization*, 589–98.

12. "Who is the Greatest Man in the World," New York, The Community Church, 61 East 34st Street, New York, 1921, in Chatfield, *Americanization*, 599–621. Quote at 620.

13. Holmes, *My Gandhi*, 33. Holmes told his audience that he first came across Gandhi's name in 1918 in an article by the Oxford classicist Gilbert Murray in the *Hibbert Journal*. Murray's article on the concept of the soul went on to discuss saints including recent ones such as Gandhi. Murray warned Great Britain in connection with Gandhi that a nation whose government prosecuted saints is neither wise, generous, nor high minded. Voss, "Discoverer of Gandhi," in Chatfield, *Americanization*, 589.

As we shall see below, the Angelican missionary in South Africa and India, Charles F. Andrews, "discovered" and "canonized" Gandhi four years earlier in 1914 when he met him for the first time in South Africa, but no public word of Andrews' experience seems to have reached Europe or America until after Murray's article.

The discovery in 1986 of 260 letters written between 2/09 and 12-5-44 by Gandhi "to his close friend and disciple," the Polish-German Jewish architect Hermann Kallenbach, forcefully reminds us that Kallenbach should be recognized as the first non-Indian to acknowledge Gandhi. In 5/10 Kallenbach, "mesmerized by Gandhi," donated to him the eleven-hundred-acre farm near Lawley, twenty miles from Johannesburg, that became Tolstoy Farm. In 1914, he [Gandhi] compared Kallenbach with C. F. Andrews, and wrote: "Though I love, almost adore, Andrews so, I would not exchange you for him." In a letter to another friend in 1946, the year of Kallenbach's death, Gandhi spoke movingly of his "old friend." Ramesh Chandra, "The Mahatma's Letters," *India Today*, 12-31-31, 1986, 52–53.

14. Both were important members of the pacifist Fellowship of Reconciliation and active supporters of Norman Thomas, who had abandoned his ministerial career in 1917 to lead the Socialist Party in New York. Holmes' younger colleague, friend, and incipient rival, Niebuhr, had recently left his well-publicized socially concerned pastorate of Detroit's comfortable Bethel Evangelical Church to become a professor at the Union Theological Seminary in New York where, in November 1930, his candidacy for a State Senate seat attracted more publicity than votes. Richard W. Fox, *Reinhold Niebuhr: A Biography* (New York: Pantheon Books, 1985), 129–30.

15. Fox, 130.

16. Mark Juergensmeyer, *Fighting with Gandhi* (San Francisco: Harper and Row, 1984), 127.

17. Holmes, *My Gandhi*, 35–36.

18. John Haynes Holmes Papers, Box 3, Autograph Collection, A-1 folder (Gandhi), Library of Congress, Washington, D.C. AS a Sabarmati, 7-30-31 [Typewritten]. "There is no certainty about my going to London as yet. There are difficulties which may prove insuperable. I feel I must not leave India unless some glaring breaches of the Settlement are repaired. I am straining every nerve to avoid a conflict, but the result is in God's hands. But if I do succeed in going too we must meet."

19. Gandhi' co-workers broke the law by taking salt—protected by government monopoly—from the area at the government's Dharsana Salt Works one hundred fifty miles north of Bombay near Dandi; four hundred policemen brutally assaulted the nonviolent marchers who remained courageously steadfast in their commitment. Miller's account is reproduced *inter alia* in Homer Jack, ed., *The Gandhi Reader; a Source Book of his Life and Writings* (Bloomington: Indiana University Press, 1958). William L. Shirer in his *Gandhi, a Memoir* (New York: Simon and Schuster/Touchstone, 1979) described Miller four decades after the Salt March as "one of the great American foreign correspondents." "His story," Shirer says, "was flashed around the world" and "published in more than a thousand newspapers at home and abroad," 97–99.

20. Webb Miller, *I Found No Peace: The Journal of a Foreign Correspondent* (New York: Simon and Schuster, 1936). See ch. 16 through 19 and 21 for Miller's coverage of India and Gandhi.

21. The account of Holmes' advice to Gandhi on the Walker interview and invitations to America is given in his *My Gandhi*, 48–51, and in Manoranjan Jha, *Civil Disobedience and After*, 181–83.

22. J. L. Garvin, editor of the *Observer*, described Gandhi's call for Indian independence as "a vain dream" and warned that without strong British rule, anarchy, worse than that in China, would follow. "Though Gandhi is a gifted and fascinating agitator, his exalted but unconstructive ideology suggests that breaking and not the making of India." Lord Beaverbrook's *Sunday Express* ran a lead editorial entitled "The Failure of Gandhi." "Gandhi," it opined, "is out of his depth in England. He has gained publicly which a film star might envy, but he has been a complete failure in solving Indian problems. Unless he provokes a miracle, the Conference will break up in two or three days, and the last remnants of his prestige will disappear," Shirer, *Gandhi*, 168, 177, 191–92.

23. Soon after World War II, Niebuhr became a "Prophet to politicians": the "Establishment theologian," and a "celebrity intellectual," Fox, *Niebuhr*, 273. The phrase "prophet to politicians" was used as the subtitle of Ronald Stone's 1972 biography, *Reinhold Niebuhr*. The often-quoted phrase "father of us all" has been attributed to George F. Kennan, but Richard Fox reports that in 1980 Kennan "did not recall" describing Niebuhr in these terms. Fox, *Niebuhr*, 238.

24. Fox, *Niebuhr*, 130.

25. "What Chance Has Gandhi," *Christian Century*, 12-16-31, in Chatfield, *Americanization*, 705.

26. Reinhold Niebuhr, *Moral Man and Immoral Society* (New York: Scribner's Sons, 1953), 234; Chatfield, *Americanization*, 705.

27. Fox, *Niebuhr*, 136.

28. Chatfield, *Americanization*, 706.

29. *Moral Man*, 242.

30. Fox, *Niebuhr*, 138.

31. *Moral Man*, 234, 247–49, 255–56.

32. *Moral Man*, 256.

33. Fox, *Niebuhr*, 142–43.

34. Fox, 136, 143, 152–53.

35. Fox, *Niebuhr*, 134.

36. Among those he read while a divinity student at Boston University was Holmes' book on Gandhi. King told Stanley Katz, Holmes' grandson-in-law, that the book had been a factor in his move toward Gandhi. Personal letter, 7-20-88. William Stuart Nelson in his "Gandhian Values and the American Civil Rights Movement," in Paul F. Power, ed., *The Meanings of Gandhi* (Honolulu: University of Hawaii Press, 1971), reminds us that the first known contact between Gandhi and American blacks (then Negroes) occurred when Howard Thurman, then a professor at Howard University, and the Reverend Edward Carrol, and their wives, met Gandhi in India on 2-28-36. Among other things, Gandhi told his guests that "one cannot be passively nonviolent," 155.

37. See for example Joan Bondurant, *Conquest of Violence: The Gandhian Philosophy of Conflict* (Princeton: Princeton University Press, 1958; reprint, Berkley and Los Angeles: University of California Press, 1967); Gene Sharp, *The Politics of Nonviolent Action* (Boston: Porter Sargent Publishers, 1973); Richard Gregg, *The Power of Nonviolence* (New York: Schocken Books, second revised edition, 1971); Staughton Lynd, ed., *Nonviolence in America: A Documentary History* (Indianapolis: Bobbs-Merrill, 1966); Karl Potter, "Explorations in Gandhi's Theory of Nonviolence" and William Stuart Nelson, "Gandhian Values and the American Civil Rights Movement"

in Power, ed., *Gandhi*; and Mulford Sibley, ed., *The Quiet Battle; Writings on the Theory and Practice of Nonviolent Resistance* (Garden City, NJ: Anchor Books, 1963). *Gandhi Marg* (New Delhi) and *The Journal of Conflict Resolution* have published over the years many articles on nonviolent civil resistance and collective action.

38. Martin Luther King, *Stride Toward Freedom; The Montgomery Story* (New York: Harper and Row, 1958), 85, 97.

39. For King on these matters see his *Where Do We Go from Here: Chaos or Commentary* (New York. Harper and Row, 1967), particularly ch. 2, "Black Power," where he remarks *inter alia* that the bible of Black Power advocates such as Stokely Carmichael is Frantz Fanon's *The Wretched of the Earth.* "They don't quote Gandhi or Tolstoy."

40. For a vivid, insightful firsthand account of these troubled and turbulent years that attends to the Gandhian dimension see Harris Wofford, *Of Kennedys and Kings: Making Sense of the Sixties* (New York: Farrar Straus Giroux, 1980). See also William Stuart Nelson, "Gandhian Values and the Civil Rights Movement," in Power, ed., *Gandhi*, 153–64. Nelson reminds us that Gandhi's influence on the civil rights movement among American blacks precedes King's. James Farmer was founding director of the Congress of Racial Equality (CORE), program director of the National Association for the Advancement of Colored People (NAACP), and an assistant secretary in the Department of Health, Education, and Welfare in the Nixon Administration. His book *Freedom When?* (New York: Harper, 1965) gives an account of his understanding of Gandhi, Gandhi's relevance to American blacks, and Farmer's use of Gandhi's ideas and practice in the civil rights movement. See also James Farmer, *Lay Bare the Heart: An Autobiography of the Civil Rights Movements* (New York: Plume, 1986).

41. These familiar quotes are drawn from a letter to the *Times of India* of 3-2-88 by Sita Ram Goel.

42. See Raymond Schwab, *The Oriental Renaissance: Europe's Rediscovery of India and the East 1680–1880* (New York: Columbia University Press, 1984), trans. Gene Patterson-Back and Victor Reinking from the original 1936 French publication, shows how much Europe in the eighteenth and nineteenth centuries learned about and from the Orient. In America leading figures such as Ralph Waldo Emerson and Walt Whitman were carriers of what might be called the "oriental renaissance." For orientalism with reference to India, see Ronald Inden, "Orientalist Constructions of India," *Modern Asia Studies*, vol. 10, no. 3 (July 1986), 401–46.

43. His *Mahatma Gandhi's Ideas, Including Selections from his Writings* (New York: Macmillan, 1930) and subsequent writings about Gandhi were among the earliest and certainly among the most read in America. Romain Rolland's 1924 biography was probably the first account of Gandhi available in America.

44. See his "Saint Gandhi," in John S. Hawley, ed., *Saints and Virtues* (Berkley and Los Angeles: University of California Press, 1986), for a more detailed account of these formative events. While I learned a great deal from this important paper, this essay is in part a rejoinder to it and to George Orwell's 1949 *Partisan Review* essay, "Reflections on Gandhi," which articulates a similar grudging and skeptical admiration. Republished in Sonia Orwell and Ian Angus, eds., *In Front of Your Nose*, 1945–1950 (New York: Harcourt Brace Jovanovich, 1968), vol. IV, *The Collected Essays, Journalism and Letters of George Orwell.* Juergensmeyer's earlier *Fighting with Gandhi* (San Francisco: Harper and Row, 1984) provided a "step-by-step strategy for resolving everyday conflicts" at home and in public life by translating Gandhi's

method of *satyagraha* into a language familiar to Americans and contracted dialogues between Gandhi and Marx, Freud, Niebuhr, and the Mahatma himself that were not always to Gandhi's advantage.

45. The absence of an equivalent to "saint" may be discerned from the meanings of Hindu terms loosely translated as saint: *Saint*, in "proper" Hundu usage an adjective (rather than a noun) indicating devotion to a *guru* or his text, has under the influence of English usage come to be used for "saintly" and as an equivalent for the noun "saint"; *sadhu* is a person who practices asceticism (mental and spiritual control), more loosely a religious mendicant, a holy man, or simply a good man but often translated as a saint; *sannyasi*, a monk or ascetic, has taken the vows of *sanyas*, i.e. to leave all worldly things including wealth and property, a state often identified with the fourth and final stage of life; *guru*, teacher, mentor, or spiritual guide, can be applied to any teacher of any subject but is usually used specifically for religious teachers; *rishi* is a sage or seer who expounds or comments on the *vedas*, the oldest Hindu scriptures; and *swami*, master or lord, is usually used for a religious ascetic but can be used to refer to a master in any context, i.e. proprietor of land, a craft, or a trade, a husband.

Karine Schomer, in the introduction to *The Sants; Studies in a Devotional Tradition*, a book that she and W. H. McLeod coedited (Delhi: Motilal Banarsidass for Berkeley Religious Studies Series, 1987), refers to sants as "those who sincerely seek enlightenment. . . . [C]onceptually as well as etymologically, it [sant] differs from the false cognate 'saint' which is often used to translate it," 30.

46. Mark Juergensmeyer, "Saint Gandhi," in John Stratton Hawley, ed., *Saints and Virtues* (Berkeley: University of California Press, 1987), 194, 201, 188.

47. For these quotations and a more extended discussion of Gandhi's *darshan* dilemma see Susanne Hoeber Rudolph and Lloyd I. Rudolph, *Gandhi: The Traditional Roots of Charisma* (Chicago: University of Chicago Press, 1983), 75–76. Diane L. Eck has dealt with *darshan* in the context of religious worship in *Darshan: Seeing the Divine Image of India*, second edition (Chambersburg, PA: Anima Publications, 1985).

48. Juergensmeyer, "Saint Gandhi," 202. In 1962, when he was seventy, Susanne Rudolph and I talked to Reinhold Niebuhr about Gandhi. He was living in Quincy House while teaching part-time at Harvard. He told us that Gandhi was too clever, too calculating to be a saint, a remark that presumably distinguished Gandhi's from Jesus' "dazzling" nonemulable qualities of selfless love. Saints were innocent of the strategy and tactics that distinguished Gandhi's conduct and message. Niebuhr's remark in 1962 was consistent with his characterization of Gandhi, after he saw him in London in 1931, as a "prophet" and a "statesman." In assimilating "St. Gandhi" to Jesus in the context of Niebuhr's remark about Jesus, Juergensmeyer was, presumably, constructing an argument rather than representing Niebuhr's view of Gandhi.

49. Margaret Chatterjee, *Gandhi's Religious Thought* (London: Macmillan, 1983), 49.

50. *New York Times*, 2-2-86 and 2-12-86.

51. Kenneth Scott Latourette, *A History of Christianity* (New York: Harper and Brothers, 1953, 1442; New Haven: Yale University Press, 1985).

52. For Merton's view see his introduction, "Gandhi and the One-Eyed Giant," in his *Gandhi on Non-Violence* (New York: New Directions, 1964).

53. This account draws on and quotes from Mary T. Clark's introduction to *Augustine of Hippo: Selected Writings* (New York: Paulist Press, 1984), and Kenneth Scott Latourette, *A History of Christianity* (New York: Harper and Brothers, 1953),

"Augustine and Pelagius," 173–81, and "Semi-Pelagianism," 181–82. Peter N. Brown's "Pelagius and His Supporters: Aims and Environment," *Journal of Theological Studies* 19, Pt. I (April 1968), and "The Patrons of Pelagius: The Roman Artistocracy between East and West," *Journal of Theological Studies*, vol. 21, Pt. I (April 1970), have been very helpful. Also relevant to the Pelagius-Augustine struggle are aspects of Peter Brown's *The Body and Society: Men, Women and Sexual Renunciation in Early Christianity* (New York: Columbia University Press, 1988) and Elaine Pagels' *Adam, Eve, and the Serpent* (New York: Random House, 1988).

54. *The Modern Review*, 10/41, 406, as quoted in Chatterjee, 55.

55. *Harijan*, 4-18-36 and 6-12-37, as quoted in Chatterjee, 55.

56. *New York Times*, 2-2-86.

57. *New York Times*, 2-12-86.

58. *New York Times*, 2-2-86 and 2-9-86. For a Catholic commentary on Gandhi, see also John Chathanatt, S. J., "In Pursuit of Truth: The Gandhian Experiment," unpublished paper, Divinity School, University of Chicago, 1986.

59. Hertzberg's reply to Richard Grenier, to be dealt with below, and to Elie Kedourie's "False Gandhi," in *The New Republic*, 3-21-83, appeared in *The New Republic*, 4-25-83 under the title "True Gandhi."

60. For an account of the controversy over the film and the man, see my "The *Gandhi* Controversy in America," in Robert M. Crunden, ed., *Traffic of Ideas between India and America* (Delhi: Chanakya, 1985). This article and one by me and Susanne Hoeber Rudolph, "Gandhi Critic's Article Distorts History," in *Views, Sunday Sun-Times*, 4-3-83, deal in some detail with Grenier's many errors and distortions. So too before the fact does our *Gandhi: The Traditional Roots of Charisma*. Also relevant to the controversy raised by Grenier's attack on Gandhi is the television program *Firing Line*, hosted by William F. Buckley, Jr., during which Richard Gernier and I spent an unrehearsed hour contesting facts and interpretations. The program was taped in New York on 6-9-83, and appeared subsequently on Public Broadcasting Service (PBS) stations in July and August. Video cassettes, audio cassettes, and published transcripts are available from Firing Line, P.O. Box 5966, Columbia, South Carolina 29250.

61. One of Mayo's earlier books, *The Isles of Fear: An Examination of America's Task in the Philippines*, helped to block the Wilson administration's efforts to move toward self-government in the Philippines by "showing" that the Filipinos were neither ready nor desirous of independence. The message of *Isles of Fear* led the British to believe that they could count on a book supportive of British rule in India, a belief in which they were not disappointed. Here and below I rely primarily on the late Manoranjan Jha's careful and detailed research in *Katherine Mayo and India* (New Delhi: People's Publishing House, 1971). Jha's account of Mayo on the Philippines is at p. 20 and elsewhere.

62. These are Manoranjan Jha's words at p. 69 in *Katherine Mayo*. Jha reproduces as Appendix I a six-page version of a typescript that Mayo had sent to Gandhi (106–11) and that Gandhi in turn had "taken pains to fill in the gaps and amplify some of her statements" (88). He also sent her long quotations from W. W. Hunter and Romesh Hunder Dutt on the causes of India's poverty. A reading of Mayo's account of Gandhi's view when compared to these texts supports Jha's characterizations.

63. Nashville, Tennessee, Thomas Nelson, 1983, 4. Diana L. Eck's chapter in this volume provides a keen analysis of recent American responses to what is perceived as Hinduism.

15

The Availability of Mahatma Gandhi: Toward a Neo-Gandhian Praxis

Makarand Paranjape

1

In order to formulate what I would call a Neo-Gandhian praxis I would like to use the broader issue of the availability of tradition, more specifically the availability of Mahatma Gandhi himself. I would like to suggest that Indian traditions—I deliberately use the word in plural—are readily available, but their availability places a special burden or responsibility upon us. This is especially true of a figure such as Gandhi. Almost no Indian can claim that Gandhi is unavailable to him or her. There is, to begin with, an iconic recognition, which one notices even in very young children. Thereafter, there is a gradual introduction to Gandhian ideas, which usually ends at a certain level of familiarity from which it becomes comfortable to deal with Gandhi. This chapter is about going beyond this "comfort zone" into the more uncomfortable and messy business of taking Gandhi seriously and, further, of trying to be a Gandhian, or in the special sense in which I use the term here, a "neo-Gandhian."[1]

This paper, then, is a personal testimony of what it means to be a neo-Gandhian. Though there are disadvantages in labeling oneself, sometimes such identifications are necessary because they indicate one's position without fear or embarrassment. So, while I am proud rather than ashamed of such a label, yet I must confess in the same breath that I am not sure that I have done enough to deserve it. This uncertainty and doubt have direct bearing on the central argument of this paper which, as I shall go on to clarify, is that being a neo-Gandhian means being not a Gandhian as much as being Gandhi-like. There is an enormous difference, to my mind, between the two.

Being a Gandhian, at least of the official kind, is to be a follower, an imitator.[2] But Gandhi himself was never a follower or an imitator; he was original, innovative, and dynamic. Being a Gandhian is hard enough; it may or may not be possible to achieve it. But being Gandhi-like, whether difficult or easy, is more than a matter of choice for those who understand the present world crisis; it is urgent and imperative. Of course, one would have to define clearly what being Gandhi-like entails. This I shall attempt later, but right now I only wish to say that neo-Gandhianism is, for me, not merely a creed or an ideology; it is not merely a set of beliefs or practices: it is the assumption of personal and social responsibility; it is the commitment to individual and collective amelioration; it is a process of self-realization and community-making.

In what follows, I shall first narrate how Gandhi became available to me; I shall then discuss the pitfalls of a certain kind of easy availability of Gandhi; thereafter, I shall attempt a description of what a more fruitful engagement in Gandhi might result in; finally, I shall try to spell out a minimum agenda for a neo-Gandhian approach to contemporary problems.

I assume that I qualify to be called a neo-Gandhian by virtue of a book I wrote a few years back called *Decolonization and Development: Hind Svaraj Revisioned*. The central thesis of the book was that at the end of the century, Gandhian ideas as outlined in *Hind Swaraj* (1909) are still vitally relevant. Though technomodernity has made inroads into the very vitals of our civilization, it has by no means conquered or destroyed us. The contradictions of our times—ecological, economic, social, scientific, political, cultural, and personal—have proved again and again that the necessity and urgency of resistance has never waned. The fight against modern civilization is an ongoing one, every inch of territory lost has been, and must be, bitterly contested.

Moreover, because of a variety of factors, both internal and external, it looks more and more certain that the complete triumph of modernity is impossible, at least in India. The huge inflow of capital, whether in the form of World Bank loans or multinational corporation investments, channeled through a rapacious bureaucracy in the third world metropolis, gradually runs aground as it meanders into the countryside. Then, another few hundred kilometers into the hinterland, it finally vanishes into the sandy marshes and wastes of rural poverty and underdevelopment. The trickle-down theory, after all, doesn't work, as we know only too well. Thus, the whole project of development has been discredited, if not derailed.

To escape from this dystopia of consumption and triage, it is essential to recognize the links between decolonization and development, between *swaraj* and *sarvodaya*. We have to reorder our minds and change our lifestyles to bring them into harmony with our civilizational genius. Such, in brief, is the argument of my book. My purpose in mentioning it was only to draw attention to the process by which I began to see myself and thus be seen as a neo-Gandhian. I would like to say a few other things about this process.

As a student of English literature, I have been well acquainted with what might be called the other mind of Europe. However, it took me several years to realize the apparently self-evident fact that canonical texts of literature were usually at odds with the dominant trends of their age. The relationship between literature and society, portrayed by Western critics as continuous, was actually contradictory. Canonical texts did not reflect the major trends and values of the times but opposed them. Consequently, a curious paradox was engendered: while the values that these texts embodied were defeated, the texts were hailed as the seminal works of their age.

I encountered this paradox again and again. Industrial capitalism, which nearly every major British writer from Blake to Wordsworth, Dickens to Hardy criticized, was not defeated, but instead triumphed totally. Similarly, across the Atlantic, the ideals enunciated by Emerson and Thoreau, Lincoln and Whitman, were disregarded; America turned its back upon them. But these very writers were revered and exalted. Literature was permitted to occupy what used to be the sacred space of religion as the increasing secularization of society proceeded apace. No wonder many of the writers now considered great were unknown or ignored by their contemporaries.

There is a notion that literature can disempower modernity. I wish I were so optimistic as to believe this. True, literature can give us a safety valve, an escape, but perhaps that is because it is the officially sanctioned and approved Other of modern society. Modernity allows literature to take care of the personal while it controls the societal. Artists and writers are given a license to be creative; they are also permitted to ruin their lives, drink themselves to death, or commit suicide. What is worse, by considering the aesthetic space as purely apolitical, the whole sordid engagement of the arts with capitalism and colonialism was easily forgotten.[3] This, then, was what was wrong with the way I was taught literature.

The other path toward self-discovery that I took was not Western, but indigenous. I became a student of modern Indian spirituality. This was one realm wherein I thought we were second to none. I began to regard the world as a self-created illusion, a projected fantasy in which we participated only too readily. The challenge, then, was to develop inner peace and harmony, an intelligence which could withstand the pressures of life. Perhaps, I wanted to develop a resilience, an insulation which would shield me from the harsh realities of the world.

Starting with Sri Ramakrishna, I began to read the lives and works of the major mystics, sages, and saints of modern India. Reading backwards, I also began to perceive an unbroken tradition, rich and varied, beginning with Vedic literature or perhaps even earlier, continuing to the present day. Interestingly, Gandhi flowed into this tradition quite effortlessly, having all the wherewithal of a traditional practitioner of spirituality. In fact, he was a full-fledged holy man, a *guru* and lawgiver to millions.

But what made him special was that it was only Gandhi who helped me connect the personal with the political. My intense dissatisfaction with the colonized mind that I had inherited and my retreat into the solace of Indian spirituality seemed to force upon me two separate lives. In fact, I often wondered if my interest in spirituality was because of the failure of the official intellectual discourse to supply the answers. But it was my reading of Gandhi which showed me a way of producing a consonance between the two, between spiritual questing and social responsibility. Gandhi radicalized me; he gave me a politics. Without him, I would have been in a state of continuous retreat which, for someone living in a poor country, was somehow inadequate, if not dishonest.

2

The official legacy of Mahatma Gandhi, not just that part of it which the state has appropriated and internalized, but the remaining portion distributed among several Gandhian organizations, old and new, now lies in a shambles. The Government's Gandhian posturing has long ceased to be credible; in fact it presents the ultimate defeat of Gandhism and its deterioration into hegemonized hypocrisy.

Similarly, various Gandhian institutions, not only those started by the Mahatma himself but various others which his associates, disciples, and followers founded, are today in a disarray. A visit to the Gandhi Smriti, Gandhi Darshan, Gandhi Sanghralaya, Gandhi Peace Foundation, or to any other major Gandhian institution in the capitol will prove my point. More often than not, these places have declined into a state of disutility. Not only are the premises badly maintained, but what is more depressing is that the workers there are devoid of commitment or enthusiasm. The most ironic comment on the decline of such institutions is the shameful fact of their dirty toilets, evident even in Birla House, the site of the Mahatma's martyrdom. Gandhi, who used to scavenge himself to set an example of cleanliness and dignity of labor, would be horrified that today nobody bothers to keep these Gandhian toilets clean.

Interestingly, despite the decline of this official Gandhi, there has been a spate of seminars and discussions on him during and after his 125th anniversary. I must confess that I have grown a bit impatient of such seminars and discussions, having attended my share of them. A major cause for this impatience is my feeling that they do not bring us closer to Gandhi. They reveal less of Gandhi and more of the mindset of those who are making the presentations. Many of those who frequent these seminars are also seen elsewhere, speaking with equal ease and authority on other topics and issues. As usual, the gulf between their lives and their ideas is glaring. I must not exclude myself from such criticism because I am, alas, one of these seminar-hopping Indian academics myself. In other words, let me hasten to clarify that my impatience with such seminars arises out of my impatience with myself.

It was Prabodh Parikh who reminded me once that Gandhi cannot be appropriated by the intellectuals. There is something about exemplars like him which resists such appropriation. Creating new knowledge about Gandhi, in the conventional, academic sense in which such knowledge is routinely produced, is, thus, useless. The challenge that Gandhi poses is that we live our ideas, that we alter our lives and lifestyles in keeping with our beliefs, that we radicalize ourselves instead of merely mouthing radical slogans. The strength and force of the Gandhian praxis, therefore, derives not from discursive cogency or clarity, but from the integrity of the lives of its practitioners. In a word, Gandhi resists the schizophrenic division between fact and value or between thought, word, and deed. To be Gandhian is to seek and find a holistic praxis in which one's lifestyle, modes of living, patterns of consumption, and processes of thinking are integrated and congruent.[4]

At the same time, we must beware of the opposite pitfall of the all-too-obvious pattern of imitation which has now come to characterize the last vestiges of the old Gandhism. Being a neo-Gandhian does not necessarily mean literally following the Gandhian dogma. As Rajiv Vora once told me, "*Charkha kaatne vale sochte nahin hain*" (Those who spin the *charkha* don't think). To be Gandhian in the older sense is, today, unfortunately not very effective *or* inspiring. The spirit of the times seems to rebel against the self-denying asceticism, the obsession with ritual purity, the emphasis on external conformity. While neo-Gandhians cannot ignore these aspects, they mustn't follow them blindly.[5]

Certain obvious questions arise. Can a neo-Gandhian be a nonvegetarian? Consume alcohol? Or wear expensive synthetic clothes? Indulge in free sex? And so on? I think the answers to such questions are getting harder, more challenging. Yet, what neo-Gandhism means to me is not so much a set of rigidly laid down beliefs or practices, but an approach to life which encompasses the personal and the social. If so, then yes, ultimately, the aim is to make one's lifestyle as nonviolent as possible, consume as little as is feasible, control the senses, not indulge them, refrain from intoxicants, and so on—but within reasonable limits and without an obsessive self-righteousness. Paradoxically, then, being a neo-Gandhian means parting company not only with the official versions of Gandhi but also with the official versions of modernity. It is the path for the independent and the self-reliant, not for those who seek conformity and security. Only an independent person can become an effective neo-Gandhian.

Coming back to the all-too-frequent seminars on Gandhi from such a perspective, it is obvious that these meetings are not merely for Gandhi or for the values that he stood for; they are for us. It is our role and function as postcolonial intellectuals that we must interrogate through such exercises, not only Gandhian ideas. If so, then we realize that such seminars are often self-serving. By making Gandhi the subject of our deliberations, we feel we are doing something more useful than the run-of-the-mill topic.

But the fact is that we suffer from a guilty conscience; we are afraid that we might be turning our backs on the Mahatma and his legacy; we are insecure that other nations and cultures may make better use of Gandhi than we have; we are worried that we might become irrelevant to our societies. And so on. So we all flock to Gandhi. It is not the other way round. Gandhi will never lose his relevance or be discredited; it is we who face the prospect of failure and dishonor. The seminars then are for us, though we pretend they are for Gandhi. They are meant as face-saving measures, as devices of legitimation. That is why I am impatient with myself when I attend them.

Then, again, perhaps I am mistaken. Perhaps, these meetings do serve an important purpose. Perhaps, they are meant to demonstrate their own futility, to remind us that Gandhi's cause will not be served merely through such discussions. Like the negative results of scientific experiments, we shall have to admit our failures at the end of such exercises—it can be done, but not this way. If so, let me repeat: Gandhi cannot be appropriated by the intellectual community; he demands a heavier price from us.

3

In effect, I have been trying to argue that one cannot follow Gandhi, one can't become a Gandhian, but one has to become Gandhi-like. It is only when one accepts this unlikely and unlikable piece of advice that one actually starts experiencing the actual difficulty or even impossibility of undertaking it. This is somewhat like saying that you must not merely be a Christian but be Christ-like. But that is almost impossible. Because, like Christ, Gandhi occupies an extreme position, not only in his views but in his life as well. And we are placed in the position of the rich man who, when asked by Christ to sell all his goods, donate the proceeds to charity and follow him, could not do so. At this inability, Christ is said to have remarked that it was harder for a rich man to enter the kingdom of heaven than for a camel to pass through the eye of a needle.

Like the rich man in the Biblical story, we neo-Gandhians are unable to do what we know is right. For those who wish to change themselves and thereby change the world, neither thought nor action poses a problem. The fact of the matter is that we want to continue as we are—greedy, selfish, and exploitative—and yet pretend that we are among the salt of the earth, the do-gooders who live for others and work for the revolution. Being a neo-Gandhian, then, is to confess our drawbacks and disabilities, to acknowledge them openly. By beginning with an autocritique, we can set the terms for a meaningful critique of society. Thus, I must confess that truly, I have more than I need, yet I cannot give it away or share it fully with others. Property is theft, as Gandhi himself said, and I must acknowledge that I am a thief.

What Gandhi did, then, cannot be replicated. It cannot be repeated. With our limited ability and determination, we must instead bear witness to our own rather restricted and impoverished truths. What is required is not so much an application as a rethinking of Gandhian ideas in the immediate contexts of our lives. In other words, being a neo-Gandhian means that I stop talking about Gandhi, stop analyzing his works, stop trying to quote him by chapter and verse, stop making a quasi-religious text out of him, stop debating over the merits and demerits of his positions on specific issues, stop, in a word, making academic and professional capital out of Gandhi. Because that is the easiest way of killing him, of making him irrelevant and obsolete, or fetishising him and his ideas.

I realize, of course, that I have locked myself into a rather narrow corridor here, having closed most of the exits. I have not only undermined my own position as a professional intellectual, but I have also disallowed the possibility of a truly Gandhi-like alternative to it. What, then, is the way out? A way out, in my opinion, becomes available when we treat Gandhi in the manner in which Gandhi himself treated traditions. Gandhi never claimed to found a new philosophy, a new religion, or a new political ideology—though, willy-nilly, he did all this. He only claimed to reapply Truth, which was as old as the hills. He himself said, "There is no such thing as 'Gandhism,' and I do not want to leave any sect after me."[6] He was against a personality cult, against turning his ideas into a creed. Similarly, when he looked back upon what he had inherited, he was more than critical. He refused to be cowed down by the weight or authority of tradition. He did not passively accept his legacy, but vigorously engaged with it. He, perhaps more than any other person in recent times, abandoned many beliefs, ideas, values, and customs. He totally reinterpreted Hinduism, giving new meanings not only to *varnashrama* (the institution of *varna* or caste and of *ashrama* or stages of life) but to *dharma* itself. He redefined the *purusharthas* (the cardinal aims of life), locating them in the context of his day. He gave us a *svadharma* (dharma unique to each person) and a *yugadharma* (the dharma for the epoch).

Now that Gandhi has passed from our midst and become a part of our tradition, we must treat him in a similar fashion, engaging with his ideas vigorously, reinterpreting and refashioning from them a praxis for our times. That is the need of the hour, not any literal reading or imitation. Becoming Gandhi-like, then, is to assume responsibility for ourselves. In fact, not just for ourselves, but for those around us, for the whole world in which we live. We have to take ourselves seriously, not mortgage our lives to some bygone or newfangled creed. We need to be far more confident, far more self-reliant.

This is how, after changing our perspectives, we can get back all that we were prepared to renounce, including our flawed and corrupt academics. Change of consciousness is the beginning of social and institutional transformation. By rethinking ourselves and our roles we can reclaim for ourselves a meaningful vocation, irrespective of how modest the scale may be. Thus, it is not my intention entirely to deny the salience of the institutional space which we occupy, but to make it accountable to the people and culture of this country. Following such a reorientation, those very seminars and discussions which earlier seemed futile and self-seeking may be made productive and stimulating, provided their basic assumptions and intentions are sound.

Jawaharlal Nehru said that "the greatest gift for any individual or nation . . . is abhaya, fearlessness" and it was for this that Gandhi raised his "quiet and determined voice."[7] Gandhi made everyone fearless. We have read Gandhi, but we are not fearless. Why? What is the source of our fear? Is it not our attachment to the privileges that we enjoy, all the security and benefits of the intellectual class, without really having earned and deserved them? This surplus elitism is, however, not free. We have had to pay a very heavy price for it. The postcolonial state, which is largely undemocratic, oppressive, and exploitative, patronizes us. We are also maintained by neoimperialistic foreign agencies, which wish to maintain their hold on the cultural products of the erstwhile colonies. The fact is that we have been kept and coopted, contained and silenced. If we open our mouths to cry out, it is not to change the system but only because we wish to have them stuffed with more mouth-stopping handouts. It is, thus, against our class interests to discharge our true intellectual responsibilities.

It is here that we need Gandhi most. Gandhi teaches us to rebel against these very class interests which gag and emasculate us. He makes us break the solidarity of the exploitative classes. What is more, he does this without accepting modernity as Marx had done. He does this without creating an imperialistic and oppressive master narrative. He does this without recourse to the violence of psuedoscience. What is more, he does this without making the oppressor's position attractive. Gandhi enables us to fight not only against, but also on behalf of, the oppressor. Unlike Marx, he believes that what the oppressor has is not worth fighting for, that in fact it is not good for the oppressor himself to have it. Though neo-Gandhian politics entails class cooperation, not class war, its aims are as radical and far-reaching.

4

It remains for me to spell out a minimum agenda for being neo-Gandhian, or if you prefer Gandhi-like, today. First of all it requires a deep social and economic awareness and an accompanying commitment to change. This was what Gandhi's talisman was all about. It is Gandhi who forces us not to be merely spiritual, ignoring the material basis of society and culture. In other words, if what we are doing today, or indeed every day, is irrelevant to the lives, needs, and requirements of the poorest of the poor, then it is not just useless, but positively harmful and counterproductive. To be a neo-Gandhian means necessarily to be pro-poor in one's orientation.

But this heartfelt concern for the poorest and least privileged of our compatriots mustn't remain merely a sentimental attitude, leading to occasional acts of charity or social service. It requires us to make ourselves, our lifestyles, our professional practices, our institutions, and our cultural choices continuously accountable. It is precisely this accountability that modern consumerism seeks to destroy. Consumerism is an ideology which liberates us from all responsibilities except consumption. We need only think of ourselves and the pleasures that can be multiplied through the acquisition of goods. Thus, it kills any sense of the community and social responsibility.

The moment we undertake to make ourselves accountable, we have an in-built yardstick to guide us in our conduct. We can now go into the very roots of poverty and inequality instead of tackling its offshoots. It is only by making such a linkage between the local and the universal that we realize that ecological conservation begins not in Tehri or in the Silent Valley, sites of recent resistance, but in the cities, in our very homes. I have to realize that I am directly supporting big dams by living in a city and using an air conditioner at home. My city, with its excessive consumption of electricity, is destroying the lives of people who live hundreds of kilometers away in the hills. It is uprooting them, destroying an ecosystem, and destabilizing the flora and fauna of an entire region. Thus, environmental degradation has a causal relationship with lifestyles. Being a neo-Gandhian therefore means changing one's lifestyle.

This accountability must extend to our professional lives. As an intellectual worker, I must strive to make my work as nonviolent and socially beneficial as possible. This, of course, goes completely counter to the prevailing climate of academic professionalism, which is just another name for self-centered self-aggrandizement. The modern academy is a part of a larger ideological-political system in which money and power are the most important motivators. That is why the academy is an arena of ruthless competition and self-promotion. As such, it cannot be conducive to public good. It cannot be nonviolent. It can only lead to a strengthening of the ego and the will to power. Such an academics is immoral, irresponsible, and destructive. Being a neo-Gandhian means to fight this prevailing trend, to devote one's energies not to personal power and glory, but to meaningful and fulfilling common causes. It is to reorder one's priorities, to resist blandishments, to cut a lonely furrow.

Ultimately, of course, one has to oppose the prevailing trends of our times, the amoral and self-destructive consumerist capitalism. This consumerism weakens us, enslaves us, and corrupts us. But what is behind this consumerist ideology? Surely it is the enshrining of the body and the denial of the nonmaterial—call it spiritual—basis of our being. If a human being is essentially a spirit and not merely a body, then no amount of material wealth can totally satisfy us. The happiness that we all seek, then, cannot come merely from a fulfillment of all our physical needs and desires.

Once this is recognized, there is a fundamental change in our lives. We stop being acquisitive and greedy and learn to moderate our needs and desires. If this attitude is called spirituality, so be it. I don't like the word because of its negative connotations. It suggests a hazy impracticality, a retreat from the real world into some sort of mystical vaguology, a status-quoism. But actually, the word spiritual is connected with breath in Latin. Breath, which is akin to *prana*. Thus, in fact, we are spiritual beings; every breath that we take confirms it. Watching the breath, going to its source is, in many mystical traditions, a means of going to our very source, to that infinite energy and consciousness that motivates and animates each one of us. Being spiritual, thus, does not mean that we deny our bodily existence, our corporeality, but cease to believe that we are primarily or exclusively identified with our bodies. A spiritual civilization does not deny the body, but it does not give it primacy either.

A spiritual civilization allows for, nay ensures, the minimum satisfaction of bodily needs and comforts, and then encourages the person to strive for that realization which is conducive to permanent happiness. From an exclusive and self-destructive obsession and identification with the body, one moves to a state where the body—without being denied, negated, or tortured—is put in its proper place. All of a person's energies in such a civilization need not be consumed in tending to the body's requirements and comforts, but a major portion of such energies can be saved for self-development and self-perfection.

Gandhi believed that, essentially, this is what Indian civilization offered. Its entire social, economic, and civil organization was meant to be conducive to the inner growth of the human being, not merely to his or her bodily comforts. Gandhi's notion of *swaraj*, too, I believe, was designed to create a community of such complete, robust, fearless, self-reliant individuals, living together in a relationship of mutual harmony and cooperation. That is why he emphasized that a belief in God would be one of the essential prerequisites of *swaraj*. This insistence may seem strange to modern man, who is used to living in a Godless universe. But to Gandhi, it was important that we recognized a force, a power, a cosmic order greater than ourselves, to which each of us must relate and submit.

Personally, I don't consider a belief in God as essential to a neo-Gandhian praxis as long as God is substituted by *dharma*. *Dharma* refers to a cosmic law, to a pattern, an order in accordance to which we must regulate our lives. Gandhi used the terminology of *bhakti*; we may invoke the notion of the *purusharthas*, the fourfold scheme of *dharma*, *artha* (wealth/power), *kama* (pleasure), and *moksha* (liberation). Some have suggested that *moksha* be substituted by *jnana* (wisdom, knowledge), to allow for modern science to be included in our schema. So be it. Further modifications may also be possible or desirable, but the total denial of such a framework would not be admissible. That would lead to the kind of unbridled and atomized individualism which we find so prevalent in modern society. Modern civilization, at its worst, is hedonistic, individualistic, consumerist, and materialistic. We have therefore to practice self-restraint, moderation, communitarianism, and spirituality.

Finally, we shall have to acknowledge that there are many ways of practicing these values rather than one, tried and tested, officially approved path. We must accept not the moral relativism of our times, nor the singularism of several dogmatic religious and Marxian ideologies, but a healthy and confident pluralism which is in tune with the best Indic traditions. This pluralism, at its most benign and compassionate, may extend even to the tolerance of intolerance, but in its defensive form must never go beyond an intolerance of intolerance. Pluralism disallows intolerance of tolerance; that, instead, is how singularism may be defined.

In conclusion, let me just say that neo-Gandhians need not be preoccupied with speaking for or in place of Gandhi, reading and rereading his works, becoming experts and authorities on Gandhi, or interpreting and reinterpreting his words like some sacred text. We must not be afraid of speaking for ourselves, of finding our own truth, of bearing witness to it, however frail or flawed it is. The idea is not to make ourselves dependent and helpless, running back to Gandhi for cover, but to align ourselves with his broader civilizational agenda and to push on further from where we are. To sum up, to what avail is it if a person is an authority on the life and works of Gandhi, but he or she doesn't live and die as a *vaishnava jan* (a godly person)?[8]

POSTSCRIPT

Since this essay was first presented, both India and the world seemed to have changed, arguably for the worse. Certainly, there has been an escalation of violence and coercion in the management of civil society and the affairs of the state. Every day, the media reports bomb blasts and killings attributed to "terrorists" and the use of retaliatory, often fatal, force by armed forces. 9/11 and its aftermath in Afghanistan, the U.S. invasion of Iraq, the internecine conflicts in Palestine and Kashmir, communal riots in India, and so on, have left their indelible imprints on the new century. Besides these more obvious forms of violence, the perennial issues of structural and economic violence stubbornly refuse to disappear. AIDS in Africa, hunger and starvation across the so-called third world, coupled with mindless consumption and conspicuous hedonism by a global middle class, seem to characterize our self-contradictory lifestyles. What is most disturbing is that the very idiom of change and transformation seems to be undergoing a tectonic shift. In India, an outcome of these trends is the total marginalization, if not erasure, of what might be termed the "discourse of the poor." It is not that the poor themselves have disappeared, only that no one seems to be concerned about them any more. For neo-Gandhians, it couldn't be a worse time to live in.

In India, more specifically, the rise of the ideology of Hindutva in the last ten years has, to all appearances, pushed Gandhism into the background. I would argue that the dominant version of *sanatani* (orthodox) Hinduism used to be Gandhian until the very 1990s. So it was Gandhian *sarva dharma samabhava* or equal respect for all faiths and Nehruvian secularism that defined the two poles of the modern Hindu mind. The last decade or so has spelt the death of Nehruvian secularism as the prevailing state ideology, substituting it with a more self-assertive, if not militant Hinduism commonly known as Hindutva. But what has happened to the Gandhian legacy? I believe it has gone into a state of hibernation or dormancy. The excesses of Hindutva may, ultimately, lead to a correction and return to Gandhism. But for this to happen, Gandhians and their like will have to redefine a new kind of *sanatanism* for the Hindu middle and ruling classes. Unfortunately, before this can happen, Hindu hegemony of a certain kind will have to be "acknowledged" in India. This is still severely challenged and combated not so much by the "minorities"—Muslims, Christians, Sikhs, and so on—but by another section of Hindus themselves, who do not wish to be seen or identified as Hindus.

These latter form a large section of the present ruling elite, whose claim to power is precisely their avowal of a nonreligious, and therefore secular, identity. Self-assertive Hindus, on the other hand, claim that this class is successor of the colonial powers and can therefore never act in the interests, not just economic or political, but also cultural, of the majority. So, India is in a state of civil war. Gandhians in India today are a divided lot too. Some find themselves on one side, others on the other. But I suspect they are comfortable with neither. India lost its opportunity to opt for a Gandhian model of development when Nehru and the Indian state turned their backs on village *swaraj*. India, however, still seeks *swaraj* as a part of its larger civilizational enterprise, but more through information technology and export of what may be called "mindware." Nuclear deterrence, strong foreign exchange reserves, and a prosperous diaspora are the new bulwarks of Indian *swaraj*. In these times, India and the world await a new incarnation of Gandhi and what he stood for.

NOTES

1. An earlier version of this paper was first presented at a national seminar on "Interpretations of Gandhi," organized by the Indian Institute of Advanced Study in New Delhi on 3-21/23-96, and then published in *DES Journal of Social Sciences and Languages, Punjab University*, vol. 1., no. 1 (Jan. 2000): 3–16.
   To the best of my knowledge, the earliest use of the word "neo-Gandhian" is by Y. G. Krishnamurti in his book *Neo-Gandhism* (Bombay: Nalanda, 1954): "The neo-Gandhian is an experimenter in political thinking and action. In his literary baggage he carries no glib futilities and worn clichés," 8.
2. Ashis Nandy makes a similar point in his op ed essay, "Gandhi after Gandhi: Disturbing People after Death," *Times of India*, 1-30-96, 8. He talks of four Gandhis: the first belongs to "the Indian state and Indian nationalism"; the second is the

"Gandhi of the Gandhians"; the third is "the Gandhi of the ragamuffins, eccentrics and the unpredictables"; and finally, "the mythic Gandhi." Nandy seems to approve of the third and the fourth Gandhis, who still inspire intellectual and social change the world over. My idea of the "official Gandhi" corresponds with the first two categories. I am not sure, though, if "neo-Gandhians" resemble Nandy's third and fourth Gandhis or if they fit into Nandy's schema fully despite the similarities in ideas. For instance, Nandy does not emphasize the difference between being a Gandhian and being Gandhi-like.

3. The work of Edward Said has consistently addressed this contradiction. See, for instance, *Orientalism* (New York: Random House, 1978) and *Culture and Imperialism* (New York: Viking, 1993).

4. See Raghavendra Rao's unpublished paper, "The Exemplar versus the Ideologue: The Issue of Friends and Foes," circulated first at the seminar on "Interpretations of Gandhi" mentioned above in March 1996, and later presented at a seminar on "Social Criticism, Cultural Creativity and the Contemporary Dialectics of Transformation," at Madras Institute of Development Studies, Madras, 12-4/7-96. Rao argues that "the notion of someone being a Gandhian seems irrelevant, if not absurd." The exemplar, as opposed to the ideologue, is not concerned primarily with enunciating a coherent body of theoretical knowledge, but with embodying and practicing a certain way of life. Rao argues that the very category "Gandhian," thus falls outside a Gandhian frame of reference, and must consequently be dissolved. Rao still allows for its use if and only if it is wedded to actualizing the kind of life that Gandhi himself lived, if one "has tried to live like Gandhiji and become some version or edition of Gandhiji. . . . Gandhiji . . . demands that he should be re-incarnated, not repeated and imitated. In short, you either live like Gandhiji or you do not. But you cannot become a Gandhian in the tradition of the ideologue."

5. I do not imply that none of the older Gandhians were Gandhi-like. As Ramachandra Guha said in response to this paper, there is an unwritten history of Gandhi-like Gandhians such as Nirmal Kumar Bose, Verrier Elwin, Gora, J. C. Kumarappa, Sarla Behn, Mira Behn, Mridula Sarabhai, and so on.

6. Paradoxically, he also said, "They might kill me but they cannot kill Gandhism. If truth can be killed, Gandhism can be killed." The contradiction can be resolved if we separate the message from the messenger: "I hold my message to be far superior to myself and far superior to the vehicle through which it is expressed." See S. R. Tikekar, compl. *Epigrams from Gandhiji* (1971; rpt. New Delhi: Publications Division, 1994), 48.

7. See *Mahatma Gandhi: Reflections on His Personality and Teachings* by Jawaharlal Nehru (Bombay: Bharatiya Vidya Bhavan, 1960; rpt. 1989): "The essence of his teaching was fearlessness and truth and action allied to these," 30.

8. Though this is necessarily a personal report, it does not rule out collective action of various kinds. To be Gandhi-like may be a way of planning one's own life, but it contains the wherewithal for powerful political action. I have not considered it the job of this paper to spell out the techniques of such action; that would require a separate treatment. But I can only end with the assertion that Gandhi-like individuals can never remain alone and isolated from the larger social and political issues that surround them. They will automatically become the nuclei of radical social transformation.

·

16

Gandhi, Contemporary Political Thinking, and Self-Other Relations

Douglas Allen

Gandhi was the most admired person in India and perhaps in the entire world. There is, however, considerable doubt about his contemporary relevance both to political thinking and to political and other developments in India and in the world. Gandhi's basic philosophical and religious assumptions and positions at the heart of his political thinking seem antithetical to what is happening in most political and other worldly developments. My own position is that Gandhi's approach is extremely relevant to the concerns of contemporary political thinking, offers a radical critique of most of contemporary life, and can serve as a catalyst for rethinking political positions. However, I also maintain that Gandhi's approach contains many contradictions and some of it is reactionary, irrelevant, and must be rejected. We must be very selective in appropriating and reconstituting what is of value in Gandhi's thought for contemporary political thinking.

In the first section of this chapter, I raise a number of challenges from modern political thinking that would contend that Gandhi's approach reflects a premodern antimodern orientation, assumes an essentialist metaphysical and spiritual approach, and is largely outdated and irrelevant to contemporary political thinking. In the second section, I submit that Gandhi's political approach, when selectively appropriated and reconstituted, can provide a radical critique of and positive alternative to modern political thinking; it can serve as an urgently needed catalyst for rethinking dominant modern political positions. In the third section, I maintain that there is not one correct, absolute, decontextualized political thought of Mohandas Gandhi; that his political thinking is eclectic and at times contradictory; and that relating Gandhi's approach to contemporary political thinking involves a dynamic domain of contestation and the reconstitution, revalorization, and development of diverse Gandhian positions. In the fourth section, I briefly formulate Gandhi's metaphysical and spiritual framework at the foundation of his political thinking by focusing on his key concepts of truth *(satya)* and nonviolence *(ahimsa)*. In the fifth section, I focus on a particular feature of this essential framework: Gandhi's analysis of self and self-other relations with his radical inversion of the dominant models of self-other relations that have constituted modern Western political thinking. Finally, I show that there are key unresolved questions about Gandhi's analysis of self and self-other relations, especially arising from ambiguities in his formulations about the individual self, the social self, and the spiritual self, and reflections on such questions can give rise to new developments in contemporary political thinking.[1]

CONTEMPORARY POLITICAL THINKING: REJECTION OF GANDHI

Dominant contemporary political thinking is completely at odds with Gandhi's basic assumptions, principles, and spiritual philosophical framework. Hundreds of foundational formulations by Gandhi about the nature and purpose of politics, economics, and law would strike modern Western thinkers as, at best, well-intentioned but naive and irrelevant or as, at worst, revealing dangerous, traditional, premodern residues.[2] Political scientists, for example, typically assume a political orientation of realpolitik in which Gandhi's ethical, religious, and other observations are largely irrelevant and are often an affront and embarrassment to modern critical political thinking. Legal thinkers typically assume, usually without any need of justification, a legal system of inherent adversarial relations, free of Gandhi's ethical and religious considerations, in which the modern objective is to win in a confrontational relational system of win-lose alternatives. Economic thinkers typically assume an anti-Gandhian view of human beings as economically calculating persons in which the modern objective is to maximize one's own economic return and in which Gandhi's ethical, spiritual, and other considerations play no part. Political commentators and analysts assume an anti-Gandhian orientation in which the purpose of politics is to win, to raise huge amounts of money to be used for political advantage, to control and manipulate media images, to do polls so that one can use political language and craft political messages to maximize voter appeal, to acquire and distribute wealth and power to supporters, to engage in negative advertising and other attacks on political opponents and to thwart the objectives of political opponents, and so forth. Gandhi's political thinking, by contrast, is seen by modern political scientists and other political analysts as out of touch with such political reality. Applying Gandhi's approach produces uncritical, romantic, utopian, irrelevant political thinking and is counterproductive in achieving modern political results.

It is not the case that all Indian political thinking, from ancient times to the present, is so at odds with dominant contemporary political thinking. In terms of the classical Hindu four aims or ends of life *(artha, kama, dharma, moksha)*, there is a vast literature that functions on the preethical and prere-ligious (nonethical and nonreligious) *artha* level of economic accumulation and political power. Kautilya's approach in his classical *Arthashastra* is cer-tainly closer to Machiavelli, Hobbes, and modern political thinking than is Gandhi's approach, which tends to subsume economics and politics under the "higher" aims of social and ethical duty *(dharma)* and religious transfor-mation and spiritual freedom and release *(moksha)*.[3]

The contrast to Gandhi can be seen in dominant characteristics assumed by most contemporary Western political thinking: primary focus on means-ends instrumental rationality and on structures of power and domination; adoption of capitalist assumptions, values, and objectives with regard to individuals, nation-states, foreign relations, and relations to nature; aggressive materialism with maximization of consumption and endless proliferation of insatiable needs; huge investment in militarism with acceptance of a large permanent war economy; primary focus on technological development and industrial-ization; easy recourse to political, economic, psychological, and other forms of violence; strengthening of globalization with military-industrial-political in-terlocking relations of power; concentration and centralization of power with top-down technological control of the flow of information; glorification of egoism and individualism with the socialization and reinforcement of ego-cravings and ego-attachments, and so forth.

The assumption and sometimes explicit conclusion of such contemporary political thinking, epitomized in Francis Fukuyama's famous chauvinistic re-formulation of Hegel's "the end of history," is that "we" in the modern West have achieved the final decisive political victory.[4] Gandhian and other polit-ical alternatives have been defeated and rendered obsolete. Those who at-tempt to adopt a Gandhian political orientation at odds with the dominant features of contemporary political thinking will create dysfunctional political structures, will be smashed by modern political forces, and will be shown to be historically irrelevant.

Modern political thinking is largely a child of the Enlightenment. Many nineteenth- and twentieth-century Indian political reformers, revolutionar-ies, and leaders in the Indian National Congress and in other developments in India's independence and freedom struggles were also strongly influ-enced by Enlightenment thinking. This helps to explain the internal contra-dictions and tensions between Gandhi and many other Indian leaders, even those who admired Gandhi's courage and supported or paid lip service to his leadership in political struggles. By describing major characteristics of the Enlightenment, we may better appreciate the sharp contrast between Gandhi and much of contemporary political thinking.[5]

In broadest terms, the Enlightenment defines leading characteristics of modernity, including modern political thinking. It begins in seventeenth-century England, especially with John Locke's approaches to knowledge, pol-itics, and religion. The French Enlightenment includes Voltaire, Montesquieu,

Diderot, D'Alembert, and Rousseau. The English and Scottish Enlightenment includes Priestly, Hutcheson, Adam Smith, Gibbon, Hume, and Bentham. The German Enlightenment includes Christian Wolff, Moses Mendelssohn, Lessing, and Kant. The North American Enlightenment includes Paine, Franklin, and Jefferson and finds expression in the Declaration of Independence of 1776.

The dominant medieval European pre-Enlightenment approach to politics emphasizes the hierarchical supremacy of supernatural or religious authority. Upheld are divine or supernatural revelation, religious scripture and tradition, religious institutions, and clerical or priestly authority. This is also the orientation of the Vedic, traditional Indian religious approach to politics and political thinking.

The Enlightenment rejects such an approach to politics and upholds the primacy of reason and of nature, not the supernatural realm, as the source and authority for political thinking, objective knowledge, and human progress. Emphasized are critical reasoning, laws of nature, objectivity, universality, a scientific outlook, progress, natural rights, liberty, equality, utility, toleration, and freedom from superstition, irrationality, and dependence on religious and other forms of external authority.

According to Kant's famous definition of 1784, enlightenment is characterized by the emergence of human beings from self-imposed immature tutelage in which they lack the determination and courage to use their own capacity for understanding and instead depend on the external authority and guidance of another. Individuals must have the courage and will to think for themselves about politics and religion instead of depending for their views on political and religious authorities.

Human beings must be true to their nature and exercise their central capacity for reason as the sole means for gaining objective knowledge and understanding of politics. Gandhi's many nonrational appeals to special political insight and disclosure of truth and to justification of his political choices are not based on objective, rational, intersubjectively verifiable criteria and must be rejected. Critical reasoning undermines irrational dogma and externally imposed religious and political structures of domination. Reason can free us from religious dogma, irrational and oppressive legal systems, and political and moral injustice and suffering. Since rationality is a universal human capacity, the Enlightenment emphasizes a new sense of egalitarianism in which individual human beings are free to exercise their own critical reason, enjoy individual liberty, are equal before the law, and are treated with equal tolerance. There was and continues to be a huge gap between such Enlightenment ideals and their limited applications and actual practices in modern political life.

Unlike many counter-Enlightenment thinkers, the Enlightenment emphasizes that the methods of investigation and the procedures for verification of true knowledge for politics and for religion are the same. Uncritical dogma, superstition, and irrationality are to be uprooted whether in religion or politics. Natural law, natural rights, critical reasoning, and objective knowledge are to be upheld whether in religion or politics.

The Enlightenment affirms both religious and political tolerance. Toleration is necessary for human beings to develop their natural capacity for reasoning to decide what they will believe. Both political and religious intolerance restrict our capacity to develop our universal, natural, rational capacity to arrive at objective knowledge and to establish political and other relations that maximize our potential for human development and the realization of liberty and happiness.

Compared with pre-Enlightenment views, Enlightenment thinkers tend to be very critical of past interactions and intersections of politics and religion. While religious and political phenomena are to be approached using the same fundamental conceptions and the same methodology, there is a strong tendency to undermine their intersection and to affirm a separation of religion and politics. This is clear in formulations of atheists of the Enlightenment who see no value in religion and are determined to free politics from religious authority, dogma, ignorance, and superstition. Other Enlightenment thinkers affirm a natural and rational deism, a rational theology, and a natural religion over a religion of supernatural revelation. However, even these religious figures of the Enlightenment oppose the use by religion of supernatural revelation, dogma, scripture, and institutional and clerical authority to interact with and restrict political life.

Any legitimate view of religion and politics is based on our critical understanding arising from our own nature as rational beings. Religion, which is based on reason and nature, must respect the rational natural foundation of politics and the universal, equal political rights and liberties of others, including those of nonbelievers and believers in other religions. Politics, which is based on reason and nature, must ensure our freedom from religious and other forms of domination while at the same time protecting our liberties, including religious liberty, so that we can freely and critically pursue the truth or falsity of religious, political, and all other matters.

It should be obvious to anyone familiar with Gandhi's writings and his political engagement that he was very critical of most of this Enlightenment approach and its profound influence on modern political thinking. Gandhi, for example, would evaluate many of these features as expressing an unjustified and dangerous rational and scientific reductionism, an arrogant deification of the sufficiency of human reason and human progress, and a devaluing of the spiritual basis of reality. He did not accept the modern separation of the political and the religious. Not only did he insist on the religionization of politics but also on the politicization of religion, especially in the sense that his spiritual orientation did not involve traditional Indian patterns of withdrawal from active political engagement.

At the same time, while showing how dominant post-Enlightenment modern political thinking is clearly at odds with Gandhi's approach, it is important to emphasize that Gandhi is really a much more subtle, complex, and flexible political thinker than is usually assumed. In many respects, he is just as critical of premodern superstitions, dogmatism, intolerance, and appeals to transcendent exclusivistic religious authority as are the modern political thinkers. In some cases, he can endorse certain Enlightenment characteristics, such as the need for tolerance and for respecting the ultimate authority of the individual self, but he usually gives justifications for such political positions that are at odds with modern political thinking. For example, in justifying a political position upholding political and religious pluralism and tolerance, Gandhi does not appeal to the ultimate authority of critical human reason: the Enlightenment view of rationality as the universal human capacity in which individuals must be free to exercise their own critical reason and be treated with equal tolerance. Gandhi, as will be seen, is more likely to justify such pluralism and tolerance by claiming that there is absolute spiritual Truth, but then submitting that we, as finite fallible human beings, are capable of having only partial limited "glimpses" of the Absolute. Therefore, we should be tolerant, recognizing the unavoidable fact that there are many diverse paths to the Truth and that each approach at most expresses relative truth.

CONTEMPORARY POLITICAL THINKING: GANDHI'S ALTERNATIVE

Although it is tempting to classify Gandhi's political thinking as reflecting a premodern, antimodern, religious essentialism at odds with modern political thinking, it is important to note two significant qualifications to our previous formulations. First, many contemporary political thinkers reject the major characteristics of the Enlightenment and how these characteristics defined modernity and modern political thinking. Second, in his rejection of much of modern political thinking, Gandhi shares some characteristics with recent postmodernist orientations.[6]

In the twentieth century, there have been widespread attacks on post-Enlightenment assumptions and values that shape modernism and modern political thinking. For example, confidence in objective human rationality and progress through scientific and technological development has often been shaken by devastating wars of mass destruction and by the "irrational" behavior of so-called rational scientists and scholars in contributing to and justifying the attempted genocide of Jews and others in the Holocaust; the development of nuclear and other weapons threatening the survival of humankind; and the production of various technologies that destroy the environment and seem to produce even greater oppression, exploitation, poverty, domination, dehumanization, and suffering. Modern political and other attempts to conceive of the human being as in essence a rational animal and to conceive of political thinking in terms of means-ends instrumental rationality are often criticized as too narrow, reductionistic, provincial, and oppressive. Many of these critiques of modernity raise the same kinds of concerns as those raised by Gandhi.

Existentialism, phenomenology, depth psychology, feminism, deconstructionism, postmodernism, and other twentieth-century developments have presented powerful critiques of modernity and modern political thinking in which the theoretical privileging of modern rationality and other post-Enlightenment political values have been analyzed as excluding gender, race, class, and other "voices." Foucault and many other contemporary political thinkers have deconstructed and demystified modern Western political models as revealing ideological justifications for dominant relations of power. Communitarians and various socialist and Marxist political thinkers have analyzed the modern individual as the alienated dehumanized person and have proposed political alternatives for realizing a sense of meaningful community and our human development and fulfillment as social individuals. Once again, Gandhi, in his criticism of the dominant features of Western modernism, raised many of these same concerns.

When noting Gandhi's metaphysical, spiritual, essentialized framework at the foundation of his political thinking, as well as his sweeping generalizations and negative judgments about the modern mode of being in the world, it is tempting to classify him as antimodern premodernist. Certainly this is how most severe critics of Gandhi, who identify with contemporary political thinking, evaluate his political approach.

However, it is also possible to interpret Gandhi's negative judgments about modernity and modern political thinking as sharing many characteristics with antimodern postmodernist approaches. "Postmodernism" is a very fashionable term among many contemporary philosophers, literary theorists, and other scholars, although the term tends to be very vague. Postmodernism encompasses all kinds of fragmented, contradictory positions. It tends to resist any clear definition or coherent formulation because it often upholds the inviolability of differences and sees attempts at coherence as oppressive forms of intellectual, political, and cultural hegemony.

Nevertheless, the following typical assertions of much of postmodernism can be related to Gandhi's approach to politics and political thinking. We must resist the tyranny and domination of the modernist idols of science, rationalism, and "objectivity." The Enlightenment gave us narrow, oppressive, hierarchical, reductionist projects of rationalistic and scientific hegemony. But rational scientific discourse is only one of many possible ways that human beings construct their "stories" about political reality. The scientific narrative does not have exclusive privileged access to political truth. Metaphysical spiritual narratives, as other ways of constructing accounts that shed light on political truth and reality, should not be reduced to scientific, rational, historical, and other nonethical and nonspiritual discourses. Ethical and religious approaches to politics that reject the major characteristics of post-Enlightenment

modernism must be respected as legitimate expressions of a multiplicity of ir-
reducible, incommensurable stories about political truth and reality. None of
the particular stories mirrors or exhausts all of political reality. Each of the stories has its own nature, structure, function, and significance; makes different
claims about truth and reality; fulfills different emotional, imaginative, conceptual, aesthetic needs for different people; and functions differently in different historical and cultural contexts.

Gandhi would undoubtedly have been uncomfortable with some of this
postmodernist language and with what I consider the vague, uncritically
eclectic, facile nature of many postmodernist formulations. Nevertheless, the
emphasis in Gandhi's political thinking on the relativity of truth and the tolerance of and respect for multiple voices, diversity, and an enriching pluralism of significant differences is similar to what one finds in various postmodernist political orientations.

Although Gandhi sometimes sounds like this postmodernism when arguing
against modern forms of political thinking, in many fundamental respects he
clearly rejects such a postmodernist orientation. For example, Gandhi, in his
critique of modernity, is not simply insisting on a separate, metaphysical, spiritual space so that he can tell an alternative political story. He is not embracing
some postmodernist relativism by endorsing the legitimacy of a plurality of ir-
reducibly autonomous stories about political reality. In his political thinking,
he makes highly normative, universal, absolute judgments about human nature, the human condition, and ultimate reality. He often judges the political
perspectives of modernity as culture-specific and oppressive, inauthentic, dehumanizing, incapable of solving our economic and political and cultural
crises, and denying human and cosmic reality. He privileges a metaphysical religious approach to political thinking as providing access to the deepest structures and meanings of the human condition as such and reality as such. Therefore, from the above typical postmodernist perspective, Gandhi, along with
dominant modernist thinkers, would be criticized for formulating another universalizing, totalizing, essentializing, hegemonic project.[7]

In the previous section, we delineated characteristics of dominant modern
political thinking, showed how such modern thinking is at odds with
Gandhi's approach, and indicated ways that the modern political orientation
would reject Gandhi's approach as premodern, outdated, and irrelevant. I
shall now present very briefly my view that some of Gandhi's political approach also provides a radical critique of and positive alternative to the dominant modern Western political thinking and to modern political developments.

My own position is that Gandhi's political, philosophical, religious, economic, and social approach is relevant to understanding many contemporary
political concerns. Gandhi's approach offers a valuable radical critique of
much of contemporary political thinking and of developments in contemporary political life. While being selective in appropriating what is of value in

Gandhi's political thought, his approach can serve as an urgently needed cat-alyst for rethinking modern political positions.[8]

Despite some of its socioeconomic, political, and other limitations, a Gandhian perspective presents a powerful critique of many features of modernity, Western materialism and models of development, domestic and foreign domination, and the bureaucratic state. It offers challenges, valuable insights, and alternatives to modern political thinking in its proposals about nonviolence, ego-construction and attachment, consumption, decentraliza-tion, community, appropriate technology, more harmonious relations with nature, more sustainable economic and political institutions and structures, and Gandhian socialism. It offers alternatives for personal and political trans-formation, ways to empathize with and communicate with oppressed and exploited masses and indigenous cultures, and ways to resist modern and other forms of domination, hatred, violence, class exploitation, gender and caste and religious and political oppression. What is needed is to con-textualize and integrate certain Gandhian political insights, perspectives, and alternatives with certain compatible non-Gandhian approaches that may have analyzed various aspects of modern political life in greater depth than did Mohandas Gandhi and his followers.

In the "Summing Up" to *Gandhian Economics: A Humane Approach,* Rashmi Sharma summarizes the following alternative to dominant modern economic thinking. I shall insert "politics" and "political" since this formula-tion also gets at Gandhi's valuable alternative to dominant modern political thinking.

> Mahatma Gandhi had formulated his economic [political] ideas in terms of his conception of an ideal social order. He wanted to build a non-violent and non-exploitative social order, peopled by truthful, non-violent and pure hearted sim-ple individuals. His approach to Economics [Politics] is through the avenue of truth and non-violence. Its goal is not pure material benefit [and political gain] but the advancement of whole humanity on the road to progress by strength-ening the character and development of the personality of each and every per-son in the society. No one's gain should be anybody's loss whether financial, physical, moral or spiritual. If there is to be a choice, the preference should fall on the eternal constituents of man rather than on the material. His conception of an ideal economic [political] organisation is directed towards the moral and spiritual development of all human beings rather than towards a blind pursuit of economic [and political] growth—a sustained increase in per capita real Gross National Product. Actually he believed that a blind pursuit of economic abun-dance [and political power] through accumulation, competition, and technolog-ical innovation would lead to economic [and political] aggression, exploitation and violence in the society. This led him to denounce the conventional eco-nomics [and modern political thinking].[9]

Many of these key features of Gandhi's political thinking will be analyzed in the following sections.

CONTEXTUALIZING GANDHI'S POLITICAL THOUGHT

Gandhians, as well as non-Gandhians, are divided on what constitutes "the true Gandhi" and the true Gandhian approach to political reality. Both proponents and opponents often appeal to an essential decontextualized Gandhi, usually identified with a rather clear, static, and rigid political approach, and then disagree on whether this essential Gandhi is relevant or irrelevant to contemporary political developments.

By contrast, I maintain that there is not one true, decontextualized political thought of Mohandas Gandhi. Not only was Gandhi's political thinking flexible, eclectic, and at times contradictory, but our attempts at relating Gandhi's approach to contemporary political thinking always involve a dynamic process of contestation with the reinterpretation, reconstitution, and development of diverse Gandhian positions.

In denying that we have access to one authentic Gandhi with his one true Gandhian approach to politics and political thinking, I in no way intend to deny the historical existence of this particular human being who expressed his views through his political writings and his political practices. This is not similar to the contemporary cases of, say, mythico-religious-historical claims by certain Hindus in India or Buddhists in Sri Lanka or fundamentalist Christians and Muslims, whose claims defy historical, scientific, and archaeological analysis and verification. In Gandhi's case, we have a tremendous amount of factual documentation about his political thinking, his political struggles, and his thoughts about modern Western political thinking. In many ways, our problem in interpreting and formulating Gandhi's political approach is that there is so much, often unsystematic and contradictory, evidence.

Mohandas Gandhi himself contributed to this problem of comprehending his political thinking. He emphasized political practice and had little interest in formulating theoretical arguments and resolving inconsistencies by writing coherent, systematic political works. Gandhi never wrote a lengthy book, and yet he left one of the most extensive collections of writings ever assembled. *The Collected Works of Mahatma Gandhi* has now grown to one hundred volumes. These largely unsystematic writings, full of political, philosophical, religious, social, and cultural assumptions and claims, have allowed interpreters to maintain that they have discovered so many blatantly contradictory Gandhis and Gandhian political perspectives.

Others have also contributed to this problem of comprehending Gandhi's true political thinking. It sometimes seems as if everyone who ever met Gandhi felt compelled to write something about this man, his views, and his struggles. What they wrote, even about the same political events and about what they attributed to Mohandas Gandhi, is often highly contradictory. Sometimes followers transformed a political speech or demonstration into a *darshan,* deifying Gandhi and embellishing his words and actions with supernatural meaning and significance. Gandhi was sometimes given credit or blame for political developments over which he had little or no control.

However, the problem with making any essentialized decontextualized claims to one true Gandhi or one true Gandhian political approach is more basic than the above considerations of historical verification and textual consistency and coherency. The more basic methodological problem has to do with the dynamic, ever-changing relations that are constituted between political and other texts, contexts, and interpretations. This is true even of texts that are less inclusivistic, eclectic, and unsystematic than are Gandhi's political writings.

My own position is that every reading of a text is to some extent a rereading, every interpretation a reinterpretation, and every philosophical or political formulation a reconstruction. What a political text by Gandhi means to us cannot be fully understood outside its contexts, both the specific contexts within which Gandhi constructed the text and how our understanding of that text is mediated by our own changing social, economic, political, religious, ethical, and other contexts. That is why any attempt to interpret, reconstitute, and relate Gandhi's political approach to contemporary political thinking must take into consideration how our views of Gandhi and his political thought are at least partially filtered through variables defining contemporary political and other contexts that did not exist during Gandhi's lifetime. How we read and interpret the meaning and significance of *Hind Swaraj* or some other political work by Gandhi, how we understand Gandhi's political actions and commitments, what we emphasize and what we ignore in Gandhi's political formulations, which voices in the Gandhian text speak to us and which voices are silenced, and how we evaluate political values and political change are all filtered through and at least partially structured by our historical, social, political, and cultural contexts. Indeed, I would even maintain that there is not one "M. K. Gandhi" in the sense that however we describe, as well as analyze, this particular human being involves a historical, social, political, and cultural reconstruction that is never completely detached from our own contextual framework.

The contradictory interpretations of the political Gandhi and his political thinking involve diverse, competing Gandhian projects, each attributing the major figure of authorship and authority to Mohandas Gandhi but also encompassing the contributions of many other individuals, including Gandhi's predecessors, contemporaries, and successors. Not only in the debates between Gandhians and non-Gandhians, but also in the sharp disagreements reflected in diverse Gandhian perspectives, there is an unavoidable domain of contestation. Any political perspective, including any Gandhian perspective, must be viewed as dynamic, open-ended, and continually changing. There is no exclusive, nondialectical, absolute, static, eternal, true Gandhi or Gandhian political perspective. Therefore, what follows should be seen as several of many possible ways to reinterpret and reconstruct a Gandhian approach to the nature of truth, nonviolence, self, and self-other relations as essential to political reality.

Such an approach is consistent with Gandhi's own dynamic, open-ended, relative experiments with truth. As a conditioned, temporal, historical, finite, fallible being, Gandhi rejected any human perspective that claimed to experience unconditioned, exclusive, absolute, static, eternal, noncontextualized, political Truth. Through concrete praxis, Gandhi continually attempted to move from one relative political truth to another greater relative political truth. According to Gandhi, one of the greatest evils in political and other human relations has been our tendency to absolutize what is necessarily relative. As we noted, Gandhi's insistence on the relativity of all political, religious, and other human perspectives is a justification for Gandhian tolerance and respect for other relative perspectives to truth and reality.

The challenge to such an approach to Gandhi's political thinking is to avoid the kind of facile relativism reflected in most of postmodernism and many other contemporary Western approaches and so clearly rejected by Gandhi. In maintaining that there is no exclusive, nondialectical, absolute, static, eternal, noncontextualized, true Gandhian (or non-Gandhian) political perspective, I do not want to maintain that "everything goes," that all political views are of equal value, or that all political views reflect nothing more than relative, personal, subjective, contextual viewpoints. Even without an exclusive, absolute, noncontextualized, normative foundationalism, I think that we can formulate criteria for evaluating different Gandhian political perspectives in terms of their explanatory power to illuminate the nature, meaning, and significance of different phenomena, their tendency to exacerbate or free us from structures of exploitation, oppression, and domination, and so forth.

GANDHI'S METAPHYSICAL AND SPIRITUAL FRAMEWORK

At the beginning of *Rediscovering Gandhi,* Yogesh Chandra makes the dramatic claim that "Gandhi's greatness—nay, uniqueness—lies in his role as an innovator in politics. . . . In fact, he endeavoured to found a new human order. He was the first in human history to extend the principle of nonviolence from the individual to the social and the political plane."[10]

What is probably most striking when contrasting Gandhi's uniqueness as a political innovator with dominant modern political thinking is how his political approach is grounded in a general ethical, metaphysical, and spiritual framework. To understand Gandhi's specific political concepts and practices, including his key analysis of self and self-other relations that we shall examine in the following section, one must become aware of this underlying philosophical and religious foundation. The two most important concepts constituting this essential Gandhian foundation are Truth *(satya)* and nonviolence *(ahimsa)*.[11] In general terms, Gandhi's spiritual philosophical presuppositions and framework affirm the essential unity of all existence, the indivisibility of Truth, and the interrelatedness of Truth, Self, and Nonviolence.

Glyn Richards in *The Philosophy of Gandhi* correctly emphasizes Gandhi's metaphysical concept of Truth as key to understanding the theoretical and practical dimensions of his philosophy.[12] Gandhi may appear to be an unsystematic thinker, but his underlying concept of Truth *(satya)* provides a rationale and coherence to his political theory and practice.

Gandhi frequently expressed his view of reality and of political truth in terms of the formulation "Truth is God." In his reflections on Truth, Gandhi expressed a personal preference for the Hindu impersonal formulations of the nondualistic Advaita Vedanta with its view of the all-encompassing, spiritual Self as *Atman* and its identification of *Atman* with the impersonal absolute Brahman.[13] Gandhi was also extremely flexible in his formulations of Truth, frequently referring to God, Rama, and many other personal and impersonal terms. Gandhi acknowledges that God "is a personal God to those who need His personal presence."[14] At the same time, Gandhi "would say with those who say God is Love, God is Love. But deep down in me, I used to say that though God may be Love, God is Truth, above all."[15] Gandhi wrote that he then "went a step further and said that Truth is God. You will see the fine distinction between the two statements, viz., that God is Truth and Truth is God."[16] In his attempt to be as inclusive as possible, Gandhi reverses the traditional theistic formulation of God is Truth, in which Truth is one of many essential attributes of the reality that is God. By focusing on reality as Truth, God can include religious and nonreligious approaches that reject "God" and other theistic concepts. For example, Gandhi states that atheists may deny the existence of God, but they still have a passion for discovering truth. Therefore, "rather than say that God is Truth, I should say that Truth is God."[17] This often allows those who have rejected theistic or other traditional religious formulations to relate to Gandhi's concept of Truth.

Analyzing the relation of "Truth is God," James Hart uses a philosophical phenomenological approach to interpret the relations and meanings of Gandhi's Truth, God, Self, and *ahimsa*.

> Truth is the *omega*, the *telos*, of life; as identified with the impersonal Brahman it is also the *alpha*. The theme of Truth is experientially available in everyday life as *telos*, as what we want as the cognitive fulfillment of the emptiness which manages to pervade even the objects which are given to us in a filled intention of evidence. Perhaps we can say that the theme of Truth, as what the mind seeks foremost, moves G [Gandhi] in the direction of a kind of "transcendental reduction." Such a reduction is already adumbrated by the Indian tradition which holds that the self must "go back" to its Self, its foundation, by relinquishing its attachment to itself.[18]

On 8 June 1927, Gandhi wrote to Basil Matthews: "If God who is indefinable can be at all defined, then I should say that God is TRUTH. It is impossible to reach HIM, that is, TRUTH, except through LOVE. LOVE can only be expressed fully when man reduces himself to a cipher. This process of reduction to cipher is the highest effort man or woman is capable of making. It is the only effort worth making, and it is possible only through ever-increasing self-restraint."[19] He concluded *An Autobiography or The Story of My Experiments with Truth* by stating: "But I know that I have still before me a difficult path to traverse. I must reduce myself to zero. So long as a man does not of his own free will put himself last among his fellow creatures, there is no salvation for him. *Ahimsa* is the farthest limit of humility."[20]

Reminiscent of passages in the Upanishads and Vedanta giving expression to a view of reality in terms of an all-encompassing, permanent, spiritual Self, Gandhi often writes of Truth or God as an impersonal Absolute, an unseen power or unifying force pervading all things, pure consciousness, the changeless essence of life beyond name and form.

> There is an indefinable mysterious Power that pervades everything. I feel It, though I do not see It. It is this unseen Power which makes Itself felt and yet defies all proof, because It is so unlike all that I perceive through my senses. It transcends the senses. . . . I do dimly perceive that whilst everything around me is ever changing, ever dying, there is underlying all that change a living Power that is changeless, that holds all together, that creates, dissolves and recreates. That informing Power or Spirit is God. And since nothing else I see merely through the senses can or will persist, He alone is.[21]

Consistent with the Advaitin monistic identification of *Brahman* (Reality, Being) with *Atman* (the Self), Gandhi often uses the terms Truth, God, and Self interchangeably. Gandhi's political life and political thought are profoundly influenced by presuppositions of the indivisibility of Truth, the identification of Self with Truth or God, and the essential unity of all existence.

This approach to Truth and Self informs Gandhi's entire philosophy and political thinking regarding *ahimsa* (nonviolence, noninjury, nondestruction of life). Gandhi attempts to correct a common misconception that his primary emphasis is always on ahimsa. "Ahimsa is not the goal. Truth is the goal. But we have no means of realizing truth in human relationships except through the practice of ahimsa. A steadfast pursuit of ahimsa is inevitably bound to truth—not so violence. That is why I swear by ahimsa. Truth came naturally to me. Ahimsa I acquired after a struggle. But ahimsa being the means we are naturally more concerned with it in our everyday life."[22] Here and in many other places, Gandhi focuses on nonviolence as the political means for realizing the goal of Truth or Reality, including the realization of the true Self.[23]

Since means and ends are convertible terms in Gandhi's political philosophy, *ahimsa* and *satya* are "so intertwined that it is practically impossible to disentangle and separate them." Attaining nonviolence involves the realization of Truth; attaining Truth involves the realization of nonviolence. Now if the essence of the individual is the higher universal Self that is at one with Truth or God or Reality, then to inflict unnecessary, deliberate violence and suffering on another is to negate or violate Truth, God, Reality, and one's Self.[24]

It is imperative to emphasize an important, often overlooked, distinction between the absolute and the relative in Gandhi's political approach. Gandhian perspectives which do not emphasize this distinction are of limited relevance for analyzing political values and political change today. Gandhi's writings, as seen throughout *An Autobiography,* often seem so full of absolute ideals and uncompromising judgments that one can easily ignore this distinction and misinterpret his political approach. Gandhi is more complex and more flexible than the common interpretations of him as a person with philosophical, ethical, and spiritual absolutes who, for sympathetic followers, was courageous in sticking to his lofty principles, or, for critics, was inflexible and even dictatorial in forcing his absolutes on his wife, children, striking workers, and others.

Gandhi himself confesses that he has only had "glimpses" of Truth. He begins *An Autobiography* by affirming that for him "truth is the sovereign principle" and is "not only the relative truth of our conception, but the Absolute Truth, the Eternal Principle, that is God." Gandhi continues that "as long as I have not realized this Absolute Truth, so long must I hold by the relative truth as I have conceived it." This relative truth must serve as his guide. Often Gandhi "had faint glimpses of the Absolute Truth, God, and daily the conviction is growing upon me that He alone is real and all else is unreal." Only when the seeker of political truth practices *ahimsa* and expresses great humility can she or he "have a glimpse of truth."[25]

Gandhi repeatedly tells us that a human being cannot fully realize Truth as the absolute ideal. "Nobody in this world possesses absolute truth. This is God's attribute alone. Relative truth is all we know. Therefore, we can only follow the truth as we see it."[26] Human beings as political beings can at most approximate the absolute ideal through their understanding of their relative, imperfect, historically and culturally conditioned political truths about self and self-other relations. Indeed, the relative understanding of self, gained through political and other limited experiments in truth, is our only means for gaining some partial, imperfect understanding of the absolute Self.

This absolute-relative distinction is essential for an understanding of Gandhi's approach toward Truth and other interrelated concepts and their application to political, social, economic, and educational concerns. In his numerous specific positions on untouchability and caste, political resistance to colonialism, educational priorities, and socialism and decentralized economic institutions, Gandhi has general concerns about which imperfect political theories and practices least violate or best approximate the ideals of the indivisibility of Truth, the oneness of existence, and the identity of Truth, Self, and nonviolence.[27]

Ahimsa in its inextricable relation to Truth and Self-realization is an absolute ideal. At best, human beings gain some partial realization of this ideal through the formulation and application of imperfect relative political concepts of non-violence as seen in dynamic, changing, political self-other relations. "Ahimsa in theory no one knows. It is as indefinable as God. But in its working we get glimpses of it as we have glimpses of the Almighty in His working amongst and through us."[28] Since our understandings are imperfect, we sometimes, even with the best of intentions, violate the absolute ideal of nonviolence. We commit violence in our political and other relations with the other. What is more surprising, and runs counter to a common stereotype of the absolutist Gandhi, is his justification for sometimes committing political and other forms of violence.

Using numerous examples from Gandhi and especially Peter Winch's analysis of "'the perspective' of the action" in *Ethics and Action,*[29] Richards repeatedly shows that Gandhi has absolute philosophical ideals but also recognizes the complexity of specific situations, especially those involving moral dilemmas. Gandhi struggled over how the self should relate to all kinds of others. He struggled over what to do not only about unintentional violence to other forms of life, but also about how to relate to disease-carrying rats, mosquitoes, venomous snakes, as well as rapists, insane persons, and other humans intent on committing violence. He even worried about the destruction of plant life necessary for his vegetarian diet. Gandhi concluded, often very reluctantly, that at times we must act in such a way as to violate the ideal of nonviolence.

According to Gandhi, we must not make a "fetish" of *ahimsa*. Sometimes we must reluctantly commit violence and even destroy the life of the other in order to live and protect life. In terms of the ideal of *ahimsa*, our acts of violence would still be wrong, but they might result from moral considerations and be done for moral reasons. This doesn't mean that we are rejecting the ideal. Gandhi has not abandoned or qualified his commitment to the ideal Self and its necessary relation with the principle of nonviolence. The ideal of nonviolence is still operative, informing our circumstances, attitudes, and actions, even when we are forced to violate it.

Such an approach presents a much more flexible political Gandhi than the typically honored or condemned rigid absolutist. In addition, such a contextualized perspectivism, while needing to struggle against the dangers of the kinds of facile relativism Gandhi opposed, has the advantages of relating Gandhi's political approach and political thinking to many contemporary critiques of ahistorical, nontemporal, abstract, rigid, essentialized foundationalist political formulations.

SELF-OTHER RELATIONS: A RADICAL INVERSION

In this section, I focus on a particular feature of the essential metaphysical and spiritual framework at the foundation of Gandhi's political thinking: his key analysis of self and self-other relations with his radical inversion of the dominant models of self-other relations that constitute modern Western political thinking. There is nothing more essential for understanding Gandhi's political approach to human relations and political change than his analysis of the nature of self and self-other relations. In this regard, Gandhi is eclectic and pluralistic with many formulations of self and self-other relations, along with contrasting formulations of false and illusory constructions of self and self-other relations found in modern Western political thought. As was previously noted, Gandhi's approach to self, self-other relations, and other political concerns must be situated within a larger utopian or ideal theoretical framework grounded in the essential concepts of Truth *(Satya)*, Nonviolence *(Ahimsa)*, Self *(Atman)*, and God.

As was seen in several quotations in the previous section and in similar passages found throughout Gandhi's political writings, Gandhi advocates a radical reversal of the post-Cartesian or dominant modern Western philosophical, economic, political, social, and cultural orientation in which one's starting point and foundation is the primacy of one's own individual self or ego. In such a modern, Western, non-Gandhian orientation—which increasingly defines politics, economics, culture, advertising, and other aspects of contemporary life in India—the human being tends to assume, both for one's own self and for others selves, some view of the person as a separate, independent, autonomous, I-me individual or ego. *rejected by G*

Perhaps the best-known formulation in the history of Western philosophy is René Descartes's *cogito ergo sum* in his *Meditations on First Philosophy*. In the *Meditations*, Descartes attempted to subject everything he normally accepted as true to rigorous, logical, methodological doubt in order to determine if anything was absolutely certain and could then serve as the secure foundation for his philosophy. He found that nothing he normally held to be true—sense impressions, reasoning, memory, belief in God, and so forth—was absolutely certain. Threatened by a pervasive skepticism, Descartes finally concluded that there was only one thing of which he could be absolutely certain: the existence of his own self or ego as a "thinking thing." Even when I am doubting, imagining, dreaming, having illusions, being mislead and deceived, there must be something that is doing the doubting, being deceived, etc., and that is the "I" or self as a thinking thing.[30]

Such a modern orientation renders problematic meaningful self-other relations. This thinking thing of which I claim to be certain is my separate individual self. I come to know my own self in isolation, independent of other selves. Indeed, all of my relations to others have been subjected to methodological doubt. This thinking thing or my self is only certain of its own existence and even then only when I am doubting or thinking. Such a modern, non-Gandhian philosophical and political project is continually threatened by a pervasive skepticism and a self-imposed solipsism as it attempts to establish objective, meaningful relations with the secondary political other.

Although Descartes's specific form of philosophical orientation, and especially his Cartesian foundationalism and metaphysics, may not be widely accepted by contemporary philosophers, his focus on the primacy of the "I" or ego, the autonomous separate individual, continues to shape much of modern Western political thought. The most influential Western social and political philosophers, such as those with Hobbesian and Lockean roots, and the most influential capitalist political economists, such as Adam Smith and David Ricardo, assumed a human condition of separate I-me individual selves. The concept of the modern post-Cartesian self, the autonomous individual, continues as an essential component in modern economic, political, legal, cultural, and educational ideologies and systems.[31]

Before discussing Gandhi's ethical, political, and spiritual inversion of this post-Cartesian self-other relation, I shall simply note my rejection of this modern Western political orientation. Unlike Western political thinkers who emphasize the isolated, separate, autonomous individual, I maintain that the self is a relational self, that there is no political self without its integral positive and negative relations with the other, and that the nonsocial, independent, autonomous, modern, individual self is largely a social, economic, political, and cultural construction. My view is that Gandhi also upholds a social relational view of self, with his major focus on dynamic self-other relations. Nevertheless, as we shall see in the concluding section, Gandhi is inconsistent on this matter, as when he sometimes emphasizes an "inner voice" or "individual consciousness" completely detached from, and at times in opposition to, all social relations with the other.

In his political analysis of self-other relations, Gandhi provides a radical inversion of the modern political focus on the primacy of one's own self or ego. This inversion is grounded in proper ethical relations with the other. Gandhi would have no difficulty agreeing with the influential phenomenologist and Jewish philosopher Emmanuel Levinas that "ethics is first philosophy." Unlike much of traditional religion, philosophy, and politics, Gandhi focuses his attention on moral values and moral human relations. He has no sympathy for political thinking that claims to be value-free or value-neutral, nonethical, or focused on power relations free from moral considerations. Similarly, he has no sympathy for religious thinking that claims to transcend morality by advocating salvation based solely on faith in some supernatural deity. For Gandhi, politics and religion are grounded in morality, and one becomes more spiritual as one establishes more moral political relations.

Gandhi critiques and rejects the dominant modern political perspective by establishing an inverted asymmetrical relation between the self and the other: We establish meaningful ethical, political, and spiritual relations with the other when we focus on the primacy of the other. This radical inversion of modern self-other relations with Gandhi's primary focus on serving the needs of the other is clearly seen in Gandhi's famous "talisman." In trying to decide how to act politically, how to establish an ethical self-other relation, Gandhi advises the person to recall the face of the poorest and most helpless human being you may have seen, i.e., focus not on your own self but instead on the other with the greatest needs. Then ask whether the political or other action you contemplate will be useful to the other. Will it help the hungry and spiritually starved other human being to gain control over her or his life and destiny? Then, Gandhi concludes, you will find your doubts about what to do and your self melting away. As with Levinas, Gandhi thus claims that we uphold authentic human values and engage in authentic social and political change only when we assume moral responsibility for the welfare of the other.[32] As Gandhi repeatedly tells us, this necessarily involves "self-restraint," reducing one's ego or self to a "cipher" or a "zero."

Several Indians, including Gandhians, have claimed to find a contradiction between Gandhi's political and other formulations of this asymmetrical human relation recognizing the primacy of the other and many other political passages, such as those upholding *swaraj,* which emphasize the necessity for self-rule, self-assertion, etc.[33] My own view is that there is no such necessary contradiction within a Gandhian perspective. Gandhi does not deny but instead affirms the existence of a true moral and spiritual self (Self). When Gandhi is talking about self-restraint and reducing the self to a zero, he is focusing on the I-me, egoistic, separate ego or self. Put in traditional Indian terms, this is not the authentic spiritual Self, but the karmic, mayic, illusory self-construction that establishes unethical and unspiritual political relations. In Gandhi's perspective, it is only when one restrains and overcomes this focus on the primacy of one's own self/ego and instead focuses on the primacy of the needs of the other that one begins to experience the deeper, true moral and spiritual Self and establishes authentic self-other political relations.

It is important to avoid a misunderstanding that could arise from several of my previous formulations of an essentialized metaphysical and spiritual foundation and an essentialized inverted self-other relation at the center of Gandhi's political thinking. As I've previously indicated, it would be incorrect to analyze Gandhi's political thinking as consisting simply of rather mechanical, ahistorical, noncontextualized, universal appeals to absolute, ultimate, moral, metaphysical, and spiritual structures and values. As Richard Fox correctly emphasizes, Gandhi's political thinking and political practice focus on the concrete, dynamic social and political processes in terms of which Gandhian political perspectives, including self-other relations, constitute and reconstitute human values and enact political change. Gandhi does uphold utopian or ideal political values, but he is always engaged politically in relative, imperfect political experiments with truth that are indispensable for understanding Gandhi's approach to political values and political change.[34]

Gandhi was pragmatic in his political approach to self-other relations, human values, and political change. He was concerned with political effectiveness, with transformation of self-other power relations, with being successful in his political experiments with truth. But unlike most pragmatic political approaches, Gandhi's also upheld ethical, political, philosophical, and spiritual ideals. His experiments, attempting to reconstitute human relations and to bring about progressive political change, always to some extent pointed beyond what could actually be achieved in our finite, limited, everyday political world. Gandhi often saw himself as a utopian political experimentalist, pursuing political experiments in an elusive truth, with the intention of radically transforming politics, culture, society, the individual person, and self-other relations. *Satyagraha* and *ahimsa* powered these dynamic experiments in truth that depended on confrontation and opposition to existing cultural and political meanings and material conditions of inequality and domination. Gandhi's political experiments were sometimes successful, when political resistance was powered by his utopian vision, and sometimes failures, such as cases when the experiment was transformed into a nonconfrontational, ideological legitimation of the dominant political reality.

KEY QUESTIONS REGARDING
THE SELF AND SELF-OTHER RELATIONS

In previous sections, I have shown that Gandhi's analysis of self and self-other relations—especially as it is grounded in his ideal metaphysical spiritual framework, in his rejection of the modern Western focus of the primacy of ego/self, and in his ethical and political inversion of dominant modern self-other relations—is essential for understanding Gandhi's political thinking. In this concluding section, I submit that there are key unresolved questions, along with creative possibilities for the development of political thinking, in Gandhi's analysis of self and self-other relations, especially arising from his ambiguous and at times contradictory formulations about the individual self, the social self, and the spiritual self.

I shall now delineate, without documentation, a series of key questions relevant to Mohandas Gandhi's complex, often contradictory, analysis of self and self-other relations. Since there are such complex and contradictory formulations in Gandhi's writings, there is little wonder that later Gandhian perspectives, incorporating data from Gandhi and from other sources, should express such a wide range of diverse and contradictory positions.[35]

Among the questions arising from formulations of self and self-other relations in Gandhi's writings are the following: How is an individual self related to other individual selves? How is an individual self related to a social self? And how is an individual self and/or a social self related to some deeper spiritual self? Gandhi's many responses to these and related questions often reveal ambiguities, complexities, and dialectical tension and contradiction.[36]

Gandhi repeatedly emphasizes the importance of the individual (individual self) by focusing on the "inner voice" and the individual consciousness.

Throughout his political writings, when facing ethical and political crises, Gandhi appeals to his inner voice for guidance. Gandhians often cite the numerous antiauthoritarian passages in which Gandhi advises the other person to listen to her or his own inner voice, even if that contradicts what Gandhi's own inner voice tells him to do. Such an admirable approach is seen as upholding the values of pluralism and diversity with a respect for individual differences and a remarkable sense of tolerance.

Nevertheless, Gandhi's emphasis on the inner voice and individual consciousness raises many serious questions. Most basic, it is not clear precisely what Gandhi means by such concepts. In some passages, inner voice seems to point to conscience, and it is tempting to adopt a Kantian philosophical approach. But in such passages, Gandhi also seems to reject some essentializing, categorical, reason-based, Kantian sense of ethical universalism. Instead he emphasizes the real differences of individual selves.

Some Indians, including Gandhians, claim that India is like the United States of America (or the West) in that both place primary emphasis on "the individual." But such a supposed similarity is usually more misleading than instructive. Gandhi does not endorse some political concept of the modern, Western, nonsocial or antisocial, nonrelational, autonomous, independent individual. Just the opposite: He usually views the ideological construction of such a modern individual self as an impediment to true self-realization and to positive self-other political relations.

What complicates this question is that Gandhi—unlike most contemporary political scientists and political philosophers, historians, social and natural scientists—does not reduce this concept of the individual self to empirical, historical, psychological, social, biological, or other scientific terms. Most essentially, this inner voice, as a statement of truth, is a spiritual voice.[37] What is this individual spiritual voice/self?[38]

There are obvious questions arising from the danger of such a primary focus on this individual inner voice. As Gandhi was well aware, many individuals throughout history, often with strong religious faith commitments, have claimed strange, demonic, anti-Gandhian inner voices. This is why Gandhi places such an emphasis on moral development, adhering to moral spiritual vows, and purification of mind and body as preconditions allowing one to listen to the true inner voice. As essential to political thinking, the inner voice is a statement of political truth, and, for Gandhi, many inner voices are statements of political untruth.

A serious difficulty in distinguishing the true inner voice as a statement of political truth from the false inner voice as a statement of political untruth arises from the fact that Gandhi usually seems to pose the individual inner voice against the social, detaching it from its larger social and political context and any process of intersubjective verification. This leaves us with a tension in Gandhi's writings and with serious questions about the basis on which I can judge an inner voice as true or false and about what this does for

Gandhi's respect for pluralism and diversity. After all, a political approach that might conclude that your particular inner voice is a statement of un-truth—even if I sometimes advise you to act politically on what is really false so that you can learn from your own failed experiments in truth—doesn't seem to correspond to Gandhi's deeper sense of tolerance and pluralism based on *Satya* and *Ahimsa*.

This focus on the individual self raises crucial questions about its relation to the social self. Gandhi's individual is not the nonsocial/antisocial individual. For Gandhi the latter is the height of egotism and immorality. Such self/ego-centered and ego-attached tendencies must be restrained, even to the extent of placing primary focus on the needs and welfare of the other and placing your "self" last. In Gandhi's political approach, it is only when one restrains and overcomes the dominant modern focus on the primacy of one's own self/ego and instead establishes dynamic, social, political self-other relations focusing on the primacy of the needs of the other that one begins to experience the deeper, true moral and spiritual Self and constitutes a more moral and spiritual political order. Only by restraining the false self/ego, realizing one's nature as a social relational self, and assuming ethical, social, and political responsibility for the welfare of the other, can I begin to listen to the authentic inner voice of the true self.

Even with this clarification, there remain many questions about the individual-social relation in Gandhi's political thinking. Clearly for Gandhi the social is an essential dimension of self-realization and of developing a more moral and spiritual political order of constructive self-other relations. In his analysis of *swaraj* and many other concepts, Gandhi emphasizes the necessity of incorporating into the process of education, moral development, and self-development, including character development, cultural, linguistic, and other aspects of one's specific social and political context. To a large extent, in Gandhi's political approach, both the false individual self and the true individual self are socially and politically constructed. Gandhi's political individual is a social relational self. But Gandhi also resists reducing the individual (inner voice, individual consciousness) to social analysis. Indeed, the individual inner voice is often posed against the social.

If, as I would submit, the self is always a relational self, the self-other is a necessary structure of human consciousness, and there is no self free from dynamic dialectical relations with the other, then many of Gandhi's political assertions about the inner voice, social reality, and spiritual reality require further analysis. Although Gandhi's political thinking usually emphasizes a commitment to a social relational view of self, he sometimes attempts to detach the individual self from its social relations with the other or to point to a deeper, nondualistic, spiritual self (Self) in which the self-other relation is transcended. I would submit that these nonsocial and antisocial formulations, when detached from Gandhi's social political relational analysis, have contributed to more reactionary Gandhian political positions.

Additional questions about the self and the self-other relation arise from Gandhi's key distinction between the relative and the absolute. As we observed in our formulation of Gandhi's essential metaphysical and spiritual framework, Gandhi repeatedly warns us that everything he says about absolute ideals of Truth, Nonviolence, God, and Self remains on the level of relative truth. At best Gandhi's political experiments with truth proceed through action-oriented praxis from one relative political truth to a more adequate relative truth. But as a limited, conditioned, imperfect self, no human being can fully grasp the absolute Self and absolute Truth. This is a major justification for Gandhi's insistence on political and religious pluralism, multiplicity, diversity, nonviolence, tolerance, and respect for many authentic perspectives, glimpses of, and paths to Truth. In short, there is not one objective, universal, absolute, true view of "the Self."

As we have seen, this leads to a complex Gandhian political approach to self and self-other relations far different from the commonly presented rigid absolutist Mahatma, admired by some followers for his uncompromising insistence on absolute political and other principles and attacked by some critics for his tyrannical imposition of his absolutes on his family, workers, and others. The more accurate and more adequate political Gandhi, in my view, who upholds the relativity of all political truths about self, can be more easily related to contemporary analyses of self-other relations. Such a Gandhian approach, for example, emphasizes a situational perspectivism, as seen in the claim by Merleau-Ponty and other philosophers that all knowledge is perspectival. Such a Gandhian approach to self can be related to contemporary antiessentialist critiques, contemporary antifoundationalism (including critiques of traditional philosophical formulations of "the Self"), and the insistence on the relativity of all perspectives.

Nevertheless, there are serious problems with simply identifying Gandhi's insistence on the relative truth of any assertion about self with contemporary pragmatist, phenomenological, multiculturalist, deconstructionist, postmodernist, and other formulations of the relativity of all perspectives. Gandhi rejects the kinds of facile or unlimited relativisms, fragmented eclecticisms, and insistence on the inviolability of relative particular differences so fashionable in many contemporary approaches. On a deeper metaphysical or spiritual level, Gandhi presupposes and insists on the indivisibility of Truth, the interrelatedness and unity and even oneness of Reality, and the ultimate spiritual identity of Truth, Nonviolence, God, and Self. This raises the key question for a Gandhian political approach to self and self-other relations as to what holds together and unifies the different, limited, imperfect, often contradictory, relative views of self.

In this regard, there is a persistent tension in Gandhi's political and other reflections on self and self-other relations. On the one hand, Gandhi repeatedly emphasizes the inner voice, the individual consciousness, relative limited political truths, and respect for a plurality of diverse political perspectives on Self and Truth. On the other hand, Gandhi grounds his profound commitment to unity and oneness, to Self and Nonviolence and Truth, by assuming a metaphysical and spiritual framework. Such an ultimate framework is constituted by moral and spiritual absolute ideals. In terms of such ideals, Gandhi has faith and believes in a deeper spiritual Self—whether formulated as a monistic, Upanishadic, Vedantic *Atman*, as the divinity within, or in other terms. Such a metaphysical and spiritual foundation provides the sense of an objective universal approach to Self that unifies diverse individual and social political perspectives on self. This distinguishes Gandhi's political approach to self from the modern Western political endorsement of a plurality of diverse, ultimately separate, fragmented, particular, relative perspectives on truth and self. There are many paths to Truth, many relative truths, many diverse paths or ways to climb the mountain. But as human beings we are unified in that we are formulating or experimenting with diverse, limited, imperfect ways to climb the same mountain, to reach the ultimate Truth and experience the unifying Self.

The tension here in Gandhi's political approach to self and self-other relations arises from the fact that he has assumed a metaphysical foundation, a spiritual essentialism, that holds together and unifies the plurality of individual selves with their diverse relative perspectives on self-other political relations. How does one justify this philosophical religious assumption of such a metaphysical spiritual framework? How is the assumption of such a spiritual political foundation reconciled with Gandhi's previous affirmations of individual inner voices, the relativity of all human glimpses of truth, and a tolerant situational political perspectivism? Through faith? Through the imposition—even if well-intentioned—of a metaphysical framework and view of deeper spiritual Self and Truth on the other, even if the political other claims that this reflects a unifying Hinduization or some other imposition of an alien political perspective on one's own approach to self and self-other relations? Put in other words, how does a Gandhian political approach deal with the claim that we may not simply be taking different paths or ways to climb the same mountain? We may be climbing different mountains with different political and other views of relative truth and absolute Truth, relative self and absolute Self.

One way that several Gandhians have attempted to resolve such a tension—even claiming that there is no real tension—in Gandhi's political approach to self and self-other relations is to present a traditional Indian philosophical distinction between relative truth and absolute truth. We should not conflate or confuse these two levels of analysis expressing two radically different levels of reality. When Gandhi is discussing individual selves, inner voices, social selves, political self-other relations, glimpses of truth, and diverse political perspectives, his political thinking functions on the limited, conditioned level of empirical, political, relative truth. When Gandhi refers to Self, *Atman*, the divinity within that unifies self and other, Truth, God, and Nonviolence, his political, ethical, and religious thinking functions on the deeper, ultimate, spiritual level of unconditioned, nonempirical, transcendent, absolute Truth. Tension arises only when we confuse these two levels of analysis of self/Self by not distinguishing what may have limited, empirical, relative, political truth from absolute Truth.

Regardless of how one assesses attempts in Nagarjuna's Madhyamika Buddhism or Shankara's Advaita Vedanta to formulate such a theory of two levels of truth, such an approach does not easily remove all tension in and questions about Gandhi's political approach to self. I'll conclude by providing two of many possible complicating considerations. First, for Gandhi, relative truth is not simple empirical truth. Even his relative political truths about self and self-other relations (inner voice, individual consciousness, etc.) have a nonempirical, ahistorical, spiritual basis or dimension. This is why many of Gandhi's relative political assertions, arising from seemingly empirical political experiments with truth, can prove so frustrating to those attempting to subject them to a process of strict empirical, social, historical, political, nonreligious verification.

Second, for Gandhi—unlike many traditional Vedantists and many other advocates of ultimate spiritual realities—there is an integral necessary relation between relative truths (t , t , t , . . .) and absolute truth (T). A traditional proponent of Advaita Vedanta may claim that on the level of absolute Truth, when we experience fully and unconditionally the true Self as nondifferentiated, pure, spiritual *Atman* and experience the complete identity of *Atman-Brahman*, we reject and transcend the political order of relative truths. The relative political order, with its formulations of limited relative self-other relations, is sublated or negated as constituted by false, karmic, mayic constructions devoid of Truth and Reality. Such empirical, political, relative truths may have epistemic status but no ultimate ontological reality. But this is not Gandhi's political approach. For Gandhi, the relative is our only access to the absolute. We can only speak politically of the ideals of Self and Truth from the imperfect, limited, relative political perspectives of self and truth. At no point can we speak of transcending ethical, political, and other relative dichotomies, including self-other relations.

Therefore, for Gandhi's political thinking, unlike some of traditional Indian philosophy, even in the imperfect realization of the Self or *Atman* or in the realization of the divinity within, there remain key questions about the status of the other and about moral, spiritual, and political self-other relations.[39]

NOTES

1. Parts of what follows in this chapter appear in Douglas Allen, "Philosophical Foundations of Gandhi's Legacy, Utopian Experiments, and Peace Struggles," *Gandhi Marg*, vol. 16, no. 2 (July-Sep. 1994): 133–60 (reprinted in Naresh Dadhich,

ed., *Rethinking Gandhi* [Jaipur: Rawat Publications, 1999]) and Douglas Allen, "Gandhian Perspectives on Self-Other Relations as Relevant to Human Values and Social Change Today," in Ishwar Modi, ed., *Human Values and Social Change,* vol. 1 (Jaipur: Rawat Publications, 1999).

2. For example, particularly troubling to most contemporary political thinkers are the many passages in which Mohandas Gandhi, struggling over political and other crises, insists that God spoke to him, God showed him the way, etc. Although such formulations are capable of different interpretations, they often point to a religious origin and legitimation at odds with modern political thinking insisting on empirical, human, intersubjective, rational justification. Similar concerns of modern political thinking can be directed at Gandhi's numerous, diverse formulations seemingly extolling a religionization of politics, even if Gandhi's orientation is at odds with much of the narrow, militant, exclusivistic, intolerant religionization of politics (and politicization of religion) that one finds in India and the rest of the contemporary world.

3. Very revealing with regard to contemporary political thinking in India are comments made in Dec. 1997 at the Institute of Gandhian Studies in Wardha by Gandhian scholar Usha Thakkar of the Institute of Research on Gandhian Thought and Rural Development in Mumbai. Dr. Thakkar indicated that she does a survey of students at the beginning of her courses in which she contrasts the *artha*-level political approach of Kautilya in his *Arthashastra* with Gandhi's more ethical and spiritual political approach. She asks her students which approach they prefer. She sadly reported that her students consistently and overwhelmingly prefer Kautilya's political approach. In fact, if I recall correctly, she reported that at least 90 percent of her students prefer Kautilya. This is consistent with my clear impression from numerous talks on Gandhi I gave at Indian universities during 1997–1998. Indian students overwhelmingly identified with dominant modern Western models of science, technology, development, economics, political science, philosophy, etc., rather than with Gandhian alternatives. Indeed, several student responses at my talks, sometimes expressed in embarrassed and even defensive pronouncements, were that their parents (or more likely grandparents) admired Gandhi, but that they really know nothing about Gandhi and his political, ethical, or philosophical thinking. What they study and know a lot about are computers and other technology, science, mathematics, "modern" economics and politics, etc., but not Gandhi's alternative thinking.

4. See, for example, Francis Fukuyama, "The End of History," *The National Interest,* no. 16 (Summer 1989) and Francis Fukuyama, *The End of History and the Last Man* (New York: The Free Press, 1992).

5. The following analysis of the Enlightenment is taken from Douglas Allen, "Enlightenment," in *The Encyclopedia of Politics and Religion,* ed. Robert Wuthnow, vol. 1 (Washington, D.C.: Congressional Quarterly, Inc., 1998), 233–35.

6. Some of this analysis, completely unrelated to Gandhi, appears in Douglas Allen, *Myth and Religion in Mircea Eliade* (New York: Garland Publishing, Inc., 1998).

7. This is similar to the criticism of Gandhi's political thinking offered by various Muslim and other Indian critics, even during Gandhi's lifetime. These critics charge that Gandhi is not really respecting the other as other; he is subsuming the other within his universalizing, totalizing, essentializing, hegemonic, metaphysical and spiritual framework which incorporates particular Hindu versions of inclusivism, tolerance, and respect for multiple paths to Truth.

8. In being selective in appropriating what is of value in Gandhi's political thinking, we must avoid a typical unfortunate dichotomy found in India and elsewhere: Either Gandhi is uncritically idealized and even deified as a larger-than-life Mahatma by some admirers or he is uncritically dismissed as reactionary or completely irrelevant by some critics.

9. Rashmi Sharma, *Gandhian Economics: A Human Approach* (New Delhi: Deep & Deep Publications, 1997), 189.

10. Yogesh Chandra, *Rediscovering Gandhi* (London: Century Books, 1997), 1.

11. What follows on truth *(satya)* and nonviolence *(ahimsa)* is taken from my "Philosophical Foundations of Gandhi's Legacy, Utopian Experiments, and Peace Struggles" and my "Gandhian Perspectives on Self-Other Relations as Relevant to Human Values and Social Change Today."

12. Glyn Richards, *The Philosophy of Gandhi* (Atlantic Highlands, N.J.: Humanities Press, and London: Curzon Press, 1991 reprint, originally published in 1982 by Curzon and Barnes & Noble).

13. See, for example, *The Mind of Mahatma Gandhi,* compiled and edited by R. K. Prabhu and U. R. Rao (Ahmedabad: Navajivan Publishing House, 1967), 47–54.

14. *The Collected Works of Mahatma Gandhi* (*CWMG*) (New Delhi: Publications Division, Ministry of Information and Broadcasting, Government of India), 26:224 (*Young India*, 3-5-25).

15. *CWMG*, 48:404 ("Speech at Meeting in Lausanne," 12-8-31).

16. *CWMG*, 48:404. M. K. Gandhi, *An Autobiography or The Story of My Experiments with Truth,* trans. Mahadev Desai (Ahmedabad: Navajivan, first published in 2 vols. in 1927 and 1929; 14th reprint), 503: "My uniform experience has convinced me that there is no other God than Truth."

17. *CWMG*, 48:404.

18. James G. Hart, "Recent Works in Gandhi Studies," *Philosophy East and West,* vol. 44, no. 1 (Jan. 1994), 155–56.

19. *CWMG*, 33:452. See also Judith M. Brown, *Gandhi: Prisoner of Hope* (Delhi: Oxford University Press, 1992), 199.

20. M. K. Gandhi, *An Autobiography,* 420.

21. *CWMG,* 37:348-49 (*Young India,* 10-11-28).

22. *CWMG,* 84:229 (*Harijan,* 6-23-46).

23. M. K. Gandhi, *From Yeravda Mandir: Ashram Observances,* trans. V. G. Desai (Ahmedabad: Navajivan, 1933; 1957 edition), 12–13: "Without *ahimsa* it is not possible to seek and find Truth. *Ahimsa* and Truth are so intertwined that it is practically impossible to disentangle and separate them. They are like the two sides of a coin, or rather of a smooth, unstamped, metallic disc. Who can say which is the obverse, and which is the reverse? Nevertheless, *ahimsa* is the means; Truth is the end. Means to be means must always be within our reach, and so *ahimsa* is our supreme duty. If we take care of the means, we are bound to reach the end sooner or later. When once we have grasped this point, final victory is beyond question."

24. Similarly this view of Truth and its inseparable relation with Self and Nonviolence is key to understanding Gandhi's formulations of the interrelated concepts of *satyagraha* ("Truth-force," "Soul-force," the techniques and applications of nonviolence) and *sarvodaya* ("universal uplift," "welfare of all").

25. M. K. Gandhi, *An Autobiography,* xi–xii.

26. *CWMG,* 84:199 (*Harijan,* 6-2-46).

27. In Douglas Allen, "Philosophical Foundations of Gandhi's Legacy, Utopian Experiments, and Peace Struggles," 142–43, I maintain that Gandhi's ethical approach to self and self-other relations, arising from his key concepts of Truth, Self, and Nonviolence, cannot be classified in terms of the dominant modern normative ethical alternatives of either utilitarian consequentialism or Kantian deontological ethics.

28. *CWMG,* 71:294 *(Harijan,* 3-2-40). It should be obvious that such typical formulations by Gandhi, appealing to ultimate ethical, metaphysical, and religious values, are at odds with dominant modern Western political thinking.

29. Peter Winch, *Ethics and Action* (London: Routledge and Kegan Paul, 1972), esp. ch. 9: "Moral Integrity."

30. See René Descartes, *Meditations on First Philosophy* (Cambridge and New York: Cambridge University Press, 1986).

31. For a more developed formulation of Descartes's orientation and modern Western concepts of self, as well as Hindu, Buddhist, Marxist, and feminist alternative perspectives to this dominant modern Western orientation, see Douglas Allen, "Social Constructions of Self: Some Asian, Marxist, and Feminist Critiques of Dominant Western Views of Self," in *Culture and Self: Philosophical and Religious Perspectives, East and West,* ed., Douglas Allen (Boulder, CO: Westview Press/Harper Collins, 1997), 3–26.

32. For an introduction to Levinas's philosophy, see Emmanuel Levinas, *Ethics and Infinity: Conversations with Philippe Nemo,* trans. Richard A Cohen (Pittsburgh: Duquesne University Press, 1985). For more detailed analysis of Levinas's perspective of ethics as first philosophy and in which I must recognize the primacy of the other and assume moral responsibility for the welfare of the other, see Emmanuel Levinas, *Otherwise Than Being or Beyond Essence,* trans. Alphonso Lingis (The Hague: Martinus Nijhoff, 1981); and Levinas, *Totality and Infinity,* trans. Alphonso Lingis (Pittsburgh: Duquesne University Press, 1969).

33. I found during my presentations and research in India in 1997–1998 that some Indians claimed that this emphasis in Gandhi on restraining the self and recognizing the primacy of the other had made Indians weak, especially when competing with modern Westerners who are not so troubled by questions involving the morality of primary aggressive self-assertion. It saddened me, although it did not surprise me, that so many Indians want to imitate those very characteristics of modern Western economic and political thinking with self-other relations that I find so egotistical, oppressive, exploitative, unjust, and destructive of other human beings and of nature.

34. See Richard G. Fox, *Gandhian Utopia: Experiments with Culture* (Boston: Beacon Press, 1989).

35. What follows is not intended to convey the impression that scholars of Gandhi do not take seriously these questions. A number of Gandhian scholars have done impressive research on Gandhi's approach to self and self-other relations. What I found in India in 1997–1998 was that many Gandhian, non-Gandhian, and anti-Gandhian scholars assume that there are clear, objective, correct answers to these questions. Scholars disagree in their interpretations of Gandhi and in their Gandhian political perspectives, but the frequent assumption is that the other interpretations and perspectives simply have it wrong; that they reflect a misreading and misinterpretation of Gandhi's political and other writings; and that there is one correct, true, or essential Gandhian answer to questions about Gandhi's political approach to self. As I've indicated earlier in this chapter, I find such an essentialist approach inadequate.

36. I do not necessarily view all such ambiguity, complexity, and dialectical tension and contradiction as inherently negative. It is not always the goal of analysis to remove all ambiguity and complexity and to eliminate any sense of dialectical tension and contradiction. My position is that an adequate Gandhian political perspective on self-other relations must sometimes insist on the ambiguity and complexity of specific phenomena and that dialectical tension and contradiction may be a constructive basis for realizing more adequate human values and bringing about needed political change.

37. I am indebted to Rajiv Vora of the Gandhi Peace Foundation in New Delhi for emphasizing this important point. Dr. M. P. Mathai of the School of Gandhian Thought and Development Studies, Mahatma Gandhi University, Kottayam, Kerala, Dr. Sadhna Vora of the Peace Research Centre, Gujarat Vidyapith, Ahmedabad, and other Gandhi scholars also offered invaluable insights on Gandhi's analysis of the inner voice, individual consciousness, and self-other relations.

38. There are many controversial and ambiguous formulations of inner voice, individual consciousness, and self in Gandhi's political and other writings that I shall not consider. For example, Gandhi frequently tells us that his inner voice is the voice of God. Such formulations are open to many interpretations, and, as we've seen, Gandhi prefers the formulation "Truth is God" and sometimes uses Truth, God, Self, and Nonviolence interchangeably. But when discussing his inner voice, Gandhi often writes of the necessity of God's grace. He tells us that he is but an agent or servant of God. His formulations sometimes express a sense of complete passivity on the part of his individual self. God shows him the right path. Some truth, transcending his individual, political, relative consciousness, is disclosed to him, as the voice of God is revealed as his inner voice.

39. My formulations of Gandhi's political thinking—as grounded in his essential metaphysical and spiritual framework, as constituted by dynamic, contextualized, inverted self-other relations, and as revealing complex, unresolved, dialectical tensions and ambiguities regarding the nature of self and self-other relations—could be applied to Gandhi's controversial political analysis of issues extremely relevant to contemporary political thinking. To mention but three examples of such controversial political analysis: Gandhi's political thinking about the priority placed on *swadeshi* and face-to-face decentralized relations; his political formulations of *swaraj*, including the endorsement of certain forms of nationalism and national *swaraj*; and his analysis of legitimate and illegitimate forms of political struggle, including his rejection of class struggle.

17

Gandhi's Legacy

Bhikhu Parekh

Even a half century after Gandhi's death, opinions about his achievements remain deeply divided. For some he was too implacably hostile to modern civilization to offer an adequate understanding of its nature, let alone provide answers to its malaise. For them he was basically a man of action whose major or even sole contribution consisted in leading his country's struggle for independence. Some of his critics regard even this as a mixed legacy. They argue that his basically conservative, puritanical, probourgeois pacifist thought hindered the development of radical political movements, did much long-term harm to the cause of the Dalits (formerly untouchables), burdened the Indian psyche with a paralyzing sense of guilt about economic development, hampered the emergence of a strong and powerful state, created a national schizophrenia about the need to acquire and exercise political power, and perpetuated unrealistic and confused ideas about human sexuality.

Gandhi's admirers take a radically different view. For them he was a man of both thought and action, a rare combination. As a man of thought he saw through the malaise and madness of modernity, and offered an alternative vision that combined the best insights of both the premodern and modern worldviews while avoiding the confusions and contradictions of the currently fashionable postmodernism. Indeed, argue his admirers, if Indians were to be asked to mention their greatest twentieth-century thinker, most would unhesitatingly refer to Gandhi and would feel hard pressed to mention another. Gandhi was also a man of action, and was unique in acting at both political and personal levels. He led the greatest anticolonial struggle in history, organized his deeply divided countrymen, gave them a sense of collective pride, forged tools of collective action that continue to stand India in good stead, and developed a unique method of struggle that combined the energy and effectiveness of violence with the peacefulness and humility of

334

nonviolence. At the personal or moral level, he restlessly strove to create a beautiful soul free of all that was petty, mean, coarse, and vulgar, successfully embarked upon a most heroic struggle to conquer all his senses including sexuality, and offered a rare example of how to lead a political life without compromising one's integrity.

Some of Gandhi's admirers go even further and argue that we should not be surprised if one day he were to prove as influential, and be placed on the same footing, as Jesus of Nazareth and the Buddha. Einstein set the tone for such a view when he remarked in a tribute to Gandhi on his seventieth birthday: "Generations to come, it may be, will scarce believe that such a one as this ever in flesh and blood walked upon this earth."[1] Ralph Boultjens echoed Einstein's view in 1984: "Thirty-five years after the crucifixion of Jesus Christ there was no indication that Christianity would emerge as one of the great spiritual forces of history. Around 450 B.C., three decades after the death of Confucius, nobody could have predicted how influential his ideas eventually became. And around 1915, thirty years after Karl Marx, the Communist movement seemed doomed to be an inconsequential political aberration. Perhaps, then, we are too near Gandhi to evaluate his impact on history."[2]

In my view Gandhi's detractors underestimate the originality of some of his ideas, the depth of his political and moral influence on India and on the rest of the world, and the sheer grandeur and moral beauty of his life. By contrast his worshippers make the opposite mistake of ignoring his confusions and ambiguities as well as the dark underside of some of his ideas and actions. Since this is not the occasion to undertake a detailed critical assessment of Gandhi and to arbitrate between his detractors and worshippers, I have decided to concentrate on what I take to be of lasting value in his life and thought. Accordingly I shall take three areas for close examination. I have selected these three because they relate to issues that agonize us today and about which Gandhi has something extremely important and original to say. These are first, the nature of fundamentalism and religious identity; second, the sources of human suffering and an adequate theory of social change; and third, Gandhi's redefinition of fundamental liberal values and his attempt to give them a much-needed moral and ontological depth.

GANDHI'S RELIGIOUS UNIVERSALISM

Religious fundamentalism has been a considerable source of violence and suffering in recent years in almost every part of the world, including such developed countries as the U.S.A. and such developing countries as Iran, Pakistan, and India. Fundamentalism is a frightened religion's response to the crisis of identity and integrity, and consists in seeking to recapture and uncompromisingly assert what it takes to be its fundamental beliefs and practices. Fundamentalism cannot be countered by abstractly condemning either the religious consciousness itself or its perversions in a spirit of secularist fundamentalism. The best way to deal with it is to understand and criticize it from within, and to show how the fundamentalist approach to religion, although understandable in a specific historical context, profoundly corrupts and ultimately destroys the integrity of the religious consciousness itself. I can think of few who understood the nature of religious consciousness and undermined fundamentalism from within the religious perspective itself as sensitively and effectively as Gandhi did.

For Gandhi every major religion articulated a unique vision of God and emphasized different features of the human condition. The idea of God as loving Father was most fully developed in Christianity, and the emphasis on love and suffering was also unique to it. As he put it: "I cannot say that it is singular, or that it is not to be found in other religions. But the presentation is unique." Austere and rigorous monotheism and the spirit of equality were "most beautifully" articulated in Islam. The distinction between the impersonal and conceptions of God, the principle of the unity of all life, and the doctrine of *ahimsa* (nonviolence) were distinctive to Hinduism. For Gandhi every religion had a distinct moral and spiritual ethos and represented a wonderful and irreplaceable "spiritual composition." To a truly religious person all religions should be "equally dear."

Gandhi argued that since God was infinite and since the limited human mind could grasp only a "fragment" of Him and that too inadequately, every religion was necessarily limited and partial. Even the religions claiming to be directly revealed by God were revealed to men with their fair share of inescapable human limitations and were communicated in the necessarily inadequate human languages.

For Gandhi, every man was born into a particular religion. Since no religion was wholly false, he should be able to work out his destiny in and through it. And if he felt attracted to some aspects of another religion, he should be at liberty to borrow them. When Madeleine Slade wished to become a Hindu, Gandhi advised her against it. She should, he insisted, live by her own Christian faith and absorb into it whatever she liked in Hinduism. Merely changing over to a new religion would not improve her conduct or way of life, the only thing that ultimately mattered. When they were overwhelmed with doubts, Gandhi encouraged his Christian friends to draw new inspiration and strength from their own religion. An American missionary, Stanley Jones, spoke for many of them when he said that Gandhi had reconverted him to Christianity. In a different context he told his Jewish friend, Mrs. Polak, that she need not "become" a Christian in order to "be" one. She could draw inspiration from Jesus' life and teachings and live like a Christian without ceasing to be a Jew.

Religions are commonly thought of as closed worlds, almost like sovereign states zealously guarding their territorial boundaries. No one is allowed to belong to more than one religion, or to borrow the ideas and practices of another, without feeling guilty or threatened at the dilution of his or her religions identity. Interfaith dialogue is therefore expected to occur within and to do nothing to weaken the religious boundaries. Gandhi took a very different view. For him a religion was not a monolithic structure of ideas and practices, but a resource from which one freely borrowed whatever one found attractive and persuasive. As such, it was a collective property and a common human heritage. Every man was born into and deeply shaped by a specific religious tradition which as it were constituted his original family. He also enjoyed varying degrees of membership of other cultural and religious families, to whose achievements he enjoyed an unrestricted right of access. Gandhi said that as a Hindu he was an heir to its rich and ancient heritage. As an Indian he was a privileged inheritor of its diverse religious and cultural traditions. As a human being the great achievements of mankind constituted a collective human capital to which he had as much right as their native claimants. While remaining firmly rooted in his own tradition, he therefore felt free to draw upon the moral and spiritual resources of the others. To express the two central ideas of rootedness and openness, he often used the metaphor of living in a house with its windows wide open. His house was protected by walls and gave him a sense of security, but its windows were wide open to allow cultural winds from all directions to blow into it and to enable him to breathe fresh air at his own pace and in his own way. *Ano Bhadra ritavo yantu vishvatah* (May noble thoughts from all over the world come to us) was one of his favorite classical maxims.

Gandhi took full advantage of his self-proclaimed intellectual freedom. He abstracted what he took to be the central values of Hinduism and set up a critical dialogue, even a confrontation, between them and those derived from other religious traditions. Thus he took over the Hindu concept of *ahimsa* (nonviolence), in his view one of its central moral principles. He found it negative and passive and reinterpreted it in the light of the activist and socially oriented Christian concept of *caritas*. However, he felt that the latter was too emotive, led to worldly attachments and compromised the agent's self-sufficiency, and so he redefined it in the light of the Hindu concept of *anasakti* (nonattachment). His double conversion, his Christianization of a Hindu category after he had suitably Hinduized the Christian concept, yielded the novel idea of an active and positive but detached and nonemotive love. Again, he took over the traditional Hindu practice of fasting as a protest, combined it with the Judaic concept of representative leadership, and the Christian concepts of vicarious atonement and suffering love, interpreted and reinterpreted each in the light of the others, and developed the amazing notion of a "voluntary crucifixion of the flesh." It involved fasting undertaken by the acknowledged leader of a community to atone for the evil deeds of his followers, to awaken their senses of shame and guilt, and to mobilize their moral and spiritual energies for redemptive purposes.

For Gandhi a religion was not a sovereign system of authoritative beliefs and practices which its adherents may violate only on pain of punishment, but a great cultural resource which, like great works of art and literature, belonged to all mankind. One did not have to be a Christian in order to feel entitled to adopt Christian beliefs and practices. And a Hindu or a Muslim who did so did not become a Christian. Indeed, the very terms Christian, Hindu, and Muslim were mistaken and a source of much mischief. They reified respective religions, set up rigid boundaries between them, sanctioned false proprietary claims, and created a psychological and moral pressure toward conformity. In the ultimate analysis, argued Gandhi, there were neither Christians nor Hindus, only whole and unfragmented human beings who freely helped themselves with the moral and spiritual resources of these and other great religious traditions.

One could admire Jesus and even accept him as the son of God, but one could also hold the Buddha, Moses, Mahavira, Zarathustra, and others in equally high regard. Men and women who did so belonged to their specific religions but also to several others. They were Christians or Muslims or Buddhists in the sense that these religious traditions were their native homes or points of spiritual orientation, and satisfied them the most. However, they also cherished and freely drew upon other religious traditions, and carried parts of these into their religion. Whatever one may think of Gandhi's views, he offers the clearest antithesis to fundamentalism and shows that the religious identity, like other kinds of identity, is both rooted and open, both firm and flexible, and is constantly reconstituted in the light of the agent's constantly changing self-understanding. As Gandhi rightly stressed, cultural and religious identities are neither primordial and unalterable as the fundamentalist imagines, nor volitionalist projects to be undertaken and executed at will as the secular rationalist maintains, but products of periodic self-reconstitution based on the inherited resources of one's tradition as interpreted and enriched in the light of changing needs and knowledge of other traditions.

SOCIAL CHANGE THROUGH *SATYAGRAHA*

Gandhi saw more clearly than most other writers both the interdependence of human beings and the ways in which systems of domination were built up and sustained. He argued that all systems of domination rested on a profound misunderstanding of human nature, and wrongly assumed that it was possible for one man or group of men to harm another without also harming themselves. Human beings were necessarily interdependent and formed an organic whole.[3] An individual owed his existence to his parents without whose countless sacrifices he would neither survive nor grow into a sane human being. He grew and realized his potential in a stable and peaceful society, made possible by the efforts and sacrifices of thousands of anonymous men and women. He became a rational, reflective, and moral human being only within a rich civilization created by scores of sages, saints, savants, and scientists. In short every human being owed his humanity to others, and be efited from a world to the creation of which he contributed nothing. As Gandhi put it, every man was "born a debtor," a beneficiary of others' gifts, and his inherited debts were too vast to be repaid. Even a whole lifetime was not enough to pay back what a man owed to his parents, let alone all others. Furthermore the creditors were by their very nature unspecifiable. Most of them were dead or remained anonymous, and those alive were so numerous and their contributions so varied and complex that it was impossible to decide what one owed to whom. To talk about repaying the debts did not therefore make sense except as a clumsy and metaphorical way of describing one's response to unsolicited but indispensable gifts.

Since the debts could never be "repaid" and the favors "returned," all a man could do was to "recognize the conditions of his existence" and to continue the ongoing universal *yajna* or system of sacrifices by accepting his full share of collective responsibility. The only adequate response to the fact that he was born in and constantly sustained by *yajna* was to look upon his own life as *yajna*, an offering at the universal altar, and to find profound joy in contributing to the maintenance and enrichment of both the human world and the cosmos. As Gandhi put it, "Yajna having come to us with our birth we are debtors all our lives, and thus for ever bound to serve the universe." Not rights but obligations were the basis of moral life, and one's rights were embedded in and grew out of others' discharge of their duties.

Since humankind constituted an organic whole and since human beings were necessarily interdependent, every human action was both self- and other-regarding. Directly or indirectly, visibly or invisibly, it affected the collective ethos and shaped the duality of the prevailing pattern of human relationship. "We cannot see this, near-sighted as we are," but it remained an inescapable feature of the necessarily interdependent world.[4] "Rot in one part must inevitably poison the whole system." When human beings developed themselves they awakened others to their potentialities, and inspired, encouraged, and raised them as well. And when they acted inhumanely, both they and others suffered. Even a trivial crime was enough to create a general sense of insecurity, to heighten mutual suspicions, and to lower the moral tone of the entire community. "I believe that if one man gains spiritually the whole world gains with him, and if one man falls the world falls to that extent."[5]

For Gandhi humanity was indivisible, in the sense that no man could degrade or brutalize another without also degrading or brutalizing himself, or inflict psychic and moral damage on others without inflicting it on himself as well. This was so in at least three ways. First, to degrade others was to imply that a human being may be so treated, and thus to lower the expected level of the moral minimum due to every human being from which all alike suffered. "To slight a single human being is . . . to harm not only that human being but with him the whole world." Second, to degrade and dehumanize others was to damage their pride, self-respect, and potential for good, and thus both to deny oneself and

ιne world the benefits of their possible contributions and to add to the collective moral, psychological, and financial cost of repairing the damage they were
likely to do to themselves and to others. Third, as beings capable of morality
and critical self-reflection, human beings could not degrade or maltreat others
without hardening themselves against the latter's suffering and cries for help,
building up distorted systems of self-justification, coarsening their moral sensi-
bilities, and lowering their own and the collective level of humanity. As Gandhi
put it, no man "takes another down a pit without descending into it himself and
sinning in the bargain." Since humanity was indivisible and since basic human
interests were harmonious, every man was responsible to and for others and
should be deeply concerned about how they lived.

Gandhi's concept of indivisible humanity formed the basis of his critique
of systems of oppression and exploitation. Such dominant groups as the
whites in South Africa, the colonial governments in India and elsewhere, and
the rich and the powerful in every society, naively imagined that their exploitation and degradation of their respective victims did not in any way
damage them as well. In fact they suffered as much as their victims and
sometimes even more. The white South Africans could not deprive the
blacks of their livelihood and dignity without suppressing their inner doubts
and tender feelings, damaging their capacities for critical self-reflection and
impartial self-assessment, and falling victim to moral conceit, morbid fears,
and irrational obsessions. In brutalizing the blacks they also brutalized themselves, and were only prevented by their arrogance from noticing how sad,
empty, and pitiable their lives had become. They did enjoy more material
comforts, but they were neither happier nor better human beings. The colonial rulers met the same fate. They could not dismiss the natives as "effemi-
nate" and "childlike" without thinking of themselves as tough, hypermascu-
line, and unemotional adults, a self-image to which they could not conform
without distorting and impoverishing their potential. In misrepresenting the
natives, they misrepresented themselves and fell into their own traps. They
also took home the attitudes, habits, and styles of government acquired
abroad, and corrupted their own society. Colonialism did promote their material interests, but only at the expense of their larger and infinitely more important moral and spiritual interests. For Gandhi material interests had only
an instrumental significance, and were positively harmful when they hampered moral and spiritual development.

On the basis of his concept of human unity Gandhi arrived at a novel theory of social change.[6] He readily agreed that no dominant group ever gave
up power without a struggle. However, he was convinced that such a struggle could not be adequately conceptualized in terms of, and conducted by
means advocated by, the fundamentally flawed traditional theory of revolution. In his view the fact that almost every revolution so far had led to terror,
devoured its children, and failed to create a better society was a proof of this.
These failures were not accidental but sprang from the Manichean view of

the world lying at the basis of the traditional theory of revolution. The theory neatly separated good and evil, and saw human existence as a mortal struggle between them. Since no cause could be nobler than the elimination of evil, everything done to eliminate evil including the use of massive violence was considered justified. The misguided belief that evil had no rights lay at the basis of revolutionary morality. Those identified as evil were deemed to have forfeited their humanity, and the concomitant claims on their fellow men's understanding and charity.

Gandhi argued that far from being mutually exclusive, good and evil were conceptually and existentially inseparable. Nothing was good except in a specific context and within a specific pattern of human relationship; what was good in one context was not so in another; good turned into evil when pressed beyond a certain point; and what was good for one man might not be so for another. Given the scarcity of time, money, energy, and emotional resources, a moral agent had to make choices, and sometimes had to sacrifice or forego good in order to achieve what in his view was better. Every moral deed had a price, and good was necessarily shadowed by evil. Furthermore in a world full of evil, good could not exist, let alone be effective, without participating in evil, and no evil could last a day, without some basis of goodness to give it strength and organization. Since good and evil were inseparable and at times indistinguishable, they could not be socially separated and ascribed to different classes or groups. Groups were composed of men, each a bearer of good and evil properties. Even the apparently innocent victims of an unjust social order actively or passively, wittingly or unwittingly, collaborated in their oppression and bore some responsibility for their predicament. Mankind therefore could not be divided into two neat classes, one so fallen or corrupt that it forfeited its claim to humanity, the other so privileged that it had a right to punish the rest. This did not mean that some men or groups might not behave in an evil manner and deserve to be restrained, but rather that this reflected only one aspect of their personality and did not foreclose the possibility of their future regeneration.

In Gandhi's view the traditional theory of revolution did not fully appreciate the subtle ways in which good suffered corruption in its struggle against evil. The theory located good in the ends of an action, judging the allegedly amoral means in exclusively instrumental forms. Since the so-called ends were in turn means to some other allegedly higher ends, everything ultimately got reduced to a mere means. Violence, mendacity, cunning, duplicity, manipulation of the opponent, and so on were all considered legitimate if used in the pursuit of good ends. By resorting to such means, good subtly became transformed into evil and its victory was really its defeat.

Gandhi argued that we needed a new theory of revolution that was free from the defects of the old and structurally protected against degeneration into terror. Such a theory had to be grounded in the three central principles of the unity of man, the indivisibility of means and ends, and a non-Manichean view of the world. It should stand up not just for the interests of the oppressed but for the shared interests of all including the oppressors, and aim at a society in which all alike led richer and more humane lives. For Gandhi imperialism damaged both the British and the Indians, and needed to be ended in the interests of both. Untouchability inflicted a grave moral and emotional damage not just on the untouchables but also on the caste Hindus, and its abolition promoted the interests of both. A revolution was justified only if the society it sought to establish did not replace one set of masters by another and put an end to all forms of class rule.

Like Marx, Gandhi argued that revolutionary consciousness sprang from an intense sensitivity to human suffering, and had a special affinity with the oppressed, its natural constituency and object of concern. Unlike Marx, however, he insisted that the oppressed were never wholly innocent and free from their share of human failings, nor the oppressors wholly evil and devoid of their share of human virtues. Both alike were caught up in a self-reproducing system which debilitated and brutalized them all and from which they needed to be liberated. Being more deharmonized and brutalized than the rest, the oppressed were more acutely aware of the need for liberation and had to initiate the emancipatory process. However, even as no oppressive system could last without the cooperation of its morally implicated victims, it could not be conclusively ended without the cooperation, however grudging, of its erstwhile masters. The latter had to be assured that the revolution did not intend to physically eliminate them, that it was concerned with their well-being as well, and that it recognized them as human beings entitled to decency and respect.

For Gandhi the means-end dichotomy lying at the heart of the traditional revolutionary theory was fundamentally false. In human life the so-called means consisted not of implements and inanimate tools but of human actions, and by definition these could not fall outside the jurisdiction of morality. Furthermore the method of fighting for an objective was not external to but an integral part of it. Every step toward a desired goal shaped its character, and utmost care had to be taken to ensure that the steps taken to realize it did not distort or damage the goal. The goal did not exist *at the end* of a series of actions designed to achieve it; it shadowed them from the very beginning. The so-called means were really ends in an embryonic form, the seeds of which the so-called ends were a natural flowering. Since this was so, the fight for a just society could not be conducted by unjust means.

Gandhi's theory of *satyagraha*, the "surgery of the soul" as he called it, was his alternative to the traditional theory of revolution.[7] It was not so much a nonviolent method of achieving revolutionary ends as a novel way of defining the very idea of revolution. Like Trotsky's permanent revolution, it was a form of gentle but sustained social pressure designed to break down emotional, ideological, and moral barriers that different groups built around themselves, to unfreeze the flow of social sympathy, and to enrich and deepen their consciousness of interdependence.

Even as every community required a widespread sense of justice to hold it together, it presupposed a deeper sense of shared humanity to give meaning and energy to its sense of justice. The sense of humanity consisted in the recognition of the fundamental ontological fact that humanity was indivisible, that human beings grew and fell together, and that in degrading and brutalizing others, they degraded and brutalized themselves. It constituted a community's vital moral capital without which it had no defense, and no resources to fight against the forces of injustice, exploitation, and oppression. The slow and painful task of cultivating and consolidating the sense of humanity, and thereby laying the foundations of a truly moral community, was an essential collective responsibility, which the *satyagrahi* took it upon himself to discharge. He assumed the burden of the common evil, sought to liberate both himself and his opponent from its tyrannical automatism, and helped reduce the prevailing level of inhumanity. He overcame his opponent by refusing to see him as one, and by appealing instead to his sense of decency and their common humanity. As Gandhi put it, the old sages "returned good for evil and killed it." The *satyagrahi* took his stand on this "fundamental moral truth."

For Gandhi a *satyagrahi* relied on the power of suffering love. Confronted with untruth he sought a dialogue with his opponent. When this was denied or reduced to an insincere exercise in public relations, he took a stand and accepted whatever punishment was meted out to him. Since his sole concern was to evoke a moral response in his opponent, he did everything necessary to put him at ease and nothing to harass, embarrass, anger, or frighten him. In the meantime he suffered the punishment without hatred or ill-will in the hope of triggering off in him a slow, intensely personal, and highly complex process of self-examination. The moment his opponent showed willingness to talk in a spirit of genuine good will, he suspended the struggle and gave reason a chance to work in a more hospitable climate.

With all its limitations which I cannot here explore, Gandhi's theory of *satyagrah* offered important insights into the nature of political praxis. Like the rationalists, he stressed the importance of rational discussion; unlike them, however, he realized that what passed as rational discussion was often little more than alternative monologues or a public relations exercise, and that sticking to it under such circumstances was an act of irrationality. Even as Gandhi was aware of the limits of rationality, he was acutely conscious of the dangers of violence. He knew that narrow rationalism and violence tended to feed off each other, and that the failure of rationality rendered violence morally respectable. Accordingly he sought to break through the narrow straitjacket of the reason-violence dichotomy lying at the basis of traditional rationalism. He imaginatively explored the uncharted terrain between reason and violence and arrived at novel forms of political praxis. His *satyagraha* was basically a new form of dialogue, a new conception of discussion, embedded in a richer and more realistic theory of rationality. Although not rational in the narrow sense of the term, it was not irrational either. It was a way

of enabling human beings to realize their potential for rationality and goodness, and to reach and act on the basis of an inherently tentative and constantly deepening perception of consensual truth.

REDEFINITION OF VALUES

Gandhi's conceptualization of political life and redefinitions of such central
concepts as liberty *(swaraj)*, equality *(samata)*, citizenship *(nagarikata)*,
rights *(adhikar)*, obligation *(dharma)*, and tolerance *(sahishnuta)* also con-
tain important insights and deserve close study. We shall take the first three
by way of illustration.

Like many Hindu philosophers Gandhi took little interest in the concept of
human nature, largely because he took a radically individualistic view of
man. Each individual was unique, followed his own path of moral and spiritual evolution, and had a distinct *swabhava,* that is, a distinct and firm but
relatively open and within limits malleable constitution or nature. It was true
that all men shared certain *gunas* or qualities in common. However, these
were too general and indeterminate to account for the unique constitution of
each individual. The qualities were also largely passive, capable of neither
mechanical nor teleological causality, and unable to explain human conduct.
Since the concept of human nature had no explanatory power, it had neither
theoretical nor practical significance for Gandhi.

For Gandhi the individual's *swabhava* had two sources.[8] First, he was endowed at birth with a specific physical and mental constitution, temperament,
tendencies, and dispositions. Gandhi thought this a legacy of his previous life,
but we need not accept such an explanation. Second, each individual was a
member of a specific community which deeply shaped his habits, character,
memories, ideals, and values, and gave his personality a distinct tone and
color. The two together shaped his psychological and moral constitution
(swabhava), which was thus a unique blend of his socially transcendental and
socially acquired characteristics. It held him together, persisted over time, and
formed the basis of his personal identity. Since it was the basis of his being and
made him the person he was, it constituted his ontological foundation or truth
(satya). The Sanskrit word *satya*, meaning truth, is derived from *sat,* meaning
reality or that which endures over time. The opposite of *sat* is *maya*, meaning
illusory, ephemeral, transient, or only relatively real.

The *satya* or the truth of an individual limited and guided but did not pre-
determine his choices and decisions. As a rational being endowed with such
capacities as introspection, critical self-reflection, and choice, he was able to
uncover and take a critical view of some of the constitutive elements of his
identity and to reconstitute it in a desired manner. Many aspects of his constitution, however, were too deep to be excavated by even the most rigorous
self-examination, and remained beyond his control. And some of those as-

pects of which he did become aware were often too deeply entrenched and tenacious to be changed without superhuman courage. Human beings were therefore neither absolutely free nor totally determined, but free within limits. The depth and extent of the limits were not and could not be the same for all. They depended on such factors as their capacity for self-analysis, moral honesty, willpower, and the kind of society in which they lived. A co-operative and relaxed society, whose members freely commented on each other's conduct and contributed to their self-knowledge, was more conducive to their self-transformation and freedom than one in which they scrupulously kept their distance. Not how to be absolutely free or fully autonomous but how to change in harmony with one's truth was the central moral problem for Gandhi, as for most Hindu thinkers. Faced with a ceaselessly changing world, the self must change or risk disintegration. And critical self-reflection constantly exposed failings and limitations which a moral being should try to overcome. The art of living consisted in how to change and yet "remain true to oneself," how to grow without losing one's ontological moorings, how to assimilate the new and reconstitute one's being without losing a sense of balance and coherence. A wise man resisted attractive but impossible ideals, knew and lived in harmony with his constitution, and strove for goals that accorded with his "truth."

Unlike the traditional liberal conception of individuality which stresses differences from others and is necessarily comparative, integration or wholeness in Gandhi's sense referred to the individual's relation to himself rather than to others and to his manner of ontologically carrying himself in the world. An integrated individual had integrity and was always "true" or "honest" to himself. In being true to himself and changing at his own pace, he retained his uniqueness or individuality, which was thus a by-product of self-integration and not a form of eccentricity or an abstract desire to be different from others. Individuality presupposed inner coherence, and the latter in turn required critical self-reflection. An unreflective person, one not in the habit of reflecting on and reconstituting her being, was constantly in danger of becoming an eclectic collection of borrowed and discordant properties. Critical self-reflection was the source of self-knowledge, and a necessary condition of wholeness and individuality.

As a uniquely constituted and situated being, each individual necessarily saw and experienced the world differently and formed his own beliefs and opinions. To force him to act against his sincerely held beliefs was to violate his truth, to ask him to be untrue to himself, to plant a lie at the very heart of his being. He might be mistaken, but he must discover that for himself. Others might, indeed they had a duty to, argue with him and to show him why he was mistaken. If he remained unpersuaded, they should leave him alone. For Gandhi respect for an individual's integrity or wholeness required that his views should grow out of *his* way of looking at the world and reflect *his* truth. That was why persuasion was qualitatively different from coercion.

Unlike the latter, it respected and reinforced the other's wholeness, and ensured that the new way of looking at the world took roots in and grew out of his changed being. To seek to persuade someone was to cooperate in reconstituting his being. Gandhi thought that an individual could be legitimately compelled only when his conduct had grave social consequences and when he could not be deterred in any other way. And even then no euphemism or verbal sophistry should be allowed to obscure the fact that compulsion violated his truth or integrity and was a regrettable necessity.

For Gandhi freedom consisted in being true to oneself, in living by "one's own light" and growing at "one's own pace." It was a form of wholeness or integrity. It involved knowing and accepting oneself as one was, recognizing one's limits and possibilities, and making choices on the basis of that knowledge. If my way of life suited me and if I was content with it, I did not cease to be free simply because I had not chosen it. Or if I realized on reflection that a specific desire did not harmonize with my being and decided not to gratify it, I could not be said to be unfree simply because I had to restrain my desire. Freedom did not consist in choice *per se* as some liberals argue, nor in making choices considered to be *higher* as the idealists argue, but in making choices in harmony with and capable of being integrated into one's being. It had nothing to do with the *number* of alternatives available to the agent either. If they did not include the one she needed, they had no significance for her. And if the one she needed was the only one available to her, the absence of others in no way diminished her freedom.

Like many Indian philosophers, Gandhi subsumed freedom under truth. Only the free man, that is one able to make his choices and decisions himself, was able to discover, develop, and live by his unique ontological truth. Freedom was thus the necessary basis and precondition of one's ability to be true to oneself. To deny a man freedom was to force him to be untrue to himself and to live by someone else's truth. For Gandhi the case for freedom was simple, and the same as that for truthfulness. Respect for truth implied respect for human beings as they were constituted at a given point in time, and for their desire to live by their truth. Love of truth involved love of one's fellow men as they were constituted, and not as one would like them to be. It could never therefore justify "forcing them to be free" or sacrificing them at the altar of an abstract and impersonal ideal.

Even as Gandhi radically redefined the concept of freedom, he redefined the concept of equality. In much of the liberal and socialist literature on the subject, equality is defined in comparative, contractual, competitive, and individualist terms. As we saw earlier, for Gandhi men were necessarily interdependent, rose and fell together, and were born subject to nonrepayable debts. He located the idea of equality in this context. Relations between human beings were mediated by their membership of the social whole, and thus nonatomic and noncontractual in nature. Human beings grew and fell together, and hence their relations were necessarily noncompetitive and nonconflictual. And since they were uniquely constituted and had different needs and capacities, they were inherently noncomparable and could not be treated according to a uniform standard.

Since society was necessarily a fellowship of unique and interdependent beings, the concept of equality had to be defined in noncomparative, non-competitive, and nonatomic terms. For Gandhi it basically consisted in each individual enjoying full access to his community's economic, political, moral, and cultural resources in order to realize *his* unique potential: that is, not an abstract human potential as determined by a philosophical conception of human nature or by an arbitrary moral standard, but his potential as a *uniquely constituted being*. As a progressive and reflecting being each individual "grew from truth to truth" and strove to enrich, deepen, and reconstitute his being. Equality of human beings consisted in all alike being able to do so. It did not mean that I should get what others get, but rather that I should get what I need for my development as I define it. It was not only in my interest but that of all others that they should treat me equally, for in degrading and demeaning me they degraded and demeaned themselves and deprived themselves of the contribution I would make as a rich human being. Equality thus was not a mechanical concept or a synonym for uniformity. It was at bottom a relationship of mutuality and fellowship.

Gandhi also redefined the concept of citizenship. As a political activist he knew that not consent, nor will, nor fear, but cooperation was the basis of the state.[9] Every state, democratic or otherwise, depended on the cooperation of its citizens, be it silent or vocal, passive or active, willing or unwilling. Since the state was an agency of action, their cooperation consisted in rendering it such specific services as carrying out its orders, paying taxes, and obeying the law. The state did not exist independently of its citizens, and was ultimately nothing more than a system of institutionalized cooperation between them. Since the state was a vast and complex organization, they did not notice that it was their acts of daily cooperation that sustained it and that they were morally responsible for all it said and did.

Every government was tempted to misuse its power, and the democratic government was in that respect no better than the autocratic. What distinguished the two was the fact that one did and the other did not succumb to the temptation. And that was so because a democratic government knew that if it did, its citizens would refuse to cooperate with it. Notwithstanding all its institutional checks and balances, a democratic government could easily turn evil if its citizens became apathetic, vulnerable to corruption and manipulation, or lost their sense of moral responsibility. For Gandhi the virtues and vices of a government were not inherent in it but derived from those of its people. It was the coward who created the bully, the worm who encouraged others to trample on it, the morally irresponsible citizen who created a tyrant.

As a moral being the citizen had a duty to decide to whom to give his loyalty and support and under what conditions. His self-respect and dignity required that his loyalty should not be unconditional or taken for granted. When a law was just, he had a "sacred duty" to give it his "willing and spontaneous obedience." The duty had a dual basis. As a moral being he had a general duty to do or support good. And as a citizen he had a specific moral duty to the community into which he was born and rooted, by which he was profoundly shaped, whose benefits he had enjoyed, and to whose members he was bound by the ties of loyalty and mutual expectation. If a law was unjust or morally unacceptable, he had a duty to protest against and even to disobey it. To obey an unjust law was to "participate in evil" and to incur moral responsibility for its immoral consequences.[10] In Gandhi's view it was a "mere superstition" and an attitude worthy of a "slave" to believe that a citizen should uncritically obey all laws. To be a citizen was to be coresponsible for the activities of the government.[11] And to obey a law was necessarily to support the government. Citizenship was not an autonomous and discrete role, but a mode of expressing and realizing one's wholeness and humanity through the medium of the state. No human being could extend uncritical and absolute support to the state without forfeiting his humanity.

LIVING DIFFERENTLY

I have so far concentrated on Gandhi's thought, and that is only a small and ultimately perhaps not the most important part of his remarkable life. Unlike men of thought whose ideas can be detached from and examined in isolation from their lives, Gandhi's thought, like that of Jesus and the Buddha, is deeply embedded in and of a piece with his way of life. His ideas grew out of his reflections on his experiences, even as his life represented a determined attempt to live out the ideals he espoused. The two formed a unity such that his ideas are best articulated not in the books and articles he wrote but in the kind of life he lived. His life was his greatest book and provides the most reliable clue to his writings.

For the first thirty-odd years of his life, Gandhi was a *Grihasthi* (householder) who, in dutiful obedience to the conventions of his society, married, raised children, and discharged his social obligations. After that he felt free to disregard the social conventions and to write the script of his life as he thought proper. His central moral passion from now onwards was to attain *moksha*, a Hindu concept which had exercised him greatly for the past few years and which he radically redefined in the light of his understanding of his own religious tradition as well as Christianity and Judaism. In this redefinition *moksha* meant three things: first, total mastery of all the senses including sexuality; second, a mind freed of fear, jealousy, pettiness, meanness, vanity, and so on; and third, total dissolution of the sense of selfhood and the consequent identification with all living beings in a spirit of universal love and dedication to the cause of "wiping away every tear from every eye." The first two primarily related to the personal, and the third to the social and political areas of life. Gandhi carried on an intense struggle at all three levels and sought to forge a pure and beautiful soul. The struggle was fierce and uncompromising and marked by moments of doubts and despair, but the overall result was a life of rare moral and spiritual grandeur.

A few random incidents of his remarkable life tell the story. During one of his many periods of incarceration, a black warden was bitten by a scorpion. When Gandhi heard his screams, he rushed to the spot, called for a doctor, and in the meantime started sucking out the poisoned blood, without the slightest thought for his life and in utter disregard of his own bleeding teeth. He went on spitting out the sucked blood until the victim felt relief, and quietly left the place as if nothing had happened.[12]

Indulal Yajnik, his one-time close colleague, turned against him and wrote a vicious attack on him. He regretted this later and went to Gandhi to apologize. It was Gandhi's day of silence. He saw Yajnik among his visitors and, before the latter could say anything, greeted him with a reassuring smile and sent him a hastily scribbled note complimenting him for changing sides only once whereas he, Gandhi, had done so more often. The poor Yajnik was in tears.[13]

Maulana Azad, the Congress President, had without Gandhi's knowledge and against his wishes sent Stafford Cripps, the visiting British minister, a confidential note saying that he and the Congress had an open mind on the partition of India. When Cripps called on Gandhi, he was surprised to find that Gandhi knew nothing about the note and left it with him to mull over. When Azad went to see Gandhi the next day, the latter asked him if there was any communication between him and Cripps. Azad lied. Although his note to Cripps was lying on Gandhi's desk, Gandhi kept quiet. After Azad's departure Gandhi's secretary suggested that the note should be copied and kept for a future occasion. Gandhi rebuked him, asked him to return the original to Cripps, and blamed himself for being unworthy of Azad's trust.

At one of his prayer meetings in 1947, a bomb exploded. As the frightened crowd began to scatter, Gandhi rebuked it for being frightened of a "mere bomb," and continued to pray unperturbed. When the Government of India insisted that he should henceforth curtail his activities or at least accept protection, he rejoined that both courses of action compromised his commitment to nonviolence and were unacceptable to him.

When Indian independence was drawing near, there was extensive intercommunal violence. Gandhi was deeply distressed and thought his entire life a failure. Not given to despair and defeat, he decided to fight the wave of violence single-handed. Disregarding their physical safety, he and his followers fanned out into remote trouble spots and strove to create intercommunal peace. Believing, wrongly in my view, that he would be able to end the violence only if he eliminated all traces of violence and aggressiveness in himself, he embarked upon the daredevil experiments of sleeping naked with his female associates to achieve total purity.[14]

Although attacked and shunned by his colleagues, he stuck to his guns. Just because they had made him a Mahatma, he was not prepared to conform to their expectations of him. His life was his and it had to be based on *his* truth. If that meant losing his Mahatmahood, he was only too happy to shed the burden, and if it involved public criticism, he was prepared to brave it so long as he was convinced after deepest reflection that his action was right. Such an uncompromising spirit of moral independence is rare in any society; in a largely conventional India, it stood out as an enduring public symbol of dissent and defiance.

It is difficult to say whether or not and which of Gandhi's ideas would prove of lasting value. However, there is little doubt that his life had a rare grandeur about it. His uncompromising commitments to truth and justice, his courage to write the script of his life himself, his relentless search for coherence and wholeness, his total lack of fear, his constant experiments with the possibilities of human existence, and so on are lasting sources of inspiration. As Gandhi said in 1937, "My writings should be cremated with my body. What I have done will endure, not what I have said or written." His life is surely his greatest legacy. And since it was a carefully crafted text, his thought too shares in its permanence.

NOTES

1. See my "Einstein's Assessment of Gandhi," *The Round Table*, 1991.

2. Ralph Boultjens, "Gandhi: The Other Side of the Balance Sheet," in *Gandhi in the Postmodern Age*, eds. Krolik and Cannon (Golden, Colorado: Colorado School of Mines Press, 1984), 15.

3. From M. K. Gandhi, *Yeravada Mandir* (Ahmedabad: Navajivan, 1932), ch. 15.

4. *The Collected Works of Mahatma Gandhi (CWMG)* (New Delhi: Publication Division, Ministry of Information and Broadcasting, 1958-1994), 50:218; Raghavan Iyer, *The Moral and Political Writings of Mahatma Gandhi* (Oxford; Clarendon Press, 1986), II, 552f.

5. *Young India*, 12-4-24.

6. Iyer, *Moral and Political Writings*, II, sec. VI.

7. *Moral and Political Writings*, 298ff.

8. *Harijan*, 6-2-46 and 4-7-46; see also preface to his *The Story of My Experiments with Truth* (Ahmedabad: Navajivan, 1956) and *CWMG*, 50:216. I have discussed this more fully in my *Gandhi's Political Philosophy*, 92f. As Shankara put it, the real nature or disposition of a thing constituted its truth *(tasya bhavah tattvam)*. The *Gita*, ch. 18, verse 47, talks of *swabhavaniyatam karma*, that is, duties that are consonant with the individual's psychological and moral constitution.

9. Raghavan Iyer, *Moral and Political Writings*, 355.

10. *Young India*, 7-22-20.

11. *Young India*, 12-1-20, 6-1-21 and 1-5-22; see also *Hind Swaraj*, 80f.

12. Indulal K. Yajnik, *Gandhi As I Know Him* (Delhi: Danish Mahal, 1943), 303.

13. For this and the following incidents, see Pyarelal, *Mahatma Gandhi: The Last Phase*, two vols. (Ahmedabad: Navajivan, 1956).

14. Pyarelal, *Mahatma Gandhi* I, Bk. 2, ch. xi.

18

Gandhi's Contribution to Global Nonviolent Awakening

Glenn D. Paige

It is said that when Gandhi spoke to villagers he frequently pointed to the fingers of his left hand to represent five great calls for problem-solving action that confronted India in the struggle for independence: spinning, removal of untouchability, improvement of the status of women, abstinence from drugs and alcohol, and achievement of Hindu-Muslim harmony. Then it is said he would point to his wrist and say, "This is nonviolence."[1]

If we had the joy of his presence today, Gandhi might summarize the pressing problems confronting our global village in a similar way. Pointing to the fingers of his left hand, he might say, "Here are the problems we must solve: peace and disarmament, economic justice, human rights, preservation of the environment, and realization of problem-solving cooperation among all the peoples of the earth." Then, pointing to his wrist, he might add, "This is nonviolence, the way we must go about solving these problems."

I do not intend to belabor you with yet another detailed recitation of these crucial threats to the survival and well-being of humankind: the threat of war with weapons of increasingly suicidal lethality, and the need for disarmament; the unspeakable impoverishment of vast masses of our fellow human beings contrasted with the opulence of others, and the need to ensure the welfare of all; the massive violations of human dignity deriving from discrimination on the basis of religion, color, gender, class, caste, nationality, ideology, and other pretexts for oppression as well as the need for mutual recognition of common humanity; the threats to the life-sustaining capacity of the biosphere (land, sea, and air) posed by ignorance, greed, and noxious technologies as well as the need for all to respect the life of the planet; and finally, the divisiveness among nations and classes, rich and poor, strong and weak, exploiter and exploited as well as the need for cooperation among all to realize global *sarvodaya* (wellbeing of all).

Gradually an awareness of these problems, both individually and collectively, is beginning to enter the consciousness of humankind. This is coming about as the result of dedicated actions by many individuals, voluntary organizations, some governments, and intergovernmental organizations such as the United Nations, as well as by performing artists and the mass media.

From one perspective, these threats are being perceived as global problems requiring global solutions. From another, they are problems that we confront in our daily lives: individually, in our families, in our villages, towns, and cities, in our nations, and beyond. That is, we are faced with violence, economic needs, violations of dignity, deteriorating environments, and divisiveness in each circle of our lives from the individual to the global.

As we confront these problems, many of us are gradually becoming aware that our continued acceptance of violence—our willingness to kill—while not the only causal factor, is nevertheless a major cause of these increasing threats to human survival and well-being. Our historic readiness to kill for security and revolutionary change has brought us to a mental and technological state in which no one on earth is safe from destruction. We are now able to kill more people, more quickly, in more ways, and with more far-reaching consequences than in any other age. As ancient wisdom warned us, and as Gandhi taught, violence begets violence, and we are faced with prospects of infinite ingenuity in discovering new ways to destroy each other.

Our willingness to kill contributes to economic deprivation in many ways. It directly diverts morality, intellect, science, labor, capital, resources, and technology from service to human needs. Our gigantic global military establishment and its deadly opponents also contribute to economic death and destruction by preventing the need-responsive structural changes among nations and classes that will be required to realize the material well-being of all. The gun in service to power, greed, hatred, and ignorance—as well as to more lofty aims such as peace, freedom, and justice—kills by impoverishment as well as by force.

Our commitment to violence in pursuit of human rights places these rights in eternal jeopardy. The violent freedom and justice fighter of today becomes tomorrow's deadly threat. One righteous atrocity evokes another and hate-filled grievances echo across the centuries. No individual, family, group, organization, community, religion, culture, or nation can be safe in freedom and justice as long as right depends on might.

And the more human needs for cultural identity, material adequacy, and freedom of expression are suppressed by violence, the more the counterviolence that can be expected. Because such needs are common to all, the poor and rich, the strong and weak, the use of violence to assert human rights leaves each and all in perpetual fearfulness.

Furthermore, our continued commitment to violence threatens to kill the life-sustaining capabilities of Mother Earth. We kill directly by employment and testing of nuclear, biochemical, and other weapons of mass destruction that threaten the land, sea, and air upon which all things depend for life. The vast military consumption of fossil fuels and the wastes produced by nuclear power contribute to present and long-range environmental contamination. The resource depletion and toxic wastes produced by industries that are deemed necessary to produce weapons and services for modern warfare further contribute to environmental devastation. So great is the environmental destructiveness of global militarization and associated disrespect for ecological vitality, that environmentalist Barry Commoner has recently warned us that we are in a suicidal "war with the planet" and that the planet inevitably will win. He warns that "survival depends equally on ending the war with nature and on ending wars among ourselves. . . . To make peace with the planet we must make peace with the peoples who live in it."[2]

Finally our commitment to violence divides us into armored states that resist cooperation to solve problems in the interest of all. Militarized nationalism absolves us of responsibility for the welfare of others. With soldiers, ships, and aircraft we subdivide planetary space—forgetting that sun, wind, earth, and oceans, as well as plants and animals, have no citizenship. Every expert on global hunger tells us that the basic obstacle is not capability to produce food but the politics of inequitable distribution within and among nation/states.

Furthermore, the problems of war, human rights, and environmental pollution cannot be solved solely within national boundaries. Like economic justice, they require the life respecting cooperation of humanity.

Increasingly we are coming to understand that these five problems are both interrelated as well as derived from cultural acceptance of violence. Militarization, for example, increases insecurity, exacerbates poverty, depresses human rights, harms the environment, and divides humankind. Fearfully selfish divisiveness in turn leads to economic deprivation, lack of respect for human rights, inability to cooperate for environmental protection, and to agressive militarization. Economic injustice incites to violence, violates human rights, despoils the environment, and divides communities.

As we awaken to the threat to global survival posed by customary violence-accepting cultures, we simultaneously search for sources of nonviolent inspiration and problem-solving alternatives. This leads inevitably to the discovery of Gandhi, his life and message, of India, the society that nurtured and tested him, and of his successors in India and elsewhere as they seek to carry forward the spirit and substance of his work. Without any doubt, Gandhi, as supported by those who made his work possible, is the principal contributor to global nonviolent awakening in the twentieth century. Of course, when we turn to Gandhi, we discover not him alone but also Kasturba Gandhi, Kamala Nehru, Sarojini Naidu, Sucheta Kripalani, Sushila Nayar, Ganga Behn, and other courageous women, as well as Jawaharlal Nehru, Vinoba Bhave, J. P. Narayan, Abdul Ghaffar Khan, Maulana Azad, C. F. Andrews, Horace Alexander,

G. Ramachandran, and many others. Additionally, when we turn to India we discover not only Gandhian nonviolence but the principled nonviolence of other great spiritual and practical leaders such as that of Acharya Tulsi of the Terapanth Jains, his *anuvrat* [small vow] movement, and its associated institutions like the Anuvrat Vishva Bharat (Anuvrat Global Organization), and the Jain Vishva Bharati Institute (Deemed University).

Gandhi's nonviolent influence can be expected to increase in world affairs in the twenty-first century. Despite the darkness of the past and of the present moment, the lights of nonviolence being lit throughout the world provide signs of great hope.

So let us turn from the violent problems of the fingers of the left hand to the nonviolent promise of the fingers of the right. What are the key elements of the nonviolent legacy that Gandhiji has bequeathed to all who seek guidance in contributing to nonviolent global transformation? There are, of course, many—but to continue the imagery of the hand, let us emphasize five.

First is Gandhi's insistence that nonviolence is profoundly *spiritual*. The word is spiritual, not sectarian. In insisting that nonviolence must be based on a living faith in God—defined as truth and love—Gandhi calls upon us to root our work for nonviolence solidly in the principal teaching of all the spiritual faiths, great and small, that have inspired the development of human civilization. Surely the voice of God, the Creator, or the divine presence in life, however conceived, has not been calling upon humankind to go out and kill our fellow human beings and to destroy our planetary home. Rather this voice has been calling upon us to love one another, respect life, and care for the gift of nature into which we are born.

The proof of this assertion is that there are now and have been nonviolent adherents of every faith drawing inspiration from deep within the wellsprings of their tradition. This includes nonviolent adherents of indigenous spiritual traditions (such as Hawaiians), nonviolent Bahais, nonviolent Buddhists, nonviolent Christians (Catholic and Protestant), nonviolent Hindus, nonviolent Jews, nonviolent Muslims, nonviolent Sikhs, and nonviolent believers in many other traditions. It includes also those nonviolent humanists who disavow adherence to any religious faith but who express profound respect for life in all its forms.

In thus rooting himself deeply in nonviolent spiritual ground, Gandhi makes it possible for adherents of all spiritual, religious, and humanist faiths to share that ground as a basis from which to work for nonviolent global change, however much they may differ in other matters. Gandhi's first legacy is undoubtedly tolerant spiritual commitment.

A second legacy is respect for *science*. By this is meant an experimental attitude, as illustrated by his autobiography and subsequent campaigns, in which the validity of nonviolent approaches to problem solving is open to lessons to be gained from practical experience. By extension this opens up the possibility of pursuing nonviolent global transformation as a subject for interdisciplinary scientific investigation—engaging the natural sciences, social sciences, and the humanities.

Undoubtedly Gandhi would have been among the first to appreciate and to recognize the importance of carrying on the scientific work set forth in the May 16, 1986, Seville "Statement on Violence." In this statement twenty distinguished scientists in fields such as anthropology, ethology, and psychology with support of "the representatives of the Spanish UNESCO" met in Seville, Spain, to declare the following:

First, "IT IS SCIENTIFICALLY INCORRECT to say that we have inherited a tendency to make war from our animal ancestors."

Second, "IT IS SCIENTIFICALLY INCORRECT to say that war or any other violent behavior is genetically programmed into our human nature."

Third, "IT IS SCIENTIFICALLY INCORRECT to say that in the course of human evolution there has been a selection for aggressive behavior more than for other kinds of behavior."

Fourth, "IT IS SCIENTIFICALLY INCORRECT to say that humans have a 'violent brain.'"

Fifth, "IT IS SCIENTIFICALLY INCORRECT to say that war is caused by 'instinct' or any single motivation."

"We conclude," they explain,

that biology does not condemn humanity to war, and that humanity can be freed from the bondage of biological pessimism and empowered with confidence to undertake the transformative tasks needed in this International Year of Peace and in the years to come. Although these tasks are mainly institutional and collective, they also rest upon the consciousness of individual participants for whom optimism and pessimism are crucial factors. Just as "wars begin in the minds of men," peace also begins in our minds. The same species who invented war is capable of inventing peace. The responsibility lies with each of us.[3]

In sum, these scientists have declared that war and violence are not made inevitable by our animal nature, by our genes, by aggressive natural selection, by our brains, or by our instincts.

Therefore to spiritual faith in nonviolence as the law of life can be added the vast resources of scientific imagination and discovery that can contribute to a nonviolent world. As Albert Einstein has reminded us, "Science itself is not a liberator. It creates means, not goals. . . . We should remember that the fate of mankind [humankind] hinges entirely on man's [human] moral development."[4] In short, Gandhi's nonviolent spiritual vision combined with commitment to perfect a science of *satyagraha* provides both moral and scientific direction toward the nonviolent transformation of global civilization.[5]

But spirit and science alone are not enough. This leads to the third important legacy of Gandhi that is contributing to nonviolent global awakening.

This is his insistence upon the importance of both *individual and mass ac-tion*. This is illustrated by his view that even a single individual, if perfectly nonviolent, could free India from the British Empire. But this must be com-bined with his assertion that several tens of thousands of Englishmen could not rule India if three hundred million Indians nonviolently refused their co-operation. These keen insights into the importance of individual and mass action help to explain why individual dissenters are considered such threats by authoritarian regimes. They explain why large-scale peaceful withdrawal of obedience can lead to the collapse of seemingly unassailable regimes, as we have recently witnessed in several countries around the world, including the Soviet Union, the Baltic republics, and Eastern Europe. Two scholars who merit enormous credit for extending the theoretical and practical rele-vance of these Gandhian insights are Krishnalal Shridharani, for his book *War Without Violence,* and Professor Gene Sharp, for his classic work *The Politics of Nonviolent Action,* which continues to influence nonviolent ac-tivists seeking to liberate humankind from suffering and oppression.[6]

This leads to a fourth component of the Gandhian legacy, which can be termed *compassionate constructiveness.* Gandhi's "Talisman" that whenever we are in doubt or preoccupied with self, we should always hold in our mind's eye "the face of the poorest and weakest" human being we have ever seen and judge all our actions as to how they will benefit and empower that person, will forever stir action to remove economic and other injustices wherever they occur. Gandhi's personal example of identification with the oppressed combined with positive action to improve their condition re-mains to challenge the apathy of the comfortable and the inertness of the comfortless.

A regrettably little-known but highly significant example of Gandhi's con-tribution to awakening humankind for nonviolent action to remove eco-nomic suffering is provided by the manifesto on the global "holocaust" of hunger and underdevelopment that was issued by fifty-three Nobel Prize re-cipients in 1981, the "Manifesto of Nobel Prize Recipients."

They first declare, "All of those who denounce and combat this holocaust are unanimous in maintaining that the causes of this tragedy are political." They next call upon all the established authorities, national and interna-tional, including politicians, voters, parliaments, and governments to enact the laws and carry out the policies that will end this holocaust.

Finally, and most significantly, they appeal to the Gandhian legacy of non-violent transformative action:

> Although the powerful of this earth bear the greatest responsibility, they are not alone. If the helpless take their fate into their own hands, if increasing numbers refuse to obey any law other than the fundamental human rights, the most ba-sic of which is the right to life, if the weak organize themselves and use the few but powerful weapons [means] available to them; *nonviolent actions exempli-*

fied by Gandhi, adopting and imposing objectives which are limited and suitable: if these things happen it is certain that an end could be put to this catastrophe in our time.[7] [Emphasis added]

The Nobel Prize recipients' manifesto illustrates yet another aspect of the Gandhian legacy of compassionate constructiveness. It encompasses the powerful and the weak, the rich and the poor, the oppressors and the oppressed, men and women, within the same circle of humanity. Whereas violence divides for the well-being of some, nonviolence unites for the well-being of all.

A fifth aspect of Gandhi's nonviolent legacy is *creative courage.* Gandhi recognized that it requires a lot of creativity to be violent. As evidence, witness the creative investment of intellect that has produced the incredible killing capability of modern military forces on land, sea, and in the air. But Gandhi understood that it will take even more creativity to be nonviolent. This is clearly recognized by all who seek to discover and implement nonviolent alternatives in every aspect of life. These range from efforts to provide nonviolent personal, national, and international security—through provision of nonviolent alternatives to violence-based economies—to evocation of nonviolent expressions in science, language, art, and culture. In this regard, the midwife-inspired *maieutic* educational work of Danilo Dolci in Sicily to bring forth latent creativity in children is a direct contribution to a fundamental global need.

Courage is connected to creativity. It takes courage to stand alone or with others, sometimes at risk of life itself, to make needed changes. Gandhi calls upon us to be "truthful, gentle, and fearless." Many in India and throughout the world have responded to that call and will continue to do so. Those deserving of honor are numberless. To mention only one by way of illustration: Brian Willson in California, who refused to move from a nonviolent action on railroad tracks to block a train carrying United States weapons for use in El Salvador—and had both legs cut off as a result.

If we now bring the hand of the Gandhian legacy—spirit, science, individual and mass action, compassionate constructiveness, and creative courage—to bear upon the hand of global problems—peace and disarmament, economic justice, human rights, environmental preservation, and achievement of human cooperation—what are the grounds for confidence that nonviolent transformative action eventually can prevail?

The first is recognition that nonviolence is the fundamental condition to which all the great spiritual teachers have called upon humanity to live. The second is the fact, noted by Gandhi, that nonviolence is the law of human life. Women, who constitute half of the more than six billion humans living now, have not traditionally been warriors; and given that only a minority of men have served as soldiers, we can have confidence that a nonviolent world is not beyond human attainment. The truth is that most humans do not kill.

Further evidence of global nonviolent human capability is shown by the fact that seventy-three countries have abolished the death penalty for all crimes, and forty-seven countries legally or in practice accept some form of conscientious objection to military service, while another twenty-seven countries have no armies at all.

Since we have these important general indicators of nonviolent human potential, what we need is to develop and extend nonviolent capabilities into those areas of life now dominated or plagued by violence.

Let us now briefly examine the five problem areas for signs of nonviolent problem-solving actions, institutions, and resources. Although we are honoring Gandhi and will recognize his contributions, we must avoid placing responsibility for nonviolent global transformation exclusively upon his shoulders. In all world areas there are nonviolent cultural resources and traditions that have their own contributions to make. Gandhi's example can serve as a powerful stimulus to evoke them, as illustrated by his influence upon the African American civil rights movement in the United States. There Dr. Martin Luther King, Jr., served as a main focus for inspired leadership by many other men and women, young and old, that reached out to all Americans. But that movement also had its own roots in Christianity and in the African American experience. Similarly Tolstoy provided a source of inspiration and example in Russia that contributed to Gandhi's work, which in turn was creatively rooted in Gandhi's understanding of both Indian and British cultures.[8]

Among nonviolent world leaders of distinction, although Gandhi himself incredibly never received Nobel Peace Prize recognition, several Nobel peace laureates since his assassination clearly have drawn nonviolent inspiration from him: Dr. Martin Luther King, Jr. (1964), Mairead Corrigan and Betty Williams (1976), Amnesty International (1977), Mother Teresa of Calcutta (1979), Adolfo Perez Esquivel (1980), Bishop Desmond Tutu (1984), the Dalai Lama (1989), and Aung San Suu Kyi (1991). Other peace laureates, although not so clearly expressive of principled nonviolence, nevertheless have shown great respect for nonviolence as a compass to guide development of world civilization. One of these is Mikhail S. Gorbachev (1990), whose participation with Prime Minister Rajiv Gandhi in the Delhi Declaration of Principles for a Nuclear-Weapon-Free and Non-Violent World on November 27, 1986, constituted a significant symbolic act to encourage emergence of nonviolent global political leadership.

In addition to these outstanding individuals and countless others who remain unknown, many dedicated institutions are working toward nonviolent solutions for global problems. Each in its own way resonates with the teaching and example of Gandhi. Each also tends to work not solely on one kind of problem, but to extend its work to make changes that will bring about a nonviolent society as a whole in which people can live happy, creative, and productive lives.

We will mention here only a few examples of beautiful and dedicated nonviolent global problem-solving resources. For *peace and disarmament,* we note the War Resisters International and Peace Brigades International, to which the distinguished Gandhian worker Narayan Desai has made such an important contribution. From 1981 to 2000 the Women's Peace Camp at Greenham Common air base in England demonstrated courageous resistance to nuclear weapons. The movement to abolish armies is beginning to spread internationally after initiation in Switzerland by the Gruppe Schweiz ohne Armee (Switzerland Without Army). It succeeded in gaining the support of some one million voters in a spring 1990 referendum to abolish the Swiss Army.

For *economic justice,* we note the *Sarvodaya* movement in India and the Bhoodan-Gramdan legacy of Vinoba Bhave and J. P. Narayan; the Buddhist-based *Sarvodaya* movement in the villages of Sri Lanka under the dedicated guidance of A. T. Ariyaratne; the nonviolent United Farm Workers union in California guided by Cesar Chavez; the efforts in the United States (Jobs With Peace) and in England (Lucas Aerospace workers) to shift skills and resources from military to nonmilitary services; and even nonviolent mutual funds such as the Calvert Social Fund and the Pax World Fund.

For *human rights,* we note the universally respected Amnesty International, working since 1961 to abolish the death penalty, to end torture, and to gain freedom for all nonviolent prisoners of conscience throughout the world. Humanitas International, founded by the nonviolent folk singer Joan Baez, has done pioneering work to support victims of political, economic, social, and cultural oppression in many countries. In Latin America we note the work of the major international political, social, and economic human rights organization Servicio Paz y Justicia, guided by Nobel laureate Adolfo Perez Esquivel, that grew out of the courageous protests of Argentinian women against the violent "disappearance" of their children under a brutal military regime.

For *environmental* protection, it is important to recognize the nonviolent direct action efforts of Greenpeace International, not only to defend dolphins and whales but also to remove all threats to a life-supporting environment on land, sea, and in the air. A source of worldwide inspiration for such actions has been the Chipko ("Hug the Trees") movement in India to which a senior village woman, Gauri Devi, contributed so much: "This forest is like our mother. You will have to shoot me before you can cut it down."[9]

Many institutions are developing peaceful relations and *problem-solving cooperation* among peoples based upon nonviolent principles, including the International Fellowship of Reconciliation, the Jewish Peace Fellowship, the International Network of Engaged Buddhists, guided by Sulak Sivaraksa of Thailand, the Soka Gakkai International, inspired by Daisaku Ikeda ("life is the most precious thing"), the American Friends Service Committee, and the venerable Friends World Committee for Consultation. The work of all these, resonating with the Gandhian legacy as well as being rooted in their own spiritual and historical traditions, refuses to accept power-striving, greed, hatred, and ignorance as eternal obstacles to prevent worldwide cooperation for the well-being and happiness of all.

As further evidence of resources for nonviolent global problem solving that spring at least in part from Gandhian inspiration, four can be mentioned briefly. They stand out in the fields of political leadership, nonviolent training, nonviolent research, and nonviolent education.

Since 1980 the fastest-growing political party movement in the world has been Green parties, beginning with West Germany. In just ten years these parties spread over Western, Eastern, and Southern Europe, and are well represented in the European Parliament. They have emerged also in Australia, Brazil, Canada, Ireland, Japan, Kenya, the United States, and other countries. Green parties show every sign of continued diffusion throughout the world. According to one of the five founders of the original German Green Party, Petra Kelly, whom history will recognize as one of the twentieth century's most significant nonviolent political figures, the original Greens drew inspiration from both Gandhi and Martin Luther King, Jr.[10] Although members of Green parties and movements differ in their degree of acceptance of the principle of "nonviolence" as a way to cope with violence, it is customarily included with other Green values such as ecology, feminism, and grass-roots (rice roots) democracy as goals of Green political action. Even if somewhat qualified, the emergence of electoral parties at the end of the twentieth century prepared to espouse "nonviolence" as among their basic political values is of great historical significance. These parties shift the burden of nonviolent change from the shoulders of the victimized outside the chambers of established power so that it can be voiced by representatives within them.

Another significant institutional sign of nonviolent change is the New York State Martin Luther King, Jr., Institute for Nonviolence unanimously approved by the Assembly of the State of New York and signed into law by Governor Mario M. Cuomo on August 1, 1988. The first of its kind in the United States, the purposes of this Institute are to carry out training, research, and public outreach to help the citizens of New York State find nonviolent means to change the very serious conditions of violence that threaten their lives. The unanimity of its approval and the substantial tax-derived support given to it testify to the seriousness of that threat as perceived by New York's political leaders of every persuasion.

The chief training advisor to the New York State Institute for Nonviolence is the inspired former King associate Dr. Bernard Lafayette, Jr., who has developed a very effective seven-point summary of Dr. King's methods: (1) define the problem, (2) conduct research, (3) educate all involved, (4) negotiate until untruthfulness becomes apparent, (5) withdraw to engage in self-purification,

(6) conduct nonviolent direct action, and (7) unite in reconciliation—the constant objective throughout every one of the preceding stages.

Internationally, of course, tribute is richly merited by the training for nonviolent action that has been given by Jean and Hildegard Goss-Mayr under the auspices of the International Fellowship of Reconciliation. They made an important contribution to nonviolent political change in the Philippines in 1986 and continue to train nonviolent problem solvers for other areas plagued by violence, such as Cambodia.

In the field of research on nonviolent political action, a principal locus of innovation is the Albert Einstein Institution in Cambridge, Massachusetts, directed by Dr. Gene Sharp. The main emphasis of this Institute is to promote "research, policy studies, and education concerning the nature and potential of nonviolent sanctions, in comparison with violent ones, for solving the problems of aggression, dictatorship, genocide, and oppression." The importance of this research program is that until it is conclusively shown that effective nonviolent alternatives are available for coping with the most serious cases of political violence, both governments and citizens are unlikely to relinquish their attachment to violence.

A fourth major global resource in the field of nonviolence is Gandhigram Rural Institute (Deemed University), located in the Madurai district of Tamil Nadu State, India. Founded by the inspired, brilliant, and dedicated Gandhian educator Dr. G. Ramachandran—himself a devoted student both of Gandhi and of Rabindranath Tagore, whose qualities he combines—the history of Gandhigram Rural University is of global significance for at least two reasons. First, it offers us the example of an effort to base a whole university (natural sciences, social sciences, arts, humanities, and professions) on principles of nonviolence. That includes the effort to have the entire university respond to the needs of all who live in its surrounding area through cooperative planning and implementation of constructive service programs. Second, the Shanti Sena (Peace Brigade) of Gandhigram Rural University provides an alternative to violent military training that gradually should be adopted creatively by every college and university in the world as an important source of leadership to assist transition to a nonviolent global community. Some important features of the training are instruction in the spirit and principles of nonviolence, tolerance, discipline, fearlessness, conflict resolution, selfless work with those in need to improve their condition, and joyful recreational and artistic expression. The first pledge of the Gandhigram Shanti Sainik stands before us all as a challenging living memorial to Gandhi's life and message: "I shall work for peace and if need be lay down my life for it."

The world will always be indebted to Dr. G. Ramachandran, the founder of Gandhigram University and of its Shanti Sena, and to Professor N. Radhakrishnan, beloved of students, who joyfully and creatively served as its chief organizer for twenty-five years, drawing upon the wisdom of senior colleagues who were veterans of Gandhian campaigns.

In addition we need to celebrate the existence of all institutions in India and throughout the world that are dedicated to nonviolence. These include the Gujarat Vidyapith, the Gandhian Institute of Studies, the Center for Gandhian Studies and Peace Research, the Gandhi Peace Foundation, the Kasturba Gandhi Trust, the Harijan Sevak Sangh, the Self-Employed Women's Association, the Jamnalal Bajaj Foundation, the Navajivan Trust, the Gandhian publication projects of the Government of India, *Gandhi Marg*, the faithful journal for the global stimulation of nonviolent thought, and others. Globally the number of nonviolent individuals, projects, and institutions is increasing. It will take a major research effort to identify all of them as a basis for worldwide supportive action.

If we are to bring the hand of Gandhi's nonviolent legacy to bear upon the hand of violent global problems—in the process of global nonviolent awakening—we need the assistance of an institution with global vision. Just as there are maps of world military deployments or of world energy and food resources, we need a map of global violence overlaid with a map of nonviolent resources for global problem solving.

It is within human capability to bring about a nonviolent global community. Such a community will have no killing and no threats to kill, no weapons specifically designed to kill, and no ideological justifications for killing, and no conditions of society that depend for maintenance or change upon the threat or use of killing force.

But to realize such a community we must identify, bring together, and advance the nonviolent spiritual, scientific, leadership-followership, compassionately constructive, and creatively courageous resources that are needed to bring it about. An analogy is provided by the contemporary achievement of placing a human being on the moon. Long considered an impossible dream, it rapidly became a reality when vision, will, skill, science, technology, human organization, training, resources, and public support were combined to make it possible. Something similar can happen in nonviolent global transformation as the historical preconditions for it begin to converge and to interact with future vision.

As our brief survey has shown, there is already in existence substantial nonviolent knowledge and experience which, if acted upon by individuals and translated into policy by private and public institutions, can assist significant nonviolent change throughout the world. Furthermore, an institution to accomplish this is not a luxury but a necessity, as illustrated by the New York State Assembly's unanimous response to violence within their society—the creation of an institute to promote nonviolence. The same logic is applicable on a global scale.

A nonviolent global institution should be interspiritual, interdisciplinary, and international in composition. Its purpose should be to advance and to combine vision, knowledge, education training, and action to assist humankind to replace conditions of violence with life-respecting conditions of nonviolence. In structure the nonviolent global institution should be patterned somewhat after the United Nations University, which has its Centre in Tokyo. That is, with an international guiding council, based upon substantial endowment resources, the institution should carry out its work by assisting individuals and organizations throughout the world to advance knowledge, education, and action for nonviolence. It should devise means to be responsive to the needs of nonviolent workers everywhere. At the same time it should help to encourage and support research at the highest reaches of spiritual, poetic, and scientific imagination. Like many previous scourges that have afflicted suffering humanity, the ancient terror of violence is not likely to subside by prayer and common sense alone, although both are indispensable for its removal.

A ten-year startup program for a global nonviolence institution can readily be envisioned. For one thing we need a series of exploratory seminars to begin discovery of past roots, present manifestations, and future prospects of nonviolence in every country and region of the world. For another we need a series of advanced research seminars to explore what we know and what we need to know on subjects such as the following: (1) nonviolence in religious and philosophical traditions, (2) brain studies and nonviolence, (3) nonviolent gender relationships, (4) nonviolent economics, (5) the role of the military in nonviolent global transformation, (6) high technologies for nonviolence, (7) nonviolence and the environment, (8) problems of leadership in nonviolent movements, (9) nonviolence in the arts, (10) nonviolent training and education, (11) nonviolent communications, (12) nonviolence in the professions, and (13) the formulation and evaluation of nonviolent public policies.

The results of such explorations, research inventories, and discoveries should be brought together in forms suitable for informing humankind of its nonviolent heritage in the twenty-first century. From this basis, research, education, and policy development can be raised to higher levels of consciousness and effectiveness on a global scale. With such awareness nonviolent knowledge, leadership, and skills can be focused more precisely and diffused more widely to solve specific problems of violence.

Some will say that a nonviolent world is impossible and that therefore a nonviolent global institution is unnecessary. But for those of us who have witnessed the incredible changes taking place throughout the world over the past two years, the wisdom of Gandhi's insight into possibilities for human change shines anew: "We are daily witnessing the phenomenon of the impossible of yesterday becoming the possible of today."[11]

Therefore let us be confident that the seemingly impossible dream of establishing a Center for Global Nonviolence to help bring the legacy of Gandhiji and other nonviolent resources to bear in global *satyagraha* for global *sarvodaya* may yet become a reality. And let us also be confident that, with or without such a Center, Gandhi's contributions to global nonviolent awakening will continue to resonate throughout the world.

NOTES

1. Geoffrey Ashe, *Gandhi* (New York: Stein and Day, 1968), 243.

2. Barry Commoner, *Making Peace with the Planet* (New York: Pantheon, 1990), 243.

3. "Statement on Violence," *Journal of Peace Research,* vol. 26, no. 2 (1989), 120–21.

4. Otto Nathan and Heinz Norden, eds., *Einstein on Peace* (New York: Schocken, 1968), 312.

5. *The Science of Satyagraha*, ed. Anand T. Hingorani, (Bombay: Bharatuja Vidya Bhavan, 1970).

6. Krishnalal Shridharani,. *War Without Violence* (Bombay: Bharatiya Vidya Bhavan, 1962); Gene Sharp, *The Politics of Nonviolent Action* (Boston: Porter Sargent, 1973).

7. *IFDA*, Dossier 25, Sep./Oct. 1981, 1(61)–3(63).

8. Bhikhu Parekh, *Colonialism, Tradition and Reform: An Analysis of Gandhi's Political Discourse* (New Delhi/Newbury Park/London: Sage, 1989).

9. Mark Shepard, *Gandhi Today: A Report on Mahatma Gandhi's Successors* (Arcata, CA: Simple Productions, 1987), 75.

10. "Gandhi and the Green Party," *Gandhi Marg* (July–September, 1989): 192–202; *Nonviolence Speaks to Power* (1992).

11. *The Collected Works of Mahatma Gandhi*, 100 vols. (New Delhi: Publication Division, Ministry of Information and Broadcasting, 1958–1994), 26:68.

19

Gandhi, Nonviolence, and the Struggle Against War

Richard Falk

GANDHI'S CALL

As early as 1931 Gandhi articulated his view that change, to be beneficial, needed to be achieved by nonviolent struggle: "I personally, would wait, if need be, for ages rather than to seek the freedom of my country through bloody means." Gandhi added some optimistic words, declaring, "I feel in the innermost recesses of my heart . . . that the world is sick unto death of blood-spilling. The world is seeking a way out, and I flatter myself with the belief that perhaps it will be the privilege of the ancient land of India to show the way out to the hungering world."[1] Of course, from the perspective of 2003 this would seem to be a prime instance of false prophecy. This essay argues that although Gandhi's literal coordinates of time and place were mistaken, that we may yet be approaching a Gandhian Moment where there occurs a worldwide revulsion against war and violence. Perhaps "the world is seeking a way out," but the translation of this sentiment into political reality, given the emotional and material forces arrayed against it, was gravely underestimated by Gandhi. Nevertheless, his prophetic insight was valid then, and if anything, is far more so today.

Should this hopeful possibility be actualized in the time ahead, it will almost certainly be a result of that other side of Gandhi's vision, the struggle against the evils of oppression. In Gandhi's words, the responsibility to act is a human duty in such circumstances, not a mere political choice. On this occasion already in 1921, Gandhi was addressing his remarks to the "freedom" associated with British colonial rule: "We seek arrest because the so-called freedom is slavery. We are challenging the might of this Government because we consider its activity to be wholly evil. We want to overthrow the Government. We desire to show that the Government exists to serve the people, not the people the Government."[2] Elsewhere, Gandhi frequently makes clear that to achieve such ends of true freedom, whatever the context, no price is too great, including death, as well as the related insistence that nonviolent struggle requires the greatest personal courage.

So when awaiting a Gandhian Moment we must grow sensitive to both potentialities of the human spirit: the renunciation of violence as a political instrument and the engagement in struggle for the sake of justice. Neither is tenable without the other.

At this time in human history, it would seem that the glass is neither full, nor empty. The passions that rage on the planet suggest an impending encounter between those destructive forces that see the glass totally empty, and those that believe it is almost full; between the extremists, whether religious or secular, locked in total war, and the visionary warriors that constitute global civil society who believe in a future based on peace, justice, and sustainability. Looking back in time, we can understand that it is an error to be too literal in anticipating the Gandhian Moment; but it would be a greater error to dismiss the possibility, and reconcile ourselves either to endless and escalating cycles of violence or to the "unpeace" of injustice and oppression.

REVIVED GANDHISM OF THE 1990s

A series of developments, especially in the 1990s, created an impression that a new era of peaceful change and global justice was displacing war and violence on the world stage. The earliest indications of this trend can be connected with the rather remarkable Iranian Revolution in 1978–1979 that toppled from power the military regime of the Shah on the basis of a massive popular movement that refused to rely on violent tactics in mounting its struggle for change. Somewhat later, a similar phenomenon was evident in the Philippines where Ferdinand Marcos, a longtime corrupt dictator, was driven into exile by the People Power movement that was also nonviolent in means and ends. Other prodemocracy movements were evident in a series of Asian countries including China, Nepal, Indonesia, Burma, Taiwan, Thailand, and South Korea. And then in the late 1980s, encouraged by the new governing style in Moscow associated with Mikhail Gorbachev's leadership, impressive mobilizations of popular opposition occurred in a series of countries in Eastern Europe, culminating in the breaching of the Berlin Wall in late 1989. Two years later the Soviet Union collapsed, and the internal empire run from the Kremlin disintegrated, again without notable violence.

These developments reached their climax in some ways when the white leadership in South Africa decided to find a way to end its racist regime based on apartheid so as to avoid isolation on an international level and civil strife at home. To achieve this transformation of a country so long governed by an oppressive white minority depended most of all on Nelson Mandela's ability to step out of jail after twenty-seven years of confinement and assume the leadership of the black African majority's struggle for a constitutional democracy. This majority was willing to accommodate itself, despite massive impoverishment, to the entrenched, yet exploitative, economic interests of the white minority. Somehow, Mandela's spirit of reconciliation and moral radiance was able to guide this transition, avoiding the strong temptations to demand social justice alongside of political justice, an admittedly high price for adherence to a nonviolent approach to conflict resolution given the massive poverty and class disparities that exist in South Africa. These various moves were reinforced by a disillusionment with military approaches. Neither revolutionary warfare of the sort that existed in a series of Asian countries, nor oppressive government, seemed able to achieve stability or "victory." In world politics, the nuclear standoff symbolized the growing realization that war was no longer a viable instrument of policy in relations among major sovereign states; and yet there remained an acute fear that an unintended breakdown (either by accident or irrationality) of the precarious stability achieved by deterrence would produce catastrophic results.[3]

The 1990s witnessed also a powerful global justice movement unprecedented in history that appeared to complement this willingness to limit challenges directed at the political status quo by renouncing violence.[4] There were several different dimensions of this turn toward global justice: a series of initiatives associated with reparations for victims of the Holocaust; a greatly increased emphasis on adherence to human rights as the foundation of political legitimacy; serious inquiry into such historic injustices as the dispossession and destruction of indigenous peoples, colonialism, and slavery; the United Nations' seeming readiness to act with the support of the United States and other leading countries to prevent, or at least mitigate, humanitarian catastrophes by accepting a responsibility to protect; and greatly enhanced efforts to impose individual criminal accountability on political leaders and military commanders guilty of crimes against humanity.[5] Although none of these initiatives was directly focused on nonviolence, their overall effect was to suggest to all sides of political controversy that peaceful means based on the rule of law were the only acceptable way to resolve grievances.

Of course, not everything was rosy in the 1990s. There was evident in many parts of the world, especially in sub-Saharan Africa and the Balkans, instances of civil strife exhibiting extreme forms of indiscriminate violence. The world watched as genocide unfolded in Rwanda. AIDS ravaged many countries in the South, but especially those in black Africa. The Asian democracy movements either crashed or achieved only minimal results. The cold war ended without the nuclear weapons states moving to negotiate a disarmament treaty or at least proclaiming the prohibition of all weaponry of mass destruction. The negative effects of globalization that were causing growing disparities in wealth and income, environmental decay, and a pervasive disregard of human suffering cast a dark shadow across the achievements of the decade. A mixed picture existed as to future prospects; but there were hopeful developments underway that have now, temporarily, at least, been eclipsed by a return to an apparent preoccupation with war and the avoidance of an American global empire as a consequence of the events surrounding and following upon the September 11, 2001, attacks. Despite such an adverse turn, there are signs that we may yet be approaching a historical period during which the world will finally heed Gandhi's call to nonviolence.

THE UNCERTAIN SEPTEMBER 11 EFFECT

It is difficult to think about Gandhi's legacy for the twenty-first century without resetting the global context associated with the impact of both the September 11 attacks on the United States and the American response. Both al Qaeda and the United States seem committed to waging borderless wars on a global scale. Both sides deem their opponent to be the embodiment of unconditional evil, outside the framework of diplomacy and compromise, with the only acceptable outcome being victory for one side and defeat for the other through the medium of pure violence.[6] Neither adversary is a sovereign state in the normally understood sense, nor are the opposed antagonists engaged in a civil war for control of a state or waging some sort of self-determination struggle. Al Qaeda is an amorphous, dispersed, secretive network that is operative in as many as sixty states, while the United States is a kind of global state that claims command of the oceans and space, as well as maintaining military bases in more than sixty countries.

Such an unprecedented conflict, repudiating the restraints of international humanitarian law, is without precedent in the annals of world history. Al Qaeda proclaims that all Americans are enemies who can be killed to fulfill the goals of *jihad*, thereby repudiating the fundamental precept of the law of war that only military personnel and targets are subject to attack. The United States, on its side, targets for death civilians suspected of terrorist links in foreign countries and denies captured al Qaeda fighters prisoners of war status. It is a war, more than most wars, in which the idea of limits is rejected by both sides. Such an assessment should not be understood as romanticizing the relevance of law to the conduct of past wars, but it is an important rupture with the attempts in both world wars of the last century to avoid superfluous suffering by finding common interests, such as protection of prisoners of war and wounded combatants, and sparing civilians so far as possible.

In such an atmosphere it might seem foolish to assert the relevance of the Gandhian legacy of radical nonviolence. Indeed, even the Dalai Lama, the most prominent living advocate of nonviolent approaches to conflict resolution, now entertains doubts whether the renunciation of violence is sustainable in the face of this radical "terrorist" challenge.[7] The Dalai Lama was quoted as saying that "[t]errorism is the worst kind of violence, so we have to check it, we have to take countermeasures," coupling this assertion with a refusal to join other religious leaders in criticizing the American military approach generating the wars against Afghanistan, and especially the war against Iraq. The leader of Tibetan Buddhism did go on to say that "the real antidote" to terrorism was a reliance on "compassion, dialogue—peaceful means. . . . We have to deal with their motivation."[8] It should be noted that this admirable religious figure succumbed to the mainstream trap of associating "terrorism" exclusively with antistate violence, and exempting "state terrorism" from scrutiny.[9] Even worse, such a venerable figure calls this non-state violence "the worst kind of violence" in the face of Hiroshima and Nagasaki, and more surprisingly, the terrible violence used by the Chinese government to crush Tibetan resistance back in the 1950s. What is significant here is that the radical nature of the struggle taking place is having a disorienting effect on settled categories of assessment, including those that proceed from the most principled of Gandhian views that any reliance on violence is degenerative and ineffectual.

At the same time, a kind of secular Gandhism is becoming visible in unexpected places. The Prime Minister of Malaysia, Mohamed Mahathir, who is capable of uttering outrageous and dangerously provocative assertions on some occasions, delivered a stirring antiwar address to open the XIIIth Summit Meeting of the Non-Aligned Movement in Kuala Lumpur on February 24, 2003.[10] Mahathir acknowledges that world order, as understood in modern times by reference to state sovereignty, has been undermined by both sides. A perceptive passage by this controversial, yet significant, leader is worth quoting in full:

> We may want to remain uninvolved and to avoid incurring the displeasure of powerful countries. But our people are getting restless. They want us to do something. If we don't then they will, and they will go against us. They will take things into their own hands. Unable to mount a conventional war they will resort to guerrilla war, to terrorism, against us and against those they consider to be their oppressors.
>
> They cannot be ignored any longer. We cannot incarcerate them all for we do not always know who they are or where they are.
>
> September 11 has demonstrated to the world that even acts of terror even by a dozen [sic] people can destabilize the whole world completely, put fear into the hearts of everyone, make them afraid of their own shadows.[11]

As with the Dalai Lama, Mahathir is also complicit in the statist logic of associating terrorism exclusively with nonstate actors, but he at least condemns both sides in this bloody encounter. His words directed at the response of the United States, without naming, also are notable for their lucidity. Mahathir says that the September 11 attacks, both before and since, "have also removed all the restraint in the countries of the north. They now no longer respect borders, international laws or simple moral values. They are even talking of using nuclear weapons." The Malaysian leader goes on to insist that the American response "is no longer just a war against terrorism. It is in fact a war to dominate the world, i.e. the chromatically different world . . . the most important threat that we face now is the tendency of the powerful to wage war when faced with opposition to the spread of their dominance," and he significantly adds, "[w]e cannot fight a war with them."[12]

Then, in language unexpectedly echoing Gandhi, Mahathir notes that "[f]ortunately many of their people are also sick of war. They have come out in their millions to protest the warlike policies of their leaders. We must join them. We must join their struggle with all the moral force that we can command." The goal is also clearly expressed: "War must be outlawed. That will have to be our struggle now. We must struggle for justice and freedom from oppression, from economic hegemony. But we must remove the threat of war first." Mahathir proposes in this most important speech that "[w]ar must . . . be made illegal" and the enforcement of this illegality entrusted to "multilateral forces under the control of the United Nations. No single nation should be allowed to police the world, least of all to decide what action to take, when."[13] There is a final element here in this conception of how to cut the Gordian knot of political violence. Mahathir asks the assembled representatives of the great majority of the world's peoples a rhetorical question, receiving thunderous applause, according to press accounts: "When Japan was defeated, it was allowed to spend only one percent of its GDP on its armed forces. If such a condition can be imposed on Japan, why cannot it be imposed on all countries?"[14]

Mahathir concludes this extraordinary speech, perhaps the most visionary address by a statesman since Woodrow Wilson gave voice to some comparable statements after the carnage of World War I, by considering the dynamics of the struggle. He acknowledges that the countries of the south are "weak" but that they have allies among the peoples and governments of the north, and insists that "[w]e must work with them." And he proposes that the Non-Aligned Movement be revitalized to realize "a world order which is above all free from the age old belief that killing people is right, that it can solve problems of relations between nations."[15]

I have emphasized this one statement by this important political leader, but there are other indications that a subtle and complicated process of reassessing the dynamics of change and conflict resolution is taking place at the deeper recesses of collective human consciousness. The nuclear age highlighted the essential self-destructiveness of war and political violence. The long unresolved internal wars that have taken so many millions of lives in the decades since World War II have underscored the terrible costs of relying on political violence, and the tragedy of interactive violence in struggles of state and society in which neither side relents.[16] Scholars and academicians have increasingly looked to such goals as the abolition of war and a geopolitics of nonviolence as the only sustainable foundations of world order, accepting as pillars of such a transformation of global security the essential role of respect for human rights, the practice of democracy, and the international rule of law, as well as an energetic implementation of the global justice agenda so promisingly initiated in the 1990s.[17]

A CONCLUDING NOTE ON GLOBALIZATION IN THE TWENTY-FIRST CENTURY

Toward the end of the twentieth century there was a strong sense that war and violence were not as significant for the future as they had been in the past. There was an economic climate of opinion in which prevailing opinions viewed the main arena of struggle to involve challenges directed by global civil society against the inequities associated with neoliberal globalization that seemed to emphasize market priorities at the expense of the peoples of the world. September 11 and its sequel have demonstrated how shortsighted such views were, and suggest the need to revamp globalization to take into account the war/peace dimensions. A conceptual framework that continues to use the terminology of "globalization" remains useful to highlight the degree to which the life of the planet and its peoples must be conceived holistically, and not as patterns of interactions among territorial entities called sovereign states.[18] If the Gandhian Moment is to be realized, then it must encompass both concerns with the violence of weapons and the violence of inequitable structures of domination and exploitation. Perhaps, unwittingly, the visibility of this violence due to the globalization of media coverage, especially TV, will hasten the process by which the peoples of the world, sick from violence and the suffering entailed, will hasten the awakening of conscience and commitment needed to carry forward the struggle for a nonviolent world order. This is as much as we can hope for at present, but such a hope will certainly prove vain if we do not also act to the fullness of our individual and collective capacities to rid the world of war and violence.

NOTES

1. Homer A. Jack, ed., *The Gandhi Reader: A Sourcebook of His Life and Writings* (Indianapolis: Indiana University Press, 1956), 264.

2. Jack, ed., *The Gandhi Reader*, Note 1, 193.

3. Perhaps this precariousness was best expressed by Jonathan Schell, *The Fate of the Earth* (New York: Knopf, 1982); see also Robert Jay Lifton and Richard Falk, *Indefensible Weapons: The Political and Psychological Case Against Nuclear Weapons* (New York: Basic Books, updated ed., 1991).

4. These developments have been described and analyzed by Elazar Barkun, *The Guilt of Nations* (2000).

5. See *The Responsibility Project*, Report of the International Commission on Intervention and Sovereignty (Ottawa, Canada: International Development Research

Centre, 2001), for overview. Richard Falk, "The First Normative Global Revolution? The Uncertain Future of Globalization," in Mehdi Mozaffari, ed., *Globalization and Civilizations* (London, UK: Routledge, 2002), 51–76.

6. President Bush has made frequent statements about "hunting" and destroying al Qaeda by force of arms, as has Osama Bin Laden as the leader of al Qaeda. For instance, "[t]his hadith teaches [us] that the conflict with the enemy will be settled by killing and warfare, and not by disabling the potential of the Nation for decades by a variety of means such as the deception of democracy." And again, "[The Islamic Nation] should toughen itself and prepare for real life, a life of killing and war, of shooting and hand-to-hand combat." Both quotes from "Bin Laden's Sermon for the Feast of the Sacrifice," 14 March 2003, 3, 12, www.Memri.de/uebersetzen_analysen/themen/islamistische_ideologie/isl_binladen.

7. There is a serious ambiguity as to the nature of terrorism. The mainstream usage associates political violence directed at civilian targets as terrorism, if and only if perpetrated by nonstate actors. I have argued in the past that if "terrorism" as a term of moral and legal opprobrium is to be used at all, then it should apply to violence deliberately targeting civilians, whether committed by state actors or their nonstate enemies. See Falk, *Revolutionaries and Functionaries: The Dual Face of Terrorism* (New York: Dutton, 1988).

8. See Laurie Goodstein, "Dalai Lama Says Terror May Need a Violent Reply," *NY Times*, 9-18-03, A16.

9. For an early attempt to analyze state terror see Alexander George, ed., *Western State Terrorism* (Cambridge, UK: Polity, 1991).

10. For text see www.nam.gov.za/media/030225na.htm.

11. See, note 10, numbered para. 32–34.

12. Note 10, para. 35–36.

13. Note 10, para. 37–39.

14. Note 10, para. 43.

15. Note 10, para. 47–48.

16. The Israel/Palestine violent encounter is paradigmatic for this pattern. Saul Mendlovitz in arguing the case for the abolition of war gathers the various estimates of deaths due to large-scale political violence concluding that since World War II there have been about 180 wars that have produced more than 40 million deaths, 125 million wounded, and some 100 million who were forcibly displaced from their homes and homeland. See Mendlovitz, "The Prospects for Abolishing War: A Proposal for the Twenty-First Century," *Rutgers Law Review,* vol. 16 (2000), 621–32, esp. 621–22 and footnotes 2–4.

17. In addition to Mendovitz cited in the prior note see Jonathan Schell's comprehensive inquiry in *The Unconquerable World: Power, Nonviolence, and the Will of the People* (New York: Metropolitan Books, 2003); along similar lines with a more poetic and inspirational style of persuasion see Stuart Rees, *Passion for Peace: Exercising Power Creatively* (Sydney, Australia: University of New South Wales Press, 2003); Fred Dallmayr is preparing a more philosophically grounded book along comparable lines. For a more programmatically oriented phased approach addressed to civil society actors around the world see *Global Action to Prevent War: A Coalition-Building Effort to Stop War, Genocide, & Internal Armed Conflict*, Program Statement, 2003.

18. For one attempt see Richard Falk, "Reimagining the Governance of Globalization," paper initially presented at conference on Critical Globalization held at the University of California, Santa Barbara, 5-1/4-03

Glossary

advaita   Nonduality, monism

ahimsa   Nonviolence, noninjury, harmlessness in thought, word, and action

anasakti   Selfless action

aparigraha   Nonpossession

ashram   A spiritual community

asteya   Nonstealing

atman   Universal Self

avatar   A person who has reached moksha; an incarnation of the Divine

bapu   Father; a term of respect and endearment for Gandhi

Bhagavad Gita   Literally "Song of God," Gandhi's favorite Hindu sacred text and the source of his practice of *karma yoga*

bhakti   Devotion, faith

brahmachari   One who practices brahmacharya

brahmacharya   Chastity, control of all the senses

charkha   Spinning wheel

crore   Ten million

communal   Religious

darshan   Spiritual fulfillment from being in the presence of a person, place, or thing

dharma   Duty, righteousness, moral law; personal and social morality

Gandhiji   The -ji suffix indicates respect; Gandhiji was and is often used

goonda   Street criminal, rowdy

guru   Teacher, spiritual guide

harijan   Literally "child of God," name used by Gandhi for untouchables

hartal   Cessation of work (from Hindu religious practice as form of purification)

himsa   Violence, injury

Jain   A follower of the Indian religion Jainism

karma   Moral law, cause and effect, action

khadi   Homespun cloth

lakh   A hundred thousand

lathi   A steel-tipped stick used by the Indian police

mahatma   Great soul; a term used regularly for Gandhi

moksha   Liberation from the cycle of birth and death; self-realization

Mussalman   Muslim

Panchayat   Village council

Parsi   Indian word for a follower of Zoroastrianism, founded by Persian Prophet Zoroaster

poorna swaraj   Complete self-rule, complete independence; poorna also spelled purna

purdah   Seclusion of women from public observation

raj   Kingdom, rule; used for British rule as "the Raj"

Rama   Hindu God, an incarnation of Vishnu; Gandhi's favorite personal deity

rishi   Seer

ryot   Peasant

sarvodaya   The well-being of all; universal welfare

sanatani   Orthodox Hindu

sannyasi   One who has renounced the world

satya   Truth, Being, Reality, a foundation of Hindu thought

satyagraha   Literally "clinging to Truth"; soul force, truth force, love force, nonviolence

satyagrahi   One who practices *satyagraha*

shastra(s)   Hindu scriptures

Sikh   Adherent of monotheistic religion of India, Sikhism, founded around 1500

swadeshi   Self-sufficiency, self-reliance

swaraj   Freedom, self-rule, home-rule

tapascharya   Meditation and austerities

Upanishads   Part of Hindu Vedic scriptures, the main source of orthodox Hindu philosophy

Vaishnavite   Devotee of the Hindu God Vishnu

vakil   Lawyer

yajna   Sacrifice, system of sacrifices

Short Bibliography

Writings by and about Gandhi are quite extensive. The purpose of this bibliography is to provide a short introductory list of books for new readers of Gandhi.

The most important primary sources on Gandhi are

Gandhi, Mohandas K. *An Autobiography: The Story of my Experiments with Truth*. Boston: Beacon Press, 1993.
———. *The Collected Works of Mahatma Gandhi*. 100 vols. New Delhi: Publication Division, Ministry of Information and Broadcasting, 1958–1994.
———. *Constructive Programme: Its Meaning and Place*. Ahmedabad: Navajivan, 1941.
———. *Non-Violent Resistance (Satyagraha)*. New York: Schocken Books, 1985.
———. *Satyagraha in South Africa*. Ahmedabad: Navajivan, 1928.
Iyer, Raghavan, ed. *The Moral and Political Writings of Mahatma Gandhi*. Oxford: Clarendon *Press*, vols. 1 and 2, 1986, and vol. 3, 1987.
Parel, Anthony J., ed. *Gandhi: Hind Swaraj and Other Writings*. Cambridge: Cambridge University Press, 1997.

There are hundreds of biographies of Gandhi. Three excellent short biographies are

Easwaran, Eknath. *Gandhi the Man: The Story of His Transformation*. Tomales, CA: Nilgiri Press, 1997.
Gruzalski, Bart. *On Gandhi*. Belmont, CA: Wadsworth, 2001.
Parekh, Bhikhu. *Gandhi*. Oxford: Oxford University Press, 1997.

The two most authoritative full-length biographies are

Brown, Judith M. *Gandhi: Prisoner of Hope*. New Haven: Yale University Press, 1989.
Nanda, B.R. *Mahatma Gandhi: A Biography*. New Delhi: Oxford University Press, 1958.

For more information about India in Gandhi's time and since, read

Brown, Judith M. *Gandhi's Rise to Power: Indian Politics 1915–1922*. Cambridge: Cambridge University Press, 1972.

————. *Gandhi and Civil Disobedience: The Mahatma in Indian Politics 1928–1934.* Cambridge: Cambridge University Press, 1977.

————. *Modern India.* Oxford: Oxford University Press, 1994.

Dallmayr, Fred, and G. N. Devy, eds. *Between Tradition and Modernity: India's Search for Identity.* New Delhi: Sage Publications, 1998.

The following books seem most useful for readers who wish to pursue more in-depth study of Gandhi and nonviolence. Some have extensive bibliographies.

Ackerman, Peter and Jack Duvall. *A Force More Powerful: A Century of Nonviolent Conflict.* New York: St. Martin's Press, 2000.

Bondurant, Joan V. *The Conquest of Violence.* Berkeley: University of California Press, 1967.

Burrowes, Robert J. *The Strategy of Nonviolent Defense: A Gandhian Approach.* Albany: State University of New York Press, 1986.

Chatterjee, Margaret. *Gandhi's Religious Thought.* Notre Dame: University of Notre Dame Press, 1983.

Dalton, Dennis. *Mahatma Gandhi: Nonviolent Power in Action.* New York: Columbia University Press, 1993.

Erikson, Erik. H. *Gandhi's Truth: On the Origins of Militant Nonviolence.* New York: Norton, 1969.

Galtung, Johan. *The Way Is the Goal: Gandhi Today.* Ahmedabad: Gujarat Vidyapith, Peace Research Centre, 1992.

Green, Martin. *Gandhi: Voice of a New Age Revolution.* New York: Continuum, 1993.

Iyer, Raghavan. *The Moral and Political Thought of Mahatma Gandhi.* Oxford: Clarendon Press, 1973.

Jack, Homer A., ed. *The Gandhi Reader: A Sourcebook of His Life and Writing.* Indianapolis: Indiana University Press, 1956.

Merton, Thomas, ed. *Gandhi on Non-Violence.* New York: New Directions Paperback, 1964.

Nagler, Michael N. *Is There No Other Way?: The Search for a Nonviolent Future.* Berkeley: Berkeley Hills Books, 2001.

Parekh, Anthony J. *Colonialism, Tradition, and Reform.* New Delhi: Sage Publications, 1989.

————. *Gandhi's Political Philosophy.* Notre Dame: University of Notre Dame Press, 1989.

Parel, Anthony J. *Gandhi, Freedom, and Self-Rule.* Lanham: Lexington Books, 2000.

Rudolph, Lloyd and Susanne Hoeber Rudolph. *The Modernity of Tradition.* Chicago: University of Chicago Press, 1967.

————. *Gandhi: The Traditional Roots of Charisma.* Chicago: University of Chicago Press, 1983.

Sharp, Gene. *Gandhi Wields the Weapon of Moral Power.* Ahmedabad: Navajivan, 1960.

————. *Gandhi as a Political Strategist.* Boston: Porter Sargent, 1979.

————. *The Politics of Nonviolent Action.* Boston: Porter Sargent, 1973.

Tendulkar, D.G. *Mahatma: The Life of M. K. Gandhi,* 8 vols. New Delhi: Ministry of Information and Broadcasting, 1951–1954.

Terchek, Ronald J. *Gandhi: Struggling for Autonomy.* Lanham and New York: Rowman and Littlefield, 1998.

Thompson, Mark. *Gandhi and His Ashrams.* Bombay: Popular Prakashan, 1993.

Zunes, Stephen, Lester R. Kurtz, and Sarah Beth Asher. *Nonviolent Social Movements: A Geographical Perspective.* Malden, Massachusetts: Blackwell Publishers, 1999.

Index

About the Contributors

Douglas Allen is Professor of Philosophy at the University of Maine and served as President of the Society for Asian and Comparative Philosophy, 2001–2003. A recipient of Fulbright and Smithsonian grants to India, he is the author and editor of thirteen books focusing on phenomenology of religion, Indian philosophy, comparative philosophy and religion, and political philosophy. He was the recipient of Maine's Presidential Research and Creative Achievement Award and the Distinguished Maine Professor Award. His most recent book is *Myth and Religion in Mircea Eliade* (2002), and he is now completing edited books *Comparative Philosophy in Times of Terror* and *The Philosophy of Mahatma Gandhi for the Twenty-First Century*.

Judith M. Brown is Beit Professor of Commonwealth History at Oxford University and a fellow of Balliol College. Among her publications are *Gandhi's Rise to Power: Indian Politics 1915–22* (1972), *Gandhi and Civil Disobedience: The Mahatma in Indian Politics 1928–34* (1977), *Men and Gods in a Changing World* (1980), *Modern India* (1984, 2nd ed. 1994), *Gandhi: Prisoner of Hope* (1989), *Nehru* (1999), and *Nehru: A Political Life* (2003). She is co-editor with Martin Prozesky of *Gandhi and South Africa: Principles and Politics* (1996) and joint editor of the twentieth century volume of the *Oxford History of the British Empire* (1999).

Richard Falk is Albert Milbank Professor of International Law, Emeritus, at Princeton University where he was a member of the faculty for forty years. Since 2001 he has been a Visiting Professor, Global Studies, at the University of California, Santa Barbara. He is Chair of the Nuclear Age Peace Foundation and author of *Religion and Humane Global Governance* (2002) and *The Great Terror War* (2003).

Richard L. Johnson is Professor of German and Peace Studies at Indiana University-Purdue University Ft. Wayne where he co-founded the Women's Studies Program and the Peace and Conflict Studies Program, which he directed for fifteen years. He is the author of *Ich schreibe mir die Seele frei: Wege zue Harmonisierung des ganzen Gehirns* (I Write My Soul Free: Harmonizing the Whole Brain), and he has published many articles on German culture and nonviolence, including European peace movements, engaged Buddhism, and Mahatma Gandhi. He has been an activist for over forty years in movements seeking to provide nonviolent alternatives to war and family violence.

Michael Nagler is Professor Emeritus of Classics and Comparative Literature at the University of California, Berkeley, where he founded the Peace and Conflict Studies Program and has taught the nonviolence course. He is the author of *America without Violence* (1982), *The Upanishads* with Sri Eknath Easwaran (1987), and *Is There No Other Way?: The Search for a Nonviolent Future* (2001). He is a student of Sri Eknath Easwaran, Founder of the Blue Mountain Center of Meditation, and since 1970 has lived at the Center's Ashram in Marin County. He is President of METTA: Center for Nonviolent Education and Vice President of Peaceworkers.

Glenn D. Paige is Professor Emeritus of Political Science, University of Hawai'i and the Founder and President of the nonprofit Center for Global Nonviolence in Honolulu. He has taught at Seoul National University (1959–1961), Princeton University (1961–1967), and the University of Hawai'i (1967–1992), where he introduced undergraduates to courses and graduate seminars on political leadership and nonviolent political alternatives. A Korean War veteran, he is the author of *The Korean Decision: June 24–30, 1950* (1968), *The Scientific Study of Political Science* (1977), *To Nonviolent Political Science: From Seasons of Violence* (1993), and *Nonkilling Global Political Science* (2002).

Makarand Paranjape is Professor of English at Jawaharlal Nehru University. A poet, novelist, critic, and columnist, he is the author of *The Serene Flame, Playing the Dark God,* and *Used Book* (poetry); *This Time I Promise It'll Be Different* and *The Narrator* (fiction); and *Mysticism in Indian English Poetry, Decolonization and Development,* and *Towards a Poetics of the Indian English Novel* (criticism). The books he has edited include *Indian Poetry in English, Sarojini Naidu: Selected Poetry and Prose, Nativism: Essays* *in Literary Criticism, The Best of Raja Rao, The Penguin Sri Aurobindo Reader, In Diaspora: Theories, Histories, and Texts,* and *Saundarya: The Perception and Practice of Beauty in India.* He is also the founding editor of *Evam: Forum on Indian Representations.*

Bhikhu Parekh is Professor of Political Science at the University of Westminster and Fellow of the British Academy. He is author of several books in political philosophy. His *Rethinking Multiculturalism* was published by Harvard University Press and Macmillan in 2000. He is the recipient of the Sir Isaiah Berlin Prize for lifelong contribution to political philosophy.

Anthony J. Parel is Professor Emeritus of Political Science at the University of Calgary, Canada. He received his Ph.D. in government from Harvard in 1963 and, since 1966, has taught the history of political thought at Calgary and other universities. He specializes in the philosophies of Machiavelli and Mahatma Gandhi. His recent publications include *The Machiavellian Cosmos* (1992), *Gandhi: Hind Swaraj and Other Writings* (1997), and co-edited with Ronald C. Keith *Comparative Political Philosophy* (1992).

Lloyd I. Rudolph is Professor of Political Science and former Chair of the Committee on International Relations at the University of Chicago. Books co-authored with Susanne Hoeber Rudolph include *In Pursuit of Lakshmi, The Political Economy of the Indian State, The Modernity of Tradition, Gandhi, The Regional Imperative,* and *Education and Politics in India.* He has contributed to and edited *Cultural Politics in India* and *The Idea of Rajasthan.* He co-authored with Susanne Hoeber Rudolph and Mohan Singh Kanota *Reversing the Gaze* and *The Singh Diary: A Colonial Subject's Narrative of Imperial India.*

Michael W. Sonnleitner has a Ph.D. in Political Science from the University of Minnesota (Minneapolis, 1979) where his dissertation short-title was "Soul Force and Social Change According to M. K. Gandhi and M. L. King, Jr." His research on Gandhi involved extensive travel to India, Pakistan, Afghanistan, and South Africa where he interviewed over thirty people who had known Gandhi personally, including the late Pyarelal Nayar, Jayaprakash Narayan, Morarji Desa, Vinoba Bhave, and Khan Abdul Gaffar Khan. Currently Chair of the Peace and Conflict Studies Program at Portland Community College in Portland, Oregon, he has over twenty-five years' teaching experience. As an activist he remains a military tax resister, nonviolence trainer, and compulsive organizer who currently serves on the boards of the Oregon Peace Studies Consortium, Northwest Military and Draft Counseling Center, and the Pacific Green Party of Oregon.

Ronald J. Terchek is Professor of Government and Politics at the University of Maryland. His field of concentration is liberal democratic theory. His recent publications include *Gandhi: Struggling for Autonomy* (1998) and *Republican Paradoxes and Liberal Anxieties* (1996). His contributions to books and journals both in the United States and abroad have dealt with problems of autonomy and rationality in liberal thought, the status of community and citizenship in models of liberal democracy, and comparative political theory. He has also published on Gandhi's theories and comparative political theory.